D0969478

The Social Psychology of Language 3

General editor: Howard Giles

Sequence and Pattern in Communicative Behaviour

Edited by R.L. Street, Jr
and J.N. Cappella

Edward Arnold

© Edward Arnold 1985

First published in Great Britain 1985 by
Edward Arnold (Publishers) Ltd, 41 Bedford Square, London WC1B 3DQ

Edward Arnold (Australia) Pty Ltd, 80 Waverley Road, Caulfield East,
  Victoria 3145, Australia

Edward Arnold, 300 North Charles Street, Baltimore, Maryland 21201, U.S.A.

British Library Cataloguing in Publication Data

Sequence and pattern in communicative behavior.
  —— (Social psychology of language series; 3)
  1. Interpersonal communication   2. Conversation
  I. Street, Richard L. II. Cappella, Joseph N.
  III. Series
  302.2'242   HM132

  ISBN 0-7131-6418-2

Text set in 10/11 pt Times Compugraphic
by Colset Private Limited, Singapore
Printed and bound in Great Britain by Richard Clay (The Chaucer Press) Bungay
Suffollk

Contents

General preface

Those fascinated by the importance and complexities of language in social life might look to psychology and especially social psychology for some insights. After all, much of an individual's behaviour occurs in a social context, is manifest linguistically, and mediated by cognitive processes. While language figures prominently in many areas of psychological inquiry such as cognition and development (albeit predictably asocial and accommunicative in the former case), detailed exploration of the dynamics of language and communication within social psychology are conspicuous by their absence. Although there are admittedly important exceptions by way of certain individuals, a few books and a couple of research topics, an examination of mainstream journals and influential texts in social psychology suggests that language and communication hold at the most a peripheral status within the discipline. This is not however to suggest that important research has not been documented. Yet it does exist across an extremely wide set of outlets in the social and communication sciences. Our potential enthusiasts then are liable to be soon disappointed at the apparent dearth of mainstream interest in social psychology for the topic, and understandably reluctant to invest much effort in discovering the inevitably rich stores of information actually available.

They are more likely to be attracted by the equally important but far more accessible perspectives in other disciplines such as philosophy, sociology and anthropology which not only have long-serving labels for their endeavours (i.e. the sociology of language) but can justifiably display their wares proudly. One obvious venue for our language enthusiasts, apart from communication science (which in the interpersonal domain has an active social psychological perspective especially in methodology), is sociolinguistics. This, for many, is a healthy multidisciplinary field examining the relationships between language and society from (to name a few) political, demographic, economic and linguistic perspectives. It has in fact generated the most impressive array of interesting and societally important findings. And once again, understandable in terms of the above, neglects a coherent social psychological approach; again, there are important exceptions particularly with regard to the study of bilingualism and forms of address.

We might then ask: what *is* this social psychological approach that is so lamentably missing from language studies? It lies in two domains. First, language and society are viewed as *interdependent* not as dichotomies as reflected in much traditional sociolinguistics; it is tremendously difficult to separate linguistic and social processes in many instances. Thus, not only do speakers' language behaviours reflect the norms of the situation as perceived by them but that very language behaviour itself can often act creatively to define, and subsequently redefine, the nature of the situation for the participants involved. Second, attention is drawn to the fact that language behaviour is likely to be dependent upon how speakers cognitively represent their social and psychological characteristics and subjectively define the situation in terms of its norms and their goals as is any objective classification of that situation imposed from without (e.g. by investigators). In this sense, *cognitive representations* are seen to be important mediators between language and social context. Given that social psychological theories – as well as their methodologies – are all about the complexities and dynamics of cognitive organization and representation of the social world, it is felt that this perspective can broaden the explanatory scope of the study of language.

Notwithstanding the reasons why a social psychological approach to language and communication has never really gelled – apart from in the early days of its history and in certain national contexts such as Canada – suffice it to say that there are many indications now that it has 'arrived'. For instance, some sociolinguists are beginning to acknowledge the contributions that social psychologists of language are making toward predicting and explaining linguistic variation in social contexts, and the former are themselves integrating speakers' feelings, values, attitudes and perceptions into their research designs.

Obviously, it is timely to promote the coherence of the approach by means of a Monograph Series of interest to those in social psychology on the one hand and language and communication on the other. In this way, we can resurrect language and communication ultimately to its rightful place as a mainstream concern in social psychology as well as concurrently continuing to promote a social psychological perspective to the study of language and communication as an essential one comparable in impact to its linguistic, sociological and anthropological counterparts. In this vein, authors and editors to this Series are being asked to expend considerable energy on taking into account the cross-disciplinary nature of the potential readership. In other words, the Utopian aim is to have volumes which are not only appealing to experienced researchers in the social psychology of language but are also compelling reading for students of linguistics having little social psychological background and for social psychological students having little linguistics background.

It will be apparent from the volumes in this series that social psychologists of language can be highly self-critical on many levels with respect to what has been achieved. However, while it seems important to develop more wide-ranging and sensitive methods, more precise concepts and sophisticated theory, contributors to this Series will be at pains to stress that we do not see a social psychological approach as any more than an important *complement* to other equally important perspectives in language and communication; many of us are actually interdisciplinarians at heart.

Howard Giles

Notes on Contributors

Richard Y. Bourhis was born and raised in the French-speaking part of Montreal and educated in both French and English. After completing a BSc in Psychology at McGill University he obtained his PhD in Social Psychology at the University of Bristol in England. His main research interests are the social psychology of intergroup relations, language attitudes, the dynamics of crosscultural communication in multi-ethnic settings and issues related to language policies and language planning. He has pursued his research interests in numerous cultural settings including Quebec, Wales, England, Belgium, Switzerland and Canada. Along with numerous book-chapter contributions, he has published articles in journals such as the *European Journal of Social Psychology, The International Journal of the Sociology of Language* and the *Journal of Language and Social Psychology*. In 1984 Dr Bourhis edited a multidisciplinary book entitled *Conflict and Language Planning in Quebec* which deals with the impact of the Charter of the French Language (Bill 101) on Quebec Society. Dr Bourhis joined the Psychology Department at McMaster University in 1978 where he is now an Associate Professor.

Douglas E. Campion is a PhD candidate in the Department of Communication Studies at Northwestern University. His research interests include bargaining and negotiation, social exchange, persuasion and compliance-gaining strategies.

Joseph N. Cappella is Associate Professor and Associate Chair, Department of Communication Arts, University of Wisconsin, Madison (1974–present). His research and teaching interests include the study of verbal and nonverbal interaction, research methods for interaction analysis and human information processing. He is co-editor of *Multivariate Techniques in Human Communication Research* (Academic Press, 1980) and has published articles in *Psychological Bulletin, Human Communication Research, Communication Monographs* and *Behaviour Research Methods and Instrumentation*.

Michael J. Cody received his PhD from Michigan State University in 1978. His main areas of research are social influence processes, correlates of deception and the analysis of conversations. He publishes in *Human Communication Research, Communication Monographs* and the *Communication Yearbook*.

Kathryn Dindia (PhD, Department of Speech Communication, University of Washington, 1981) is presently teaching in the Department of

Communication, University of Wisconsin-Milwaukee. Her research interests include self-disclosure and marital communication. Her publications include 'Reciprocity of Self-Disclosure: A Sequential Analysis' in M. Burgoon, ed., *Communication Yearbook 6* and a chapter co-authored with Mary Ann Fitzpatrick on 'Marital Communication' in S. Duck and D. Perlman, eds., *Sage Series in Personal Relationships*, vol. 1.

Margaret L. McLaughlin received her PhD from the University of Illinois in 1972. Her main areas of research include the analysis of conversations, communication and the sexes, and research methods. She publishes in *Human Communication Research, Communication Monographs* and *Communication Quarterly*. She has recently published a book on the organization of conversation and is editor of *Communication Yearbooks 9* and *10*.

G.H. Morris received his PhD in Communication at the University of Texas, 1980. He is currently a communication consultant in Austin, Texas. His research interests include the investigation of meta-rule processes in social interaction, communicator alignment, and conversational effectiveness. He is co-author of an article entitled 'Remediation and Legislation in Everyday Talk: How Communicators achieve Consensus', which appeared in the *Quarterly Journal of Speech*.

Miles L. Patterson is Professor and Chairperson of Psychology, University of Missouri-St Louis. He is a social psychologist whose primary research interests are in nonverbal behaviour in social interaction. He has published numerous papers on nonverbal behaviour, including two theoretical articles in *Psychological Review*. He is also the author of two books, *Nonverbal Behaviour and Social Psychology* (1982, with Richard Heslin) and *Nonverbal Behaviour: A Functional Perspective* (1983).

Marshall Scott Poole (PhD University of Wisconsin, 1980) is Assistant Professor of Speech Communication at the University of Illinois at Urbana-Champaign. His research interests include the theory of structuration, group and organizational decision-making, organizational climate, conflict management and methodologies for studying human interaction. His work has appeared in a number of journals including *Communication Monographs, Human Communication Research* and *Academy of Management Review*, and he serves on the editorial boards of *Human Communication Research* and *Communication Quarterly*. He is co-author of a recently published book, *Working Through Conflict*.

Linda L. Putnam is an Associate Professor in the Department of Communication at Purdue University. She received her PhD in 1977 from the University of Minnesota in Group and Organizational Communication. Her research interests include communication patterns in public sector bargaining, conflict in organizations, and contradictions and paradoxes. She has published articles on sequential data analysis in *Communication*

Yearbook 5, Communication Monographs and *Human Communication Research*. Her work on bargaining and conflict in organizations appears also in *Small Group Behaviour* and *Communication Yearbook 6*. She is co-editor of *Communication and Organizations: An Interpretive Approach*.

Michael E. Roloff is Associate Professor of Communication Studies at Northwestern University. He received his PhD in Communication from Michigan State University and was Assistant Professor of Human Communication at the University of Kentucky prior to moving to Northwestern. His interests include persuasion, bargaining and negotiation, interpersonal conflict resolution, and the formation of cognitive scripts. He recently co-edited (with Gerald R. Miller) *Persuasion: New Directions in Theory and Research* and authored *Interpersonal Communication: The Social Exchange Approach*.

Carol Myers Scotton is a professor in the Department of Linguistics and Languages at Michigan State University. Her specialization is sociolinguistics and she is especially interested in the use of linguistic choices in the negotiation of interpersonal relations. She is also a Bantuist, specializing in Swahili, and many of her sociolinguistic publications have dealt with language choices in multilinguistic African settings. She holds a PhD in Linguistics from the University of Wisconsin and has taught at Howard University and Yale University (USA) as well as at Makerere University (Uganda) and the University of Nairobi (Kenya). In 1982–3 she was a visiting professor at Peking University (People's Republic of China) for one semester, where she taught sociolinguistics and stylistics, and then conducted sociolinguistic research in Kenya and Zimbabwe under a Fullbright Senior Research Fellowship.

Richard L. Street, Jr (PhD, University of Texas, 1980) is Assistant Professor of Speech Communication, Texas Tech University (1982–present). His research and teaching interests include the study of speech, language and nonverbal behaviour in various interpersonal communication contexts such as conversation, interviews, adult – child interactions and interactions of the elderly. He has published numerous articles in international journals including *Human Communication Research, Journal of Language and Social Psychology, Language and Communication* and *Communication Monographs*. He has also published chapters in *Attitudes towards Language Variation* (1982), *Social Cognition and Communication* (1982) and *Handbook of Interpersonal Communication* (in press).

Karen Tracy received her PhD from the University of Wisconsin and is presently on the faculty of the Department of Speech at Temple University in Philadelphia. Her central research interest is to explain how communicators design messages to accomplish multiple goals in conversational settings. She is co-editor of *Conversational Coherence: Form, Structure and Strategy* and has contributed articles to *Human*

Communication Research, Discourse Processes and *Communication Yearbook*.

John M. Wiemann received his PhD in 1975 from Purdue University and is now Associate Professor of Communication at the University of California, Santa Barbara. His research interests include communicative competence, the structure of social interaction and nonverbal behaviour. He has published more than 35 articles, books and book-chapters, including most recently, *Nonverbal Interaction* (ed., with Randall Harrison). He is on the editorial boards of several journals, including *Human Communication Research*, and has recently completed a three-year appointment as a W.K. Kellogg Foundation National Fellow.

To Robert Hopper and Donald Cushman, scholars whose thinking has made a difference.

1

Introduction: a functional approach to the structure of communicative behaviour

Joseph N. Cappella and Richard L. Street, Jr

Interpersonal relationships germinate, live, grow and die in human interactions. To be sure, relationships attain after a time a status that is no longer
simply the sum of the individual events that began and maintained the relationship. But relationships begin in interactions, are cultivated in interactions, and
find their moments of greatest joy and sorrow in interactions. Simply put,
social interactions are the crucible in which relationships are lived. This volume
considers features of that crucible and how those features impact on various
contexts of interpersonal relationships.

Our interest focuses on how people manage the conversations in which they
participate. Who has not come away from some conversation wishing that
he/she had avoided saying a particularly hurtful thing, or had commented when
he/she remained silent? Who has not wished that he/she could take back a
hasty comment or appeared more excited and interested than he/she was? Who
has not participated in the complex back and forth flow of information, verbal
and nonverbal, that is a conversation and wondered how it all happened and
wondered how to make it all happen differently the next time? These common
reflections are the motivating questions of this volume and are the common
intuitions that pen the connections between conversations and relationships. In
our social actions we worry and wonder, reflect and recreate the events of our
conversations in implicit recognition that the believed status of our relationships with other people are tested in those conversations, and, more importantly, changed in those conversations. How people manage such complex
events, intentionally and unintentionally, is the subject of this volume.

The chapters of this volume address a diverse set of behaviours, contexts, and
methodologies for the study of social interaction. They do not adopt the traditional single behaviour approach, choosing instead to examine the impact and
consequences of patterns of co-occurring behaviours during communicative
exchanges.

The present chapter seeks to set out the basic assumptions and basic knowledge about social interaction so that subsequent chapters may be read in a
common context. The basics upon which we focus include (1) the importance
and centrality of managing our social interactions and (2) the structure and
functional organization of the bewildering arrays of behaviour that operate in
even the simplest of conversations. We make two contentions: first that the
stimuli of social interaction are organized into functional groups and should be
studied within these groups; second, that social actors influence and are influenced by the functional behaviours of their partners in ways that are sometimes

deliberate and purposeful and at other times automatic and unintentional. It is our hope to redirect the study of social interaction toward behavioural functions and toward the patterns of behavioural interdependency that define and alter our personal relationships.

The management of social interactions

There are two important senses in which conversations can be managed. The more typical connotation of the word 'manage' implies that a person intentionally seeks to alter the content, tenor or events of a conversation toward some preordained end or purpose. For example, an overworked spouse might try to move the topic of conversation toward the stresses of the work place or home in order to let the other know about his or her experienced difficulties. This sense of management might be labelled the control sense since it suggests that actions are undertaken in order to achieve what one or the other participants perceives to be an important need or purpose.

A less typical connotation of the word 'management' will also be discussed here. Certain regularities are obtained in the sequencing of microscopic events during conversations. For example, increases in speech rate by one party tend to produce increases in the partner's speech rate (Cappella and Planalp 1981). People are in general quite unaware that such influences exist and, under most circumstances, do not employ such effects intentionally. These and other regularities are both interesting and non-obvious but are they relevant to the control of interactional events?

We believe that they are. The ability to control interaction depends upon the existence of certain regularites that can be exploited by one or the other conversational partner, and this exploitation depends upon knowledge of the regularity. For example, in order to encourage discussion of a topic of interest to me I try to get a version of that topic onto the floor. I do so because I know that there is a strong norm in discussion that people stay on the topic. I must know this norm and how to use it in order to achieve the end that I desire. The only difference between the regularities that people consciously employ to control conversations (e.g. topic continuity) and those that they do not (e.g. speech rate) is that conversationalists are not generally aware of many of the regularities that do govern conversational events. Once made aware of such regularities, people could use them to manage the content and style of their conversations.

Attention to the nature of management cannot ignore what it is that people manage in their conversations. In the world of raw stimuli conversations are a complex, information-rich mix of auditory, visual, olfactory and tactile events, simultaneous and sequential in time. But such a description of the uninterpreted events of communicative interchanges is more pertinent to the study of psychophysics than to the study of interpersonal relations. If the management of interaction is to be relevant to the study of interpersonal relations, then the events that are managed in those encounters must have an empirically strong and conceptually significant relationship to the domain of interpersonal judgements and perceptions. Put in other words, the raw stimuli of conversations must be signs of the relationship which the conversation is participating in or creating. The verbal, nonverbal and vocal events of the interaction do not

stand simply for themselves but as indicators of the perceptions that the partners have of one another. This is not to say that any given conversation is a
microcosm of a relationship, particularly a long-lived one, but rather that
certain verbal, nonverbal and vocal events carry relational information and are,
hence, symbolic of relational perceptions. These are the events that need to be
managed and understood in human interaction.

Let us try to clarify the relationship in general terms here. Consider the
example of face-directed gaze. As a raw stimulus, such a behaviour is nothing
more than gaze fixed at the general facial region of another person. Folklore,
literature and controlled research have shown that this stimulus has a number of
possible interpretations. From the point of view of the sender the gaze may have
been directed to gather more information about the other person or, more
purposefully, to signal to the other an interest that decorum requires be more
indirect than verbally straightforward. In either case the gaze means something
other than the mere act of gazing and is, therefore, a sign of some internal state
of the sender.

The second internal state that could have been signalled (namely, interest on
the part of the sender) has more immediate and direct relational implications
than does the first internal state, information gathering. The recipient of the
gaze may not notice it at all or may interpret it as impolite staring, or worse.
Although either reaction by the recipient has impact, the latter interpretation
has more immediate and severe relational implications than does the former. In
either case the first steps of this hypothetical interaction are headed for trouble
because the possible intentions of the sender and the possible interpretations by
the receiver do not overlap at all. The relational value of the act is not shared.

This example illustrates a number of principles that will undergird this discussion of interaction management. First, the uninterpreted value of interactional events can be sharply distinguished from the interpretations that those
events receive. Second, the interpretations that can be given to interaction
events are multiple with some having more powerful relational implications
than others. Third, the interpreted values of interactional events can be located
in at least three places: the motivational states of the sender, the perceptions of
the receiver, or in the shared world of senders and receivers. We assume that
interaction management is concerned with interpreted rather than raw conversational events, with interpersonally significant events, and with events whose
meaning is broadly shared by the body of the speech community.

The verbal, nonverbal and vocal events that occur within conversations have
the potential to initiate, reinforce, and change the status of relationships
between partners. The management of interaction, whether deliberate or unintentional, is in part the management of these meaningful events and in this
indirect way the management of relationships. Of course, it would be naive to
claim that relationships and interactions are equivalent. Relationships exist in
abstracted form in the memory of partners. That abstraction certainly influences the content, structure and management of interaction and in turn is
influenced by them but that is not to say that a given conversation is a replica of
the relationship in which it takes place. Rather, a given interaction is an indicator of the relationship in which it functions in much the same way that that the
monthly indicators of the nation's economic welfare are related to the nation's
actual economic condition: they are certainly related to the economic condition

but are more informative when compared to the trends that the economy has been displaying over time rather than treated as absolutes.

The sequential and vertical structure of social interaction

The streams of behaviour that make up an interaction are complex both because they are multiple in number and because their organization is not obvious. The purpose of this section is to discuss this organization among the various streams of conversational behaviour in order to categorize and simplify the complexity that faces the theorist and researcher, let alone the social actor. Subsequent chapters will consider the question of how management of social events occurs.

When one stops even for a moment to consider the diversity and kind of stimuli that are being generated during an interaction, a kind of despair creeps into the researcher's bones. How can anyone hope to study, let alone understand, the various verbal, vocal and kinesic activities that people carry out while speaking and listening? What is worse, these auditory, visual, tactile and olfactory stimuli are information dense per unit of time. This means that they are changing a great deal over time (at least the so-called dynamic features are (Kendon 1970)). Interestingly, the despair created in researchers by such information overload is not shared by interactants. They surely have developed strategies for ignoring, combining and substituting information generated by their partners. Part of the task that researchers have is to understand the organizational shortcuts that conversationalists take so that this route to the simplification of interactional structure can be profitably employed in research.

The most obvious description of the behavioural activities of conversations would be organized along two dimensions: a horizontal dimension representing time and a vertical dimension representing a particular type of behaviour, such as smiling and laughter. This description is represented in Figure 1.1. Conversational events of course occur sequentially so that the temporal organization of such events is one feature of interaction structure. Numerous types of behaviours occur during any moment of the conversation, filling the range from the microscopic and automatic, such as pauses prior to word choices, to the macroscopic and deliberate, such as justifications following accusations. These streams of behaviour are represented by the vertical categories vocal, verbal and kinesic with subcategories within each. The second dimension of conversational organization concerns these vertical categories. Are these vertical behaviour streams sufficiently independent to be treated as separate and distinct or are they interrelated in ways that would allow researchers, and conversational partners, to treat them as functionally equivalent? In the sections that follow the questions of sequential organization and vertical or functional organization will be taken up in turn.

Sequential organization

The question in this section is whether the sequential generation of verbal, nonverbal, and kinesic behaviours in conversation falls into any identifiable time-unit groupings that would permit researchers to organize conversational time into useful units for analysis. The first important distinction to make in the time domain is between real time and event time (Folger, Hewes, and Poole

1984). Real time or clock time marks the conversational event with every tick of
the clock, whether those ticks are tenths of a second, minutes, or whatever. For
example, in our laboratory talk and silence sequences have been studied so that
the presence or absence of vocalization is sampled every 300 milliseconds
(Cappella and Streibel 1979). In every 300 millisecond tick of the clock each
person is either talking or silent. Event time on the other hand marks occurrences by the presence or absence of specified interactional events. For example,
Ellis and Fisher (1975) coded the sequential structure of acts of dominance and
submission in various types of groups noting when certain types of acts were
followed by other act types. Sequential character was defined in terms of act
sequences regardless of the exact timing of the acts. Hewes, Planalp, and
Streibel (1980) point out that one need not make a choice between an event-time
and a clock-time formulation of time because, in fact, events occur in real time
with definite points of origination and termination. These authors show us that
even though some interaction behaviours seem to be more easily viewed as
occuring in real time or in event time, such a choice is neither necessary nor true
to the phenomenal description of naturally observed conversations.

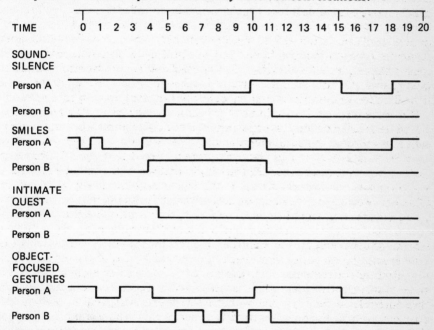

Figure 1.1 A discrete time representation of on and off patterns of selected conversational
behaviours

Two of the most influential attempts to define interactional units are based
upon the pioneering work of Chapple (1939, 1940). Interestingly, both of these
attempts focused upon the conversational turn as the most natural unit of
organization in time. Jaffe and Feldstein (1970) developed a machine-assisted
coding system that described a conversation in terms of the presence of sound
and silence. The conversational turn was the crux of their conceptualization
with a turn beginning 'the instant one participant . . . starts talking alone and

end[ing] immediately prior to the instant another participant starts talking alone' (Feldstein and Welkowitz 1978, p. 335). This base definition allowed Jaffe and Feldstein and their colleagues to define a number of other behaviours within the turn: vocalization, pause, switching pause, and interruptive and non-interruptive simultaneous speech (Jaffe and Feldstein 1970, pp. 19–20).

Their definition of a conversational turn is a purely objective one because the presence of unilateral vocalization is determined by a computer-driven decision that sound in a channel exceeds a preassigned threshold. The genuine advantage of such an approach is that the definition of turn is made objective so that agreement in its use across researchers is virtually assured. Less objective definitions of a conversational turn may be used reliably within a given research group but assuring reliability across research groups is much more difficult and is usually ignored. The objective definition suggested by Jaffe and Feldstein has some potentially serious shortcomings however. The boundaries of a turn are determined operationally by the presence or absence of sound in a channel. But conceptually one must assume that the sound is speech. No machine can currently make that distinction. Also short bursts of speech by the listener during momentary hesitations by the speaker would be coded as turns by the Jaffe and Feldstein system but not by other coding systems described below.

Matarazzo and Wiens (1972) also developed a comprehensive programme of research based upon the work of Chapple and using the turn as the fundamental unit of temporal organization. They called the turn an utterance and defined it as follows: 'The total duration of time it takes a speaker to emit all the words that he is contributing in that particular unit or exchange (as this would be judged by common social standards' (Matarazzo and Wiens 1972, p. 6)).

Pauses occurring during an utterance are ignored unless they are long, in which case they are coded as initiation time latencies. Matarazzo and Wiens also focused on the turn as a fundamental organizational unit but by insisting on judged continuity and common social standards, they side-step the problems of coding non-speech sounds as if they were talk and of coding brief intrusions by the listener as if they were turns. At the same time their definition offers little guidance as how 'common social standards' are to be interpreted. Although their own research did not lack reliability of judgement, there can be no guarantee that imitators of their work are employing the same set of common social standards.

Duncan and Fiske chose not to adopt the low inference judgement schemes of either Jaffe and Feldstein or Matarazzo and Wiens. Rather their fundamental unit of temporal organization was the turn as defined on the basis of the speaker and the hearer's intent: 'A speaker is a participant who claims the speaking turn. An auditor is a participant who does not claim the speaking turn at a given moment' (Duncan and Fiske 1977, p. 177). When a person carries out verbal and nonverbal actions whose purpose is not to wrest the floor from the speaker then that person is said to have emitted a back channel. Back channels can include nodding, brief vocal insertions such as 'yeah', and 'm-hm', smiles (Bruner 1979) and longer verbal actions such as restatements, clarifications, questions and agreements. Even though back channels ultimately depend upon the intent of the actor, coders were able to judge reliably all types of back-channel actions. The longer back channels which were most likely to produce confusion and unreliability accounted for only 10 per cent of all back-channel actions. Duncan and Fiske (1977) do not report any studies in which coders were asked to distinguish turns from back channels. However, they report good reliabilities for the judgements of each category separately, suggesting that they could be reliably distinguished.

The above three research groups were all concerned with the study of conversation and isolated the turn as their basic unit of temporal organization. Other research programmes not concerned with the structure of conversation have tended to find units of temporal organization smaller than the turn. Dittman (1962, 1972; Dittman and Llewelyn 1969) and Boomer (1963, 1965, 1978; Boomer and Dittman 1964), building on the work of Trager and Smith (1951), studied the distribution of pauses, hesitations, movements and interruptions within and between phonemic clause groupings. They concluded that the basic unit of speech encoding was the phonemic clause.

Typically a turn is longer than a single phonemic clause. Goldman-Eisler and her associates (Beattie 1978; Butterworth 1975; Butterworth and Goldman-Eisler 1979) maintain that under conditions of high cognitive load, especially as indicated by long periods of monologue, units of temporal organization of speech much larger than the phonemic clause can be expected. For example, Butterworth (1975) found that subjects talking about topics with which they agreed and disagreed exhibited cycles of hesitancy and fluency with a mean duration in the vicinity of 18 seconds. An independent group of subjects was able to mark these monologues at the 'idea boundary' such that the boundaries were related to the boundaries for periods of fluency and hesitancy. Beattie (1978) coded monologues lasting more than 30 seconds into periods of hesitancy and fluency, discovering that the periods of hesitancy also showed more gaze aversion and fewer speech focused gestures. This evidence suggests that the temporal organization of longer turns may involve macroscopic units much greater than that of the phonemic clause.

The above research on the phonemic clause and on periods of hesitancy and fluency is probably not contradictory. Each line of inquiry has used slightly different measures to label temporal units and has directed its attention to different sized units for close scrutiny. Similarly, this research does not directly contradict the research that has identified the turn (in its various versions) as the fundamental unit of temporal organization. In many ways the differences in units are due to the fundamental research questions that have been posed, whether interactional or cognitive. These different starting points reinforce the notion that the driving questions of a line of inquiry have a greater impact on what is found than the phenomena being investigated.

Although the above schemes for identifying temporal units of organization are not the only ones that have been posed (see for example Kendon 1970 and Frey 1983), they are certainly among the most provocative and influential. Of the five points of view described above, all are encoding-oriented and use the verbal stream as the point of departure for structural units. Those that have been concerned with the study of interaction have adopted the turn as the unit of analysis while those concerned with cognitive or psycholinguistic studies have adopted units that usually occur within a turn. That units of analysis match the questions under investigation is not surprising but that the encoding perspective should be so pervasive is.

The encoding perspective implies that it is the enacted behaviour of participants, verbal, nonverbal and vocal, that is the focus of research. If actors organize their output behaviour in turn units, phonemic clauses, or larger idea groups, then by focusing on these units pertinent verbal, vocal and nonverbal behaviour will not be lost. These units are like organizing nodes for the researcher. But we must be certain to note that these units are created and validated from the point of view of the actor and not from the point of view of the perceiver. Thus, although the evidence is that speakers organize their behaviour in these temporal groups, there is no evidence that receivers perceive sequential behaviour in these temporal groups. In fact, research by Newtson and his colleagues (Newtson 1976; Newtson, Enquist and Bois 1977) suggests that observers of social interaction partition those interactions more finely and more grossly as a function of their needs to attend and goals in observing the situation. Research on the sequential structure of interaction has been almost completely encoder-oriented with the result that we know a bit about how actors organize their behavioural output in conversations but little about how receivers organize their input.

No research programmes that I am aware of have failed to adopt some unit of temporal organization for their studies. An alternative to either the turn, the phonemic clause or the idea boundary would be clock-time units. Such units simply code behaviours as they occur in clock time regardless of their sequential structure. The problem with bypassing a 'natural' unit in favour of an objective but *ad hoc* unit is that even clock time must at some point be partitioned for the purpose of analysis. It is that partitioning which raises the unitizing question all over again. The number of possible partitions is of course infinite and the question of the most effective or valid partition must be addressed.

Vertical organization

For the sake of simplicity let us assume that there are three categories of behaviour that are operative during interaction: vocal, verbal and kinesic. Within these three are a variety of specific behaviours that fall into the category by definition (see Table 1.1). The behaviours summarized in Table 1.1 are not meant to be a comprehensive listing of interactional behaviours but only a listing of behaviours that have received at least modest research attention. Of course future research might modify this list considerably. The list is meant to inspire awe in the reader who is not familiar with the potential complexity of the vertical structure of conversational behaviour. The listing of Table 1.1 is also somewhat misleading. The behaviours listed are the family names of conversational behaviours and not the operational definitions of the possibe behaviour streams flowing in conversation. To illustrate, consider the family group of gestures. Most research on gestural behaviour recognizes a fundamental difference between object-focused and body-focused gestures (Freedman 1972), that is, between gestures complementing the spoken word and gestures directed at self-manipulation. These two gestural categories could be operationally defined (at least) as durational, average or rate measures. The point is that this single family name, upon closer scrutiny, quickly becomes six operational behaviours to be tracked. Table 1.1 significantly understates the vertical variety in conversational behaviour (see Duncan and Fiske 1977).

Table 1.1 An incomplete list of behaviour categories occuring in conversation.

Category	Behaviour
Verbal	Self-disclosure
	Intimate questions
	Topic structure
	Floor time
	Dialect
	Accent
	Language choice
	Type token ratio
	Dominance–submission tokens
Vocal	Pauses
	Speech rate
	Latency
	Amplitude
	Vocalization
Kinesic	Eye gaze
	Distance
	Posture and orientation
	Smiles and laughter
	Touch
	Gesture

The question to be asked in this section is whether this apparent vertical complexity is actual. Put a bit more picturesquely, are these rivulets of behaviour coursing through interactional time all separate waterways to be navigated and explored independently or are they just tributaries to a few larger streams? If they are just tributaries, then navigation and exploration can proceed in the larger streams ignoring the unproductive sloughs and backwaters. The empirical question is whether these behaviours are dependent or independent of one another. If independent, then the study of conversational management must simply resign itself to the complex world that it seeks to understand. If dependence exists, then the apparent formidable complexity of interaction is only apparent and not actual. Behaviours flowing in the same stream could then be treated as indicators of the stream and as functionally equivalent contributors to the same underlying stream.

In understanding how the vertical structure of conversation might be explored empirically it is useful to look back to an analogous research question, the connotative dimensions of word meaning (Osgood, Suci and Tannenbaum 1957). The intuitions of language users would suggest that the complexity of word connotations would be great. Not only are there a large number of words of very different function, use and etymology but the variety of connotations seems to be as complex as the word base whose connotations are being sought. The results produced by Osgood's research are counter to these intuitions. In general, three dimensions of word meaning emerged: activity, evaluation and potency. An analogous project needs to be undertaken for the complex of conversational behaviours. Such a project is nothing short of the study of the meaning of verbal, vocal and kinesic behaviours in the hopes that our intuitions about their complexity will be just as wrong as our intuitions about word connotations.

Theories of word meaning give some excellent clues about how one might establish meanings for the complex set of interactional behaviours empirically. Such meanings, if they can be found, would presumably be much less complex than the structure of the behaviours themselves, being analogous to the connotative dimensions of word meaning and analogous to the wider behaviour streams which is our operative metaphor. All comprehensive discussions of meaning offer at least two locations for meaning of a given sign: in the intentions and motivations of the sender and in the effects the sign produces in the receiver. If the sender gestures actively, motivated (not necessarily consciously) by his or her involvement in the topic of conversation, then one view of the meaning of that gestural activity is found in the motivations existing in the sender at the time of action. An alternative view of the meaning of the gestural activity is found in the perceptions that such activity produces in observers. If a set of observers typically judges such activity to be flamboyant, expressive, outgoing and animated, then these perceptions are the meaning of the gestural activity. Let us call the first approach the encoding approach and the second the decoding approach.

Both the encoding and decoding approaches have been advocated in the recent literature. Patterson (1982a, 1982b, 1983; Eidinger and Patterson 1983) has argued that the usual channel categorization of nonverbal behaviours is a convenient but uninformative means of organizing discussion of nonverbal behaviours. A more informative method would identify the functions that various behaviours could serve in interpersonal encounters. He has organized his functions into five categories: providing information, regulating interaction, expressing intimacy, and a service-task and social control function. These functions are conceived as residing in the motivational states of actors rather than in the perceptions of observers. In his comprehensive reviews of the literature Patterson (1983; Eidinger and Patterson 1983) has shown that the functional categories of his encoding approach can usefully organize and explain research findings. For example, Ickes, Patterson, Rajecki and Tanford (1982) found that persons smiled more at confederates whom they expected to be friendly and at those they expected to be unfriendly in comparison to control confederates. The authors reasoned that the subjects with the friendly confederate were smiling because they were expressing intimacy whereas those with the unfriendly confederate were trying to minimize unpleasantries by seeming to be friendly. They were exhibiting social control by managing the situation.

While acknowledging the importance of Patterson's move toward a functional categorization for nonverbal behaviour, Cappella (in press a) has argued that a decoding approach to the identification of functions could be equally valid (indeed complementary) and could take advantage of the powerful methodological tools that already exist for the mapping of behavioural spaces into perceptual spaces (Poole and Folger 1981; Wish, D'Andrade and Goodnow 1980). Neither approach is concerned with the idiosyncratic functions that an isolated sender or receiver might have but rather with broadly shared functions. Although both approaches are still at the proposal stage, an interesting question arises over the degree to which the results will overlap. Two sets of overlaps are important: overlap in the functions identified and overlap in the behaviours that map into each function. Will mismatching verbal and nonverbal behaviours be those most likely to be the source of communication breakdowns? Much elementary research remains to be done before this question can be answered.

In both the encoding and the decoding approaches two significant problems immediately arise. The first problem concerns the effect of context on the meaning (or function) of interactional behaviours. Even the simplest views of word meaning acknowledge that the meaning of words derives in part from the context of their occurrence. We would be naive to ignore this issue in interactional behaviours. The context can significantly alter perceptions of a given behaviour or be related to different motivations by a sender. Let us illustrate.

Gaze directed at another person does not in itself signify one or another function. Prolonged gaze by a stranger directed at another person in a deserted city park is likely to be interpreted as a threatening gesture while the same prolonged gaze by dating friends over an intimate dinner is likely to be interpreted as personal, warm and intimate. The prolonged gaze takes its functional interpretation as much from the situation as from the behaviour itself. Controlled research has tended to support this view certainly with respect to gaze (Ellsworth and Carlsmith 1968; Ellsworth and Langer 1976) but also with respect to touch (Whitcher and Fisher 1979). In the hypothetical example above the participants in each situation might be equally involved with one another but the character of that involvement differs from situation to situation. As researchers have come to recognize the importance of social normative factors and interpersonal factors in the interpretation of verbal, vocal and kinesic behaviours, they have begun to identify these behaviours as signs of involvement (Cappella 1981, 1983; Patterson 1982b, 1983) and to actively incorporate situational and relational expectations into their theories of the effects of conversational events (Burgoon 1978, Cappella and Greene 1982; Patterson 1982b). Researchers cannot continue to blindly label the functions of verbal, vocal and kinesic behaviours without recognizing the impact that situational and relational factors have on the labeling and without checking and validating their labels with encoders and decoders (Poole and Folger 1981).

The second concerns the complexity of either the motivations of senders or the perceptions of receivers. Obviously the set of possible motivations and the set of possible perceptions that senders and receivers can have is extremely large, if not infinite. If the complexity of these motivations and perceptions cannot be reduced, then little parsimony can be achieved through the functional approach because the domain of functions would be as complicated as the domain of behaviours. No reduction in the vertical complexity of conversational behaviour could be achieved. This same problem faced researchers studying the connotative dimensions of word meaning. They found a considerable reduction in variety from the domain of words to the domain of word connotation. Some of the evidence on the structure of the domains of interpersonal perception and interpersonal motivation will now be discussed.

The attempt to structure taxonomies of interpersonal motivations has a long and rich history that shows a unanimity remarkable to social and behavioural research (Leary 1957; Schutz 1958; Lorr and McNair 1965; Carson 1969; Wiggins 1979, 1982; Kiesler 1983). These taxonomies have differed in their level of behavioural specificity, in the detail of their structure in each category, and in the clarity and validity of their empirical results. But despite these differences all have concluded that two fundamental dimensions constitute the basis of interpersonal motivation. Variously labelled, they include a dimension of control or dominance–submission and a dimension of affiliation or associativity, bounded by friendly and warm at one end and by hostile and cold at the other end. Kiesler's (1983) recent review and empirical reassessment of interpersonal motivation gives solid basis for Patterson's (1982a, 1983) categories of affiliation and social control as motivations prompting verbal, vocal and kinesic actions in conversation. Patterson's service-task, information and regulation functions are not represented but if Bales's work (1970) in interpersonal dimensions of personality were included, then the service-task and information functions would have received some support.

On the decoding side taxonomies of interpersonal judgement exhibit a unanimity equal to that found in interpersonal motivation although not the historical nor the empirical depth. An array of empirical techniques using a variety of methodologies have consistently uncovered at least two categories and sometimes four categories of perceptions of others. The two commonly unearthed include an associativity or affiliation dimension, sometimes called social evaluation, and a control or dominance–submission dimension. Other categories include an activity dimension (Wish, Deutsch and Kaplan 1976; Norton 1978) and a formality–informality (intimacy) dimension (Wish *et al.* 1976, Triandis and Vassiliou 1972). The two common categories of perception have been found across a variety of relationships (Wish *et al.* 1976), across a variety of situations (Wish and Kaplan 1977), and across at least two quite different cultural groups (Triandis, Vassiliou and Nassiakou 1968; Triandis and Vassiliou 1972). Studies that use perception items that are behaviourally based rather than evaluatively based have also unearthed the two common dimensions (Bochner, Kaminski and Fitzpatrick 1977; Norton 1978, 1983). Most of these studies have subjects rate hypothetical relationships, either their own or those of others, on behavioural or evaluative rating scales. Wish, D'Andrade and Goodnow (1980) took the next step having subjects evaluate actors from 20 brief scenes from the television documentary, 'An American Family'. The structure of these responses resulted in a dominance dimension and a social evaluation dimension, as well as a task and an intensity category. This last study makes an important addition to the taxonomic structure of interpersonal perception because it comes closest to investigating the perceptions created immediately after observation of interpersonal interactions.

Empirical studies of both interpersonal motivation and interpersonal perception yield strong evidence that the most common categories are in each case an associativity and a control category. Other categories arise as a function of the rating scales employed and other methodological and procedural features, but the structure of encoding functions and of decoding functions is relatively simple at its core. If these functions represent the basic intentions of encoders and the basic reactions of receivers, then research can ask how behaviours are related to these underlying functions or meanings. How do interpersonal motivations relate to verbal, vocal and kinesic actions? How do these behaviour actions relate to interpersonal perception? Answers to these questions are answers to questions about the vertical structure of conversation. Brief consideration of these issues is undertaken below.

The encoding perspective has been much more widely researched than the decoding perspective. Part of the reason for this bias may be due to the fact that encoding studies can be carried out on a single subject population while decoding studies require the senders and receivers to be different groups. But the more significant reason is the long history of the study of personality and affective states of people generally. Operationally the study of interpersonal motivations includes the study of affective states such as liking and hostility as well as the study of more permanent personality traits of dominance, affiliation, extraversion, and the like. To understand the relationship between the verbal, vocal and kinesic events of interaction and their encoding functions, both personality and affective states should be considered.

Such a topic is too large for this chapter. Excellent and up-to-date reviews are available in Patterson (1983), Burgoon (in press) and Eidinger and Patterson (1983) (for transient affective states) and in Scherer (1979) and Giles and Street (in press) (for personality factors). In brief, these reviews find that personality factors and transient affective states are predictive of a variety of verbal, vocal and kinesic behaviours though often the relationship is complex and highly qualified by situational, relational, and other factors.

On the decoding side extensive and comprehensive research on the perceptual outcomes of various behaviours is not available except for certain behaviours. No single study has tried to assess simultaneously the impact of a variety of verbal, vocal and kinesic behaviours upon a set of interpersonal perceptions. Mehrabian's research (Mehrabian 1971; Mehrabian and Ksionsky 1970, 1972) led the way in large-scale coding of subjects' behaviours. Using factor analytic and other techniques (Mehrabian 1972, Chapters 1 & 2), he was able to show that behaviours grouped into categories labelled affiliation, relaxation, intimacy and responsiveness. Behaviours grouping into the affiliative-intimate categories included statements, questions, duration of speech, duration of gaze, head nods, facial expression, verbal reinforcers, positive verbal content, gestures per minute, pleasant vocal expressions, shoulder orientation and proximity. The relaxation category (generally associated with perceptions of status, power and control) included leg/foot movements, rocking motions and body lean. These studies did not directly assess perceivers' reactions but rather inferred those reactions. A more recent study by Shrout and Fiske (1982) coded 49 nonverbal behaviours derived from eight behaviour groups from brief segments of videotaped interactions. Subjects who viewed the videotapes evaluated the persons on tape by using the sociability subscales of the Adjective Checklist. By regressing these evaluations on the values of the coded behaviours the authors were able to show that five behaviours (number of smiles, filled pause rate, nod rate, gaze rate and short back-channel rate) accounted for substantial portions of the variance in perceived sociability.

Although no other studies have carried out as extensive behavioural coding, individual behaviours have been manipulated and their effects on subject perceptions assessed. Earlier we argued that context effects on the 'meaning' of conversational events must be taken into account if our attempts to find structure in conversational behaviours is not to be fatally flawed. Situational and relational factors are two such contextualizing factors. One of the implications of including situational and relational factors is that the perception of a behavioural level as insufficiently low or excessively high is made relative to the situational and relational expectations. No simple linear relationship between behavioural intensity and observer perception should be expected (Cappella 1983). More specifically, Cappella and Greene (1982) have argued that the other's perception of an actor's behaviour is an inverted U function of the behaviour relative to the expectation where the expectation is determined by situational, relational and personal dispositional factors.

Few studies have manipulated enough levels of a behaviour to assess the curvilinear relationship to perception. However, speech rate (Smith, Brown, Strong and Rencher 1975; Street, Brady and Putman 1983), eye gaze (Cook and Smith 1975; Argyle, LeFebvre and Cook 1975), social distance (Patterson and Sechrest 1970; Thompson, Aiello and Epstein 1979), verbal disclosure (Cozby 1972, Derlega, Harris and Chaikin 1973), and duration of participation (Hayes and Meltzer 1972, Hayes and Sievers 1972) all show the expected inverted U relationship to perceptions of attraction and associativity.

The relationship between conversational behaviours and perceptions of control and power is not very extensive. The most widely researched of behaviours is percentage of time holding the floor in small-group situations. Cappella's (in press a) review of this literature found that the evidence for a monotonically increasing relationship between floor time and perceptions of the speaker's control and power is solid (Stang 1973, Sorrentino and Boutellier 1975; Daly, McCroskey and Richmond 1977; Hayes and Meltzer 1972). Dovidio and Ellyson (1982) have conducted one of the first decoding studies on eye gaze, finding that as the proportion of looking while speaking increases so does the perception of the actor's control and power. The dearth of decoding studies makes strong conclusions difficult but their absence, we hope, will not be taken as a sign of their lack of importance. Without both encoding and decoding studies of the verbal, vocal and kinesic behaviours of conversation, research will continue to study isolated behaviours with little sense of how behaviours work together either in encoding or in creating perceptions and, secondly, the microscopic elements of conversation will remain distinct from the life of relationship formation, growth and change.

A taxonomy of social interaction functions

Although the call for a functional approach to the grouping of verbal, vocal and kinesic events in interactions is relatively recent, some research has gone forward that implicitly takes a functional perspective. This section recognizes that work and tries to make explicit what has been implicit. The functions that emerge during interaction depend on (1) the conscious or subconscious intentions of the interactants, (2) their behavioural repertoires, (3) their definitions of the situation, and (4) other personal factors such as emotional state and experienced arousal level (Cappella 1983; Giles and Street in press).

Table 1.2 presents a list of some common functions that have been identified as operating within social interaction as well as the behaviours associated with them. Although not exhaustive, this taxonomy demonstrates the rather complex relationships between behaviour and function as well as the diverse ways researchers have approached functional analysis of social interaction.

Coherence

If our social exchanges are to be comprehensible and sufficiently orderly to accomplish personal and group goals, they must be coherent. Communicators accomplish this through an array of behavioural and interpretive strategies. *Interpretive procedures* refer to rather general cognitive principles that serves as

Table 1.2 Verbal and nonverbal behaviours accomplishing selected interaction functions

Coherence
Discussion management tactics
Alignment moves
Discussion structuring moves
Object-focused gestures

Speech and lexical adaptations given cognitive
level of listener
'Issue' extensions when topic is clear
'Event' extensions when topic is ambiguous

Intimacy
Close interpersonal distances
Direct body orientation
Forward lean
Verbal intimacy
Facial expressiveness

Reciprocal touch
Mutual gaze
Postural openness
Personal resource exchange

Reinforcement (positive)
Direct body orientation
Positive head nods
Friendly touch
Positive back-channel responses
Praise
Gaze at the other

Speech convergence
Postural convergence
Gestural convergence
Reciprocal self-disclosures
Smiles
Relatively long talk durations

Impression management
Moderate to fast speech rates
Moderate to long talk durations
Few and brief pauses (unless topic is
highly intimate)
Speech with little or few disfluencies
Prestigious or similar (to the interlocutor)
accents
Accounting for untoward behaviour

Speech convergence
Smiles
Forward lean
Positive head nods
Appropriate self-disclosure
Gestures
Lexical diversity
Erect posture (formal settings)

Control
  Turn-taking sequencing
    Turn-yielding cues

Turn suppressing cues

Persuasion
Gazing at target
Increasing loudness
Moderate to fast speech rates
Gestures

Lexical diversity
Dialect similarity
Gestural matching
Facial expressiveness

Dominance and power
Gazing at listener when talking
Gazing away while listening
Non-reciprocal touch
Lack of facial expressiveness
Relaxed posture
Control–acquiescence speech act sequences

Interruption
Long floorholdings
Lexical style shifts
Moderately loud speech (when vying for
dominance)

interpretive guides when interactants impose meaning on the speech stream.
Hopper (1981) has identified some of these, such as the 'etc.' principle (a
receiver's willingness to fill in the meaning in ambiguous language), the assumption of relevance (assuming interlocutors' responses are relevant to the preceding utterance), the retrospective–prospective sense of occurrence (the reliance
on present or future utterances to interpret past or present remarks), and role-
taking.
Poole's chapter (Chapter 11) focuses on group discussion identifying several

discussion-management tactics applicable to most interaction. The tactics represent linguistic choices which help coordinate a coherent communicative exchange. The 'elementary devices' that he identifies are those semantic and syntactic items that facilitate meaning by linking clauses to sentences, sentences to conversational turns, and turns to episodes (e.g. references to previous statements, paraphrases, conjunctions). 'Alignment moves' (Hopper 1981; Morris and Hopper 1980, Ragan 1983) seek to remedy actual or potential problems of understanding or appropriate behaviour. Examples of alignment moves include motive talk ('Now the reason why I did that . . .'), disclaimers ('I haven't read much in that area but . . .'), and accounts ('I did poorly on the exam but you see my roommate . . .'). The understanding fostered by alignment moves may not only promote comprehension but also help remedy untoward behaviour. Structuring moves include *quid pro quo* (making concessions to gain compliance from another), procedural messages and fractionation (breaking the discussion into several issues to be considered separately).

Topic continuity is fundamental to smooth, efficient and indeed coherent verbal exchanges. Tracy (1983, Chapter 2) has demonstrated that utterances which extend the immediate conversational topic generally facilitate comprehension more than do extensions of the earlier conversational topic. These in turn are viewed as more competent than extensions of the conversational environment and background knowledge. Extensions of the theme or global topic are viewed as more relevant than extensions relating only to the immediate prior topic regardless of its relation to the global theme. However, if the issue is vague, receivers generally rely upon event extensions to promote comprehension.

Other, less obvious, behaviours also contribute to the coherence of conversation. Kendon (1983) reviews research supporting the notion that object-focused gestures (including facial, head, eye, arm and hand gestures) closely parallel linguistic units. The gestural and verbal modalities appear to share a communicative function, the representation of meaning.

To facilitate understanding, speakers frequently produce speech adaptations such as slowed speech rate and matched lexical choices toward the comprehension level of receivers. Thus, adults typically speak faster and with more complex language forms to other adults than do children (Street 1983). Audiences unfamiliar with the speaker's topic generally prefer slower, simpler utterances (Giles and Smith 1979). Speech that is excessively fast or complex exceeds the cognitive processing capacity of listeners (MacLachlan 1979). However, excessively slow, simple or redundant speech does not sufficiently engage the receiver to maintain interest and attention toward the topic or to think positively of the speaker (Bradac *et al.* 1979; Street *et al.* 1983). Thus coherence is likely when interactants discover and adapt toward mutually preferred speech formats.

Intimacy

Patterson (1983, Chapter 10) discusses nonverbal behaviour patterns typifying intimacy levels. As intimacy increases, nonverbal involvement also increases. Relative to their non-intimate counterparts, intimate relationships are typically characterized by closer interpersonal distance, more direct body orientation, more mutual facial gaze, more touch, more postural openness and less self-touching. The pattern for non-romantic but close personal relationships is comparable with more talking, more intimate disclosures (Dindia Chapter 8), and more facial expressiveness than for impersonal relationships.

Intimacy levels are also dependent upon the resources exchanged (including affection, love, supportiveness, money and services) and the patterns of exchange themselves. Roloff and Campion (Chapter 9) describe intimate relationships as exchanging more personal resources than less intimate relationships. Family members exchange love, status and supportiveness; supervisors and subordinates exchange information; buyers and sellers exchange money and services. Non-intimate relationships appear to reciprocate homomorphic resources of an identical type with the exchange completed rather quickly. Intimate relationships exchange heteromorphic resources with the exchange being completed over a longer duration of time. For example, a spouse's support during a crisis may be repaid much later with more time spent in activities of that spouse's preference.

As relationships develop toward greater intimacy, reciprocation of non-intimate self-disclosure tends to decrease. However, a curvilinear relationship appears to exist between relational development and reciprocity of intimate disclosures (Dindia Chapter 8, Gilbert 1976; Roloff and Campion Chapter 9; Won-Doornink 1979). The latter trend suggests that self-disclosure reciprocity of intimate information is important for relational growth. Once a desired level of intimacy is achieved, reciprocity among intimates may become less crucial.

Feedback and reinforcement

Several verbal and nonverbal behaviours serve as reinforcers or give communicators feedback cues for the extent to which current behaviours are approved or disapproved. Whether in the classroom, interview or conversation, these include direct body orientation, smiles, positive head nods, positive verbal utterances, gazing, friendly touch, and speech, postural and gestural convergence. On the opposite side, nondirect body orientation, gaze avoidance, neutral facial affect, criticism, punishing touch (e.g. slaps or spankings), little talk of short durations, and speech and postural divergence reflect disfavour (Bassett and Smythe 1979; Bourhis Chapter 7; Patterson 1983, Chapter 10; Street and Giles 1982).

Impression management

Upon first meeting, interactants often carry out stereotypically desirable behaviour. For initial impressions, competence appears to be associated with relatively fast and fluent speech, more talk, few pauses, brief response latencies, standard or prestigious accents, moderately loud speech, lexical diversity, speech convergence and gaze (Street and Hopper 1982, Patterson 1983). Impressions of social attractiveness are often linked to moderate to relatively fast speech (especially for males, Street *et al.* 1984), speech and accent similarity, moderate amounts of pauses and disfluencies, moderate amounts of talk (Street and Hopper 1982), smiles, head nods, appropriate self-disclosures and forward leans (Patterson 1983).

Of course behaviours contributing to judgements of competence and social attractiveness are likely to vary as a function of context. During counselling interviews, counsellor expertise is enhanced by increased gaze, forward lean and gestures directed toward the client, facial expressiveness, head nodding, gestures and interpretive statements. Trustworthiness and warmth are enhanced by facial expressiveness, gestures toward the client, gaze, postural change, open hand movements and little talk (Patterson 1983).

Job applicants are generally perceived more favourably when employing a high level of gaze, dressing appropriately, having erect posture, smiling frequently, using frequent head movements and gestures, speaking fluently (Patterson 1983), using correct grammar, displaying vocal variety, asking questions and using gestures (Stano and Reinsch 1982). Street *et al.* (1983) found that a more moderate, deliberate rate of speaking may be preferred in employment interviews relative to casual conversation.

Finally it is reasonable to assume that, with increasing relational development, stereotypically desirable behaviours assume less salience for impression management relative to behavioural patterns more unique to the relationship itself (Knapp 1978).

Interactants often attempt to defuse actually or potentially untoward behaviour through some *remedial process*. A three-step sequence typifies accounting for socially untoward behaviour: reproach, account and evaluation. Morris's (Chapter 4) elaborated model suggests that this process can be quite complex as the interactants often negotiate not only the acceptance of the remedy but also the rules presupposing a remedy is warranted and, if it is, the nature of the remedy. Cody and McLaughlin (Chapter 3) explicate two classes of variables influencing account sequences: (1) how the reproacher reproaches and (2) how the accounter perceives the offence and related situational constraints. Cody and McLaughlin describe two trends regarding the reproaches: Mitigating reproaches rarely elicit aggravating accounts, and aggravating accounts generally do. Concerning the accounter's perceptions, excuses appear to be used when offenders feel guilty and when the relationship between actors is less intimate. Justifications tend to occur with intimate and familiar others and when the offender feels highly responsible for the act.

Control

Relational control has been examined at a variety of levels. Wiemann (Chapter 5) reviews research and models of how interactants negotiate through *turn-taking sequences* during interaction. Conversational turns are yielded and assumed via subtle but powerful behaviours. Turn-yielding cues include termination of gestures, completion of a grammatical clause, sociocentric sequences such as 'you know' and 'but ah', decrease in pitch or loudness at the end of a sociocentric sequence, prolonging the last syllable in a clause, change in pitch of the last word of a clause, and asking a question. Turn beginnings are frequently characterized by head shifts away from the speaker, gesturing, overloudness of speech and audible inhalation (Duncan 1972, 1983; Duncan and Niederehe 1974). Wiemann notes that these cues assume salience when placed at speaker 'transition-relevance' places and as a function of context.

When attempting to *persuade* others, communicators usually display more nonverbal involvement behaviours (Patterson 1983, Chapter 10) such as increasing gaze, head nodding, facial expressivenes, loudness, speech rate and gestures (Mehrabian and Williams 1969). Attitude change and perceived persuasiveness have been enhanced by moderate and fast speech rates (Apple *et al.* 1979; Miller *et al.* 1976), intense language (for credible sources and attitudinally congruent messages) and diverse lexical choices (Bradac *et al.* 1979), accent similarity between speaker and listener (Giles and Powesland 1975), and postural and gestural matching (Dabbs 1969).

Related to persuasion, the *compliance-gaining* literature has reported subjects' preferences for the following strategies in the following situations: (1) married couples stated a preference for emotional appeals (agent appeals to target's love and affection) and personal rejection (agent attempts to make target feel worthless or stupid) whereas non-intimates preferred non-negotiation tactics (Fitzpatrick and Winke 1977), (2) justification strategies (e.g. providing reasons, disclaiming), exchange strategies (e.g. offering promises or compromises), and personal rejection strategies were more likely in intimate settings, (3) when the decision involves short-term consequences (e.g. postponing a date, trade-in on a used car), exchange and manipulation strategies are more likely than when the decision has long-term consequences (e.g. moving to another town, cutting down a shade tree (Cody *et al.* 1981), and (4) conciliatory strategies are likely where the agent desires liking from the target (Clarke 1979). Other compliance-gaining strategies appear to vary in complex ways with situational and relational factors (see Cody *et al.* 1981 for review).

Regarding patterns of *dominance and power* in relationships, Patterson (1983, Chapter 10) proposes that when the power relationship is stable, the more powerful interactant gazes more while speaking, less while listening, touches more, has less facial expressiveness, and is generally more relaxed (i.e. more leg and arm asymmetry and sideways lean) than the less powerful partner. Fisher (1983) demonstrated that dyads with cooperative interaction patterns are characterized by speech-act pairs of 'control-acquiescence'. When the power relationships are being negotiated among interactants, participants emerging as more dominant or having greater control frequently interrupt more (Rogers and Jones 1975; Wiemann Chapter 5; Zimmerman and West 1975), talk more (Shaw 1981), touch more (Major and Heslin 1982), shift lexical styles (e.g. from more formal to more casual, Scotton Chapter 6), and have louder and faster speech (Scherer 1979).

Task

Behavioural patterns may differentially evolve depending on the task at hand. While we will not address these issues at this time, Poole (Chapter 11) and Putman (Chapter 12) discuss interaction development for small-group decision-making and bargaining negotiation tasks respectively.

Conclusion

The comprehensive research necessary to study the encoding and decoding functions of verbal, vocal and kinesic behaviours has not yet been systematically carried out. The vast majority of research studies focus upon single behaviours relative to one or more personality traits or affective states or study the single perceptions that a particular behaviour might produce. The methodologies for simultaneously mapping complexes of personality or complexes of affective states into comprehensive codings of behaviour are available.

The necessity of such research is not merely blind empiricism but is rather an attempt to carry out a kind of behavioural scale building. Just as we would never permit a set of ill chosen questions to be accepted as a test of a theoretically important construct, similarly we should not pick a set of behaviours to describe conversations without going through the same winnowing and sifting that is done in test construction. In this section we have argued that this process must be carried out and have tried to provide some criteria for choosing what 'items' might go together in our 'test'. The criteria have included the functions or meanings that the behaviours have as evidenced by their correlations with senders' motivational states or receivers' perceptions. These criteria were chosen because it is *not* sufficient that the behaviours merely correlate with one another, the typical test of internal consistency, but that the behaviours correlate with an underlying construct which is itself meaningful to people's common interpersonal motives and interpersonal judgements. In this way behaviours that are a part of the same stream are so because of their relation to a common interpersonal motive or perception. Further, the study of the microstructures of interaction will be assured of an important place in the study of interpersonal relationships.

Summary

To summarize this overview chapter, we present a descriptive account of an interaction in Figure 1.2. This example can be discussed in terms of its vertical and sequential structure as they perform particular functions. The example consists of a brief excerpt from an employment interview. The employers' first remark, 'So you worked in food service during college?', presumably contains linguistic markers for making sense and appropriately extending the topic. The nonverbal and vocal displays – indirect body orientation, gazing when speaking, not gazing when listening, slow speech, neutral facial affect – are typical of higher-status persons when interacting with lower-status persons. In essence, these behaviours index the dominant–submissive complementarity of the two interactants. The rising vocal intonation on 'college' represents a turn-yielding cue which functions as control in the sense that the employer intends for the applicant's remark, 'Yes, I worked for three years as a student supervisor at . . .,' pragmatically and semantically to follow the previous remark. The verbal and nonverbal behaviours – smiles, head nods, gazing at the employer, upright posture, direct body orientation, relatively fast speech – represent the submissive complement of the dominant position maintained by the employer. These behaviours are also related to impression management as a show of deference and stereotypically desirable behaviours. Note also, the rather formal nature of the interaction promotes the applicant's perceived competence. In sum, the verbal and nonverbal pattern of this exchange reflects the dominant–submissive roles of the participants, coherent connections and impression management by the applicant.

This pattern changes dramatically with the subsequent remarks. After realizing that they have something in common, the employer demonstrates

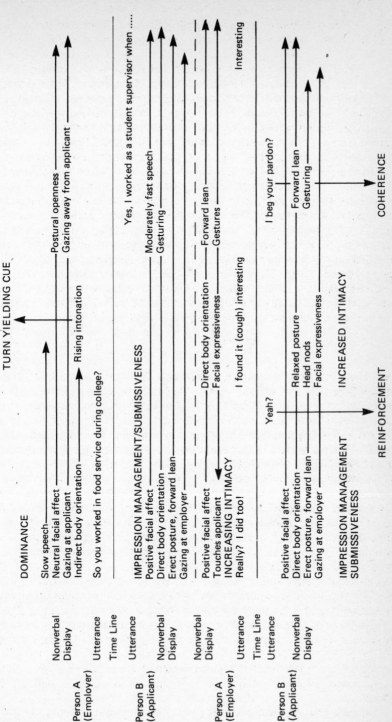

Figure 1.2 An example of behavioural patterns and their functions

greater nonverbal involvement, approval of and friendliness toward the applicant through the use of smiles, direct body orientation, patting the applicant on the back, head nods, gazing at the applicant, and a more animated vocal style. In short, the employer is defining the interaction in more egalitarian and personal terms. The applicant, apparently accepting this redefinition, reciprocates smiles and head nods, relaxes posture somewhat, and perhaps matches the employers' vocal pitch, vocal intensity and postural adjustments. Note however, that while the friendlier, more intimate setting is created, the more dominant position of the employer is maintained through the employer's licence to interrupt, the non-reciprocated touch, and the applicant's use of politeness terms. Two other behavioural functions are apparent. The applicant's 'Yeah' is for the most part a back-channel response which, along with head nods and smiles, reinforces the employer's verbal contributions and encourages continuation. The phrase 'I beg your pardon' is defined as a side sequence move designed to achieve clarity of the meaning of the previous response. As such, it functions to maintain coherence.

This example is intended to demonstrate the rich and complex nature of which behavioural arrays accomplish particular functions during social interaction. Note also the hierarchical nature of these functions. Some, such as maintaining coherence, appear to be regulated implicitly or explicitly by interactants almost constantly. Others, such as the signaling of speaker switches, emerge periodically and momentarily though the effects of such moves may linger.

The chapters in this volume stake distinctive territorial claims to portions of the social interaction domain. Part I, 'Regulating Conversational Coherence and Propriety', contains an initial essay by Tracy (Chapter 2) on cognitive principles guiding interactants' selections of conversational extensions. Cody and McLaughlin (Chapter 3) and Morris (Chapter 4) follow with discussion of remedial processes, verbal methods of fixing false steps in social interaction. Their respective explanations are quite different from one another, however. Part II, 'Power, Status and Dominance,' begins with Wiemann's analysis of turn-taking as a conversational resource whose control can mean control within the conversation and perhaps within the larger relationship. Scotton (Chapter 6) follows with a discussion of lexical style-shifting and its role in marking and even in enhancing the speaker's status and power. This section concludes with Bourhis's paper (Chapter 7), a theoretically and empirically innovative account of how the use of French or English impacts upon impression formation in bilingual Canada.

Part III concerns itself with 'Affiliation and Resource Exchange'. Dindia (Chapter 8) discusses the manner in which self-disclosure interacts with nonverbal behaviours in the expression and regulation of intimacy. Employing a social exchange model, Roloff and Campion (Chapter 9) examine conversation as the exchange of symbolic resources between interactants. This section concludes with Patterson's essay (Chapter 10), a synopsis of his sequential functional model of nonverbal behaviour.

Part IV is labelled the 'Task Function' in recognition of the fact that interactions are consciously and unconsciously purposeful, aimed at achieving group and individual, shared and unshared goals. Poole (Chapter 11) presents his theoretical and empirical work on structuration, coherence, cohesion, and decision-making in small groups. Putnam (Chapter 12) analyses the evolution of interaction patterns in different types of bargaining and negotiation. Finally in Chapter 13 we provide an empirical synthesis and suggest directions for a general theoretical account of sequential structure and pattern in communicative behaviour.

References

APPLE, W., STREETER, L.S. and KRAUS, R.M. 1979: Effects of pitch and speech rate on personal characteristics. *Journal of Personality and Social Psychology*, **37**, 715-27.

ARGYLE, M., LEFEBVRE, L. and COOK, M. 1975: The meaning of five patterns of gaze. *European Journal of Social Psychology*, **4**, 125-36.

BALES, R.F. 1970: *Personality and interpersonal behaviour*. New York: Holt, Rinehart, & Winston.

BASSETT, R. and SMYTHE, M.J. 1979: *Communication and instruction*. New York: Harper & Row.

BEATTIE, G.W. 1978: Floor apportionment and gaze in conversational dyads. *British Journal of Social and Clinical Psychology*, **17**, 7-15.

BOCHNER, A.P., KAMINSKI, E.P. and FITZPATRICK, M.A. 1977: The conceptual domain of interpersonal behaviour. *Human Communication Research*, **3**, 291-302.

BOOMER, D.S. 1963: Speech disturbance and body movement in interviews. *Journal of Nervous and Mental Disease*, **136**, 263-6.

—— 1965: Hesitation in grammatical encoding. *Language and Speech*, **8**, 148-58.

—— 1978: The phonemic clause: Speech unit in human communication. In Siegman, A.W. and Feldstein, S., editors, *Nonverbal behaviour and communication* (Hillsdale, NJ: Erlbaum).

BOOMER, D.S. and DITTMAN, A.T. 1964: Speech rate, filled pause, and body movement in interviews. *Journal of Nervous and Mental Disease*, **139**, 324-7.

BRADAC, J.J., BOWERS, J.W. and COURTRIGHT, J.A. 1979: Three language variables in communication research: Intensity, immediacy, and diversity. *Human Communication Research*, **5**, 257-69.

BRUNER, J.S. 1979: Smiles can be back channels. *Journal of Personality and Social Psychology*, **37**, 728-34.

BURGOON, J.K. 1978: A communication model of personal space violations: Explication and initial test. *Human Communication Research*, **4**, 129-42.

—— (in press.) Nonverbal communication. In Knapp, M.L. and Miller, G.R., editors, *Handbook of interpersonal communication* (Beverly Hills, CA: Sage).

BUTTERWORTH, B. 1975: Hesitation and semantic planning in speech. *Journal of Psycholinguistic Research*, **4**, 75-87.

BUTTERWORTH, B. and GOLDMAN-EISLER, F. 1979: Recent studies on cognitive rhythm In Siegman, A.W. and Feldstein, S., editors, *Of speech and time* Hillsdale, NJ:, Erlbaum).

CAPPELLA, J.N. 1981: Mutual influence in expressive behaviour: Adult-adult and infant-adult dyadic interaction. *Psychological Bulletin*, **89**, 101-32.

—— 1983: Conversational involvement: Approaching and avoiding others. In

Wiemann, J.M. and Harrison, R.P., editors, *Nonverbal interaction.* (Beverly Hills, Cal.: Sage).

—— in press: Controlling the floor in conversation. In Siegman, A.W. and Feldstein, S., editors, *Nonverbal communication* (Hillsdale, NJ: Erlbaum).

CAPPELLA, J.N. and STREIBEL, M.S. 1979: Computer analysis of talk-silence sequences: The FIASSCO system. *Behavioural Research Methods and Instrumentation*, **11**, 384–92

CAPPELLA, J.N. and PLANALP, S. 1981: Talk and silence sequences in informal conversations III: Interspeaker influences. *Human Communication Research*, **7**, 117–32.

CAPPELLA, J.N. and GREENE, J.O. 1982: A discrepancy-arousal explanation of mutual influence in expressive behaviour for adult–adult and infant–adult interaction. *Communication Monographs*, **49**, 89–114.

CARSON, R.C. 1969: *Interaction concepts of personality*. Chicago: Aldine.

CHAPPLE, E.D. 1939: Quantitative analysis of the interaction of individuals. *Proceedings of the National Academy of Sciences*, **25**, 58–67.

—— 1940: Personality differences as described by invariant properties of individuals in interaction. *Proceedings of the National Academy of Sciences*, **26**, 10–14.

CLARK, R.A. 1979: The impact on selection of persuasive strategies on self-interest and desired liking. *Communication Monographs*, **46**, 257–73.

CODY, M.J., MCLAUGHLIN, M.L. and SCHNEIDER, M.J. 1981: The impact of intimacy and relational consequences on the selection of interpersonal persuasion tactics. *Communication Quarterly*, **29**, 91–106.

COOK, M. and SMITH, J.M. 1975: The role of gaze in impression formation. *British Journal of Social and Clinical Psychology*, **14**, 19–25.

COZBY, P.C. 1972: Self-disclosure, reciprocity and liking. *Sociometry*, **35**, 151–60.

DABBS, J.M. 1969: Similarity of gestures and interpersonal influence. *Proceedings of the 77th Annual Convention of the American Psychological Association*, **6**, 337–8.

DALY, J.A., MCCROSKEY, J.P. and RICHMOND, V.C. 1977: Relationships between vocal activity and perception of communicators in small-group interaction. *Western Journal of Speech Communication*, **41**, 175–87.

DERLEGA, V.J., HARRIS, M.S. and CHAIKIN, A.L. 1973: Self-disclosure, liking and the deviant. *Journal of Experimental Social Psychology*, **9**, 277–84.

DITTMAN, A.T. 1962: The relationship between body movements and moods in interviews. *Journal of Consulting Psychology*, **26**, 480.

—— 1972: The body movement speech rhythm relationship as a cue to speech encoding. In Siegman, A.W. and Pope, B., editors, *Studies in dyadic communication* (New York: Pergamon).

DITTMAN, A.T. and LLEWELLYN, L.G. 1969: Body movement and speech rhythm in social conversation. *Journal of Personality and Social Psychology*, **11**, 98–106.

DOVIDIO, J.F. and ELLYSON, S.L. 1982: Decoding visual dominance: Attributions of power based upon relative percentages of looking while speaking and looking while listening. *Social Psychology Quarterly*, **45**, 106–13.

DUNCAN, S.D. 1972: Some signals and rules for taking turns in conversations.

Journal of Personality and Social Psychology, **23**, 283–92.

DUNCAN, S.D. 1983: Speaking turns: Studies of structures and individual differences. In Wiemann, J. and Harrison, R.P., editors, *Nonverbal interaction*. (Beverly Hills, Cal.: Sage).

DUNCAN, S.D. and FISKE, D.W. 1977: *Face-to-face interaction*. Hillsdale, NJ: Erlbaum.

DUNCAN, S.D. and NIEDEREHE, G. 1974: On signalling that it's your turn to speak. *Journal of Experimental and Social Psychology*, **10**, 234–47.

EIDINGER, J.A. and PATTERSON, M.L. 1983: Nonverbal involvement and social control. *Psychological Bulletin*, **93**, 30–56.

ELLIS, D.E. and FISHER, B.A. 1975: Phases of conflict in small group development: A Markov analysis. *Human Communication Research*, **1**, 195–212.

ELLSWORTH, P.P. and CARLSMITH, J.M. 1968: The effects of eye contact and verbal content on affective response to dyadic interaction. *Journal of Personality and Social Psychology*, **10**, 15–20.

ELLSWORTH, P.P. and LANGER, E.J. 1976: Staring and approach: An interpretation of the stare as a nonspecific activator. *Journal of Personality and Social Psychology*, **33**, 117–22.

FELDSTEIN, S. and WELKOWITZ, J. 1978: A chronography of conversation: In defense of an objective approach. In Siegman, A.W. and Feldstein, S., editors, *Nonverbal behaviour and communication*. (Hillsdale, NJ: Erlbaum).

FISHER, B.A. 1983: Differential effects of sexual composition and interactional context on interaction patterns in dyads. *Human Communication Research*, **9**, 225–38.

FITZPATRICK, M.A. and WINKE, J. 1979: You always hurt the one you love: Strategies and tactics in interpersonal conflict. *Communication Quarterly*, **27**, 3–11.

FOLGER, J.P., HEWES, D.E. and POOLE, M.S. 1984: Coding social interaction. In Dervin, B. and Voigt, M., editors, *Progress in communication sciences*, Vol. 4, (Norwood, NJ: Ablex).

FREEDMAN, N. 1972: The analysis of movement behaviour during the clinical interview. In Siegman, A.W. and Pope, B., editors, *Studies in dyadic communication*, (New York: Pergamon).

FREY, S. 1983: Integrating speech and movement with the sequel-analysis-model. Paper presented at the Second International Conference on Social Psychology and Language, Bristol, England.

GILES, H. and POWESLAND, P.F. 1975: *Speech style and social evaluation*. London: Academic Press.

GILES, H. and SMITH, P.M. 1979: Accommodation theory: Optimal levels of convergence. In Giles, H. and St Clair, R.N., editors, *Language and social psychology* (Oxford: Blackwell).

GILES, H. and STREET, R.L. in press: Communicator characteristics and behaviour: A review, generalizations, and a model. In Knapp, M.L. and Miller, G.R., editors, *Handbook of interpersonal communication* (Beverly Hills, Cal.: Sage).

GILBERT, S.J. 1976: Empirical and theoretical extensions of self-disclosure. In Miller, G.R., editor, *Explorations in interpersonal communication* (Beverly Hills, Cal.: Sage).

HAYES, D.P. and MELTZER, L. 1972: Interpersonal judgments based upon talkativeness: I. Fact or artifact. *Sociometry*, **35**, 538–61.

HAYES, D.P. and SIEVERS, S. 1972: A sociolinguistic investigation of 'dimensions' of interpersonal behaviour. *Journal of Personality and Social Psychology*, **24**, 254–61.

HEWES, D.E., PLANALP, S. and STRIEBEL, M.J. 1980: Analyzing social interaction: Some excruciating models and exhilirating results. In Nimmo, D., editor,*Communication yearbook 4* (New Brunswick, NJ: Transaction).

HOPPER, R. 1981: The taken for granted. *Human Communication Research*, **7**, 195–211.

ICKES, W., PATTERSON, M.L., RAJECKI, D.W. and TANFORD, S. 1982: Behavioural and cognitive consequences of reciprocal versus compensatory responses to pre-interaction expectancies. *Social Cognition*, **1**, 160–90.

JAFFE, J. FELDSTEIN, S. 1970: *Rhythms of dialogue*. New York: Academic Press.

KENDON, A. 1970: Movement coordination in social interaction: Some examples described. *Acta Psychologica*, **32**, 100–25.

—— 1983: Gesture and speech: How they interact. In Wiemann, J.M. and Harrison, R.P., editors, *Nonverbal interaction* Beverly Hills, Cal.: Sage).

KIESLER, D.J. 1982: The 1982 interpersonal circle: A taxonomy for complementarity in human transactions. *Psychological Review*, **90**, 185–214.

KNAPP, M.L. 1978: *Social intercourse: From greeting to goodbye*. Boston: Allyn & Bacon.

LEARY, T. 1957: *Interpersonal diagnosis of personality*. New York: Ronald Press.

LORR, M. and McNAIR, D.M. 1965: Expansion of the interpersonal behaviour circle. *Journal of Personality and Social Psychology*, **2**, 823–30.

MacLACHLAN, J. 1979: What people really thing of fast talkers. *Psychology Today*, 113–16.

MAJOR, B. and HESLIN, R. 1982: Perceptions of cross-sex and same-sex nonreciprocal touch: It's better to give than to receive. *Journal of Nonverbal behaviour*, **6**, 148–62.

MATARAZZO, J.D. and WIENS, A.N. 1972: *The interview: Research on its anatomy and structure*. Chicago: Aldine-Atherton.

MEHRABIAN, A. 1971: Verbal and nonverbal interaction of strangers in a waiting situation. *Journal of Experimental Research in Personality*, **5**, 127–38.

—— 1972: *Nonverbal communication*. Chicago: Aldine-Atherton.

MEHRABIAN, A. and KSIONSKY, S. 1970: Models for affiliative and conformity behaviour. *Psychological Bulletin*, **74**, 110–26.

—— 1972: Categories of social behaviour. *Comparative Group Studies*, **3**, 425–36.

MEHRABIAN, A. and WILLIAMS, M. 1969: Nonverbal concomitants of perceived and intended persuasiveness. *Journal of Personality and Social Psychology*, **13**, 37–58.

MILLER, N., MARAYAMA, G., BEABER, R.J. and VALONE, K. 1976: Speed of speech and persuasion. *Journal of Personality and Social Psychology*, **34**, 615–24.

MORRIS, G.H. and HOPPER, R. 1980: Remediation and legislation in everyday talk: How communicators achieve consensus on rules. *Quarterly Journal of Speech*, **67**, 266–74.

NEWTSON, D. 1976: Foundations of attribution: The perception of ongoing behaviour. In Harvey, J.H., Ickes W.J. and Kidd, R.F., editors, *New directions in attribution research*, Vol. 1. (Hillsdale, NJ: Erlbaum).

NEWTSON, D., ENQUIST, G. and BOIS, J. 1977: The objective basis of behaviour units. *Journal of Personality and Social Psychology*, **12**, 847–62.

NORTON, R.W. 1978: Foundations of a communicator style construct. *Human Communication Research*, **4**, 99–112.

—— 1983: *Communication style*. Beverly Hills, Cal.: Sage.

OSGOOD, C.E., and SUCI, G. and TANNENBAUM, P. 1957: *The measurement of meaning*. Urbana, Ill.: University of Illinois Press.

PATTERSON, M.L. 1982a: A sequential functional model of nonverbal exchange. *Psychological Review*, **89**, 231–49.

—— 1982b: Personality and nonverbal involvement: A functional analysis. In Ickes, W. and Knowles, E.S., editors, *Personality, roles, and social behaviour* (New York: Springer-Verlag).

—— 1983: *Nonverbal behaviour: A functional perspective*. New York: Springer-Verlag.

PATTERSON, M.L. and SECHREST, L.B. 1970: Interpersonal distance and impression formation. *Journal of Personality*, **38**, 161–6.

POOLE, M.S. 1981: Decision development in small groups I: A comparison of two models. *Communication Monographs*, **48**, 1–24.

POOLE, M.S. and FOLGER, J.P. 1981: A method for establishing representational validity of interaction coding systems: Do we see what they see? *Human Communication Research*, **8**, 26–42.

RAGAN, S.L. 1983: A conversational analysis of alignment talk in job interviews. In Bostrom, R.N., editors, *Communication Yearbook 7* (Beverly Hills, Cal.: Sage).

ROGERS, W.T. and JONES, S.E. 1975: Effects of dominance tendencies on floor-holding and interruption behaviour in dyadic interaction. *Human Communication Research*, **1**, 113–22.

SCHERER, K.R. 1979: Voice and speech correlates of perceived social influence in simulated juries. In Giles, H. and St Clair, R., editors, *Language and social psychology* (Baltimore, Md.: University Park Press).

SCHUTZ, W.C. 1958: *The interpersonal underworld*. Palo Alto, Cal.: Science and Behaviour Books.

SHAW, M.E. 1981: *Group dynamics: The psychology of small group behaviour*. (Third edition.) New York: McGraw-Hill.

SHROUT, P.E. and FISKE, D.W. 1982: Nonverbal behaviours and social evaluation. *Journal of Personality*, **49**, 115–28.

SMITH, B., BROWN, B., STRONG, W. and RENCHER, A. 1975: Effects of speech rate on personality perception. *Language and Speech*, **18**, 145–52.

SORRENTINO, R.M. and BOUTELLIER, R.G. 1975: The effect of quality and quantity of verbal interaction on ratings of leadership quality. *Journal of Experimental Social Psychology*, **11**, 403–11.

STANG, D.J. 1973: Effect of interaction rate on ratings of leadership and liking. *Journal of Experimental Social Psychology*, **27**, 405–8.

STANO, M.E. and REISCH, N.L. 1982: *Communication in interviews*. Englewood Cliffs, NJ.: Prentice Hall.

STREET, R.L., Jr, 1983: Noncontent speech convergence in adult–child interactions. In Bostrom, R.N., editor, *Communication Yearbook 7* (Beverly

Hills, Cal.: Sage).

STREET, R.L., Jr, BRADY, R.M. and LEE, R. 1984: Evaluative responses to communicators: The effects of sex, speech rate, and interaction context. *Western Journal of Speech Communication*, **48**, 14–27.

STREET, R.L., Jr, BRADY, R.M. and PUTMAN, W. 1983: The influence of speech rate stereotypes and rate similarity on listener's evaluative judgements of speakers. *Journal of Language and Social Psychology*, **2**, 37–56.

STREET, R.L., Jr, and GILES, H. 1982: Speech accommodation theory: A social cognitive approach to language and speech behaviour. In Roloff, M. and Berger, C.R., editors, *Social cognition and communication* (Beverly Hills, Cal.: Sage).

STREET, R.L., Jr, and HOPPER, R. 1982: A model of speech style evaluation. In Ryan, E.B. and Giles, H., editors, *Attitudes towards language variation: Social and applied contexts*. (London: Edward Arnold).

THOMPSON, D.E., AIELLO, J.R. and EPSTEIN, Y.M. 1979: Interpersonal distance preferences. *Journal of Nonverbal behaviour*, **4**, 113–18.

TRACY, K. 1983: The issue–event distinction: A rule of conversation and its scope conditions. *Human Communication Research*, **9**, 300–14.

TRAGER, G.L. and SMITH, H.L. 1951: *An outline of English structure*. Norman, Okla.: Battenburg Press.

TRIANDIS, H.C. and VASILIOU, V. 1972: A comparative analysis of subjective culture. In Triandis, H.C., editor, *The analysis of subjective culture* (New York: Wiley).

TRIANDIS, H.C., VASILIOU, V. and NASSIAKOU, M. 1968: Three cross-cultural studies of subjective culture. *Journal of Personality and Social Psychology*, Monograph Supplement, **8**, 1–42.

WHITCHER, S.J. and FISHER, J.D. 1979: Multidimensional reaction to therapeutic touch in a hospital setting. *Journal of Personality and Social Psychology*, **37**, 87–96.

WIGGINS, J.S. 1979: A psychological taxonomy of trait descriptive terms: The interpersonal domain. *Journal of Personality and Social Psychology*, **37**, 395–412.

—— 1982: Circumplex models of interpersonal behaviour in clinical psychology. In Kendall, P.C. and Butcher, J. N., editors, *Handbook of research methods in clinical psychology* (New York: Wiley).

WISH, M., D'ANDRADE, R.G. and GOODNOW, J.E. 1980: Dimensions of interpersonal communication: Correspondence between structures for speech acts and bipolar scales. *Journal of Personality and Social Psychology*, **39**, 848–60.

WISH, M., DEUTSCH, M. and KAPLAN, S.J. 1976; Perceived dimensions of interpersonal relations. *Journal of Personality and Social Psychology*, **33**, 409–20.

WISH, M. and KAPLAN, S.J. 1977: Toward an implicit theory of interpersonal communication. *Sociometry*, **40**, 234–46.

WON-DOORNINK, M.J. 1979: On getting to know you: The association between the stage of a relationship and reciprocity of self-disclosure. *Journal of Experimental Social Psychology*, **15**, 229–41.

ZIMMERMAN, D.H. and WEST, C. 1975: Sex roles, interruptions and silences in conversation. In Thorne, B. and Henley, N., editors, *Power and dominance* (Rowley, Mass.: Newbury).

2

Conversational coherence: a cognitively grounded rules approach

Karen Tracy

To initiate talking or continue listening, to smile or frown, to gaze away or toward, to speak quickly or slowly, to pause briefly or for an extended time, to use a formal or informal dialect, to talk about intimate or superficial topics – all these conversational actions, to name but a few, are influenced by one's conversational partner (Cappella 1981; Street and Giles 1982). For a number of these actions, communicators appear only marginally aware of choosing a response based on their partner's actions (Cappella and Planalp 1981; Giles 1980). This limited awareness about choice is not true for all conversational behaviours. Perhaps the decision about which communicators appear most aware concerns what to say next in conversation. That this is indeed perceived as a communicator choice influenced by the partner is suggested by the kinds of comments and criticisms communicators make about themselves and others. Comments like 'I didn't know what to say to him', 'I said the wrong thing', or 'She changed the topic' imply that communicators hold themselves and others responsible for how the conversation is continued. Moreover, the comments suggest that communicators feel constrained in their selection of what to say next and likewise expect their partner to feel similar constraints.

What are these constraints? Where do they reside? How do we explain them? Stated more technically, what is conversational coherence and how is it best explained? In this chapter I take as a central goal the explanation of conversational coherence – the fact that comments produced in conversation seem connected to each other in meaningful orderly ways. In particular I argue for the value of a cognitively grounded rules approach to explaining conversational coherence. I begin by considering the different functions served by topic management, then describe and give a critique of two alternative explanations of conversational coherence: discourse-based, and situation–interpreter based;

and finally, present a cognitively grounded rules approach, showing how it accounts for many of the regularities that exist in conversational sequencing, while at the same time allowing for irregularity. In addition, I also show how a cognitively grounded rules approach accounts for judgements communicators make about what are appropriate and competent responses in a variety of conversations.

Functions of topic management

The achievement of conversational coherence – successful topic management – can be seen as serving two major functions. First, it serves self-presentational and relational goals (Brown and Levinson 1978). By staying on the topic the partner has introduced, the speaker grants the other the freedom to define the nature of the interaction (i.e., what will be talked about) and therein indicates deference to the other. Staying on the partner's topic is also a gesture of friendliness. It indicates that a speaker is interested in what interests the partner. On the other hand, changing the topic from the speaker's focus is a way of establishing one's own importance and right to define the interaction. Changing the topic may indicate that the speaker is self-confident, assertive, full of interesting things to say, not obsequious or submissive, Yet it may also be construed as evidence that the speaker is overly dominant, rude or stupid (e.g. when a topic change is seen as a failure to 'get the point'). In the extreme, radical topic change with complete and consistent failure to provide relevant linkages will be taken as evidence that one is 'not normal', either schizophrenic (Rochester and Martin 1979) or mentally retarded (Bedrosian 1979).

Other conversational behaviours besides the way the topic is managed have implications for self-presentation and the relationship, but the fact that communicators are seen as choosing what to say next, where they might not, for instance, be seen as choosing speech rate or eye-gaze behaviour, gives topic management a special role in assessing one conversationist's intentions toward the other. Thus the degree to which a communicator extends or changes the topical focus and the manner in which it is done carry a host of implications for how each person in the interaction will be perceived by the other.

While self and relationship presentation goals are important functions of topic management, they are not the only ones. In fact these functions may be seen as resting on an even more basic one – interaction management. Interaction management concerns the establishment of a smooth and easy pattern of exchange, the meshing of one person's contributions with the other's (Argyle 1969). This meshing is difficult, if not impossible, if the conversation consists of non-sequiturs. Vuchinich (1977) illustrates how failure to relate one's contribution to the ongoing discourse may cause awkward silences and other signs of disrupted flow. Unless each conversationist gives some attention to making his or her contribution relevant, smooth and continous interaction is impossible. Thus, adherence to relevancy expectations (Grice 1975) both creates a structure that we recognize as 'conversation' and is the behavioural basis for higher-level personality inferences about self and other.

Approaches to coherence

Discourse-based

Discourse-based approaches to coherence include a number of distinct theories, most notably sequencing rules models (Searle 1969, 1975; Sacks *et al*. 1978), the cohesion model (Halliday and Hasan 1976), and the move model (Goldberg 1983). While differing in a number of respects, soon to be mentioned, these approaches explain coherence by appealing primarily to discourse features. Sequencing rules models explain the connectedness of discourse by positing a set of rules which specify which type of act may follow others. These rules exist not at the surface level of the discourse but at the level of the act performed. Typically, identification of a unit of discourse as a particular act (e.g. request, order, promise) is based on a set of felicity conditions. Although theorists disagree about what felicity conditions apply to specific acts – Searle (1969), for example, posits an invariant set of conditions necessary for the accomplishment of any act where Kreckel (1981) maintains that felicity conditions vary from social group to social group – once a discourse unit is identified as an act, sequencing rules models specify which acts may follow each other.

The most explicit formulation of sequencing rules is seen in the work on adjacency pairs (Sacks *et al*. 1978). Essentially an adjacency pair consists of two parts, the 'first pair part' and the 'second pair part'. Utterance of the second part is expected or in Schegloff's term, 'conditionally relevant' upon the first part's expression. So, for example, sequencing rules specify if a question has been uttered, an answer should follow. If the appropriate second part does not follow the initiating utterance, the sequence will be notably deviant. Speech acts may have more than one acceptable second part; for instance while grants are preferred in response to requests, refusals are also acceptable (Jackson and Jacobs 1980). In all cases, however, sequencing rules models identify constraints on what act may follow another (Levinson 1981).

Sequencing rules explanations of relevance have been criticized on three counts. First, they make predictions that do not hold up; conversational data do not demonstrate the level of regularity claimed to exist. Plausible examples of relevant utterance sequences may be provided that violate the sequencing rules. For instance if a speaker posed the question, 'What does Joe do for a living?', the partner could respond:

    i: Do you need to know?
    ii: Oh, this and that.
    iii: I've no idea.
    iv: What's that got to do with it?
    v: He doesn't.
    (Levinson 1981, p. 107)

As Levinson (1981) summarizes, 'responses to first parts of adjacency pairs are a lot freer than question–answer stereotypes would suggest. Questions may be happily followed by questions, by partial answers, statements of ignorance, denials of the relevance of the question, details of the presuppositions of the question and so on' (p. 107).

A second problem is that sequential rules models make no predictions where they are needed (Jacobs and Jackson 1983; Levinson 1981). Much of conversational discourse consists of the speech act of asserting; yet this is just the act for which the sequencing rules model has the least to say. It does not seem plausible, for example, that any assertion may follow any other assertion. Besides act structure, it seems likely that semantic and lexical properties need to be considered in formulating what may count as relevant.

A third criticism of sequencing rules models is the quality of the explanation offered. Sequential rules models provide no basis to explain *why* a rule takes the form it does (Jacobs and Jackson 1983). Not only is the lack of an explanatory principle dissatisfying in and of it itself (see Berger 1977; Miller 1978), it also means there is no way to generate other rules of conversation. Before retreating to a position that sees conversational rules as no more than a set of arbitrary, although agreed upon, conventions (Lewis 1969) we need to consider principles that might link and explain the regularities we do see.

In contrast to sequencing rules models which aim to explain, the goal of the move system (Goldberg 1983) is to provide an adequate descriptive account of the utterance sequences that occur in natural discourse. Explanation, Goldberg argues, is premature without an adequate descriptive basis. Discourse in her system is classified into moves – units roughly analogous to sentences – based on whether they tie semantically to propositions in the immediate discourse (progressive holding moves or holding moves), earlier discourse (reintroducing moves) or have no semantic ties (introducing move). When the move system is applied to natural discourse, clear sequencing preferences are not obvious; there appear to be no absolute constraints on what type of move may follow another. Goldberg's failure to find absolute constraints may be related to the units of analysis used; that is, her units may be too gross to capture the constraints that exist. More likely, however, is the possibility that absolute constraints do not exist. Thus, the move system and the sequencing rules approach emphasize opposite characteristics of conversational data; sequencing rules models emphasize regularity; the move model emphasizes the lack of regularity. Both of these probably exist. The crucial task, then, is to account for the utterance sequences that are more probable in a way that does not prohibit the occurrence of other sequences.

A quite different discourse-based approach is seen in the work of Halliday and Hasan (1976) on cohesion. They catalogue a host of linguistic devices – for example pronomial reference, ellipsis, lexical connectives – used to create connectedness in discourse. Of particular importance is their idea that cohesion is a matter of degree. Thus for any text a cohesiveness score may be computed by counting the cohesive devices present. Halliday and Hasan's primary concern is for written texts produced by a single individual, yet their approach is applicable to conversation. Conversants would be expected to use various cohesive devices to signal the connectedness of their discourse with what preceded it. The apt use of particular cohesive devices is, in fact, one way normal adult speakers differ from schizophrenics (Rochester and Martin 1979). Moreover noncohesive turns are followed by longer latencies, more terminations, and are better remembered and marked as unusual (Vuchinich 1977).

The cohesion approach provides insight into the nature of conversational relevancy. A relevant remark is one that ties to earlier discourse through the use of any number of devices. However just as with the sequential rules, the cohesion model is unduly rigid. Utterance sequences may have no cohesive devices and still appear relevant or possess them and appear lacking in relevancy. Consider the following two examples:

A: Are you ready for dinner?
B: The time is 4 o'clock.

A: The weather is wonderful today.
B: But, it's sad that it had to happen that way.

The first sequence seems like a sensible reply if both conversants come from an area where dinner is usually served at six p.m. and both know that the other knows that. However no cohesive devices have been used. In the second example, cohesive devices are present (conjunction and several types of pronominal reference) but it is hard to imagine response B as other than bizarre from a point of view that takes only the discourse into account. While it is undoubtedly true that cohesion devices are usually present between consecutive utterances and usually do help to create a sense of connectedness, we need to consider more than just the discourse.

Two other factors are used to explain the connectedness of conversation: the situation or context, and the mind of the interpreter. Since these two factors are often invoked jointly to explain coherence the next section considers them together. Situation–interpreter approaches are better seen as reactions to, and criticisms of, discourse-based approaches rather than independent explanatory positions; as such, their primary value is to highlight problems with discourse-based approaches that a satisfactory theory of conversational coherence will need to consider.

Situation–interpreter approaches

Situation–interpreter approaches focus on how communicators draw upon situational and relational background knowledge to determine whether an utterance sequence seems connected and reasonable. For instance, consider the following sequence between two co-workers on Monday morning as they ride out work:

Woman 1:   We saw that new movie Saturday night. It was good.
Woman 2:   Jack and I also went . . . uh, bowling . . . on Sunday.
(Sigman 1983, p. 180)

The sequence seems connected, not because of specifics about the discourse but because of our situational knowledge that reports on weekend activity are a frequent conversational activity between friendly acquaintances. The relevance of one utterance to another, then, depends on the context in which it is said (Hymes 1974). If, for example, at bedtime a child says to a parent 'I'm hungry', and the parent responds, 'No, it's past your bedtime', the sequence seems coherent because of our situational knowledge of the strategies children use to avoid going to bed. However, this utterance sequence would be bizarre and incoherent if it occurred between a pedestrian and a beggar on a public street.

That coherence depends on the relationship between an utterance sequence and the situation is a proposition with which few people would quarrel. Differences, however, exist in opinions about the degree to which situational knowledge is shared and situations are interpreted similarly. On the one hand are

scholars who emphasize the idiosyncracy of situational knowledge and interpretation. Beach (1983), for instance, shows how utterance sequences between
friends and acquaintances are understandable as coherent only by bringing to
bear very specific background information about the interactants. Thus, the
categorization of an utterance sequence as coherent or not becomes virtually
impossible from the perspective of an observer. Hopper (1983, p. 81) goes even
further; he suggests that coherence is not so much explained by features of the
discourse or even of the situation but by communicators' 'will to cohere'.
Interpreters, he argues, are motivated to see things as connected and hence will
supply some type of connection regardless of what they have to work with. A
similar sentiment is expressed by Sanders (1983, p. 69): 'Whether an item is
relevant depends entirely on the interpreter's ability (or willingness) to infer or
invent a situationally plausible, topically relevant motive for the communicator's having included the item: no principled basis for saying categorically
that an item is relevant or not seems to exist.'

On the other hand are scholars (e.g. Forgas 1979; Frentz and Farrell 1976;
Hymes 1974; Pearce and Conklin 1979) who stress the shared nature of situational knowledge. Participants within a culture, they argue, share expectations
about appropriate sequences of action and dialogue in particular situations.
These contextual or 'episodic' expectations constrain whether, and to what
degree, utterance sequences will be perceived as coherent. In other words, the
social episodes within which participants are engaged create particular rules of
relevancy. In the courtroom, for example, the necessity to make all information
explicit to the jury and available in a written record leads to different kinds of
conversational sequencing than seen in everyday interchange (Nofsinger 1983).

Sigman (1983) documents three influences that situations generally have on
how communicators construct and understand message sequences. Drawing
upon examples from conversations in nursing homes among patient and staff,
he shows how the situation – including both the larger institution and the social
relationship between the conversants – constrains: (1) the information that is to
be taken for granted, (2) the information that must be excluded from an interchange, and (3) the information that is generally expected to be shared. In
summary, situation–interpreter approaches alert us to two problems in strictly
discourse-based views: situation variability and individual variability. Clearly
an adequate theory of conversational coherence will need to take into account
the role of situation. This requires, however, more specific identification of
general situational dimensions or the important social episodes that influence
discourse choices. Without this type of specificity we have little more to go on
than the vague, although certainly true, claim that 'it depends on the situation'.
The second problem, the potential individuality of interpretation, while true, I
believe, is overstated. When we take the interpreter position to an extreme, the
apparent connectedness of discourse becomes a myth. Experience of social
situations is not completely or even highly idiosyncratic. If it were, there would
be no way to account for the similarities in judgements communicators share
about good and poor things to say (Tracy 1982), nor about the similarities in
reactions (i.e. silences, topic termination) to specific types of sequences
(Vuchinich 1977). Second, a radical interpreter position fails to consider regularities in how any cognitive system may be structured. In other words, it seems
reasonable to expect regularities because humans all use the same tool, that is

the brain, and that tool has constraints on how it may be used.

Summary

Based on the research and arguments made thus far, let me suggest several findings that need to be considered in a theory of conversational coherence: (1) Regularities exist concerning what units of discourse may follow other units but the regularities are far from perfect. (2) Coherence is not an all or none phenomenon but is better conceived of as a matter of degree; some utterance sequences are more coherent than others. (3) An adequate account of conversational coherence needs to show, or at least suggest, the nature of the ties between text, situation and interpreter. In the next section I describe a cognitively grounded rules approach to conversational coherence and illustrate how it deals with these three concerns.

Cognitively grounded conversational rules

Overview of perspective

Before focusing in on our central question, 'what counts as relevant?', let us consider the two key parts of our perspective: rules and cognitive grounding. For some time communication theorists have argued over the advantages and limitation of a variety of perspectives for the study of human interaction (Berger 1977; Cushman 1977; Delia 1977; Monge 1977). One perspective that has received considerable attention is that of rules. While this perspective is not a uniform viewpoint (Pearce and Conklin 1979); there are points of commonality. Shimanoff (1980) specifies four. First, rules pertain to behaviour; they specify how people should act rather than focusing on what they should think or feel. Second, a rule while preferred or in some cases mandatory, is not deterministic. People may choose whether or not to manifest the identified behaviour in any particular situation. Third, a rule is prescriptive. While communicators in any particular situation may choose not to follow the rule, they cannot avoid the negative evaluations that generally follow should they do so. Finally, a rule is contextual; it applies only under certain circumstances.

A *rules* approach to conversational sequencing, then, would specify: (1) preferred types of conversational extensions; (2) provide evidence that identified response types, indeed, are seen as more appropriate and preferred over other types of responses; (3) provide evidence that people actually respond in the preferred manner a good portion of the time; and (4) describe the conditions when the preference operates.

A *cognitively grounded* approach to conversational rules adds one more component. Not only does the perspective identify the regularities that exist in the sequencing of conversational units and communicator judgements of appropriateness but it explains *why* these regularities occur. The perspective shows how conversational regularities derive from general cognitive principles. In a nutshell, communication is a complex task which taxes the mental resources and capacities of conversants. Thus, any way of proceeding that makes the cognitive work easier will be preferred response types (see Hewes and Planalp 1982; Planalp and Hewes 1982 for a good overview of this perspective).

With regard to utterance sequencing this implies that conversational extensions which draw upon typical inference patterns will be preferred over those that draw upon atypical ones.

The cognitive approach outlined here bears some similarity to two other approaches to conversation. The first approach, seen in the work of Brown and Levinson (1978), argues that people are universally concerned about self-presentation and relational concerns, and pursue those goals in a rational manner where means are selected judiciously to accomplish particular ends. Discourse choices, then, are explained by particular goal configurations. A second approach, seen in the work of Jacobs and Jackson (1983), attempts to formulate rules of rationality communicators typically use to pursue goals. Here regularity in the discourse is explained by appeal to a set of underlying rational principles that guide human action. Like these rational approaches, the cognitive approach also assumes humans are rational beings that seek goals. However, unlike these approaches, the focus is on the mental operations (information processing, storage and retrieval) that undergird rational behaviour.

The following section presents a series of studies, carried out by colleagues and myself, elaborating and assessing this perspective. Three decisions communicators need to make about conversational sequencing are considered. For each decision I describe the conversational extension options available, provide evidence of which options are used most often or are judged most appropriate, and illustrate how these preferences and behavioural regularities can be accounted for by a small set of cognitive principles.

Selection of a context

The first task for speakers when uttering a remark, or listeners when interpreting one, is the establishment of a context in which the remark can be understood. Without understanding, conversation, as we recognize it, has not occurred. Thus, the establishment of interaction requires that conversationists say at least minimally understandable things to each other. Understanding involves relating an input (e.g. a conversational remark) to a context or background information (Bransford and Nitch 1974; Kintch and van Dijk 1978; Ortony 1978). This context may be of three types: the conversation itself (what has already been said), the particular situation within which the conversation occurs, and the general cultural knowledge that interactants have at their disposal (Keenan and Schieffelin 1976; Planalp and Tracy 1980). Each of these sources of information when paired with an input may yield understanding; yet each of these types of background information will not be equally salient. As a result information that is most salient will be searched first. If a conversationist cannot make a connection between the salient context and the input, only then are the less salient contexts searched (Hobbs 1979).

The principle of salience provides a basis for evaluating conversational extension types and formulating a preliminary conversational rule. This we did in our first study (Planalp and Tracy 1980); the rationale was as follows: The conversation, we argued, is likely to be more salient to participants than non-conversational contexts. In general participants are expected to be involved in the conversation and focused upon what the other is saying (Goffman 1957). Hence a remark which extends a part of the conversation will be easier to understand than one that links to a source outside. Within the conversation, comments that link to the immediate topic will be more understandable than remarks that tie to a topic that may have occurred much earlier. Since the current topic is expected to be, and usually is, the focus of attention for both participants, the easiest comment to understand will be one that links to it. Comments that extend topics that occurred much earlier in the discourse require the listener to search prior topics to find one the input comment may be tied to. Earlier topics, then, were predicted to be less salient than the immediate one.

Besides the conversation, communicators may introduce remarks that respond to the environment (e.g. commenting on someone walking by) or general background knowledge (non-environmental and non-conversational knowledge). Both of these types of conversational extensions should prove difficult to follow. While neither are likely to be the focus of communicators' attention in a typical conversational setting, environmental extensions were expected to be more salient than background-knowledge extensions. At least for the environment, participants share it; for background knowledge, even this may not be true. Because the background knowledge that may be brought to bear in understanding any utterance is vast, links to the unspecified and potentially unshared context are likely to be least successful.

Given this rationale, we predicted the following competence ordering for contexts: (1) immediate conversation, (2) earlier conversation, (3) conversational environment, (4) unspecified background knowledge. In other words, the more salient the context in which a remark was to be understood, the more favourably we expected people to evaluate that remark. One more distinction regarding contexts is important. For each context type we can inquire whether the identification was done explicitly or left implicit. Explicit identification (e.g. 'talking about X', 'going back to X', 'not to change the topic but') would cue the listener as to the appropriate context to search for a link. Implicit identification, on the other hand, would offer the speaker no advice about how to search for a connection. Thus, we expected conversational extensions which explicitly cued the context would be seen as more competent than their implicit counterparts: Explicit cues ease the task of the comprehender and direct his/her search. In summary, then, we expected communicators to judge conversational extensions which eased the task of comprehension as the most socially appropriate and competent type of responses.

These claims were evaluated by (a) presenting people with written conversational segments followed by responses that extended one of the four contexts either explicitly or implicitly, and (b) having people evaluate the appropriateness, relevance, etc. of the responses. The results indicated strong support for the claims; with two exceptions, the predictions were accurate (Planalp and Tracy 1980). Examination of the exceptions suggests a way in which a cognitively grounded rules approach could be refined. Let me sketch out the two 'exceptions' and suggest a more complex version of this approach that would account for the results. Of course, this speculation requires empirical testing.

The first exception concerned extensions of non-conversational contexts. We had expected links to the environmental context to be more competent than links to unspecified knowledge but, in fact, comments that tied to the background context were judged more competent than remarks which tied to the conversational environment. Consider why this may have happened. In the study all of the conversational stimuli communicators examined came from initial interaction between unacquainted college students taped in a small, quiet, nondescript room. As has been noted (Berger *et al.* 1976; Knapp 1978), initial interaction is quite scripted. Conversants typically elicit certain specific types of information ('What do you study?', 'Where are you from?', 'what are your interests?'). These questions seem like a reasonable sequence not because of semantic connections at the level of the discourse text but because they are information slots in a frequently engaged in script. Thus, in this experimental situation, where the environment was neutral with few interesting or novel stimuli, and the initial interaction script was probably quite salient, it is not so surprising that links to this type of 'unspecified knowledge' were judged more competent than environmental links.

This exception to our predictions raises a more general question. Are the contexts for interpreting conversation fixed in their likely salience ordering, as initially assumed, or do they vary? While it would be nice to have a fixed ordering, conceptually simpler and more elegant, it seems more likely that salience will vary with the nature of the conversational interaction. Consider a situation where a group of friends are watching a football game on television. One frequent conversational pattern (Lull 1980) is to offer comments on whatever is occurring on the screen. In this situation, we might expect the environment (i.e., the TV) to be more salient than the prior conversation. Or to take another example, imagine that an expert and apprentice are assembling a machine. Here too we might expect the conversants to consider aspects of the situation (what is going on with the machine) as more salient and attempt to understand talk, first in terms of the situation, and only if that fails in terms of prior talk (Grosz 1977). In most interactive situations, the conversation itself is likely to be the most salient context. Hence, responses to the immediate conversation are likely to be preferred and seen as more appropriate. However, it is important to keep in mind that this regularity exists because of its usual correspondence with information search procedures.

The second exception to competence predictions (Planalp and Tracy 1980) involved the ranking of immediate conversational extensions that were explicit and implicit. Recall that we had predicted that explicitly cued topic changes would be judged more competent than those that were not. While this proved true for three contexts (earlier conversation, environment and background knowledge), it was not true for extensions of the immediate conversation. No difference was found between implicit and explicit versions of this type.

Let me offer a recasting of this finding that I see as more consistent with a cognitive rationale than the one initially offered. When the context for a comment is not highly salient, a cue aids a listener's mental search by providing direction. However, if a context is highly salient, it will be the first place a listener searches. Under these circumstances an explicit cue is unneeded. In fact, an explicit cue might even prove counterproductive. If cues are used principally when the referent of a speaker's topic is not obvious, the presence of a cue could suggest that an utterance is *not* to be understood in terms of the most salient context. Thus, when a conversational remark links to the most salient context – most usually the immediate conversation – cues are unneeded.

In summary, this study (Planalp and Tracy 1980) provides evidence that the possible contexts within which a conversational remark may be understood can be arrayed on a competence continuum: Responses which extend the immediate conversation are the most competent; when an immediate extension is used, an explicit cue is unnecessary. Furthermore, the reason for these communicator preferences is not arbitrary but can be explained in terms of people's comprehension procedures.

Selection of units from the immediate topic

When the conversation is the most salient context, as it is likely to be in most interactive situations, links to the immediate topic are more competent than other types of links (Planalp and Tracy 1980). Unfortunately what is meant by 'topic' is unclear; two different definitions are seen in the literature. The first conception of topic is a local one. Topic in this sense is an aspect of sentences: a comment is extending the topic if it chains to the immediately prior sentence. Once a comment has been spoken, the entire sentence becomes that which is given, in other words, the potential topic for a subsequent response. Within this conception, topic is a continuously changing entity, modified sentence by sentence (Schank 1977). This conception of topic is seen in studies of discourse comprehension (Haviland and Clark 1974), children's development of topicality skills (Bloom *et al.* 1976) and models of adult 'small talk' (Schank 1977). The local conception of topic places a heavy premium on *temporal* sequencing of ideas. Ideas which have just been mentioned are in some sense more on the immediate topic than those mentioned several sentences earlier.

In contrast, the global conception sees topic as the main point of a unit of discourse. According to the global conception, assessments of topic are determined by the structure of the entire message. An idea is the 'topic' because of its position in an information hierarchy, not because of its temporal immediacy. That information, ideas or goals are organized hierarchically is a basic tenet in most cognitive models, whether the model be of memory structure (Collins and Loftus 1975; Rosch 1977), discourse text (van Dijk 1977) or macroscopic theories of human activity (Miller *et al.* 1960; Schank and Abelson 1977). For different types of discourse, different kinds of hierarchical structure have been suggested.

For instance, Mandler and Johnson (1977) and Rumelhart (1975) describe variations of a discourse structure – what they label a story grammar – that people use to produce and understand narratives. Story grammars include units of differing levels of abstraction which are hierarchically related to each other. For informational prose, van Dijk (1977) provides a detailed model wherein the main point or topic is ascertained by breaking the discourse into 'propositions', meaning units roughly equivalent to a single idea. Propositions, then, are related to each other using both general and situation-specific knowledge, and a set of rules to produce the topic or 'macro-structure'.

Conversation is unlikely to be as organized as written discourse; yet hierarchical relations, albeit simple ones, also come into play. One hierarchical structure that occurs with some frequency is that of issue–event (Labov and Fanshel 1978; Reichman 1978; Ryave 1977; Tracy and Moran 1983). In this structure an issue is an abstract principle, a generalization, what we typically think of as the main point; the event is an episode, a concrete example of the more abstract issue. Consider the following message:

(1) Reading *Time* is just like the advertisements say. I find it interesting – it's a good way to pass time and I learn something. Last week I learned about those sets of separated twins who grew up not knowing each other and yet are still very similar.

In this message, the issue is the speaker's claim that reading *Time* is a worthwhile activity; the event is the brief story about twins growing up apart.

When a conversational remark is no longer than a sentence, local and global conceptions yield the same topic. This is not so, however, for longer messages. For instance in (1) the global conception predicts the issue to be the topic, the local focuses on the temporally immediate event. Thus local and global conceptions lead to quite different predictions for what it means to 'stay on the immediate topic'. Essentially the global predicts that extensions of issues are more on topic and more socially competent; the local predicts the superiority of event extensions.

Elsewhere (Tracy 1982) I argue that global predictions are more likely to account for conversational extension preferences because of their greater consistency with cognitive principles. Put specifically, extensions of the issue are expected to be judged as 'better things to say' because they will be easier to understand. The main point is retained longer in memory, is likely to be most salient, and if extended will be understood most easily. In reference to the *Time* magazine example this means that extension (2) would be judged more competent than (3).

(2) It's good to get a weekly news magazine but I like *Newsweek* better than *Time*.
(3) Were there two women twins who both wore seven rings on their hands?

A test of these predictions (Tracy 1982) revealed communicators selected the issue as the topic whenever the message included issue and event, irrespective of ordering, and generally, although there was an exception, saw issue extensions as more appropriate than event ones. The exception occurred in one conversation which a post-hoc analysis revealed to be significantly more difficult to understand than the others. This deviation suggested another way in which communicators' processing influences what would be judged as preferable responses in conversation. If some aspect of discourse structure, or the comprehender's background knowledge, make understanding of the issue difficult, then the issue is less likely to be uppermost in memory and the most salient part of the discourse. Under the condition of low issue clarity, extensions of other parts of the discourse, such as the event, should become more competent.

In a follow-up study (Tracy 1983) to test this proposed influence, respondents heard tape-recorded messages following an issue–event structure in which the clarity of the issue was varied, and rated the competence of issue and event extensions. In both high and low comprehensibility conditions the issue was stated using vague pronominal references (e.g. '*It's* just like the advertisements say . . .'). In the high comprehensibility condition, respondents were also provided background information in the form of a short cue (e.g. The speaker had previously been talking about *Time* magazine) that made it possible for respondents unequivocally to identify 'it'. Results supported the prediction: Issue extensions were judged more competent than event extensions under all circumstances; but when background information was absent, thereby making issue identification more problematic, preference for issue extensions was much less marked. Event extensions were rated more positively in the low-understandability condition.

The research discussed so far (Planalp and Tracy 1980; Tracy 1982, 1983) gives support for the value of a cognitively grounded rules approach to conversational coherence. We have considered some of the conversational extension options available, indicated which ones communicators prefer, when this preference operates, and offered an explanation that accounts for the pattern of preferences. So far, however, I have not shown that people actually respond in the described ways. Since communicators do not always act in the ways they report as best (Clark 1979), it is important to show the conversational relevance rule accounts for a significant portion of conversational extension behaviour.

In a subsequent study (Tracy, in press) rather than rating responses, communicators constructed their own. In reaction to short tape-recorded comments, communicators wrote down how they would respond. These responses were rated by two expert judges on scales that measured the degree of issue extension and degree of event extension. In addition, responses were examined to see if they included types of patterned extensions other than issue or event extensions. Results indicated that respondents extended issues significantly more than events, and, as predicted, the degree of issue extension was less marked when the discourse was difficult to comprehend. The reverse was true for event extensions: Events were extended more directly when the conversational issue was difficult to comprehend. In addition, a number of response types occurred in the low-comprehensibility condition that, while not issue extensions, appeared to be attempts to avoid extending peripheral parts of the discourse.

For instance, in one conversation respondents in the low-comprehensibility condition heard the speaker say how 'it put him in a good mood' but did not hear the cue that made it evident that 'it' referred to television watching. In this case, a number of responses suggested communicators were attempting to respond to the issue but had inferred it unsuccessfully, the most frequent inference being that the speaker was talking about taking drugs. Another type of response seen frequently was one that directly queried the respondent about his or her main point (e.g. So what in the world are you talking about?). Essentially a direct query avoids responding to peripheral parts of the discourse, as could have been done, and questions the speaker about his/her intended main point. Both of these response types, as well as a number of others discussed elsewhere (Tracy, in press) can be seen as attempts to avoid extending nonsalient parts of the discourse when the most salient unit is unclear and fuzzy.

Notably absent from conversational responses in this study (Tracy, in press) were attempts to introduce new topics. That is, respondents limited themselves to extensions of speakers' remarks with few attempts to move the conversation in another direction. While this is not unusual in some conversational situations, it is not representative of all of them. Conversants frequently do seek to guide the direction of talk to a particular topic. It seemed important, therefore, to discover how communicators extend conversation when they possess their own topic agenda, as well as concerns about being an appropriate conversational partner.

In the most recent study (Tracy and Moran 1982), communicators were given two goals they were likely to possess in everyday discourse: (1) a desire to be an attentive conversational partner, and (2) a desire to introduce a new topic. For half the subjects the first goal was top priority, for the other half, the second goal was. In addition the comprehensibility of the speaker's message was also varied. Communicators heard taped messages in one of four conditions and wrote down how they would respond. Each response was rated for its degree of issue extension, degree of event extension, and degree of new topic introduction (in all cases, a recently seen movie). While a number of predictions were made, one is especially pertinent to our concerns about cognitively based rules.

We predicted respondents would achieve a lower degree of success on whichever goal was lower priority. Our reasoning was as follows: Tasks requiring simultaneous attention to multiple goals are more cognitively difficult than ones that have only a single goal (O'Keefe and Delia 1982). Moreover, the more complicated a mental task, the more likely all components of it will not be accomplished equally well. Thus we expected conversants whose primary goal was new topic introduction to construct links to speakers' issues that were less direct than those whose primary goal was being an attentive partner. Similarly, respondents whose primary goal was being an attentive partner would be less successful in introducing their desired new topic because of the sheer difficulty of constructing an understandable conceptual bridge. While links were formed with every possible part of speaker messages, when the issue was easily inferrable the most frequent unit continued to be the issue.

We have considered thus far two choices communicators have in deciding what to say next: (1) what context to tie their remark to, and (2) assuming they select the conversational context, what unit in the conversation to link to. In the next section we consider the types of possible linkages.

Selection of linkage strategy

A qualitative analysis on the conversational comments generated in the study on goals (Tracy and Moran 1982, 1983) suggested three general ways communicators responded to the demands to be attentive to the partner and introduce a new topic. One way was to abandon the goal of introducing the new topic and merely extend the speaker's original remark. This type of action was seen most often when a respondent's primary goal was to be attentive. A second type of response was simply to abandon the goal of being attentive and introduce the new topic. Respondents made introduction of the new topic understandable by explicitly marking that they were closing off the speaker's topic (e.g. 'Let's talk about something on the brighter side. Have you seen *Raiders*?').

By far the most interesting type of response, and in fact the kind made most frequently, was a response that attempted to accomplish both goals (i.e., extending the partner's topic and introducing one's own). Four kinds of strategies were used to link the new topic to the speaker's issue or event. In the first strategy, communicators made use of schematic or script knowledge (Schank and Albeson 1977). For instance in response to the *Time* magazine message, respondents made use of their world knowledge that *Time* had a film review section to introduce the desired new topic (e.g. 'I also enjoy reading the cinema section of *Time*. They do a good job analysing new movies. You know they just gave a bad review to that movie *Private Lessons*.')

A second strategy used was a direct link to an idea mentioned in the speaker's message. Here, for instance, in response the speaker's claim that one could learn from *Time*, respondents suggested you could learn from other things as well (e.g. 'Yes magazines can be informative, as well as leisure – just like movies – which is why I went to see this movie. Maybe you've heard of it – *The French Lieutenant's Woman?*')

A third strategy communicators used was to show how the speaker's issue was an instance of some larger issue – what we labelled a meta-issue – and then show how the new topic was linked to the meta-issue. One meta-issue seen was an appeal by respondents to the fact that all activities take time, of which people have a limited amount. Thus to talk about activity X raises the issue of how to spend time generally (e.g. 'The way I like to do away my time is to party. I just saw a great movie called *Boys in the Band* which had a great party scene.')

The last type of link seen, and the least common type in these data, was a procedural link (see Poole Chapter 11). The procedural link maintained there was a mental connection between the speaker's topic and the respondent's (e.g. 'I know exactly what you mean', 'That reminds me of') but substitution of the speaker's issue in the slot where the vague pronominal reference occurred caused confusion rather than clarity. In essence, then, the procedural strategy cued the partner inappropriately, suggesting the issue was being continued when it was not.

The social competence of these four strategy types has not yet been tested but following from the cognitively grounded rules rationale developed so far, it seems probable that procedural links would be judged the least competent. Not only do they not aid the partner's mental search procedures they actually miscue him or her. For the other three strategies no one type is obviously better; most likely it will depend upon the salience of the script, meta-issue, or particular message idea.

Summary

The ways communicators extend conversation may be described in terms of three choices. The choices are not necessarily conscious ones, but reflect options that are logically available. The first decision concerns the selection of context. That is, is the extension to be understood as relevant to the conversation (immediate or earlier), the situation, or background knowledge? Second, if the immediate conversation is selected as the context, what unit is extended – the issue or an event? Finally, what type of strategy is used to link the respondent's new topic with the prior speaker's issue or event? For these choices I have shown that what communicators say, and how they evaluate the choices of others, may be explained by cognitive principles.

Conclusions

In this chapter I have attempted to show how a cognitively grounded rules approach can help us explain many of the patterns in, and preferences for, conversational sequences. As is true of any framework, the cognitively grounded rules approach cannot do everything. It is better suited to deal with some issues and questions than others. Let me mention two potential limitations for the framework.

One possible problem is that of perspective. If we freeze a conversation at any moment in time, interactants will be in one of two roles: message constructor or message interpreter. Each of these roles requires significant cognitive activity. Message constructors take sets of thoughts and convert them into appropriate words and sentences that are clear and understandable to the partner. Message interpreters start with a set of words and sentences and attempt to extract the other's intended meaning, including the expected relationship to prior discourse (Huttenlocher 1974). The cognitive work required by communicators in these two roles, while having overlap, is not identical. In fact under certain circumstances – most notably when conversants possess large differences in cultural background – the amount of cognitive effort expended by a person in one role is likely to be inversely related to the amount needed in the other. The more work a speaker expends in designing a message, the less work a listener will need to do to understand it. The less work a speaker gives to message design, the more cognitive effort the listener will need to expend to extract the speaker's meaning. Thus, the cognitive rules perspective does not tell us whose cognitive processing (a speaker's or a listener's) is more important in explaining what occurs in conversation. To the extent that the cognitive effort required of one partner is directly related to the amount of effort required by the other, there is little problem; to the extent that this is not true, cognitively grounded rules theories will need to develop a more complex rationale that mesh the competing requirements of two cognitive systems. Some of the research discussed here begins to address this issue in a preliminary manner; more research is obviously needed.

Second, while it seems likely that many of the regularities in communication can be tied to cognitive principles, it is unlikely that all regularities can be. Goals other than clarity and cognitive efficiency are important. The most obvious set of 'other goals' are communicators' concerns about social appropriateness and face (e.g. Brown and Levinson 1978; deBeaugrande 1980). Thus it should be expected that certain regularities in discourse, while influenced by cognitive processes, are better explained by social principles (see, for example, Cody and McLaughlin Chapter 3; Morris Chapter 4). Moreover although we know that the goals communicators have influence what they say because of cognitive constraints, we do not know what motivates people to select particular goals. In other words, the cognitively grounded perspective does not help us understand *why* communicators would have one goal rather than another or why, if communicators have multiple goals, they prioritize them in particular ways (Planalp and Hewes 1982).

A cognitively grounded rules approach may not be the best way to investigate all communicative phenomena; but as I have attempted to show it is especially helpful for understanding the complexities of conversational behaviour. Unlike either discourse-based or situation–interpreter approaches, the cognitively grounded rules approach provides a way to make sense of both the variety and the regularity in everyday discourse. Because conversational behaviour is the product of intentional choice, rule rather than law-governed, variety is expected. Because communicators understand information presented in some ways better than others, regularity is expected. Second, the cognitively grounded rules perspective enables us to account for what types of conversational extensions people see as most skilful. It provides a generative basis to explain the preferences conversants possess. Finally the perspective seems promising for understanding other areas of conversational activity. For example the meshing of rules and cognition could help us explain how communicators decide how much to say on any particular topic – Grice's (1975) quantity maxim – or why certain patterns of gaze and gesture are seen as more socially skilful.

References

ARGYLE, M. 1969: *Social interaction*. Chicago: Aldine Atherton.

BEACH, W.A. 1983: Background understandings and the situated accomplishment of conversational telling-expansions. In Craig, R.T. and Tracy, K., editors, *Conversational coherence: Form, structure, and strategy* (Beverly Hills, lal.: Sage).

BEDROSIAN, J. 1979: Communicative performance of mentally retarded adults: A topic analysis. Paper presented at the American Association of Mental Deficiency. Miami, Fla.

BERGER, C.R. 1977: The covering law perspective as a theoretical basis for the study of human communication. *Communication Quarterly* 25, 7–18.

BERGER, C.R., GARDNER, R.R., CLATTERBUCK, G.W. and SCHULMAN, L.S. 1976: Perceptions of information sequencing in relationship development. *Human Communication Research* 3, 29–46.

BLOOM, L., ROCISSANO, L. and HOOD, L. 1976: Adult–child discourse: Developmental interaction between information processing and linguistic knowledge. *Cognitive Psychology* 8, 521–52.

BRANSFORD, J.D. and NITSCH, K.E. 1977: Coming to understand things we could not previously understand. In Kavanagh J.F. and Strange, W., editors, *Implications of basic speech and language for the school and clinic* (Boston: MIT press).

BROWN, P. and LEVINSON, S.L. 1978: Universals in language usage: Politeness phenomena. In Goody, E.N., editor, *Questions and politeness: Strategies in social interaction* (New York: Cambridge University Press).

CAPPELLA, J.N. 1981: Mutual influence in expressive behaviour: Adult–adult and infant–adult interaction. *Psychological Bulletin* 89, 101–32.

CAPPELLA, J.N. and PLANALP, S. 1981: Talk and silence patterns in informal conversations III: Interspeaker influence. *Human Communication Research* 7, 117–132.

CLARK, R.A. 1979: The impact of self-interest and desire for liking on the selection of communication strategies. *Communication Monographs* 46, 257–73.

COLLINS, A.M. and LOFTUS, E.T. 1975: A spreading activation theory of semantic processing. *Psychological Review* 82, 407–28.

CUSHMAN, D.P. 1977: The rules perspective as a theoretical basis for the study of human communication. *Communication Quarterly* 25, 30–45.

DE BEAUGRANDE, R. 1980: *Text, discourse and process: Toward a multidisciplinary science of texts*. Norwood, NS: Ablex.

DELIA, J.G. 1977: Alternative perspectives for the study of human communication: Critique and response. *Communication Quarterly* 25, 46–64.

FORGAS, J.P. 1979: *Social episodes: The study of interaction routines*.

London: Academic Press.

FRENTZ, T.S. and FARRELL, T.B. 1976: Language-action: A paradigm for communication. *Quarterly Journal of Speech* **62**, 333–49.

GILES, H. 1980: Accommodation theory: Some new directions. In de Silva, S., editor, *Aspects of linguistic behaviour* (York: University of York Press).

GOFFMAN, E. 1957: Alienation from interaction. *Human Relations* **10**, 47–59.

GOLDBERG, J.A. 1983: A *move* toward describing conversational coherence. In Craig, R.T., and Tracy, K., editors, *Conversational coherence: Studies of form and strategy* (Beverly Hills, Cal.: Sage).

GRICE, H.P. 1975: Logic and conversation. In Cole, P. and Morgan J.L., editors, *Syntax and semantics, Vol. 3: Speech acts* (New York: Academic Press).

GROZ, B.J. 1977: The representation and use of focus in a system for understanding dialogs. *Proceedings of the international joint conference on AI* (Cambridge, Mass.: MIT).

HALLIDAY, M.A.K. and HASAN, R. 1976: *Cohesion in English*. London: Longman.

HAVILAND, S.E. and CLARK, H.H. 1974: What's new? Acquiring new information as a process of comprehension, *Journal of Verbal Learning and Verbal Behavior* **13**, 512–21.

HEWES, D.E. and PLANALP, S. 1982: There is nothing as useful as a good theory . . .: The influence of social knowledge on interpersonal communication. In Roloff, M.E. and Berger, C.R., editors, *Social cognition and communication* (Beverly Hills, Cal.: Sage).

HOBBS, J.R. 1979: Coherence and coreference. *Cognitive Science* **3**, 67–90.

HOPPER, R. 1983: Interpretation as coherence production. In Craig, R.T. and Tracy, K., editors, *Conversational coherence: Form, structure, and strategy* (Beverly Hills, Cal.: Sage).

HUTTENLOCHER, J. 1974: The origins of language comprehension. In Solso, R.L., editor, *Theories of cognitive psychology* (Potomac, Md: Lawrence Erlbaum Associates).

HYMES, D. 1974: *Foundations in sociolinguistics: An ethnographic approach*. Philadelphia: University of Pennsylvania Press.

JACKSON, S. and JACOBS, S. 1980: Structure of conversational argument: Pragmatic bases for the enthymeme. *Quarterly Journal of Speech* **66**, 251–65.

—— 1983: Speech act structure in conversation: Rational aspects of pragmatic coherence. In Craig, R.T. and Tracy, K., editors, *Conversational coherence: Form, structure, and strategy* (Beverly Hills, Cal.: Sage).

KEENAN, E.O. and SCHIEFFELIN, B.B. 1976: Topic as a discourse notion. A study of topic in the conversations of children and adults. In Li, C.N., editor, *Subject and topic* (New York: Academic Press).

KINTSCH, W., and VAN DIJK, T.A. 1978: Toward a model of text comprehension and production. *Psychological Review* **85**, 363–94.

KNAPP. M.L. 1978: *Social intercourse: From greeting to goodbye* (Boston: Allyn & Bacon).

KRECKEL, M. 1981: *Communicative acts and shared knowledge in natural discourse*. London: Academic Press.

LABOV, W. and FANSHEL, D. 1977: *Therapeutic discourse: Psychotherapy as conversation*. New York: Academic Press.

LEVINSON, S.C. 1981: Some pre-observations on the modelling of dialogue. *Discourse Processes* **4**, 93–116.

LEWIS, D.K. 1969: *Convention: A philosophical study*. Cambridge: Cambridge University Press.

LULL, J. 1980: The social uses of television. *Human Communication Research* **6**, 197–209.

MANDLER, J.M. and JOHNSON, N.S. 1977: Remembrance of things parsed: Story structure and recall. *Cognitive Psychology* **9**, 111–51.

MILLER, G.A., GALANTER, E., and PRIBRAM, K.H. 1960: *Plans and the structure of behavior* (New York: Holt, Rinehart, & Winston).

MILLER, G.R. 1978: The current status of theory and research in interpersonal communication. *Human Communication Research* **4**, 164–77.

MONGE, P.R. 1977: The systems perspective as a theoretical basis for the study of human communication. *Communication Quarterly* **25**, 19–29.

NOFSINGER, R.E. 1983: Tactical coherence in courtroom conversation. In Craig, R.T. and Tracy, K., editors, *Conversational coherence: Form, structure, and strategy* (Beverly Hills, Cal.: Sage).

O'KEEFE, B.J., and DELIA, J.G. 1982: Impression formation and message production. In Roloff, M.E. and Berger, C.R., editors, *Social cognition and communication* (Beverly Hills, Cal.: Sage).

ORTONY, A. 1978: Remembering, understanding and representation. *Cognitive Science* **2**, 53–69.

PEARCE, W.B. and CONKLIN. F. 1979: A model of hierarchical meanings in coherent conversation and a study of 'indirect responses'. *Communication Monographs* **46**, 75–87.

PLANALP, S. and HEWES, D.E. 1982: A cognitive approach to communication theory: Cogito ergo dico? In Burgoon, M., editor, *Communication Yearbook 5* (New Brunswick, NJ: Transaction).

PLANALP, S. and TRACY, K. 1980: Not to change the topic but . . .: A cognitive approach to the management of conversation. In Nimmo, D., editor, *Communication Yearbook 4* (New Brunswick, NJ: Transaction).

REICHMAN, R. 1978: Conversational coherency. *Cognitive Science* **2**, 283–327.

ROCHESTER, S. and MARTIN, J.R. 1979: *Crazy talk: A study of the discourse of schizophrenic speakers*. New York: Plenum Press

ROSCH, E.H. 1977: Classification of real-world objects: origins and representations in cognition. In Johnson-Laird, P.N. and Wason, P.C., editors, *Thinking: Readings in cognitive science* (Cambridge: Cambridge University Press).

RUMELHART, D.E. 1975: Notes on a schema for stories. In Bobrow, D.G. and Collins, A. editors, *Representation and understanding: Studies in cognitive science* (New York: Academic Press).

RYAVE, A.L. 1979: On the achievement of a series of stories. In Schenkein, J. editor, *Studies in the organization of conversational interaction* (New York: Academic Press).

SACKS, H., SCHEGLOFF, E.A., and JEFFERSON, G.A. 1978: A simplest systematics for the organization of turn-taking for conversation. In Schenkein, J., editor, *Studies in the organization of conversational interaction* (New York: Academic Press).

SANDERS, R.E. 1983: Tools for cohering discourse and their strategic utilization: Markers of structural connections and meaning relations. In Craig, R.T. and Tracy, K., editors, *Conversational coherence: Studies of form and strategy*

(Beverly Hills, Cal.: Sage).

SCHANK, R.S. 1977: Rules and topics in conversation. *Cognitive Science* 1, 421–41.

SCHANK, R.C. and ABELSON, R.P. 1977: *Scripts, plans, goals and understanding: An inquiry into human knowledge structures.* Hillsdale, NJ: Lawrence Erlbaum.

SCHEGLOFF, E.A. 1972: Sequencing in conversational openings. In Fishman, J.A., editor, *Advances in the sociology of language* (Vol. 2) (The Hague: Mouton).

SCHEGLOFF, E.A. and SACKS, H. 1973: Opening up closings. *Semiotica* 8, 289–327.

SEARLE, J.R. 1969: *Speech acts.* London: Cambridge University Press.

—— 1975: Indirect speech acts. In Cole, P. and Morgan, J.L., editors, *Syntax and semantics, Vol. 3: Speech acts* (New York: Academic Press).

SHIMANOFF, S.B. 1980: *Communication Rules: Theory and research.* Beverly Hills, Cal.: Sage.

SIGMAN, S.J. 1983: Some considerations of the multiple constraints placed on conversational topics. In Craig, R.T. and Tracy, K., editors, *Conversational coherence: Form, structure, and strategy* (Beverly Hills, Cal.: Sage).

STREET, R.L. and GILES, H. 1982: Speech accommodation theory: A social cognitive approach to language and behavior. In Roloff, M.E. and Berger, C.R., editors, *Social cognition and communication* (Beverly Hills, Cal.: Sage).

TRACY, K. 1982: On getting the point: Distinguishing 'issues' from 'events', an aspect of conversational coherence. In Burgoon, M., editor, *Communication Yearbook* 5 (New Brunswick, NJ: Transaction).

—— 1983: The issue-event distinction: A rule of conversation and its scope condition. *Human Communication Research* 9, 320–34.

—— in press: Staying on topic: An explication of conversational relevance. *Discourse Processes.*

TRACY, K. and MORAN, J.P. 1982: Competing goals and conversational extensions. Paper presented at the Speech Communication Association, Louisville, Kentucky, 1982.

—— 1983: Conversational relevance in multiple-goal situation. In Craig, R.T. and Tracy, K., editors, *Conversational coherence: Form, structure, and strategy* (Beverly Hills, Cal.: Sage).

VAN DIJK, T.A. 1977: Semantic macro-structures and knowledge frames in discourse comprehension. In Just, M.A. and Carpenter, P.A., editors, *Cognitive processes in comprehension* (Hillsdale, NJ: Lawrence Erlbaum).

VUCHINICH, S. 1977: Elements of cohesion between turns in ordinary conversation. *Semiotica* 20, 229–57.

3

Models for the sequential construction of accounting episodes: situational and interactional constraints on message selection and evaluation

Michael J. Cody and Margaret L. McLaughlin

Accounting sequences (Sykes and Matza 1957; Scott and Lyman 1968; Hewitt and Hall 1973; Rogers and Buffalo 1974; Blumstein 1974; Harré 1977; Ditton 1977; Shields 1979; Schonbach 1980; McLaughlin *et al*. 1983 a; b; Morris Chapter 4) are manifestations of a systematic provision in the organization of social interaction for the management of *failure events*. Such sequences revolve around the proposition that one of the parties to a relationship has committed an *offence* (Blumstein 1974) or has neglected some obligation, and that a *remedy* (Remler 1978) should be proposed by the offending party for evaluation by him/her who was offended. The kinds of offences which have been observed to precipitate a request for repair have ranged from the grave to the trivial. In long-term interpersonal relationships or in the workplace, persons are often reproached for behaviour which appears to violate the requirements of a role (for example, lover, child, subordinate) vis-à-vis some focal counter-role (lover, parent, superior) (Gouldner 1960). The following example, collected by McLaughlin *et al*. (1983a), is a case in point:

> One Saturday night I was out all night and was feeling kind of good. That night I spent the night with a friend. I didn't call home and tell my parents that I was spending the night with a friend. I knew that my parents were going to be mad. I took a shower and got dressed. Then I hopped in my car and started on my way home. When I entered the house there was my mother cooking over the stove with her angry look on her face.

Accounting sequences have also been found in the conversations of persons who do not have established relationships, and in fact are subject to no interlocking sets of rights and obligations. In interactions between strangers, requests for accounts or more generally for repair seem to be commonplace and appear to be motivated by one of three factors: (1) a *misapprehension* of some kind (Jefferson 1972), for example, a misunderstanding or 'non-hearing' (Grimshaw 1981); (2) *disagreement* with or disbelief of the propositional content of an utterance by one of the speakers (McLaughlin *et al*. 1983b); or (3) *exploitation* of differences in perspective as a conversational resource (McLaughlin *et al*. 1983b). The following examples from conversations between strangers represent the first two of these three factors:

> B: Medical illustration. I'm majorin' in Advertising Arts and minoring in Biology.
> A: But what- what do you want to do- be a- be an artist for uh one of those T.V. - not T.V. those uh- newspaper-newspaper funnies or somethin'?
> B: No. Ha ha.

A: I don't know. I always thought that they had a whole lot of acclaim, you know, 'cause everybody knows who they are. I thought that was fame right there.

B: No, no, a MEDICAL illustrator – MEDICAL illustrator, yeah. Yeah, see, if I had a minor in Biology I wouldn't be doin' so good in cartoons. (McLaughlin *et al.* 1983b, p. 111)

A: Well, I'll probably work Christmas Day. I

B: (*CHRISTMAS DAY?!!*)

A: I worked Thanksgiving Day, see.

B: Oo-o. Ha ha.

A: See, we're open- it's cotton season-

B: (   )
                                        Yeah.

A: Shipments are right now – we're open twenty-four hours a day, you know, so =

B: = you have to be there.

A: Yeah. (McLaughlin 1984)

Accounting sequences, regardless of the relationship of the parties involved, seem to conform to a canonical form (Remler 1978), consisting minimally of three moves: a request for repair, an utterance which communicates that something requires attention; a remedy, which is usually supplied by the offending party but which may be developed collaboratively; and an acknowledgement, an evaluation by the offended party of the remedy which has been proposed. This basic skeletal structure is usually subject to expansion by pre-sequences, insertion sequences, or post-sequences (Jacobs and Jackson 1979; Jackson and Jacobs 1980).

The basic sequence has been noted by a number of different scholars, under a variety of labels, including the misapprehension sequence (Jefferson 1972), the correction sequence (Jefferson and Schenkein 1978), the account episode (Schonbach 1980), the remedial episode (Morris Chapter 4), the corrective interchange (Goffman 1967), and the remedial cycle (Goffman 1971), although some of these writers include as a fundamental move in the sequence such features as the precipitating failure event (Schonbach 1980), a display of 'relief' that a remedy has been provided (Goffman 1971), or an expression of thanks by the offender that a proposed remedy was acceptable (Goffman 1967).

The order of events in an account sequence is rather strictly determined; that is, a request for repair, or a *reproach* (Schonbach 1980; McLaughlin *et al.* 1983a) always precedes the remedy, or *account*, which always precedes an acknowledgement or the *evaluation* of the account. The order of moves within an account sequence is heavily constrained by demands of conditional relevance (Schegloff 1972); that is, the account is a reply to the reproach, and the evaluation a reply to the account. Jefferson (1972, p. 305) has formulated two rules which cover the way in which moves within the sequence are assigned to parties. First, 'if a statement is made and is followed by a demonstration/assertion that a hearer did not understand, then the one who made the statement may/must provide a clarification.' Thus the *account* move is assigned to the author of the repairable utterance or action. Second, the opening and closing moves in the account sequence are allocated to the party who 'calls' the violation (Jefferson 1972; McLaughlin 1984). Thus, the *reproach* and *evaluation* moves are assigned to the 'offended' party.

While the series of moves which comprises an account sequence, their serial order, and their allocation among interacting parties have all been well established in the literature, only recently has much attention been given to uncovering the constraints, both interactional and situational, on the kinds of moves which parties to an accounting episode are likely to make. We propose that there are two broad classes of factors which influence the choice of an account and the manner in which it is received. First, an interactional factor which we describe as the *aggravation–mitigation continuum* (Labov and Fanshel 1977) affects the way in which reproaches influence accounts, and similarly the way in which accounts are evaluated. Simply put, in accounting sequences moves which are more polite, deferential or 'mitigating' tend to elicit like subsequent moves, while actions which are 'aggravating' (impolite, unresponsive, challenging) appear to provoke actions in kind. For example, McLaughlin *et al.* (1983a) found that one of the best predictors of an actor's selection of a remedial strategy was the manner in which he/she was reproached, with aggravating reproaches such as predicting that the other would try to deny the offence generally resulting in aggravating moves in the account 'slot', such as challenging the reproacher's right to demand repair. This could be attributed in part to the effects of the reciprocity norm or interpersonal accommodation effects (Giles *et al.* 1973; Larsen *et al.* 1977; Giles 1980), and in part to the interlocking preconditions (Searle 1975) for the performance of the speech acts such strategies would embody (for example, *accuse* and *deny*). Similarly, more mitigating accounts such as excuses (for example, claiming that one 'didn't mean to') have been found to be more likely to lead to mitigating replies in the evaluation slot, such as honouring the account or retreating to a less antagonistic position (McLaughlin *et al.* 1983b).

A second set of factors which has been found to influence actors' account strategies as well as reproachers' evaluations of the accounts they hear is the offending party's *perceptions of the situation* in which the account sequence is embedded. These factors include the extent to which the alleged offender feels guilty about the failure event, the severity of the offence, the relative dominance of the reproacher, the importance to the offender of maintaining the relationship with the reproacher, the importance attached to securing honouring, the degree of intimacy between the two parties, the relational consequences of failing to secure honouring (McLaughin *et al.* 1983a), and the nature of the offence (McLaughlin *et al.* 1983b).

In subsequent sections we will present: (1) a typology and some examples of reproaches and accounts, arrayed along an aggravation–mitigation continuum; (2) a closer examination of the situation perception variables which seem to influence the sequential unfolding of account episodes; and (3) a comprehensive model of the role of the interactional and situational factors in the construction of account sequences.

Reproaches and accounts: typologies and examples

McLaughlin *et al.* (1983a) found that in dealing with failure events reproachers generally employed one of five strategies in soliciting repair. Four of the strategies were verbal: (1) *projected concession* ('Aren't you sorry you did it?'); (2) *projected excuse* ('Were you stuck in traffic?'); (3) *projected justification* ('Did you have something more important to do?'); and (4) *projected refusal*

('Don't try to pretend you didn't see me'). One of the strategies was nonverbal: *silence*, a 'pregnant' absence of comment. Cody and McLaughlin, in a study of patrolman–driver encounters, on which we will report in a subsequent section, found two of these reproach types to be used by police officers when they pulled drivers over to cite them for a moving violation: projected excuse and projected justification. Nonverbal reproaches, or suggestions that the offender would or should apologize (or on the other hand that he/she would refuse to be cooperative) were apparently inconsistent with the patrolman's role, his understanding of his responsibilities, and his relationship to the driver.

Types of reproach may be arrayed along a mitigation–aggravation continuum, with projected concessions and excuses as most mitigating and silence and refusals as most aggravating. Justification seems to be somewhat intermediate with respect to the continuum. With respect to reproaches, our continuum is less than perfect, for projected concessions and projected justifications have both been found to have a significant likelihood of eliciting an aggravating response (McLaughlin *et al.* 1983a). Some of our data indicate that a reproach in which one projects that the actor will concede is regarded as 'pro-offender', in that the reproacher recognizes that the offence is something for which the offender as a good person will wish to make amends. However, a significant number of persons recalling account episodes in the McLaughlin, Cody and O'Hair study clearly perceived projected concessions as aggravating. We have tended to treat projected concessions as mitigating because they usually result in mitigating responses (apologies and concessions). However, this relationship may well be accounted for under the interlocking preconditions hypothesis; for example, the *assertion* 'you are sorry' receives an *acceptance* ('yes, I am sorry'). In any event, we give below some examples of each of the five types of reproach, with examples taken from our several studies.

In a *projected concession*, the reproacher projects that an apology or an admission of guilt is forthcoming:

> My grandparents and my younger brother came to campus from Greenwood to bring me items for my room at school, and when they arrived on campus, I wasn't home. When I got back, my grandmother said, '*Well, it sure was nice of you to have us come down so you could be gallivanting all over the country.*' (McLaughlin *et al.* 1983a, p. 214)

In a *projected excuse*, the reproacher implies that the offender may have erred unintentionally, or that he/she may be planning to claim to have done so. Implicit here is the notion that the offender will agree that the action was bad, but will report being unaware of it or being unable to prevent its having occurred. For example, in the patrolman–driver encounters, the following were typical reproaches relating to a projected denial of intent to do wrong:

> Did you realize you just ran a red light?
> Are you aware that your exhaust pipes need repair?
> Do you know the speed limit here?

In a *projected justification*, the reproacher implies that the offender knowingly and deliberately erred, but that he/she might claim to have had a good reason for doing so.

> Is there some reason why you are driving in the passing lane?

Is there some emergency?
What are you doing out this late?

The reproacher may also suggest that the offender will try to minimize the severity of the failure event.

In a *projected refusal*, the reproacher suggests that the offender will try to deny the offence, or to deny him or her the right to reproach in the first place:

> The theater owner called me into his office one night with the manager present, and began degrading me for what he felt were inaccurate doorman reports I was to fill out daily (bathroom cleanliness, theater temperature, etc.). The owner at first was withholding. '*Now why haven't you been filling these out with the truth*?' he said. '*You can't lie to me*. I saw the bathrooms downstairs and they're absolutely filthy.' (McLaughlin *et al*. 1983a, p. 215)

Synthesizing the earlier work by Scott and Lyman (1968), Sykes and Matza (1957), and Harré (1977), Schonbach (1980) provides the most exhaustive taxonomy of accounts: *concessions, excuses, justifications* and *refusals*. The first three categories were obtained in McLaughlin *et al*. (1983a, b), and in the Cody and McLaughlin patrolman–driver study. The category *refusal* was obtained in both McLaughlin, Cody and O'Hair and in McLaughlin, Cody and Rosenstein. In some contexts, *silence* was also a response which appeared in the account slot. Concessions and excuses appear to be the most mitigating forms of account, and silence and refusals the most aggravating.

In the *concession*, the accounter acknowledges his/her guilt and/or apologizes and offers restitution. In the guilt admission, the accounter simply accepts responsibility for the offence:

> My dad said, 'What did you do with all the money you made from January through June?' *I admitted I blew it all*. (McLaughlin *et al*. 1983a, p. 209)

> Officer: I clocked you going seventy-one miles per hour.
> Driver: *That's about right. I had my cruise on*.

The apology, however, is a somewhat more mitigating tactic. According to Schlenker and Darby (1981; see also Darby and Schlenker, 1982), apologies can be used in a perfunctory manner ('pardon me'), but also include saying one is sorry, expressing remorse, offering to help the victim, employing self-castigation and requesting forgiveness. Apologies parallel the penitence variable adopted by Blumstein (1974), and to some extent the confessional approach noted in Coleman's (1976) account of self-defence in traffic courts. Blumstein found that perceived penitence was related to honouring of the account. An example of an apology from the police officer–driver data set is given below:

> Officer: Ma'am, you didn't come to a full stop back there.
> Driver: Well, I'm sorry. I guess I was talking to the children about Christmas shopping and I wasn't paying enough attention. I'm usually more cautious than that.

Excuses include strategies in which the accounter admits that the offence occurred, but denies that he/she was able to do anything about it. Subsumed under the category of excuses are denials of intention and denials of personal responsibility. In denials of intention the offender admits that the offence occurred, but claims that he/she didn't intend to engage in the behaviour. As in the 'appeal to accidents' (Scott and Lyman 1968), denials of intention are mitigating because the offender claims or implies that anyone can fall victim to circumstances beyond his/her control, and that the offence would not have occurred had circumstances been otherwise.

> Officer: You in a hurry, lady?
> Driver: No, sir, and if I appear to be, it was unintentional. This is my husband's car. It's more powerful than mine, and I had no idea how rapidly it would gain speed, since I've only driven it a couple of times previously, and I came through the alley, not having realized it was a school zone, so I assumed that the speed limit was thirty miles per hour.

Denials of personal responsibility are strategies used by offenders to place the blame for the offence on other persons ('deferred responsibility', Coleman 1976; 'scapegoating', Scott and Lyman 1968), or on environmental obstacles. Again, these excuses are somewhat mitigating because the accounter implies that he/she would not have committed an offence had he/she been in full control.

> Officer: Do you realize you were weaving and speeding?
> Driver: Well, the truck was loaded wrong back in _____. It shifts and I've had a hard time maintaining a constant speed.

Justifications include those replies in which the actor accepts responsibility for the offence, but attempts to redefine it in terms of its positive outcomes. Forms of justification include minimizing the severity of the offence, denying that anyone was victimized, claiming the right to self-fulfilment, appealing to one's positive intentions, and appealing to loyalties or higher involvements (Scott and Lyman 1968; Coleman 1976; Schonbach 1980; McLaughlin *et al*. 1983a). One common form of account offered to police officers was the appeal to higher involvement, in which the accounter admits that he/she was responsible for the offence, but attempts to argue that personal commitments and loyalties outweigh the transgression:

> Officer: Is there some emergency?
> Driver: Yes, sir. Kinda. You see, my grandmother died yesterday and I'm going to pick up my brother and sister and my fiancee so we can get on our way because we have a long way to drive so we can be on time for the funeral.

Justifications also include accounts in which the offender argues that the violation was acceptable because something worse might have happened had it not been committed:

> Officer: You made an illegal U-turn there. What are you doing this early in the morning?
> Driver: I was at the library and I was scared down here alone. I just wanted to get home.

In a *refusal*, the offender explicitly takes issue with the propositional content of the reproach, and/or with the reproacher's implicit assumption of the right to reproach.

> Officer: We clocked you first at eighty-three and then at sixty-five.

Driver: I never drive over sixty-five, especially at night. There's no way I was going eighty-three!

Officer: I'm going to cite you for changing lanes without properly signalling.

Driver: You're kidding!

Situation perception variables

Our work to date has examined more than a dozen different factors of situation perception, which along with pertinent examples are presented in Table 3.1. The situation factors include: intimacy of the reproacher–offender relationship; relational consequences of the account's not being accepted; relative dominance of the reproacher; the importance of securing honouring; the importance of face-maintenance goals; the severity of the alleged offence; the expressed guilt of the offender; the degree of the offender's familiarity with the reproacher; perceived responsibility for the offence; perceived right to persuade; the reproacher's perceived resistance to persuasion; the offender's felt situation apprehension; and the perceived hostility of the reproacher.

A number of these situation perception factors have been found to be good predictors of message construction strategies in studies other than our own. For example, perceived responsibility for the offence was found by Darby and Schlenker (1982) to be directly associated with the use of apologies. Darby and Schlenker also found that apologies were more likely to be constructed as offence severity increased. Perceived resistance to persuasion (perceived lack of cooperation on the part of a roommate) has been implicated by Sillars (1980) in the avoidance of persuasive tactics in roommate conflicts. Similarly, Kipnis *et al.* (1980) found that perceived resistance (refusal to comply with a first request) interacted with dominance/status in predicting the use of particular social influence tactics. When superiors had to overcome resistance on the part of subordinates they were likely to use persistence and personal negative sanctions, but when subordinates had to overcome resistance on the part of superiors there were few choices available to them.

Not all of the situation perception factors which we have examined have turned out to be good predictors. In the scheme which we are about to present, we include those factors which we have found to show significant, consistent, and interpretable patterns of association with the actor's choice of accounting strategy and its subsequent evaluation by the reproacher.

A model for the prediction of account tactics and their evaluation

A model for predicting accounts and their evaluation is given in Figure 3.1. Two classes of variables associated with the type of account tactic individuals employ are included: the type of reproach and the individual's perception of the situation in which the accounting sequence is embedded. The reproach types, as noted above, represent the interactional constraints on account selection, while the account types represent the interactional constraints on the form of evaluation. Situation perception variables included are perceptions of the offence and the accounting episode itself (offence severity, current goals, rights to persuade, and so on); the feeling state of the accounter (guilty, responsible, etc.); the offender's perception of his/her relationship to the reproacher; and

Table 3.1 Situation perception factors and representative rating scales, Studies I and II

Situation perception factor	Representative rating scale, Study I
Intimacy of the offender–reproacher relationship	'This situation involved an intimate relationship'/ 'This situation involved a superficial relationship'
Relational consequences of the account strategy	'The outcome of this situation could have potentially harmed the relationship between me and the other person'/'The outcome of this situation could *not* have potentially harmed the relationship between me and the other person'
Dominance of the reproacher	'The other person in this situation usually dominates me'/'The other person in this situation usually did *not* dominate me'
Importance of instrumental goals	'It was *not* very important to me that the other person in this situation believe me'/'It was very important to me that the other person in this situation believe me'
Importance of positive face-maintenance goals	'I was very concerned with the image I presented to the other person in this situation'/'I was *not* very concerned with the image I presented to the other person in this situation'
Importance of relational maintenance goals	'It was very important to me whether or not I disrupted the normal relations I have with the other person'/'It was *not* very important to me whether or not I disrupted the normal relations I have with the other person'
Severity of the failure event	'The behaviour I felt obligated to account for was a severe offence'/'The behaviour I felt obligated to account for was not an offence at all'

Situation perception factor	Representative rating scale, Study II
Perceived right to persuade	'I felt that I have a right to talk my way out of being ticketed'
Perceived responsibility	'I felt I was falsely accused of the offence'
Perceived importance of instrumental goals	'It was very important for me to avoid getting ticketed'
Perceived importance of positive face-maintenance goals	'I was very concerned with maintaining a good image in this situation'
Severity of offence	'The violation for which I was stopped was very serious'
Familiarity	'I've met the police officer before'
Perceived situation apprehension	'I was very nervous when stopped by the police officer'
Perceived reproacher hostility	'The officer seemed very angry when he/she stopped me'
Perceived resistance	'I thought the officer would be very agreeable to letting me go without giving me a ticket'

perceptions of the reproacher (resistance, hostility, and so forth). These variables can be arrayed on the basis of their association with aggravating and mitigating strategies. Generally, when the offence is severe, face-maintenance or instrumental goals are important, and/or the offender feels guilty about the offence, accounts take the form of concessions or excuses. On the other hand (and still speaking generally), when the offender feels less guilty, or when relational goals are unimportant, refusals and/or silence may be the most probable response to a reproach. Honouring tends to be associated with the use of concessions (apologies), excuses and justifications, while refusal to honour appears to be associated with silence, refusals to account, and the admission of guilt.

We next summarize the results of three studies which link various situation variables and reproach types to accounts; this process should help to fill in some of the pieces in Figure 3.1. In Study I (McLaughlin *et al*. 1983a), we explored how reproach types and several of the situation variables impact on the selection of account strategies. In the second study, we surveyed a particular domain of events where we could investigate the impact of account strategy selection on a *behavioural* measure of honouring: whether or not the accounts offered to police officers for traffic violations led to citations. In the third study (McLaughlin *et al*. 1983b), we explored how individuals account for potential 'disagreeables' in ongoing dyadic conversation between strangers. While somewhat different forms of reproach or account were employed in the three studies, our general purpose was to explore the generality of the mitigation–aggravation hypothesis.

Study I

Study I involved a survey in which 278 undergraduates reported what they and an interlocutor had said in a situation in which they believed, for one reason or another, that they had to answer to the other person because of something they did or failed to do (see details in McLaughlin *et al*. 1983a). No stipulation was made concerning the types of events the individuals could recall; we wanted to sample contexts which varied considerably in type of relationship and type of offence. Two situation variables were used to measure characteristics of the offence: perceived severity of the offence and expressed guilt. It was hypothesized that more mitigating strategies would be used when severity and guilt were low. Three characteristics of the reproacher–offender relationship were assessed: intimacy, dominance of the reproacher and the relational consequences of the account episode. The latter perception deals with whether or not the account selected for use would have a potential impact on the future of the relationship (see Miller and Steinberg 1975; Cody *et al*. 1983). It was predicted that intimacy would be associated with more mitigating accounts (concessions, excuses and justifications), that long-term relational consequences would be associated with excuses and refusals, and that short-term relational consequences would be related to the use of justifications. High reproacher dominance was predicted to increase the use of concessions, with a decrease in the use of refusals. Finally, Clark and Delia's (1979) three goals associated with strategy selection were assessed: importance of instrumental goals, importance of maintaining positive face, and importance of maintaining the relationship. It was predicted that as these goals increased in importance, level of mitigation in the account selected for use would increase.

The study also attempted to assess the impact of the reproach forms silence, projected concession, projected excuse, projected justification, and projected refusal on each of the five forms of account we have examined so far: silence, concession, excuse, justification, and refusal.

The results of the data analysis indicated that there were a number of significant links between reproach type and account type, and between situation

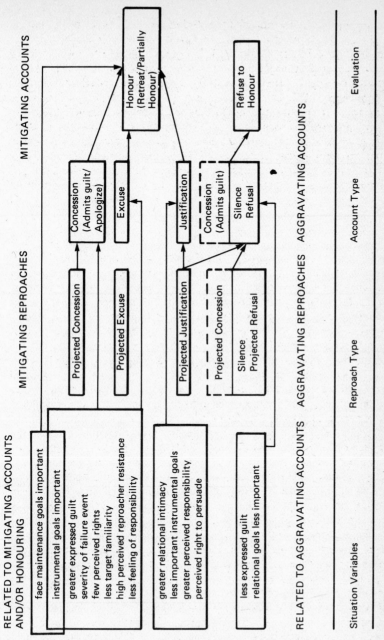

Figure 3.1

perception factors and account types, for the following five types of account:

1 *Concessions* were more likely to occur when
   a the reproacher projected a concession;
   b the reproacher used a 'silence' approach;
   c the accounter felt guilty;
   d instrumental goals were very important to the offender; and
   e the offence was severe.

2 *Excuses* were more likely to occur when
   a guilt was low;
   b the reproacher did not use projected refusal;
   c relational consequences were short-term;
   d the reproacher–offender relationship was of low intimacy; and
   e instrumental goals were important to the offender.

3 *Justifications* were more likely to be used when
   a the reproacher did not use silence;
   b the reproacher–offender relationship was intimate; and
   c instrumental goals were not important to the offender.

4 *Silence* was used more often when
   a the reproacher also was silent;
   b the offender felt little guilt;
   c the importance of maintaining the relationship was not very great; and
   d the reproacher was not dominant.

5 *Refusals* were likely to be used when
   a reproachers used either a projected refusal, projected justification, or projected concession;
   b the accounter felt falsely accused;
   c the relational consequences were short-term; and
   d the reproacher was dominant.

The results of this study lent some support to the mitigation–aggravation notion as an important dimension along which the reciprocity norm is organized. For example, projected concession led to concessions, while projected refusal led to refusals, and were negatively related to excuses. However, there is evidence that several of the reproach forms may not possess the same strength of implicature as the ones noted above. For one, projected excuses were not associated with the selection of any account type. Second, projected justification did not lead to justifications, but led instead to the use of the more aggravating form refusal. Finally, while projected concession did lead to concessions, the same reproach type also led to refusals. It may be the case that when the offender is falsely accused of having committed an offence, a tactic which presupposes a concession is perceived as a fairly aggravating reproach type, while a projected excuse, which was not associated with refusals, may not be so perceived.

Study II

Several of the same situation variables were employed in Study II, the study of patrolman–driver encounters, as were employed in Study I. In Study II 156 volunteers contacted through students enrolled in a senior-level persuasion course completed questionnaires in which they described what happened when they were pulled over for an ostensible traffic violation. The 72 females and 84 males, whose ages ranged from 15 to 48, recalled instances involving a variety of traffic offences and violations in small towns in west and central Texas, and freeway violations in Texas, New Mexico, and Oklahoma. Variables examined in both Study I and Study II were perceived responsibility (similar to expressed guilt in Study I); importance of instrumental and face-maintenance goals; severity of the offence; and familiarity (loosely paralleling intimacy, but phrased more appropriately for the patrolman–driver relationship). We did not include an assessment of dominance, since by virtue of the situation the police officer occupies the dominant role position, nor an assessment of the importance of maintaining a positive relationship, since, typically, no relationship exists. Several additional situation variables were included to improve prediction of account strategy selection. Perceived right to persuade was included to assess the extent to which accounters felt that they had reasonable grounds on which to persuade police officers not to ticket them (see Cody and McLaughlin 1980; Cody *et al*. 1983). Such grounds, in the present context, obviously would have to do with minimizing the level of severity of the offence (that a violation occurred for justifiable reasons), and thus high rights to persuade should lead to an increase in the use of justifications. Similarly, low rights to persuade should lead to more frequent admissions of guilt.

Perceived resistance to persuasion is the perception that the reproacher would not be likely to honour any account that might be put forward. High perceived resistance means that direct and rational forms of persuasion are judged as potentially less effective, leaving persuaders little choice other than to use less traditional forms of getting their way, or to give up altogether. Since the typical individual attributes power to the police officer, at least for the duration of an encounter, we anticipated that drivers would merely admit guilt when perceived resistance is high.

Perceived situation apprehension deals with the accounter's level of tension or uneasiness during the encounter with the police officer (see Cody *et al*. 1983). This variable has not been examined carefully in the face-to-face persuasion literature, and was examined in Study II because it seemed logical to expect that some accounters would feel more intimidated by police officers and more fearful of the consequences of being stopped than others. While it is clear that people will vary in felt apprehension, it is not clear whether apprehensive accounters would be more or less likely to employ apologies, excuses and/or justifications. Instead, it seems likely that they would be less able to think of an appropriate rationalization, and would want to keep the encounter as brief as possible. Under these circumstances, a simple admission of guilt would be highly likely to occur.

Operating under the assumption that the level of mitigation in the reproach would lead to a like level of mitigation in the account, a variable was included which measured the perceived hostility of the reproacher – probably a more direct measure of the officer's apparent level of annoyance, anger and unfriendliness that the overt propositional content of his reproach. To be sure, perceived hostility is likely to be correlated with perceived resistance and severity of the offence, but it is also possible that a reproacher may be annoyed even when the offence is trivial, and that offenders may believe that the reproacher would be resistant even if not hostile. Further, the mood of the officer may be partially independent of the accounter's current offence. If the mitigating reproach/mitigating account, aggravating reproach/aggravating account relationship is an important one, then we would expect that the more hostile the mood of the officer is perceived to be, the more likely offenders would be to admit guilt or refuse the reproach, and the less likely they would be to make excuses or offer justifications.

Analyses of the essays for Study II indicated that only three varieties of reproach were employed by police officers: projected excuse, projected justification, and 'simple statement of the offence'. In the simple statement of the offence, the patrolman explicitly and flatly cited the reason why the driver was pulled over:

> I stopped you for violation of the speed limit.
> I clocked you at seventy-eight miles per hour.
> You failed to come to a complete stop back there.

Projected excuse and projected justification seem to be comparatively mitigating reproach forms relative to a straightforward assertion that an offence has occurred, in that they indicate that the patrolman might be receptive to an account, and as reproach strategies are focused less on the fact of wrong-doing than on the reasons for it.

The typology of account strategies developed in our first study would have served nicely to categorize the drivers' accounts had it not been for two factors: (1) silence in the face of the police officer's reproach was not reported by any of the subjects; (2) apologizing and admitting guilt, which had both been treated as concessions in the earlier work, behaved quite differently in the present data set, particularly in regard to how they were received; that is, the officer's obligation toward a 'concession' is very different than, say, a friend's or parent's, and a guilt admission in the patrolman–driver encounter is likely to have an aggravating effect (i.e., *not* lead to honouring). Consequently, the taxonomy was slightly altered to accomodate the special circumstances presented by the police officer–driver encounters. The five account types examined in Study II thus were apologies, excuses, justifications, admissions of guilt and refusals, roughly ordered from most to least mitigating.

The results of Study II may be summarized as follows:

1 *Apologies* were more likely to occur when
  a face-maintenance goals were highly important;
  b instrumental goals were highly important; and
  c the level of perceived resistance was low.
2 *Excuses* were more likely to be given when
  a the reproacher was a stranger (low familiarity);
  b the reproacher was perceived to be highly resistant to persuasion; and
  c the accounter felt little responsibility for the offence.
3 *Justifications* were more likely to occur when
  a the reproacher used a projected justification;
  b the accounter felt responsible for the offence; and
  c the accounter felt he/she had a right to use persuasion.
4 *Admissions of guilt* were more likely to be made when
  a perceived rights to persuade were low;
  b the offender felt apprehensive; and

c the reproacher was a stranger (low familiarity).
5 *Refusals* were more likely to occur when
a the reproacher simply stated the offence;
b the reproacher was perceived as hostile; and
c the reproacher used a projected excuse.

Further, the analysis linking accounts and situation variables to honouring indicated that honouring was more likely to occur when: (a) instrumental goals were highly important; (b) an apology was used; (c) an excuse was used; (d) a justification was used, and (c) face-maintenance goals were highly important.

The results of this study also provided some support for the mitigation-aggravation hypothesis. Projected justifications led to justifications, and the 'states offence' reproach led to refusals, as did perceived reproacher hostility. Mitigating accounts, and two situation variables related to mitigation (see Figure 3.1), resulted in honouring. However, projected excuses led to the selection of the aggravating refusal tactic, not to the selection of mitigating tactics. One explanation for this finding may be that projected excuses conveyed the impression that the patrolmen were receptive, and that many individuals used this potential receptivity to deny wrongdoing; possibly due to the (false) expectation that if they convinced a receptive patrolman that they did nothing wrong, then they wouldn't be ticketed. Consequently, there were more projected excuses–refusal sequences (i.e., 'Did you see the stop sign there?' 'Yes, sir, and I did come to a complete stop.') than projected excuses–excuse sequences ('Did you see that stop sign there?' 'Well, sir, I came through the alley and I was trying to see the signs, but with the construction going on and with some signs covered up . . .'). Also, the results of this study indicated that some tactics (apologies, excuses and admissions of guilt) were more strongly influenced by the accounter's goals and feeling states than by the interactional constraint. However, the situation variable–account selection relationships which were significant generally support our hypotheses concerning mitigation and aggravation (see Figure 3.1): the importance of communicative goals and the perception of low resistance led to apologies; low familiarity, high perceived resistance and lack of felt responsibility led to excuses; low rights to persuade, high apprehension and low familiarity led to admissions of guilt; and high rights to persuade and felt responsibility led (along with projected justifications) to justifications.

Study III

In the third study exploring the generality of the mitigation–aggravation hypothesis, we moved away from reliance on survey data toward studying the full account sequence (offence–reproach–account–evaluation) as it unfolds during dyadic conversations among strangers (McLaughlin *et al.* 1983b). Consequently, no questionnaire data concerning situation perception was used; analyses of the full sequence required, instead, a typology of 'disagreeables' (assertions or behaviours with which partners take issue), a typology of reproaches, a typology of accounts and a typology of ways in which conversationists evaluate accounts (beyond 'honouring'). In this study, the original typology of accounts proved adequate for coding account types (doesn't account (silence), concessions, excuses, justifications and refusals), but some clarification of types of offences, reproach types and evaluation responses relevant to conversation is required.

Analyses of 50 half-hour conversations (25 same-sex and 25 opposite-sex dyads) revealed that the topics found to be disputed in self-disclosure conversations can be subsumed under four categories. In the *taste/attitude/belief* type of offence the reproacher takes issue with the attitudes or beliefs his/her partner has adopted, such as the amount of funding for women's athletics. *Personal identity* offences included those components of personal identity claimed by the accounter to which the reproacher took exception, such as being a male secretary, a male nurse, a male who fails in math, being prejudiced, etc. *Work/study* offences included the accounter's activities with which the reproacher took issue; such as not having a major, working on Christmas Day, taking too many credits, taking too few credits, etc. *Interaction offences* included activities which occurred during the conversation which were found to be questionable: failing to listen, misunderstanding, yawning. Since personal identity and work/school offences involve offences usually reflecting only that the accounter is not behaving in accordance with a norm or stereotype, we anticipated that such offences would be addressed by concessions, excuses or justifications. However, since folk wisdom suggests that 'there's no accounting for taste', and since both taste/attitude/belief and interactional offences reflect idiosyncratic behaviours, we anticipated that such offences would lead to refusing or neglecting to account.

Analyses of reproach types indicated that there were four general ways in which reproachers requested (or implied the offering of) accounts in ongoing conversations. In the *moral/intellectual superiority* reproach, the reproacher suggests that something about the accounter's taste, life style, etc., is not quite up to the reproacher's high standard of conduct. When a speaker, for example, asserts that he/she enjoys watching soap operas, a moral/intellectual superiority reproach may follow:

> Oh, Lord! But they – *I have enough problems of my own without getting all involved in some little fictional problem.* (McLaughlin *et al.* 1983b, p. 110).

In the *direct rebuke* the reproacher explicitly and flatly categorizes (and occasionally even labels) some aspect of the accounter's behaviour as offensive, incorrect or unacceptable:

> Oh, *you're prejudiced.*
> That's uh – *female chauvinism right there.*

In the *surprise/disgust* reproach, the reproacher expresses befuddlement, amusement, amazement or puzzlement over the partner's statement (e.g. 'What??' 'Yuk!' 'You're ah – you're a secretary??'). In the *direct request for account* the reproacher asked questions seeking reasons for a behaviour or for clarification of a response: for example, 'Why did you do that?' This reproach type parallels both the projected justification and the projected excuse noted above, but does not specifically forecast whether the accounter will deny responsibility (excuse) or minimize severity (justify). Clearly, direct rebuke and moral/intellectual superiority reproaches are the more aggravating reproach types, and direct requests are mitigating. The surprise/disgust reproach type is less clearly related to a general influence of mitigation or aggravation, though it is clearly less aggravating the direct rebuke or moral/intellectual superiority reproaches.

Evaluation behaviours included four general types of responses to the account (see McLaughlin *et al.* 1983b). In *honouring*, the reproacher explicitly indicates, through laughter, agreement, positive endorsements, etc., that the account has been accepted and is adequate to achieve closure of the account sequence. In a *retreat*, the reproacher provided partial honouring (agreeing with some subtopic of the accounter's statement), withdrew the original objections and made excuses for the accounter's untoward behaviour. In *reject account/take issue/reinstate reproach*, the reproacher restated the reproach as if no account had been given. In *drop issue/switch topic*, either of the conversational partners may terminate the account–evaluation sequence by introducing new topics (which may serve the function of finding other topics on which the two may establish agreement). We anticipated that concessions, excuses and (lastly) justifications would be related to honouring and retreating responses, while 'doesn't account' and refusals would led to reject/take issue/reinstate responses. Drop issue/switch topic, however, is neither aggravating or mitigating because the issues of the offence and the accountability of the offence are left unresolved. One would expect, however, that if the offence was not severe (and many offences in dyadic conversations were not severe), the reproacher may drop issue/switch topic if the accounter didn't account – both would tactfully move to new topics on which agreement may be secured.

Two stages of analyses were conducted, predicting account type and predicting evaluation behaviours. Analyses predicting account strategy selection can be summarized as follows:

1 *Didn't account* tactics were used
   a more frequently for interaction offences and less frequently for work/ school and personal identity offences; and,
   b more frequently when moral/intellectual superiority or direct rebuke reproaches were used, and less frequently when disgust/surprise reproaches were used.
2 Neither offence type of reproach form predicted the use of *concessions*.
3 *Excuse* tactics were used
   a more frequently for offences of taste/attitude/belief, work/school, and personal identity, and were less frequently used for interaction offences; and,
   b reproach type was not associated with the use of excuses.
4 Neither offence type or reproach form predicted the use of *justifications*.
5 *Refusal* tactics were used
   a more frequently for offences of personal identity and taste/attitude/ belief; and,
   b more frequently following direct rebuke, direct request for account and moral/intellectual superiority reproaches.

Analyses predicting evaluation can be summarized as follows:

1 *Honouring* occurred
   a more frequently when accounters used excuses; and,
   b less frequently when accounters didn't account.
2 *Retreating* occurred
   a more frequently when accounters used justifications; and,

    b more frequently when accounters used concessions.
3 The *reject account/take issue/reinstate* reproach tactic occurred
    a more frequently when accounters didn't account;
    b more frequently when accounters used justifications; and,
    c more frequently when accounters used refusals.
4 The *drop issue/switch topic* tactic occurred
    a more frequently when accounters didn't account.

Predictions based on the mitigation–aggravation hypothesis were, for the most part, confirmed. The more aggravating refusal tactic followed the more aggravating reproach forms of moral/intellectual superiority and direct rebuke. Excuses led to honouring, and concessions and justifications were reciprocated with retreats. Failing to account, justifications and refusals led the reproacher to restate the reproach. Partial support was also obtained for hypotheses linking type of offence to the selection of accounts (see McLaughlin *et al*. 1983b).

Conclusions

The evidence presented here, and in Blumstein (1974), clearly indicates that the level of mitigation (or penitence) in the account is the most important determining factor in how interactants achieve closure of the account sequence. Mitigating accounts lead to honouring or retreating. However, it does not appear that levels of mitigation in the reproach led to mitigating accounts. Instead, the results of these studies indicate that aggravating forms of reproaches lead to aggravating accounts and that aggravating reproach forms rarely lead to mitigating accounts. Specifically, the consistency with which projected refusal (states offence, perceived hostility, and both moral/intellectual superiority and direct rebuke) led to refusal suggests a generalizable sequence of response matching. Further, in three studies conducted, the aggravating forms of reproach never predicted mitigating accounts, while in one study (Study I) projected refusals were negatively associated with the use of excuses.

    Two limitations exist in the mitigation–aggravation hypothesis: (1) there were no consistent relationships between mitigating reproaches and mitigation accounts; and, (2) in a few instances, mitigating reproaches led to aggravating accounts. In the former, projected concessions led to concessions in the first study, projected justifications led to justifications in the second study and reproach type was not associated with concessions, excuses or justifications in the third study. In the latter limitation, projected concessions led to refusals in the first study, projected excuses led to refusals in the second study and direct requests led to refusals in the third study. Obviously, then, aggravating reproach forms convey a more pressing interactional constraint on behaviour than do mitigating ones. Why?

    The results of three studies suggest to us that when individuals enter into an account sequence, they may already perceive the event along a number of lines (i.e., guilt, severity of offence, etc.) and/or possess routine ways of accounting (for example, reasons for why one is male and a nurse). Consequently, many contexts exist where individuals have accounting preferences and when a reproacher conveys the impression of being receptive (by using a mitigating reproach), the level of mitigation doesn't interfere with planned social behaviour. Thus, individuals respond in predictable ways as dictated by their perceptions of responsibility, etc. Mitigating reproaches are thus evenly distributed across a wide range of possible mitigating (concessions, excuses and justifications) and aggravating accounts (refusals). On the other hand, perceived hostility, projected refusals, moral/intellectual superiority reproaches may constitute reproach forms one is less likely to expect under normal conditions (due to the preference for agreement principle). Consequently, the use of aggravating reproach forms represents a thwarting of what one plans to (or usually would) communicate. The driver–patrolmen essays provided a number of examples attesting to the viability of this conclusion. For example, if a driver had exceeded the speed limit by 10 m.p.h. he/she may consider, while the officer approaches, using an excuse (it was a long drive, late at night in stormy weather, etc.). But as a hostile patrolman accuses the driver of driving 83 m.p.h. the driver's preferred plan becomes inoperative and he/she feels compelled to deny the charge. This framework also is useful in explaining those instances in which the mitigating reproach led to aggravating accounts. In the case of projected concession–refusal sequences, the accounter's perception of being falsely accused of an offence may result in the projected concession being perceived as aggravating. In the projected excuse–refusal sequence, the accounter may, given the impression that the officer is receptive, select tactics he/she thinks should be related to honouring (i.e., innocence).

Stemming from this conclusion, one of the pressing issues involved in extending research on the account sequence rests in *a priori* specification of how 'aggravating' an aggravating reproach must be if the level of aggravation operates as the primary constraint on behaviour. Consequently, future research may well benefit from exploring the paralinguistic cues operating when a reproach is made. Further, we plan in subsequent stages of our research to (a) uncover how the respondents themselves perceive the level of mitigation–aggravation in the reproach (since, as noted above, the particular context may have an impact on perceived aggravation), and, (b) assess the accounter's preferred account tactic (i.e., socially planned or routine behaviour) in different situational contexts. Implementing these extensions should cast more light on understanding how people go about selecting accounts, and understanding how people collaboratively make or resolve 'trouble'.

Finally, in passing we can recommend to theorists interested in research on accounts that we have found excuses and justifications (which were not predicted by reproach type as a general rule) to be regarded as 'utility' strategies for use regardless of the form of reproach (see McLaughlin *et al.* 1983b). Since these account types represent the majority of types of accounts which are used, scholars may find it useful in their own research to employ subcategories of excuses and justifications, since some types of justifications may be more mitigating than others. Scott and Lyman (1968) and Schonbach (1980) provide some relevant means for differentiating between different subcategories.

References

BLUMSTEIN, P. 1974: The honoring of accounts. *American Sociological Review* **39**, 551–66.

CLARK, R.A. 1979: The impact on selection of persuasive strategies on self-interest and desired liking. *Communication Monographs* **46**, 257–73.

CLARK, R.A. and DELIA, J. 1979: Topoi and rhetorical competence. *The Quarterly Journal of Speech* **65**, 187–206.

CODY, M.J. and MCLAUGHLIN, M.L. 1980: Perceptions of compliance-gaining situations. *Communication Monographs* **47**, 132–48.

CODY, M.J., WOELFEL, M.L. and JORDAN, W.J. 1983; Dimensions of compliance-gaining situations. *Human Communication Research* **9**, 99–113.

COLEMAN, R.V. 1976: Court control and grievance accounts: Dynamics of traffic court interactions. *Urban Life* **5**, 165–87.

DARBY, B.W. and SCHLENKER, B.R. 1982: Children's reactions to apologies. *Journal of Personality and Social Psychology* **43**, 742–53.

DITTON, J. 1977: Alibis and aliases: Some notes on the 'motives' of fiddling bread salesmen. *Sociology* **11**, 233–56.

GILES, H. 1980: New directions in accomodation theory. *York Papers in Linguistics* **9**, 105–36.

GILES, H., TAYLOR, D.M. and BOURHIS, R.V. 1973: Towards a theory of interpersonal accomodation through language: Some Canadian data. *Language in Society* **2**, 161–79.

GOFFMAN, E. 1967: *Interaction ritual: Essays on face-to-face behaviour.* Chicago: Aldine Publishing Company.

—— 1971: *Relations in public: Microstudies of the public order.* New York: Basic Books.

GOULDNER, A.W. 1960: The norm of reciprocity: A preliminary statement. *American Sociological Review* **25**, 161–79.

GRIMSHAW, A.D. 1981: Instrumentality selection in naturally occuring conversation: A research agenda. In Werth, P., editor, *Conversation and discourse: Structure and interpretation* (New York: St Martin's Press).

HARRÉ, R. 1977: The ethogenic approach: Theory and practice. In Berkowitz, L., editor, *Advances in experimental social psychology* (vol. 10) (New York: Academic Press).

HEWITT, J.P. and HALL, P.M. 1973: Social problems, problematic situations, and quasi-theories. *American Sociological Review* **38**, 367–74.

JACKSON, S. and JACOBS S. 1980: Structure of conversational argument: Pragmatic bases for the enthymeme. *The Quarterly Journal of Speech* **66**, 251–65.

JACOBS, S. and JACKSON, S. 1979: Collaborative aspects of argument production. Paper presented at the meeting of the Speech Communication Association, San Antonio.

JEFFERSON, G. 1972: Side sequences. In Sudnow, D., editor, *Studies in social interaction.* New York: Free Press.

JEFFERSON, G. and SCHENKEIN, J. 1978: Some sequential negotiations in conversation: Unexpanded and expanded versions of projected action sequences. In Schenkein, J., editor, *Studies in the organization of conversational interaction* (New York: Academic Press).

KIPNIS, D., SCHMIDT, S.M. and WILKINSON, I. 1980: Intraorganizational influence tactics: Explorations in getting one's way. *Journal of Applied Psychology* **65**, 440–52.

LABOV, W. and FANSHEL, D. 1977: *Therapeutic discourse: Psychotherapy as conversation.* New York: Academic Press.

LARSEN, R.S., MARTIN, H.J. and GILES, H. 1977: Anticipated social cost and interpersonal accomodation. *Human Communication Research* **4**, 303–308.

MCLAUGHLIN, M.L. 1984: *Conversation: How talk is organized.* Beverly Hills, Cal.: Sage.

MCLAUGHLIN, M.L., CODY, M.J. and O'HAIR, H.D. 1983(a): The management of failure events: Some contextual determinants of accounting behaviour. *Human Communication Research* **9**, 208–24.

MCLAUGHLIN, M.L., CODY, M.J. and ROSENSTEIN, N.E. 1983(b): Account sequences in conversations between strangers. *Communication Monographs* **50**, 102–25.

MILLER, G.R. and STEINBERG, M. 1975: *Between people: A new analysis of interpersonal communication.* Chicago: Science Research Associates.

REMLER, J.E. 1978: Some repairs on the notion of repairs. *Chicago Linguistic Society, Papers from the Ninth Regional Meeting* 391–402.

ROGERS, J.W. and BUFFALO, M.D. 1974: Neutralization techniques: Toward a simplified measurement scale. *Pacific Sociological Review* **17**, 313–31.

SCHEGLOFF, E.A. 1972: Notes on a conversational practice: Formulating place. In Sudnow, D., editor, *Studies in social interaction* (New York: Free Press).

SCHLENKER, B.R. and DARBY, B.W. 1981: The use of apologies in social predicaments. *Social Psychology Quarterly* **44**, 271–8.

SCHONBACH, P. 1980: A category system for account phases. *European Journal of Social Psychology* **10**, 195–200.

SCOTT, M.B. and LYMAN, S.M. 1968: Accounts. *American Sociological Review* **33**, 46–62.

SEARLE, J. 1975: Indirect speech acts. In Cole, P. and Morgan, J.L., editors, *Syntax and Semantics: Speech acts* (vol. 3) (New York: Academic Press).

SHIELDS, N.M. 1979: Accounts and other interpersonal strategies in a credibility detracting context. *Pacific Sociological Review* **22**, 255–72.

SILLARS, A.L. 1980: Attributions and communication in roommate conflicts. *Communication Monographs* **47**, 180–200.

SYKES, G.M. and MATZA, D. 1957: Techniques of neutralization. *American Sociological Review* **22**, 667–9.

4

The remedial episode as a negotiation of rules

G.H. Morris

The study of problematic situations (Hewitt and Hall 1973) and failure events (Schonbach 1980) concerns how inappropriate behaviour is remedied through the provision of accounts and other aligning actions (Goffman 1971; Scott and Lyman 1968; Stokes and Hewitt 1976). Problematic situations are important theoretically, because they shed light upon issues of social order and social change (Stokes and Hewitt 1976), interaction management (Jefferson 1972; McLaughlin *et al*. 1983; Cody and McLaughlin Chapter 3), and alignment (Morris and Hopper 1980).

Alignment is considered here as the process of tuning social interaction to meet participants' preferences (Stokes and Hewitt 1976; Morris and Hopper 1984). A central part of alignment research concerns matters of appropriateness, such as: Is it appropriate to call the doctor by her first name? Is it appropriate to notify teachers in advance of absences? Is it appropriate to broach a certain topic? Is it appropriate to call someone after midnight? or Is it appropriate to refuse a friend's request for a favour? The thrust of alignment research has been to ascertain how social interactants 'calibrate' behaviour to match what they think is preferable. When engaging in alignment, participants can come to agreements about what is preferred, what situations call for the preferred behaviour, and precisely what counts as full enactment of that behaviour. (Morris and Hopper 1980). The alignment approach is thus quite different from other approaches to action in problematic situations, because it emphasizes communicators' cooperative efforts to guide their activity, as opposed to the efforts of 'offenders' to account for admittedly deviant behaviour.

This chapter employs the alignment approach, and characterizes a type of problematic situation, the remedial episode, as a negotiation of rules for social interaction.

Discussion unfolds as follows: I first characterize extant research about problematic situations and failure events, claiming that this research stresses issues of identity (e.g. 'Is the actor foolish?') over substantive issues (e.g. 'Is what the actor did inappropriate under the circumstances?'). Second, I argue that substantive issues (relating to rules) are inherent in problematic situations, and deserve research attention. Third, I propose a rules meta-language used to describe and explain substantive issues in problematic social interaction. Fourth, I address three types of problematic situations called remedial episodes, including accounting sequences, remedial interchanges, and more extensive negotiations. Fifth, I work through an analysis of a remedial episode featuring negotiation of rules. Finally, I discuss implications of the alignment approach taken here for the conduct of future inquiry into rules and the regulation of social interaction.

The focus on identity in problematic situations

As Cody and McLaughlin (Chapter 3) point out, most studies of failure events have focused on discriminating types of excuses and justifications (Scott and Lyman 1968) or on elaborating the taxonomy of speech acts in failure events, to include apologies and pretexts (Goffman 1971), disclaimers and quasi-theories (Hewitt and Hall 1973; Hewitt and Stokes 1975), or concessions and refusals to account (Schonbach 1980). The conditions under which the various remedial moves might be successful (Blumstein *et al.* 1974) and the situational influences over what kind of remedial move will be made (McLaughlin *et al.* 1983) have also been explored.

The developing account language emphasizes identity as opposed to substantive aspects of social behaviour. Throughout his work, Goffman (1971; 1974) has maintained that inappropriate behaviour damages the impression that an 'offender' is a competent, responsible actor. It is not the offence which is harmful, but rather the *virtual offence* to one's identity, and it is the virtual offence that must be rectified. To illustrate: An apology, to Goffman, is 'a gesture through which an individual splits himself in two parts, the part that is guilty of an offence and the part that dissociated itself from the delict and affirms a belief in the offended rule' (1971, p. 113). Similarly, the motive behind giving accounts is that 'the more an actor can argue mitigating circumstances successfully, the more he can establish that the act is not to be taken as an expression of his moral character' (1971, p. 112).

One consequence of the emphasis on identity has been that researchers have tended to assume that participants in problematic situations *agree* that an offence has been committed. To investigate the conditions under which accounts will usually be successful, and the kinds of accounts likely to be produced under certain conditions, researchers have relied upon cases of transparent, agreed upon, inappropriateness. Blumstein and his colleagues (1974) state that remedial interchanges (Goffman 1971) are triggered by an offence. They state further that 'An account should be honoured when the moral character of the offender has been restored' (1974, p. 552). Holding such views about the impetus for remedial interchanges led the researchers to pass over the substantive issue of the appropriateness of conduct, and instead to use vignettes of obviously inappropriate behaviour in their research design. Similarly, in instructions to subjects in a study of situational influences over account types, McLaughlin *et al.* (1983) gave the following examples:

> you might have to account to your boss for why you were late to work; your girl/ boyfriend might expect you to account for your failure to call when you were expected to; your professor might expect you to account for your absence from the mid-term exam (p. 218).

The assumption that participants agree that an offence has been committed has also been reflected in the typologies of accounts that have been generated. Schonbach's (1980) extended taxonomy of accounts includes concessions, excuses, justifications and refusals as major categories, as well as 22 sub-categories. Only one of the possible account types (a type of refusal) applies to a case in which the accused and reproacher differ about whether or not an offence has occurred.

In sum, investigators have favoured an approach to problematic situations and failure events that ignores substantive considerations. They have generally assumed actors' consensus about what counts as an offence. To elaborate on the significance of this move, I turn now to a discussion of rules and their part in regulating social behaviour.

Rules as substantive issues

Rules find their places in communication theory as parts of explanations for why behaviour occurs as regularly as it does. If actors repeat certain discourse strategies it might be because they know and follow rules that prescribe such behaviour (Shimanoff 1980). For instance, if they regularly say 'Thank you' upon receiving gifts, it might be explained that they know that this is the prescribed behaviour, and have elected to conform to the prescription. Similarly, if employees ordinarily make appointments before discussing problems with their employers, it might be because they know an organizational rule that prescribes this advance notice, and they have elected to follow the rule. Viewing rules as prescriptions for situated behaviour allows theorists to explain recurrent behaviour of persons belonging to a homogeneous community (Donohue *et al.* 1980).

Other rules approaches treat rules more as individuals' constructions for recognizing and selecting behaviours in recurrent contexts (Pearce 1976; Pearce and Cronen 1980; Cronen *et al.* 1982). Recurrent behaviour, to such theorists, stems from the coordinated interpenetration of one person's rules with those of another. Actors are considered to be heterogeneous, and successful coordination between actors is alleged not to depend upon communicators' consensus on rules.

In this essay, rules are considered as behaviour standards (Carver and Scheier 1981); that is, rules are the individual's 'comparison values' for social behaviour. In action, persons compare contemplated actions with rules much like a chef measures the quantity of an ingredient. Rules are also used for comparison when evaluating completed actions of self and other. I do not assume that this rule-matching process is continuous; on the contrary, I am in accord with Berger and Douglas (1982) that some social interaction is simply scripted, and interactants sometimes perform with very little mindfulness. With Cronen *et al.* (1982), I assume that rules are hierarchically organized, with relatively abstract rules (e.g. Be cooperative; Protect everyone's face; or Make sense) warranting more particular rules (e.g. Give help when it is needed; Don't reprimand someone loudly in public; or Accomodate your language use to that of your interlocutors).

Rules become substantive issues for communicators when dispreferred outcomes are experienced. It is under such conditions that people wonder what is going on, why action went awry, and what to do about it (Hewitt and Hall 1973). Experiencing dispreferred outcomes is most likely when participants' rules are substantially different, the participants are highly interdependent, and the interaction highly consequential. Additionally, more problems may be expected in enigmatic than in highly scripted interaction (Harre and Secord 1973). This is not to say that scripted interaction does not generate problems. Berger and Douglas (1982) outline some conditions under which people may become highly conscious of behaviour, including when scripts are interrupted by external forces, when more of a behaviour is required than ordinarily, when discrepant outcomes are obtained, and when competing scripts exist. I presume that the explanation of this higher consciousness of behaviour is the perceived likelihood of interactional problems.

I should disclaim one apparent implication of this approach to rules, which is that since they are individuals' constructions, they are entirely disconnected from normative conceptions of what is supposed to happen. I assume, to the contrary, that individuals' rules will develop in concord with the most abstract rules of their communities, but that individuals' rules are more extensive and particular. At least part of individuals' rules are developed, as we shall we, through processes of remediation and legislation which generate more particular guides for behaviour (Morris and Hopper 1980). People will have rules, for instance, which guide their conduct in specific relationships.

I have attempted to establish, in this section, that rules may become substantive issues for interactants, that when problematic situations erupt, at least part of participants' concern will be collectively to determine what is supposed, and not supposed, to happen. Unfortunately though, because previous research has passed over these substantive issues in favour of investigating how actors combat the destructive implications of offensive behaviour, the language that has been developed to describe problematic situations is inadequate to deal with substantive issues when they crop up.

In the section that follows, I reveal a rules meta-language developed to capture the substantive aspects of talk during problematic situations. The language evolved out of a study of remedial episodes in teacher–student conferences (Morris 1978), which sought to discover the structure of remedial episodes, and to account for the episodic force (Frentz and Farrell 1976) of individual utterances contained in the episodes. Excerpts from these episodes are examined later in this chapter.

Aspects of a rules meta-language

The rules meta-language I devised to account for substantive aspects of remedial episodes is as follows:

1   A *rule* is a proposition that: *Act A is appropriate in Context C* (Morris and Hopper 1980).
2   A *statement of rules* explicitly or implicitly expresses the author's understanding of a rule. For example, one of the teachers in the 1978 study said: 'I guess I sort of resent you coming in here and saying "hey, I didn't do it, now you tell me how to fix it", without coming up with any ideas, and I think it's your responsibility to do it.' This obvious reproach also serves as a statement of rules, since it states that it is appropriate for the student to suggest ways to make up missed work. An affirmed rule statement is the product of 'legislation', and establishes expectations for future interaction.

3   A *statement of conformity* is a claim that the actor either conformed with or violated a rule. For example, when it was recommended to a student that she notify teachers in advance of future absences, she replied: 'I called my boyfriend and asked him to call you', which claims conformity with a 'notification' rule. An affirmed statement of conformity can overturn accusations, because it is agreed that the appropriate act was actually performed. Affirmed statements of conformity indirectly ratify the rule.

4   A *statement of conditions* relates to the context, or circumstances of action, and is a claim that the conditions warrant an exception to the rule. For example, a student who missed an assignment explained: 'I didn't get better until Thursday. Found out I had some sort of flu.' The force of this statement is that the student falls into a category of persons (sick ones) for whom a violation of the rule (to do assignments on schedule) is warranted. An affirmed statement of conditions modifies the rule, in that qualifications are considered to be warranted exceptions. Such a statement, in effect, establishes an 'escape clause' in an interpersonal contract.

This meta-language is employed in a subsequent section in an analysis of an elaborate remedial episode. Before commencing that analysis, however, I address the notion of 'remedial episode', showing various types, and explaining how the more elaborate episodes develop.

Remedial episodes

Remedial episodes are restorative sequences of behaviour occurring in problematic situations. The briefest form of remedial episode is perhaps the account sequence (Cody and McLaughlin Chapter 3) which includes a reproach, an account, and an evaluation of the account. Slightly more involved than this is the remedial interchange, conceptualized by Goffman (1971) as a four-move exchange involving a remedy (e.g. an account), relief (acceptance of the remedy), appreciation (a statement expressing gratitude for having been relieved) and minimization (a denial that elaborate appreciation is necessary). An imaginary episode will clarify the difference between these sequences:

(01) A: Why didn't you show up to meet my parents? (reproach).
(02) B: I didn't realize they'd be leaving so early (account/remedy)
(03) A: Well, alright, you can catch them next time. (evaluation/relief)
(04) B: Thanks. (appreciation)
(05) A: Oh, it's nothing. (minimization)

The first three of these utterances comprise an accounting sequence, while utterances (02) through (05) make up a remedial interchange.

Goffman (1971) acknowledged that the remedial interchange may be modified in various ways, including the recycling of moves. Remedies are recycled, for instance, when immediate relief is not provided. A similar extension of the remedial episode occurs when a remedy is compounded or extended over several turns, or when a succession of different remedies are involved. The following transcript of conversation between a teacher and student features a justification ('family illness') that is extended over several turns:

(01) T: I haven't seen you for so long. And I need to know, you know, what the deal is. (reproach)

(02) S: Ok. Um, I was thinking

(03) T: (Interrupting) You know, I can't kinda just give you a blanket, 'That's fine', you know to

(04) S: I understand, perfectly. Um well see my grandmother has been real sick. She has cancer, she's always in the hospital and lately she's been getting, you know, a lot worse, and my parents have been very upset. My father works at an oil company (Account/statement of conditions).

(05) T: Uh huh.

(06) S: And, um, had to go to Hague, to Holland, you know, he does work over there. (extension)

(07) T: Uh huh.

(08) S: My father does. And my grandmother got a lot worse and there's nobody else to go over there and I had to, the hospital, you know. (extension)

(09) T: Oh.

(10) S: and since I'm the only ma- ma- since I'm, I'm not a minor, I'm the only grandchild who is not a minor, you know, I have to go and sign papers and stuff (extension).

(11) T: Yeah.

(12) S: Cause she, you know, they were afraid she was going to die with my parents gone. (extension)

(13) T: Yeah.

(14) S: OK, and I'd go up there – she's in Dallas – and I came down with my parents.

(15) T: Yeah. That must have been hard. (relief)

The strength of the student's remedy, in this example, is compounded as she offers each extension. Although having a sick grandmother might not fully justify a lengthy absence from college, it is more legitimate to miss school when the grandmother is seriously ill (04), getting worse (04), when the parents are upset but are unable to attend the grandmother and hospital business (04, 06, 08), when the student is the only person who could step in to help (10) and when the grandmother is close to death (12). Modifications like these can lead to quite elaborate remedial episodes, the structure of which is diagrammed in Figure 4.1.

This diagram begins at the point of reproach – the point at which a violation of rules is noted, and it is made an issue. The first decision-point in the model is whether or not a remedy is offered. The remedy will either be a statement of conditions (as in the above example), a statement of conformity to rules under these conditions, or a statement that proposes a rule applicable to the situation and behaviour in question.

If this statement is affirmed, that is, if the reproacher feels that the statement is consistent with his or her view of the condition, behaviour or rule at issue and speaks accordingly, the person who provided the remedy may provide appreciation, and this may be followed by minimization. On the other hand, if (as in the above example), the reproacher does not affirm the remedy statement, one of four kinds of symbolic acts may be offered. Either the reproacher solicits clarification of the preceding statement, or openly disputes the statement, or accuses the other of the same or another rule violation, or makes an indirect response.

Often the one reproached responds with a recycling of the original statement of conditions, conformity or rule, or provides additional information to support such statements. The cycle of remedy followed by disaffirmation may continue until all options have been tried. Also, it is not uncommon for alleged

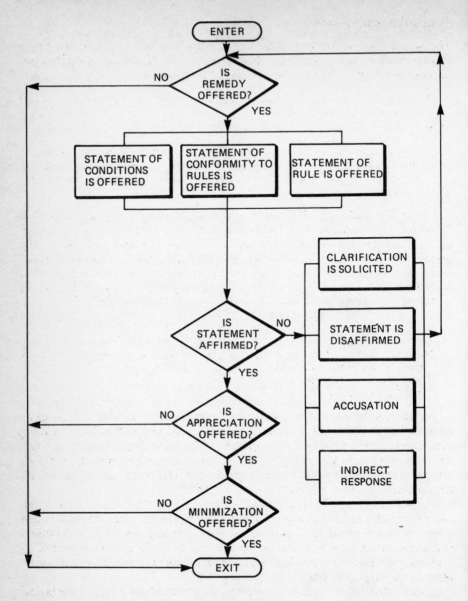

Figure 4.1 Sequencing of moves in remedial episodes

violators to attempt to turn the tables on the other participant by claiming that although they may be in violation of rules, so are the others. Thus the positions of accuser and accused may be exchanged in the remedial process.

To illustrate the negotiation of rules in remedial episodes, I offer next an analysis of an elaborate remedial episode. This episode was selected as the best illustration from the episodes analysed in an earlier study. Participants in this episode, more than any other, lack consensus about rules.

Sample remedial episode

The episode to be considered here begins with a reproach (an implication by a teacher that a student's performance is substandard). It ends, after much negotiation, with a topic change to supportive interchange.

> (01) S: And then I want to, I got that unsatisfactory on my self-concept (exercise), and I want to get that taken care of.
> (02) T: OK. I'm
> (03) S: Well
> (04) T: I was thinking about that and what I would like you to do instead of rewriting it is to really look at the um, comments that I wrote on there, and just make sure that you understand the difference in what I was asking for and what you gave me. Is that clear to you?

The student had received a grade of 'unsatisfactory' on an assignment that called for her to write about a 'Self-concept exercise' that had been performed during class. The teacher replies to the student's concern about the exercise by implying that the student failed to comply with requirements of the assignment, and suggests a course of action. This utterance quite vividly *makes* the situation problematic, insofar as it claims that a gap exists between what the student did and what she should have done.

> (05) S: Yeah. It was just, it was just my opinion differed a whole lot with yours, that's what I found, you know. I just, you and I just differed a whole lot.
> (06) T: I don't think it was a matter of differing opinions, it is just that you didn't talk about improvement, or talk about
> (07) S: (interrupts) Oh, but I did.
> (08) T: Do you have it with you?

The student replies with a statement of conformity, claiming that she conformed with requirements for the assignment, and implies that the teacher's judgement of her performance was influenced by the teacher's holding a different opinion of the exercise than she did. Her implication seems accusatory, since teachers are supposed to evaluate work strictly on its merits, not on its consonance with their own views.

The teacher disaffirms the student's statement of conformity, and at the same time (06) reasserts that a difference exists between what the student did and what was required. She supports this with the claim that the student failed to discuss a required topic ('improvement'). Evidently, the teacher uses a rule to evaluate performances on this assignment, that students should include statements about improvement.

By uttering (07), the student recycles the statement of conformity, displaying consensus between her and the teacher that statements about improvement are necessary. It would be pointless to argue conformity with a rule that does not apply to the case in question.

Presumably in order to find out if the required statements were present, and thus to resolve the issue of conformity, the teacher responds indirectly, requesting to review the student's paper (08).

To this point in the episode, a rule violation is being alleged by the teacher and contested by the student. Both parties agree on the rule that students' papers must include statements about improvement, but they disagree about whether or not an 'offence' has been committed, and if so, by whom. Because her statements of conformity have not been affirmed, the student's choices now are either to terminate the episode or to offer another remedy. If she offers a remedy, she might either recycle her statement of conformity, offer a statement of conditions which would explain why she didn't include more about improvement, or switch to a statement of another rule.

> (09) S: Yeah. I didn't put a whole lot, I put, I know I didn't put a whole lot, but I put a sentence of like, a sentence of dislike and a sentence of improvement, I really did, 'cause that's all I could come up with.
> (10) T: You know, I felt like this wasn't a, uh, an evaluation of the exercise that really reflected all that you were capable of looking at.

The student (09) softens her statement of conformity by admitting that she did not write very much about improvement, and offers a statement of conditions: As she was doing the assignment, one sentence about improvement was all she could generate. This statement does not detail what might have transpired which limited her to a single sentence, though any of a broad range of excuses or justifications might have been offered here. Schonbach (1980) might code this an 'appeal to human shortcomings'.

If this episode were primarily a negotiation of participants' identities, we would predict that the teacher would honour the student's account, because if she did the best she could, what more can be expected? Instead, the teacher disaffirms both the statement of conformity and the statement of conditions. The teacher (10) asserts that the 'evaluation' is substandard, and that the student was capable of more work. Use of the term 'evaluation' in place of improvement clarifies the rule in dispute: the assignment was to have been an evaluation, of which some notion of how the exercise would be improved must be a part. Again, the student's choices are to exit, to recycle a remedy, or to offer a statement of rules. If she does not continue her insistence that she has conformed, she will be admitting nonconformity.

> (11) S: But if that's all I got out of it, you can't really knock it, you know?
> (12) T: No. I am asking you to make an analysis of it though. I am asking you to look at what was effective and what was ineffective, and looking at how effective the dynamics of the class and the dynamics of the learning situation.

In turn (11), the student recycles the statement of conditions, and denies the teacher's right to reproach her for her performance on the assignment, since, as she said in turn (09), she did the best she could. Clearly, the student is reproaching the teacher's conduct, claiming that the teacher has been overly critical. We should expect a remedy from the teacher, particularly if the main issue is identity. The teacher's initial reply, 'NO', is difficult to code. Either it counts as disaffirmation of the student's statement (to the effect that she can indeed reproach the student), or it is an elision of 'No, you are correct, I shouldn't knock you for not doing more.', or 'No, I'm not trying to knock you, but rather to instruct you about how to do an evaluation.' The use of the present tense after this reply makes the last alternative seem plausible. If so, then the teacher has not provided the expected relief, and instead has argued a statement of conformity: She is not being overly critical. The remainder of this turn further clarifies the rule she has been seeking to establish; not only must the assignment be an evaluation, including statements about improvement, the evaluation has additional critical components.

(13) S: But you didn't explain that.

(14) T: Yeah, I said that.

(15) S: You, you just said evaluate the self-concept exercise, and when I was evaluating it, evaluation is just putting what you liked about it, what you thought was good, what you thought was bad, and ways of improving, and that's the way I understood the exercise.

Turn (13) is both an accusation and a statement of conditions. The teacher is accused of requiring performances on the assignment that were not explained to students. If that is the case, then the student was unmindful of these requirements when she did the assignment, and so ought not to be bound by them now.

The teacher (14) denies the accusation, offering a statement of conformity. The teacher claims to have detailed the required components of an evaluation at the time the assignment was made.

The student's reply (15) begins by recycling her accusation; the teacher only said 'evaluate the self-concept exercise'. If this is so, then, the student claims, her understanding of what counts as an evaluation is all she has to guide her performance. Moreover, if she and the teacher have different views of what constitutes an evaluation, her view is not necessarily wrong, particularly if the teacher failed to articulate her viewpoint. In the student's view, an evaluation contains statements about what she liked and disliked, and statements about how it could be improved. We should note, parenthetically, that this part of the episode nicely illustrates how problems may be generated when parties agree on a superordinate rule (Evaluate the assignment), but disagree about rules at a more concrete level.

(16) T: OK. And I think I am asking for that. But, I'm asking for it in more detail, with more insight than what you did with this. I mean, this is just very, very brief. I guess I don't have anyone else's now, I've given them all back.

(17) S: Like, like what? I couldn't, I probably, I just dug in my head and that's all, 'cause I didn't, I just

(18) T: See you have to look at what the purpose of it was, whether it was effective in achieving that purpose. When you do an evaluation.

(19) S: OK.

The teacher next (16) affirms the student's understanding of the rule, agreeing that an evaluation should contain the elements the student has listed. She adds, however, that even though the student's understanding is sufficient, she could have been expected to provide a more detailed and insightful evaluation than she did. This seems to be a critical point in the episode, because either new remedies are going to be offered and scrutinized, or student and teacher will be essentially in the same position as they were in immediately before turn (09), when the rule had been partially clarified, and the degree of conformity was an issue.

The student begins (17) by eliciting further clarification of the rule, then offers the same statement of conditions she did in turns (09) and (11). It appears as though the student realized here that she wasn't succeeding in the negotiations.

In turn (18), the teacher provides the required clarification: The evaluation involves looking at the purpose of the exercise, and determining whether or not it was effective.

The student's 'OK' in turn (19) pre-empts further clarification, and might also count as acknowledgement that she did not do what was necessary. To this point in the episode, substantive issues about what was to have been done and about whether or not they were performed have predominated.

(21) T: See what I mean? I mean an evaluation isn't just whether you like or dislike it, it is how effective it was at accomplishing a goal.
(22) S: What, what was the purpose?

Turns (21) and (22) show that substantive issues have largely been resolved. When the teacher tries to solidify their understanding of what counts as evaluation, the student initiates a discussion of the purpose of the exercise – something she would have known had she performed the exercise as required. I have deleted the discussion of the exercise's purpose from this analysis. That discussion spanned five turns.

(27) S: I thought, I thought it was good for that. I don't know maybe I just didn't take it as seriously as some other people did. 'Cause I don't know, when I was doing it, I don't know, I just felt sort of weird, 'cause well, I didn't know anyone in the class and I felt kind of strange getting up there and doing it.
(28) T: Yeah.

Identity considerations come forward with turn (27) and beyond. The student gives a brief bit of evaluation of the exercise, then justifies her performance on the grounds that since she was doing the exercise in front of strangers, she had trouble taking it seriously. Basically, she is saying that the conditions surrounding the assignment were such that ideal performance was unlikely.

In her reply (28), the teacher admits that the assignment may have made the student uncomfortable, but she does not affirm the student's justification, thereby letting the student off the hook for appearing to take the assignment less than seriously.

(29) S: See. I do think that it helped to get to know other people.
(30) T: Right. And you did get that part of it. But there were other things involved in it, too. Maybe because I know that you are the kind of person who tends to look at and analyze things that I thought this was a way you were trying to get out of doing it. Really. You just did like, 'Oh shit. I've got to do this.' So you did this little bit, and it is not at all reflective of the work you are capable of doing.
(31) S: (Squeals) Well! I, I promise I did think about it. I sat down and thought 'OK now, what did we do? We told everybody about ourselves.' It helped me to listen to other people, But I don't see, but I don't feel it helped me to do the exercise. See what I mean? It helped me, it helped other people for me to do it, and it helped me to listen to other people, but for me to do it, it didn't benefit me, it benefitted everyone else.

The student (29) does not interpret the teacher's statement as relief (and follow this with appreciation, as we might expect). Instead, she merely remarks about the effectiveness of the assignment. She appears to be trying to accommodate to the teacher's more positive opinion of the exercise.

Turn (30) counts as an accusation that the student did not take the assignment seriously, something that the student already admitted. The teacher fortifies her accusation with a left-handed compliment about what the student is capable of doing. At no point in the episode is the 'virtual offence' committed by the student more salient; her substandard performance on the assignment 'means' that she is the kind of person who would squander a personal resource, her analytical ability.

The student denies the accusation, vociferously, in her reply (31). She clarifies that she did think about the assignment, and offers a justification to the effect that she found no personal value in the exercise.

(32) T: Did it encourage you at all to explore your own self-concept?
(33) S: Uh-uh. (Laughs) Well
(34) T: No, that is fine. I think that some of what is happening is that you weren't looking at it seriously.

In turn (32), the teacher elicits information about the value of the exercise, as if to question the student's statement that it held no value for her. The student replies (33) that it held no value for her, whereupon the teacher allows that it is permissible for the student to hold this opinion. Since there is a gap between their opinions of the exercise (something the student alleged at the very beginning), the teacher explains the difference by recycling her accusation that the student did not take the assignment seriously. Presumably, had the student done so, her opinion of the assignment would have been more positive, and her evaluation of it more thorough.

(35) S: Well, 'cause I didn't exactly see the point of it. I think that if we did it again it would be a little bit different. Because I can't, I can't remember what other people put on theirs. But it would be interesting if we did it again.
(36) T: Wouldn't it be neat if we had saved them? And then on the last day, gone back and looked at each other's self-concept.
(37) S: Uh huh.

As the episode winds down, the student acknowledges that she didn't take it seriously (35), and justifies this (she didn't see the point of it). The remainder of this turn initiates a topic change, to the idea of repeating the exercise. If she were granted a second chance, knowing what she now knows about the purpose of the exercise, the assignment would interest her. The teacher's reply (36) is the only unqualified agreement she has made with the student's ideas in the entire episode; this supportiveness is met with a similarly agreeable reply (37). It has finally been established that although the student performed poorly on the assignment, she is a capable student who can be expected to perform acceptably from now on. In the teacher's eyes, at least, the student's identity has been restored.

Discussion

In the episode just reviewed, a teacher and student negotiate a rule of conduct. During the negotiations, this rule evolves from a rather imprecise and general prescription, that students are to evaluate an exercise in writing, to a detailed one calling for students to include several elements in their evaluations. Additionally, the final statement of the rule prescribes that all of these elements be considered in detail and with insightfulness. This more elaborate rule is actually legislated throughout the negotiations (Morris and Hopper 1980).

Woven through the episode, but especially through the last 11 turns, are many utterances that address identity issues, particularly, the 'virtual offences' teacher or student may have committed. These offences include the student's not taking the assignment seriously, squandering known potential to perform well, and also the teacher's being a biased judge of the assignment, an unduly harsh accuser, and an ill-adroit explainer of performance requirements. It is interesting to note that none of these virtual offences is ever entirely relieved; the best participants accomplish is a shared wish to repeat the whole experience, and thereby to erase the faults revealed in their characters.

Hopefully, analysis of the episode has suggested that it is an error to ignore substantive issues in remedial episodes, that substantive and identity issues can be expected to co-occur in at least some discourse, and that the rules meta-language used here is sufficient to handle substantive issues when they crop up.

In some ways, this remedial episode is admittedly peculiar, thus it might be suspected that alignment of the kind I have been discussing is confined to similar episodes, and that these occur very infrequently. For instance, the teacher and student in this episode have unequal status, the teacher occupying a social position that legitimizes rule making and enforcement (Ragan and Hopper 1982). Furthermore, the setting is generally instructional in purpose, which might make in-depth discussion of how to do a kind of performance more likely than in other settings. Finally, teacher and student seem to 'care enough' about the alleged offences to devote considerable attention to resolving them, whereas in less involving encounters participants might content themselves with more perfunctory, ritualistic moves.

None of these considerations, however, substantially limits the range of discourse episodes that may feature rules negotiation. Status differences between episode participants are common, and there is reason to anticipate *more* negotiation among equals (say, between marriage partners or children at play). Similarly, instructional settings, in schools, offices and homes, are hardly a rarity, and the requirement for instructor and students to achieve consensus about rules is no greater than the same requirement on other people who must coordinate their activity. Finally, though actors may rely on ritual manoeuvres when they fall into minor social problems, social life contains enough turbulence, uncertainty and looseness that more serious and involving remedial episodes are frequent. Whatever preference there might be for high-lighting identity issues in these cases, if such happens, might be a consequence of there being a well entrenched and developing vocabulary of accounting behaviours (both in popular wisdom and among academicians), and only the barest beginnings of a substantive rules-language.

A final consideration: The possibility of negotiating rules of conduct, and, in this case, communication, should cast some light on the development of rules theories. One of the more prominent directions in rules research in speech communication, since the publication of Shimanoff's (1980) book on communication rules, has been to consider the discovery of particular communication rules as a primary object of research. Such rules would prescribe communication behaviour in given situations, and would apply to any members of a homogeneous speech community (Donohue *et al.* 1980).

The present discussion suggests another course, which is to concentrate research attention on processes of rule negotiation in the interaction of particular, heterogeneous actors. Rules that are widely applicable to all members of a community are necessarily going to be relatively abstract (e.g. if asked a question, give an informative reply), and they are going to be prone to adaptation and specification by particular interactants. Therefore, knowledge of rules negotiation and other meta-rule processes is a necessary adjunct to knowledge about rules in any fruitful discussion of how rules are used to govern and guide social interaction.

Conclusion

I have offered here a glimpse of how rules-negotiation occurs in remedial episodes, and have sought to divert some of the research attention presently being paid to identity aspects of such episodes into considerations of the substantive issues that inhere in them. A meta-language, based upon rules and statements about rules, has been proposed for use in describing and explaining substantive issues in problematic social interaction. This meta-language was used to examine a lengthy remedial episode, one in which substantive issues are raised, negotiated, and then give way to other considerations. Finally, I discussed the similarity between the sample episode and other episodes, suggesting that it represents a fairly vast array of situations, and that such situations, since they involve rules negotiation, bear importantly on recent theoretical developments in communication.

J.L. Austin (1961), in closing his essay 'A Plea for Excuses', avowed that they were a fertile field for ordinary language analysis, and highly recommended their study. I suspect that students of social interaction, particularly those interested in the regulation of interaction, will find studies of substantive issues, including rules negotiation, to be equally engrossing and theoretically rewarding.

References

AUSTIN, J.L. 1961: *Philosophical papers*. Oxford: Oxford University Press.

BERGER, C.R. and DOUGLAS, W. 1982: Thought and talk: 'Excuse me, but have I been talking to myself?'. In Dance, F.E., editor, *Human communication theory* (New York: Harper & Row), 42–60.

BLUMSTEIN, P.W., CARSSOW, K.G., HALL, J., HAWKINS, B., HOFFMAN, R., ISHEM. E., MAUERER, C.P., SPENS, D., TAYLOR, J. and ZIMMERMAN, D.L. 1974: The honoring of accounts. *American Sociological Review* 39, 551–66.

CARVER, C.S. and SCHEIER, M.F. 1981: *Attention and self-regulation: A control-theory approach to human behavior* (New York: Springer-Verlag).

CRONEN, V., PEARCE, W.B. and HARRIS, L. 1982: The coordinated management of meaning: A theory of communication. In Dance, F.E., editor, *Human Communication Theory* (New York: Harper & Row), 61–89.

DONOHUE, W.A., CUSHMAN, D.P. and NOFSINGER, R.E. 1980: Creating and confronting social order: A comparison of rules perspectives. *Western Journal of Speech Communication* 44, 5–19.

FRENTZ, T. and FARRELL, T.B. 1976: Language-action: A paradigm for communication. *Quarterly Journal of Speech* 62, 333–49.

GOFFMAN, E. 1971: *Relations in public*. New York: Harper & Row.

—1974: *Frame Analysis*. New York: Harper & Row.

HARRE, R. and SECORD, P.F. 1973: *The explanation of social behavior*. Totowa, NJ: Littlefield, Adams & Co.

HEWITT, J.P. and HALL, P.M. 1973: Social problems, problematic situations and quasi-theories. *American Sociological Review* 38, 367–74.

JEFFERSON, G. Side sequences. 1972: In Sudnow, D., editor, *Studies in social interaction* (New York: Free Press), 294–338.

McLAUGHLIN, M.L., CODY, M.J. and O'HAIR, H.D. 1983: The management of failure events: Some contextual determinants of accounting behavior. *Human Communication Research* 9, 208–24.

MORRIS, G.H. 1978: *The remedial process as a negotiation of rules.* Speech Communication Association, Minneapolis.

MORRIS, G.H. and HOPPER, R. 1980: Remediation and legislation in everyday talk: How communicators achieve consensus on rules. *Quarterly Journal of Speech* 67, 266–74.

—1984: Making problems, solving problems: A sketch of alignment talk phases. Unpublished manuscript.

PEARCE, W.B. 1976: The coordinated management of meaning. In Miller, G.R, editor, *Explorations in interpersonal communication* (Beverly Hills, Cal.: Sage), 17–36.

PEARCE, W.B. and CRONEN, V. 1980: *Communication, action and meaning: The creation of social realities.* New York: Praeger.

RAGAN, S. and HOPPER, R. 1981: Alignment talk in the job interview. *Journal of Applied Communication Research* 9, 85–103.

SCHONBACH, P. 1980: A category system for account phases. *European Journal of Social Psychology* 10, 195–200.

SCOTT, M.B. and LYMAN, S.M. 1968: Accounts. *American Sociological Review* 22, 46–62.

SHIMANOFF, S.B. 1980: *Communication rules: Theory and research.* Beverly Hills, Cal.: Sage.

STOKES, R. and HEWITT, J. 1976: Aligning actions. *American Sociological Review* 41, 838–49.

5

Interpersonal control and regulation in conversation

John M. Wiemann

The unscripted taking of turns by interactants makes conversation unique among forms of verbal discourse. This feature of conversation is important to interactants beyond the fact that it allows for the possibility of people saying something to and that being processed by their interlocutors. The theme of this essay is that turn-taking – or, more precisely, turn-taking strategies – is among the fundamental resources available to interactants to establish a definition of their relationships, especially in terms of control distribution. My purposes here are to (1) illustrate the link between the molar-level concept interpersonal (relational) control and the micro-level concept conversational regulation, and (2) present a model of the turn-taking process which facilitates the study of the control/regulation link. First, research regarding the importance of control in social, interpersonal relationships is reviewed. Following that, two conceptualizations of turn-taking are briefly presented to illustrate the importance of models for interpreting how this sort of conversational structuring is accomplished. Finally, an outline of a new model which enhances our ability to understand the role of conversational regulation in the determination of control distribution in relationships is discussed.

Control in relationships

Control (along with affiliation and/or empathy) has long been considered a central, and in some cases a defining, element of relationships in a variety of literatures (Wiemann and Krueger 1980; for earlier reviews, see Brown 1965; Carson 1969; Triandis, Vassillou and Nassiakou 1968). Many workers in this area have recently shifted their focus from the characteristics of individuals (e.g. who has the most 'power' in a dyad) to those of 'the relationship' (e.g. how is control distributed in a dyad, or how is a pattern of control established). The relational focus is adopted here, although it is clearly informed by the individual–differences research. From this perspective, control is the constellation of constraints people place on one another by the manipulation of both interactional structure and content, which limit the options appropriately available subsequently to each relational partner and the relational system as a whole (Wiemann and Kelly 1981). That is, the doing or saying of something has the potential to prescribe or proscribe next possible actions or statements. An 'interrogator' narrowly constrains what will count as appropriate responses, for example. And by so doing provides a definition of the relationship which is obvious to all present. The interrogatee accepts that definition (at least temporarily) by responding appropriately, i.e., answering questions. More will be said about the relationship of conversational structure and relational definition later.

The point here is that control is an important feature of specific interactions and relationships as a whole. Evidence has been offered supporting the centrality of control by researchers investigating such phenomena as pronoun usage (Brown and Gilman 1960), terms of address (Ervin–Tripp 1972), psychopathology in families (Bateson, Jackson, Haley, and Weakland, 1956; Watzlawick, Beavin, and Jackson 1967), communicator style (Ellis 1978; Norton 1978), interaction in families (Lederer and Jackson 1968), meaning of nonverbal behaviour (Mehrabian 1972), perceptions of role–appropriate behaviour (Marwell and Hage 1970; Triandis *et al.* 1968; Wish, Deutsch and Kaplan 1976; Wish and Kaplan 1977), and the quality of interpersonal relationships (Schutz 1966).

Much thinking about and research on control is indebted to Bales's (1950) identification of two types of interaction characteristics of decision–making groups, socio–emotional orientation and task orientation, a control dimension. Subsequent work by Carter (1954), Borgatta (1960, 1962, 1963, 1964; Borgatta, Cottrell and Mann 1958) and others has demonstrated that control–oriented components of communication can be identified in a variety of types of task groups. Several researchers using circumplex procedures (a type of factor analysis) have extended this finding into the interpersonal realm (cf. Becker and Krug 1964; Bochner, Kaminski and Fitzpatrick 1977; Foa and Foa, 1972; Leary 1957; Lorr and McNair 1965). Not only has control consistently emerged as a primary characteristic of relationships, it has done so in a variety of relational contexts, including parent–child and adult social relationships, as well as task groups. Typically, control has emerged as the factor which accounts for most of the explained variance in the way people describe their relationships (e.g., Bochner *et al.* 1977), a finding which contributes to the attention it has received by scholars interested in relational communication (e.g., Millar and Rogers 1976; Sluzki and Beavin 1977).

Although researchers referred to above have used a variety of labels in addition to 'control' for the variables with which they have worked, e.g., power, status, task orientation, it is useful here to focus on the similarities among these variables (without denying the meaningful distinctions among them). It is clear that at least one of the assumptions these researchers have in common is: The manner in which decisions are made in a relationship is an issue that must be resolved. The issue is pervasive to the point of being trans–cultural (cf. Triandis *et al.* 1968) and apparently central to the maintenance of at least small social structures like the family (cf. Watzlawick *et al.* 1967).

Although control is a pervasive issue, it doesn't seem to come up very often as an explicit topic of discussion. During the daily course of most 'normal' interpersonal relationships, the control issue is not particularly problematic. Intimates and acquaintances develop routines which reinforce the distribution of control in their relationships. Children, for example, use polite but familiar terms of address with adults in their family and formal address with other adults; spouses tacitly divide family responsibilities. Control is not often *allowed* to become an open relational topic. This 'civil inattention', of course, changes during transition periods or at crisis points in a relationship (e.g., the readjustment of family understandings evident in many teenager/parent relationships or an argument between intimates).

But just because relational–control issues are infrequently on the conversation agenda does not mean that they are not attended to nor that they are unimportant. It is precisely their importance that keeps control issues off the agenda except during crises. The lack of explicit attention to control issues necessitates that relational partners monitor and mutually 'fine tune' their understanding of the allocation of control, and thus, mutual influence. (Note that when a person has to say, 'Let's not forget who's in charge here', the situation is already out of hand!) As a result, control negotiations are typically conducted metacommunicatively, on what Watzlawick *et al.* (1967) have called the 'command' level. In stating this, I do not want to implicate all of Watzlawick *et al.* 's notions about communication, but merely to establish the position that the communicative context in which 'content' messages are exchanged has a bearing on how the conversants subsequently interpret their relationship. Specifically, the manner in which *a* conversation is structured potentially has a bearing on the definition of the relationship. Any *one* conversation will not necessarily result in the redefinition of a relationship (although *any* one could). Consequently, conversation can usefully be seen as a microcosm of relationships and, if enough conversation between relational partners is studied, an accurate description of the relationship can be drawn.

More importantly, in new or transitional relationships, variation in structurally mandated conversational enactments (e.g. the necessity of alternating turns) is one method available to interactants to negotiate the distribution of control without overtly challenging each other (to the possible detriment of the relationship). In ongoing relationships, dyad–to–dyad variation in the implementation of these structural imperatives serves to reaffirm previously, albeit tacitly, agreed–upon control allocation.

This is possible because conversation is a rule–guided activity, which is rendered predictable, in part, by the mapping of the rules onto a stable structure. Variation in the execution of turn taking may be meaningful for relational partners when the pattern of turn–taking behaviour is compared with other possible patterns, or with a previous pattern of the partners. Speaking directly to this point, Zimmerman and West (1975) argued that the pattern of men interrupting women in conversation more than they interrupted other men and more than they were interrupted in return by women was a reflection of men's dominance of women in society at large. Such behavioural variation, i.e., interrupting one type of person more than another type, can be seen as strategic in Goffman's (1969) sense of the term. Patterson's (1982) model of nonverbal exchange illustrates the relationship of function to structure. Similarly, Duncan (1983) has argued that structural features of conversation are important because of the functions interactants have them serve.

In sum, a position can be drawn that holds structural features of conversation important to relationships because interactants can vary their behaviour *vis-à-vis* these features to achieve strategic interpersonal ends. Conversational variables involved in the taking of turns have been shown to contribute to perceptions of interactants in terms of control distribution, for example, in the relationship of interrupting behaviour to perceptions of dominance (cf. Ferguson 1977; Zimmerman and West 1975). The strategic use of conversational variation has been labelled 'interaction management' (Wiemann 1977) and has been shown to be related to perceptions of communicative competence (see Wiemann and Backlund 1980, for a review). The taking of turns in conversation is an important element of interaction management and, because of the amount of attention it has received in the literature, presents us with an opportunity to explore the control/regulation link in some detail.

The importance of turn taking in structuring our social life apparently cannot be overestimated. Turn taking is more than just a characteristic of language, Kaye (1982; also see Lewis and Freedle 1973) has argued; mastery of it is necessary for the acquisition of language. He points out that the alternation of turns between mother and infant is necessary from the beginning of life – for successful breast feeding, for example. This accomplishment is the beginning of an alternation pattern that is ubiquitous in our social experience. A more communicative variety of turn taking can be seen as early as 12 days after birth, when children are capable of imitating certain facial and manual behaviour, e.g., lip protrusion and sequential finger movement (Metzloff and Moore 1977). Imitation necessarily involves turn taking since the imitative act produced by one partner is dependent upon the production of that act by the other partner. Rudimentary aspects of what will later become conversational turn taking begins to appear around three months (Lewis and Freedle 1973). Importantly, the manner in which mother (and other significant others) and infant adapt to and coordinate with each other has interpersonal and intrapsychic consequences for both (cf. Goldberg 1977).

Thus, the manner in which turns are taken in conversation plays a potentially important role in the development and maintenance of our relationships throughout our lives. The mechanism by which we accomplish turn transition, however, is not completely understood. It is to that mechanism that I now turn.

Models of turn taking

I have been using the term 'turn taking' rather loosely thus far, as if there is one standard conceptualization of the phenomenon. But that is clearly not the case. Wilson, Wiemann and Zimmerman (in press) have identified three major approaches to turn taking: stochastic modelling (cf. Cappella 1979, 1980; Jaffe and Feldstein, 1970); the signalling system offered by Duncan (1972; Duncan and Fiske 1977), and the sequential production model proposed by Sacks, Schegloff, and Jefferson (1974). Each of these approaches begins with a different set of assumptions about turn taking and, as a consequence, each produces an analysis that is not readily comparable to the others.

On the surface, it appears obvious that people alternate their turns at talk in time; that is, turns are constructed sequentially. But Wilson *et al.* (in press) point out that below the surface, things aren't always what they seem.

> Physically, one has a stream of sound and silence from each participant, and one can segment the confluence of these streams into silence, simultaneity, and one or another participant speaking by him- or herself. However, there is no agreement on which concatenations of such segments constitute turns, nor even whether the notion of a turn can be defined entirely in terms of just physical data. For, in addition to physical descriptions of the acoustic stream, there are events such as paralinguistic phenomena, body movements, grammatical closures, questions and statements, and so on, that apparently defy useful definition in purely physical terms. Just how the events observable in one way or another are arrayed in relation to turn taking, then, is handled differently in different approaches to the study of turn taking and is closely bound up with the particular conceptual framework employed.

It is not necessary – and probably not particularly useful – that one model dominate turn–taking research at this time. But a robust model of turn taking that allows for an account of the structural/functional outcomes in a relationship should lead to greater understanding of the process of defining relationships.

The approaches to turn taking most clearly relevant to social functions as experienced by interactants are signaling (Duncan and Fiske 1977) and sequential production (Sacks *et al.* 1974). Stochastic studies offer an objective but essentially asocial view of turn phenomena in that it is unlikely that people process their experiences in the manner described by such models. Thus, for the purpose of understanding the control/regulation relationship, attention will be directed exclusively to the signalling and sequential production models. Wilson *et al.* (in press) provide an in–depth review and critique of these approaches so there is no need to do that here. A brief overview of each, however, will be useful.

The signalling approach

From this view turn taking is governed by the rapid exchange of vocal and gestural signals during the course of conversation. Yngve (1970) first articulated this position, but the most influential and consistent contributor has been Duncan (cf. 1972, Duncan and Fiske 1977).

Several assumptions are necessary for signalling to be a viable explanation of how turn exchanges are managed. Some of these seem to have been *a priori* to the research and others have emerged from the empirical work. The specifics of Duncan's 'turn system' model can be subsumed by these assumptions. The primary and most obvious assumption is that participants manage turn exchanges by the display of and response to cues displayed by other interactants (see Table 5.1). These signals are composed of behaviours which are discrete and independent of one another. For the most part, they are also context free, with the exception that to be appropriate (that is, to be seen as 'signals') they must appear at specified points around the end of a phonemic clause. These signals are related to the process of turn taking by a set of rules specifying the appropriate response to a signal by the participants. For example, Duncan

Table 5.1 Speaker turn cues.

Any one of the following behaviours constitutes the 'speaker turn signal':
1 an intonation pattern other than 2 2|;
2 a sociocentric sequence;
3 completion of a grammatical clause;
4 drawl on a final syllable;
5 termination of gesticulation or relaxation of the hand.

From Duncan and Fiske, 1977, pp. 169–89.

and Fiske (1977, pp. 188–9) propose these rules to describe their 'turn signal':

> the auditor may claim the speaking turn during the active period of the turn signal
> . . . . In proper operation of the turn system, if the auditor so claims the turn in
> response to the signal, the speaker is obliged to relinquish immediately his (or her)
> claim to the turn. When the turn signal is not active, auditor claims of the turn are
> inappropriate . . . .

Similarly they specify one rule governing the 'gesticulation signal', which they claim suppresses or overrides the turn signal:

> the signal serves to inhibit any turn signal concurrently being displayed. (Duncan and
> Fiske 1977, p. 189)

Both interactants are bound by the prescriptions of the signals the speaker displays. Finally, turn signals are seen as social conventions, albeit very general ones. That is, signals are to some extent problematic until interactants have a chance to work them out for themselves. Duncan *et al.* (1979) view the question of the generality of turn–system conventions as a strictly empirical matter. But the tone of the discussion in Duncan and Fiske (1977) and evidence presented by Opliger (1980) indicate that the system is on the whole, if not in its particulars, very robust.

Duncan's signalling approach to turn taking merits careful consideration in spite of the variety of criticisms to which it has been subjected (see, e.g. Beattie 1980, 1981; Wilson *et al.* in press). In terms of control as manifested in the regulation of turns, the signalling model pictures interactants as competent to the extent that they process signals appropriately – both the ones displayed by their interlocutors and ones they might display themselves. By implication, the ability to forecast where a signal might appropriately be displayed and then acting to pre-empt the conversational prerogatives of fellow interactants would permit one to regulate, and thereby control, the conversation. By extension, the person who can regulate the conversation is in a good position to impose his/her allocation of control on the relationship.

The analysis presented above extends Duncan's work well beyond its intended scope (and Duncan might say does some violence to it in the process), but nonetheless Duncan's turn system represents one way in which regulation of conversation can be extended to describe how control is enacted at the relational level. But there are problems with Duncan's system which become particularly apparent when the relational implications of it are considered. The most important of these is the 'demand' characteristics of signals. The implication is that interactants are somehow bound by the rules invoked by signalling, that there is a penalty for violators. But, in fact, we know this not to be the case. As Wilson *et al.* (in press) point out, the conversational phenomena considered to be signals (along with other behaviours) can more usefully be seen as neutral events – resources – which interactants can construe in different ways. *Resources* do not carry with them the implied injunctions for or against specific next actions which *signals* do. The consequence of this distinction is that variations in turn–taking procedures can be interpreted as meaningful relationally and not necessarily as conversational 'errors'. For example, there are relationships where one partner consistently interrupts another but the interruptions are not reciprocated. Rather than interpret the interrupter as socially unskilled or merely rude, it is more interesting theoretically to analyse the interruptions as serving a relational function. Unilateral interruptions are a manifestation of the relationship definition in terms of control allocation. Unlike the conversational-error analysis, this one does not make an evaluative statement; both partners may be very satisfied with the asymmetrical control allocation. Conversely, mutual interruptions could be seen as either a contest for control or as an indication of interactants' involvement with each other or the topic.

The major alternative to the signalling approach, Sacks *et al.* 's (1974) sequential production model, offers some improvements in terms of functional interpretation of the use of the turn-taking mechanism. A review of its assumptions follows.

The sequential production approach

Sacks *et al.* 's (1974) basic assumption about turn taking is that it is neither probabilistic (as described by stochastic modelling) nor deterministic (as indicated by signalling research). Rather, turn taking, like conversation as a whole, must be managed sequentially by participants on a moment-by-moment basis. Following Sacks *et al.* any model of turn taking must accommodate the features of naturally occurring conversation, including:

1 . . . [S]peech exchange occurs in which the order, length, and content of turns are free to vary.
2 The length of the conversation need not be fixed in advance.
3 The number of participants may vary.
4 In multi-party conversations, the relative distribution of turns is not specified in advance.
5 Talk can be continuous or discontinuous.
6 Typically, one party talks at a time.
7 Simultaneous talk is common, but its duration is usually brief.
8 Transitions from one turn to the next occur, for the most part, with little or no gap and/or overlap.
9 Explicit turn-allocation techniques such as addressing a question or request to another party may, but need not, be used.
10 Turns may vary in their anticipated duration, for example, from one-word answers to lengthy stories. (Wilson *et al.* in press).

Note that in contrast to the signalling model, gaps in talk and simultaneous speech are seen here as expected, regular features of conversation, not breakdowns in the turn-taking system.

Another important contrast is that the sequential production of conversation is the mutual responsibility of all parties to the conversation. The signalling model implies that the speaker is in a position to determine turn allocation unilaterally by either displaying a turn signal (although Duncan and Fiske 1977, point out that the auditor may, but does not have to, accept the turn when this signal is activated) or a gesticulation signal, which suppresses others' claims to the floor. Lack of attention to these and other turn-related signals puts the auditor in jeopardy of violating a conversational rule, and thus becoming subject to some sort of sanction. (The question begged by the signalling model is 'How does one get a word in edgewise?') While Sacks *et al.* 's approach distributes responsibility for 'who talks when' more equitably between a speaker and other participants, their formulation of 'unit-types' seems to place the speaker at the mercy of his or her auditors.

Unit-types are the building blocks of speaking turns. A turn is constructed out of unit-types, which in English include sentences, clauses, phrases and single words (Sacks *et al.* 1974, pp. 702-3, 720-2). Whether or not a particular construction functions as a unit-type at any given point in a conversation depends, to some extent at least, on the context at that point. At the end of a unit-type, a 'transition relevance place' occurs, at which point a change of speaker may, but need not, take place. (And the question begged here is, of course, 'How does one string together more than one sentence?')

The speaker-change mechanism from this view can be summarized by the following set of options:

1 [At a transition relevance place] the current speaker may, but need not, select another party to the conversation as the next speaker.
2 Should the current speaker not select the next, then another party to the conversation may, but again need not, select him- or herself as the next speaker. The first party to speak at such a point acquires the turn.
3 If no other party self-selects under the provisions of (2), then the current speaker may, but need not, continue.
4 In the event that the current speaker does not continue, the option to speak cycles back to the control of (2). (Wilson *et al.* in press).

Since the ends of unit-types are easily projectable, potential 'next speakers' can legitimately interject themselves into the conversation by anticipating the completion of a unit-type and moving with precise timing. If the timing is not quite precise enough, then a system-induced overlap results (Wilson *et al.* in press). Thus, an auditor can create a transition relevance place by acting as if Option (2) was available to him or her at the time of the interjection. According to this rule set, the speaker has little recourse but to prepare to get the floor back at the end of the next unit-type. If this model is an accurate description of the turn-taking process, one consequence of it is that conversation participants are encouraged to attend closely to the conversation in all of its particulars so that they might be able to enter, if they wish, at appropriate times.

A final characteristic of the model is that it can be seen as applicable to the allocation of turns in any conversation, without regard to social, cultural or linguistic context. Thus, the model can be viewed as both context-free and context-sensitive, in that 'while the mechanism itself is independent of the particular contexts in which it is employed, its use in any specific situation requires speakers and hearers to be oriented to that context' (Wilson *et al.* in press). This is not to say that the sequential production model should be seen as a set of universal laws. Rather the model as a whole, including violation-management procedures, describes the mechanism generally available for managing turn taking. Further, it is limited to the speech-exchange system of conversation; other systems may be managed differently. Sacks *et al.* 's rules are also different in kind from those proposed by Duncan in that.Duncan's are explicitly called conventions, which are subject to alteration by negotiation or social or cultural influences. To the extent that the sequential production model is generalizable to all conversations, its rule system is not alterable in the same ways. The system is built into the nature of conversation; that is, it is a product of the structure of conversation (see Cappella 1983, p. 36, on this point).

The primary difficulty with Sacks *et al.* 's explanation of turn taking is the lack of precision in the expression of the unit-type/transition relevance place relationship. Clearly speakers (and auditors, for that matter) do not see all unit-type endings as turn endings. Sacks *et al.* (1974) note that intonational patterns and the sequential or social context may disambiguate the status of a unit-type ending – especially for sub-sentence constructions. And Schegloff (1980) has demonstrated how certain kinds of prefacing remarks can suspend transition relevance for an extended number of unit-types, e.g. so that a story might be told without interruption. But, as Wilson *et al.* (in press) point out, these observations are 'fragmentary' and do not address the problem of transition relevance in a systematic way.

In terms of relational control as manifested in conversational structure, the sequential production approach to turn taking presents a view favouring the auditor. Even though the rule system presented earlier lists the speaker as having the first option to select next speaker (including self-selection), the auditor clearly has the opportunity to 'snatch' the floor without appearing to have broken any conversational rules. That is, the floor can be taken without overtly discrediting the current speaker's right to complete an utterance. One practical consequence is that the current speaker does not have the right to say something like, 'Don't interrupt me while I'm talking.' Thus what is to count as an interruption is not very clear. And since interruptions have consequences for relational definition, this aspect of the sequential production model must be specified if it is to be useful beyond just illuminating the particulars of turn taking.

The sequential production model serves our purposes, however, because it portrays conversation as mutually constructed by all participants. This approach, therefore, seems to spread responsibility among participants more than does the view offered by the signalling model. Further, since aspects of conversation other than turns (e.g. topics, question–answer sequences, etc.) can be seen as mutually constructed, the sequential production approach is consistent with the manner in which conversation as a whole proceeds. That is, conversation is constructed on an utterance-by-utterance basis, with each subsequent utterance to some extent dependent on preceding ones for its sensibility and appropriateness (cf. Grice 1975).

This line of analysis can reasonably be extended to the issue of control as manifested in conversation, with the caveat that the extension might do violence to Sack *et al.*'s original conceptualization. Mutual construction of conversational features such as turns makes mutual influence possible. Control 'moves' become available to interactants in their use of turn-taking strategies (cf. Cappella 1983). By making strategic choices concerning how and when to accomplish a change of speaker, interactants can reinforce an existing definition of who is in control (both right now in this conversation and in the relationship over time), offer a new definition, accept a definition so offered, or enter into a *sub rosa* negotiation about how control will be distributed.

A resource model of turn taking

It should be obvious from even this brief discussion that these two approaches offer reasonable interpretations of the turn-taking process, in spite of the questions each leaves unanswered. The foundation of a new turn-taking model which, to some extent, reconciles these two approaches has been outlined by Wilson *et al.* (in press). After summarizing this 'resource' model, I will demonstrate that it has utility for informing our understanding of how relational control issues are handled through strategic use of conversational structure.

The resource model combines formal elements of both of the previously reviewed approaches to turn taking. Specifically, a modified concept of signalling is employed to elaborate the general structure of the sequential production model and to revise the conceptualization of 'transition relevance place.' In addition, the model gives the objective context in which a conversation occurs a central role and attempts to take into account how semantic features of language can be used to facilitate smooth turn transitions.

In its general form as proposed by Wilson *et al.*, the resource model resembles the sequential production model in that turn taking is accomplished by the sequence of options suggested by Sacks *et al.* (1974), which were reviewed earlier in this essay. That is, the current speaker has the option to select the next speaker; if that option is not exercised, a potential next speaker may self-select, etc. Further, a fundamental assumption of the resource model, which is shared with the other two, is that turns are managed by what people do during the course of the conversation. Thus, the appropriate place for researchers to direct their attention is at points of potential or actual turn exchange. The notion of 'transition relevance place', consequently, remains useful and is retained in the resource model in a revised form.

As was pointed out earlier, it is not very productive to consider the end of every unit-type (to use Sacks *et al.*'s terminology) a transition relevance place, at which interactants cycle through the four options available to them to determine who will utter the next unit-type. A conceptualization of transition relevance places which is more consistent with the view that interactants *mutually* construct conversation is necessary.

Schegloff (1980) and others, as was mentioned previously, have noted that there are devices available to interactants which can be used to facilitate extended turns. But research to date says little about how frequently they are employed and implies that these devices are limited to certain specific types of conversation constructions, e.g. telling a joke or a story. The concept of signals which facilitate turn exchange regardless of content or construction as proposed by Duncan and Fiske (1977) offers a practical and robust solution to the problem of identification of transition relevance places. The conceptualization of signals as independent and relatively context-free conventions is problematic given the fact that there is the implication of a demand characteristic in conventions which both extant research evidence and everyday experience belie. Rather than conceptualizing behaviours like intonation change, grammatical completions, gestures and gaze direction as signals which cue specific states, it is proposed that they be considered neutral (i.e., without predetermined meaning or use) conversational events which are inherent in speaking and listening. These conversational events are interpreted by interactants in different ways at different times, depending on the social and relational context of the interaction, as well as on their appearance relative to the overall stream of interaction. These events can thus be seen as *resources* for interactants to make use of as needed. No given behaviour necessarily carries a demand quality (e.g. tensed-hand position does not necessarily suppress the exchange of turns). One advantage of this view of conversational events is that it does not require a different theory for different physical settings in which conversations take place, such as in the dark, face-to-face, or over the telephone. Interactants use the resources available to them at any given time, and are certainly not precluded from using idiosyncratic ones if they are effective. From this view, 'what is signalled is an understanding as to what in the immediate situation will constitute a complete utterance, following which turn transition is appropriate' (Wilson *et al.* in press).

Some evidence in support of this position has recently been presented by Buzolich (1983). She found that dyads composed of a 'normal' speaker and an 'augmented' speaker (a person who has cerebral palsy with accompanying severe speech dysfunction, and communicating with either a spelling board or an electronic voice simulator) used turn signals similar to those reported by Duncan and Fiske (1977) for 'normal' dyads. The interactants in Buzolich's study were sensitive to regulation and control issues, but did not have the same resources available to dyads composed of normal speakers. Rather than ignore regulation concerns, these interactants made use of the behaviours available to them to accomplish turn exchanges. For example, augmented communicators used gaze toward their communication device to signal that they wanted to maintain the speaking turn. Gaze at the device by the normal speaker seemed to serve as a turn yielding cue. These behaviours developed signal quality over the course of the conversation, but appeared to have been interpreted as signals only in certain semantic contexts. In a conversation where resources were limited (i.e., behaviour was greatly constrained), the interactants made use of what was available to them.

The resource model does not compel researchers to seek out and identify behaviours which might at some time or other, in specific contexts, count as signals. But there is a need to develop an understanding of what behaviours might be expected to serve as signals in either typical or special circumstances. Duncan's work, and that of others in the same vein (e.g. Beattie 1980, 1981; DeLong 1974; Opliger 1980; Wiemann and Knapp 1975), points the way for our expectations for everyday face-to-face conversation. Buzolich (1983) and Rutter and Stephenson (1977) are examples of research in other sorts of circumstances.

Context, of course, plays a major role in the selection of which conversational events will be brought into play in the management of turn transitions. The context includes not only the physical setting, but the relational history of the interactants, and their reasons for the current conversation. For example, a

one-word response might be taken as a complete and acceptable turn in response to
a certain type of question (e.g. 'What's the temperature like outside?' – 'Hot!')
but not another (e.g. 'What happened in school today?' – 'Nothing!').

While the physical context probably plays only a minimal role in the management of most conversations (Buzolich's 1983, study being an example of an
obvious exception), the relational history of the dyad can play a major role. It
seems reasonable to assume that perceived status difference and intimacy level will
have an impact on who is most attentive to the other's behaviour and how that
behaviour will be interpreted. For example, one might hypothesize that people of
equal status each perceive more transition relevance places in a conversation than
do those of unequal status. Further, in dyads composed of unequal-status people,
the higher-status person might see more transition relevance places than the
lower-status person. Leet-Pellegrini (1980) offers some evidence that this is in fact
the case, although her study focuses more on general measures of dominance than
on the specifics of turn taking. These, of course, are empirical questions, but they
are suggestive of the direction in which the resource model points researchers.

Similarly the situational location of the conversation might preclude some
behaviours from serving as signals and automatically invoke others. A conversation conducted in the dark limits visual signals, for example. Or an argument
between parents conducted in front of their children might tacitly call for the
repression of paralinguistic features which indicate anger.

A final feature of the resource model is its recognition of the importance of the
semantic context in which behaviours are displayed. This is not an innovation in
and of itself. Both the signalling and sequential production approaches take into
account the significance of a sentence completion, for example. But it is not the
mere completion of a grammatical unit which is important for the exchange of a
turn. Rather the semantic component of the conversation is the environment in
which behaviours are interpreted as potential turn-taking signals or as serving
some other conversational function (e.g. emphasizing what has been said concurrently). For an auditor appropriately to assume the turn, he or she must provide
the speaker with the opportunity to finish the saying of the utterance. That is, the
speaker must be given the opportunity to come to a logical completion of the
utterance – even if the place where the turn is exchanged is not the speaker's
projected point of completion. That this is important can be seen in everyday
conversations where interrupters excuse themselves for taking the turn even
though a unit-type had been completed, there was no simultaneous talk, and no
turn suppression signal was displayed.

The resource model shows promise of accounting for both how people get a
word in edgewise and how they manage to string two sentences together. It
acknowledges the fact that some behaviours have signal-like qualities. Interactants are seen as making use of conversational events-as-signals within a social,
relational and sequential context to determine appropriate turn-transition relevance places. What is most useful about the resource model for communication
scholars is its potential for use beyond the mere explanation of the mechanics of
turn taking.

From conversation to relationship

It can be one long journey from a conversation to a (meaningful?) relationship, and the route may not always be obvious – either to relational partners or to researchers. But the route can be mapped. Relationships can be characterized in a variety of ways. Some are social/cultural definitions to which people subscribe (implicitly, at least, and not necessarily freely), e.g., married, going steady, employer–employee, sibling. Another sort of definition is emergent; during the course of having a relationship, the participants create a definition. They do this in several ways, the most important being the manner in which they communicate with each other. This 'communication definition' work is most obvious, or at least most easily captured, during extended initial interactions and at relational crisis (transition) points. For it often can be at these points in relationships that the foundation is laid for future interaction, if there is to be any. To the extent that the interactants foresee themselves in a long-term relationship of one (socio-cultural) sort or another, they usually will see as important the need to get things 'off on the right foot'. That is, they will want the emergent definition to reflect their motivations for entering the relationship.

The components or dimensions that social scientists have used to describe relationships (e.g. control, affiliation, task orientation, etc.) are attempts to capture the emergent definitions of a variety of relationships. (Note that for present purposes it is not necessary that interactants describe their relationships in the same terms as researchers or that they even be consciously aware of these characteristics.) The work reviewed at the beginning of this essay and similar research indicates that control is a central characteristic of emergent definitions in a variety of relationships. It is a relatively easy move from here to adopt the position that control is made manifest in relationships by the way interactants communicate with each other. Specifically, the manner in which interactants employ the structural features of conversation is relevant to the definition of the relationship in terms of control distribution. The very pervasiveness of turn taking in conversation makes it a useful – and possibly inescapable – device for solving control issues before they are brought to interactants' consciousness.

The model of turn taking outlined here facilitates the move beyond explanation of turn-taking phenomena to the wider social scientific significance of the strategic use of conversation structure. An example of one type of perceived control behaviour should illustrate this point. Consider the case of simultaneous talk in conversation. It is a relevant relational concern because simultaneous talk can be (and frequently is) construed as an interruption of one interactant by another. Interruptions have been linked to perceptions of dominance (Zimmerman and West 1975). More generally, interruptions have been shown to be negatively related to perceptions of communicative competence (Wiemann 1977).

The status of simultaneous speech then is an important issue. The signalling model treats it as a clear violation of the conversational rule, only one person should speak at a time. Yet, for example, Rutter and Stephenson (1977) report massive amounts of simultaneous speech in the conversations they studied. Simultaneous speech is treated a bit more ambiguously by Sacks *et al.* but the implication in their work is that it is to be avoided, that interruptions are an 'error'. But viewed as a conversational resource, interruption becomes a tactic available for interactants to use to accomplish some conversational or relational goal – e.g. to dominate a conversation, to establish dominance in a relationship, to show enthusiasm for a topic, to show interest in one's partner, etc.

It would be a mistake, from this perspective, to count all interruptions as merely rude behaviour. Some researchers have presented evidence that there are several types of interruptions, some of which are positively construed by interactants. Kennedy and Camden (1983) found that more than half of the 255 interruption sequences in their conversations served a 'confirming' function. Sexton (1980) identified four different types of interruptions in her study of empathic and unempathic dyads. 'Agreement-type interruptions' served an empathic and supportive role, while those which operated to change the topic or 'display independent knowledge' were described as unempathic and non-supportive. 'Question-type interruptions' were described as more ambiguous than the other types, but generally supportive. (Also see Jefferson 1973; Wiemann and Knapp 1975.)

Further, both the sequential production model and the signalling model limit interruptions conceptually to those instances in conversation where simultaneous talking is instigated by one interactant beginning to speak before another has ceased and which cannot be treated as being in the 'back channel'. But the model developed by Wilson *et al.* accommodates interruptions which are the result of non-simultaneous talk, those that result from an interactant initiating talk at a particular grammatical completion without regard to the unit-type ending projected by the speaker. This possibility also has been recognized by Beattie (1980), Ferguson (1977) and Zimmerman and West (in preparation) among others. Such work is consistent with the view that conversational events are intrinsically neutral and can be exploited to accomplish specific goals within concrete conversational contexts.

Clearly there are other structural features of conversation which are used to display and/or negotiate control. Two obvious variables that merit further exploration (which space limitations do not permit here) are time spent holding the floor (cf. Cappella 1983) and topic control (cf. Wiemann 1977). The available evidence suggests that these sets of behaviours work much the same way as does the management of turn exchanges in both regulating conversations and establishing control in relationships.

In summary, I have attempted to show the relevance of sequential conversational structure for relational control issues. Conversational structures provide strategic opportunities for interactants to work through relational issues without allowing those issues to become a major concern. Turn taking in conversation was used as an important example of how structural features can be manipulated to accomplish relational ends. A review of two prominent models of turn taking was undertaken to illustrate how models can influence our interpretation of conversational phenomena. Finally, the resource model, which provides a more useful view of how turn taking is accomplished in conversation, was outlined. What is especially important here is that the resource model facilitates the interpretation of conversational events so that they can be seen as resources by which people accomplish relational goals.

References

BALES, R. F. 1950: *Interaction process analysis*. Reading, Mass: Addison-Wesley.
BATESON, G., JACKSON, D. D., HALEY, J., and WEAKLAND, J. 1956: Toward a

theory of schizophrenia. *Behavioral Science* **1**, 251–64

BEATTIE, G. W. 1980: The skilled art of conversational interaction: Verbal and nonverbal signals in its regulation and management. In Singleton, W. T., Spurgeon, P., and Stammers, R. B., editors, *The analysis of social skill* (New York: Plenum) 193-211.

—— 1981: The regulation of speaker turns in face-to-face conversation: Some implications for conversation in sound-only communication channels. *Semiotica* **34**, 55–70.

BECKER, W. C., and KRUG, R. S. 1964: A circumplex model of social behaviour in children. *Child Development* **35**, 371–96.

BOCHNER, A. P., KAMINSKI, E. P., and FITZPATRICK, M. A. 1977: The conceptual domain of interpersonal communication behavior: A factor-analytic study. *Human Communication Research* **3**, 291–302.

BORGOTTA, E. F. 1960: Rankings and self-assessments: Some behavioral characteristic replication studies. *Journal of Social Psychology* **52**, 297–307.

—— 1962: A systematic study of interaction process scores, peer and self-assessments, personality and other variables. *Genetic Psychology Monographs* **65**, 219–91.

—— 1963: A new systematic interaction observation system: Behavior scores system (BSs). *Journal of Psychological Studies* **14**, 24–44.

—— 1964: The structure of personality characteristics. *Behavioral Science* **9**, 8–17.

BORGOTTA, E. F., COTTRELL, L. S., and MANN, J. H. 1958: The spectrum of individual interaction characteristics: An interdimensional analysis. *Psychological Reports* **4**, 279–319.

BROWN, R. 1965: *Social psychology*. New York: Free Press.

BROWN, R. and GILMAN, A. 1960: The pronouns of power and solidarity. In Sebeok, T. A., editor, *Style in language* (Cambridge, Mass: Free Press) 253–76.

BUZOLICH, M. J. 1983: *Interaction analysis of augmented and normal adult communicators*. Unpublished doctoral dissertation, University of California, San Francisco.

CAPPELLA, J. N. 1979: Talk–silence sequences in informal conversations I. *Human Communication Research* **6**, 3–17.

—— 1980: Talk–silence sequences in informal conversations II. *Human Communication Research* **6**, 130–45.

—— 1983: *Controlling the floor in conversation*. Paper presented at the Second International Conference on Social Psychology and Language, Bristol, England.

CARTER, L. F. 1954: Evaluating the performance of individuals as members of small groups. *Personnel Psychology* **7**, 477–84.

CARSON, R. C. 1969: *Interaction concepts of personality*. Chicago: Aldine.

DELONG, A. 1974: Kinesic signals at utterance boundaries in preschool children. *Semiotica* **11**, 43–74.

DUNCAN, S. 1972: Some signals and rules for taking speaking turns in conversation. *Journal of Personality and Social Psychology* **23**, 283–92.

—— 1983: Speaking turns: Studies of structure and individual differences. In Wiemann, J.M. and Harrison, R. P., editors, *Nonverbal interaction* (Beverly Hills, Cal: Sage) 149–78.

DUNCAN, S., BRUNNER, L.J., and FISKE, D. 1979: Strategy signals in face-to-face interaction. *Journal of Personality and Social Psychology* **37**, 301–13.

DUNCAN, S. and FISKE, D. W. 1977: *Face-to-face interaction*. Hillsdale, NJ: Erlbaum.

ELLIS, D. G. 1978: Trait predictors of relational control. *Communication Yearbook* **2**, 185–91.

ERVIN-TRIPP, S. 1972: On sociolinguistic rules: Alteration and co-occurrence. In Gumperz J. J. and Hymes, D., editors, *Directions in sociolinguistics*. (New York: Holt, Rinehart & Winston.) 213–50.

FERGUSON, N. 1977: Simultaneous speech, interruptions and dominance. *British Journal of Social and Clinical Psychology* **16**, 295–302.

FOA, U. G. and FOA, E. B. 1972: Resource exchange: Toward a structural theory of interpersonal communication. In Siegman, A. W. and Pope, B., editors, *Studies in dyadic communication* (New York: Pergamon Press) 291–323.

GOFFMAN, E. 1969: *Strategic interaction*. New York: Ballantine Books.

GOLDBERG, S. 1977: Social competence in infancy: A model of parent–infant interaction. *Merrill-Palmer Quarterly* **23**, 163–77.

GRICE, H. P. 1975: Logic and conversation. In COLE, P. and MORGAN, J. L., editors, *Syntax and semantics: Vol. 3. Speech acts* (New York: Academic Press) 41–58.

JAFFE, J. and FELDSTEIN, S. 1970: *Rhythms of dialogue*. New York: Academic Press.

JEFFERSON, G. 1973: A case of precision timing in ordinary conversation: Overlapped tag-positioned address terms in closing sequences. *Semiotica,* **9**, 47–96.

KAYE, K. 1982: *The mental and social life of babies*. Chicago: University of Chicago Press.

KENNEDY, C. W. and CAMDEN, C. T. 1983: A new look at interruptions. *Western Journal of Speech Communication* **47**, 45–58.

LEARY, T. 1957: *Interpersonal diagnosis of personality*. New York: Ronald.

LEDERER, W. J. and JACKSON, D. D. 1968: *The mirages of marriage*. New York: Norton.

LEET-PELLEGRINI, H. M. 1980: Conversational dominance as a function of gender and expertise. In Giles, H., Robinson, W. P., and Smith, P., editors, *Language: Social psychological perspectives*. (Oxford: Pergamon Press.) 97–104.

LEWIS, M. and FREEDLE, R. 1973: Mother–infant dyad: The cradle of meaning. In Pliner, P., Krames, L., and Alloway, T., editors, *Communication and affect: Language and thought* (New York: Academic Press) 127–55.

LORR, M. and McNAIR, D. M. 1965: Expansion of the interpersonal behavior circle. *Journal of Personality and Social Psychology* **2**, 823–30.

MARWELL, G. and HAGE, J. 1970: The organization of role-relationships: A systematic description. *American Sociological Review* **35**, 884–900.

MEHRABIAN, A. 1972: *Nonverbal communication*. Chicago: Aldine Atherton.

MELTZOFF, A. N. and MOORE, M. K. 1977: Imitation of facial and manual gestures by human neonates. *Science,* **198**, 75–8.

MILLAR, F. E. and ROGERS, L. E. 1976: A relational approach to interpersonal communication. In Miller, G. R., editor, *Explorations in interpersonal communication* (Beverly Hills, Cal: Sage) 87–103.

NORTON, R. 1978: Foundation of a communicator style construct. *Communication Research* **4**, 99–112.

OPLIGER, R. G. 1980: *Conversational turn taking in acquainted dyads: A t Duncan's model*. Unpublished master's thesis, University of Califo ..., Santa Barbara.

PATTERSON, M. L. 1982: A sequential functional model of nonverbal exchange. *Psychological Review* **89**, 231–49.

RUTTER, D. R. and STEPHENSON, G. M. 1977: The role of visual communication in synchronising conversation. *European Journal of Social Psychology* **7**, 29–37.

SACKS, H., SCHEGLOFF, E., and JEFFERSON, G. 1974: A simplest systematics for the organization of turn-taking for conversation. *Language* **50**, 696–735.

SCHEGLOFF, E. 1980: Preliminaries to preliminaries: Can I ask you a question? *Sociological Inquiry*, **50** (3–4), 104–52.

SCHUTZ, W. C. 1966: *The interpersonal underworld*. Palo Alto, Cal: Science & Behavior Books.

SEXTON, N. 1980: *An exploration of empathic behaviour in dyadic conversation*. Unpublished master's thesis, University of California, Santa Barbara.

SLUZKI, C. E. and BEAVIN, J. 1977: Symmetry and complementarity: An operational definition and a typology of dyads. In Watzlawick, P. and Weakland, J. H., editors, *The interactional view* (New York: Norton) 71–87.

TRIANDIS, H. C., VASSILLOU, V., and NASSIAKOU, M. 1968: Three cross-cultural studies of subjective culture. *Journal of Personality and Social Psychology, Monograph Supplement* **8,** (No. 4 Part 2), 1–42.

WATZLAWICK, P., BEAVIN, J., and JACKSON, D. D. 1967: *Pragmatics of human communication*. New York: Norton.

WIEMANN, J. M. 1977: Explication and test of a model of communicative competence. *Human Communication Research*, **3**, 195–213.

WIEMANN, J. M. and BACKLUND, P. 1980: Current theory and research in communicative competence. *Review of Educational Research*, **50,** 185–99.

WIEMANN, J. M. and KELLY, C. W. 1981: Pragmatics of interpersonal competence. In Wilder-Mott, C. and Weakland, J. H., editors, *Rigor & imagination: Essays from the legacy of Gregory Bateson*. (New York: Praeger) 283–97.

WIEMANN, J. M. and KNAPP, M. L. 1975: Turn-taking in conversations. *Journal of Communication* 25(2), 75–92.

WIEMANN, J. M. and KRUEGER, D. L. 1980: *Dimensions of interpersonal relationships revisited*. Paper presented at the meeting of the International Communication Association, Acapulco, Mexico.

WILSON, T., WIEMANN, J. M., and ZIMMERMAN, D. H. in press: Models of turn taking in conversational interaction. *Journal of language and Social Psychology*.

WISH, M., DEUTSCH, M., and KAPLAN, S. J. 1976: Perceived dimensions of interpersonal relations. *Journal of Personality and Social Psychology*, **33**, 409–20.

WISH, M. and KAPLAN, S. J. 1977: Toward an implicit theory of interpersonal communication. *Sociometry* **40**, 234–46.

YNGVE, V. H. 1970: On getting a word in edgewise. In Campbell, M. A., *et al.* editors, *Papers from the sixth regional meeting.* (Chicago, I: Chicago Linguistics Society & Department of Linguistics, University of Chicago) 567–78.

ZIMMERMAN, D. H. and WEST, C. 1975: Sex roles, interruptions and silences in conversation. In Thorne, B. and Henley, N., editors, *Language and sex: Difference and dominance.*(Rowley, Mass: Newbury House) 105–29.

ZIMMERMAN, D. H. and WEST, C. in preparation: *The concept of 'interruption.'* Unpublished manuscript, University of California, Santa Barbara.

6

What the heck, sir: style shifting and lexical colouring as features of powerful language

Carol Myers Scotton

Introduction

The purpose of this paper is to discuss the interactional functions of style shifting and lexical colouring as features of 'powerful language'.[1] 'Powerful language' is the aggregate of linguistic features negotiating the position of 'taking charge' in a talk exchange (Owsley and Scotton 1981; in press). Such language attempts to control the overall exchange, including the addressee's conversational contribution, in three main ways: it directs the amount and content of what gets said, it evaluates such talk by passing judgements or providing interpretations, and it organizes the exchange. Obvious examples of powerful linguistic features are interruptions, leading questions (*Because? Meaning?*), and challenges (*Don't you think, however. . . .*). Detailing the syntactic/semantic features constituting powerful language, Owsley and Scotton analysed the speech of six prominent American television interviewers and ranked these persons, based on the frequency and type of powerful features they used.[2] They considered style shifting and lexical colouring as powerful language because these features organize the exchange by modifying the current degree of social distance between participants. These features will be defined and illustrative data from the Owsley and Scotton study will be presented once some necessary groundwork on linguistic variation is in place.

Language use has not only a referential, but also a relational, function. That is, speakers use linguistic choices to index the social situation and to encode their attitudes about their relations to it as well as to convey information (see Wiemann Chapter 5; Bourhis Chapter 7). The tacit knowledge that social meaning is encoded by using one linguistic variant rather than another is part of the communicative competence of speakers about their linguistic repertoires and their speech community (Hymes 1972). Social meaning may be carried by the presence, absence or varying frequency of single phonological, syntactic, of

[1] I wish to thank Heidi Owsley and Stuart Hirst for helpful discussions relating to this paper and to thank Richard L. Street, Jr, and Joseph N. Cappella for comments on an earlier version.
[2] The aim of the Owsley and Scotton study was to delineate powerful language features and, at the same time, provide an explanation since it claimed to characterize the structural basis of powerful language. It used the conversational turns of television interviewers as a source of powerful language because the interview is the type of asymmetrical relationship in which such speech is likely to occur. The interviewers were chosen intuitively to represent a variety of users of powerful language. The first three minutes of three different interviews for each interviewer, for a total of 18 interviews, were analysed. The study tested several hypotheses in addition to describing powerful language.

lexical choices, or by co-occurring sets of such variants. For example, *why did you* vs *why'ja* carries a message about the tenor of the exchange. 'Linguistic variety' is a cover term for such co-occurring sets.

Differences in their phonological, syntactic and lexical systems and in their social distribution distinguish linguistic varieties. This paper views 'language', 'dialect' and 'style' as heuristic labels for varieties, the specific label applied depending on the extent a given variety differs from related varieties. That is, languages show relatively gross differences from each other; but dialects are sub-systems within a specific language and differ less dramatically from each other; and styles exist within any dialect, showing still more minor rule variations. At the same time, this paper acknowledges with Hudson (1978, p. 24) that the actual distinctions between linguistic varieties (as made by both linguists and speakers) show no consistent basis. That is, languages, dialects and styles are sometimes so defined mainly on a structural basis (How different are the grammatical systems of variety x from variety y ?), or on a functional basis (Are the speakers of variety x sociopolitically separated from those of variety y ? Is variety x used for different communicative purposes than variety y ? etc.), or by combining structural and functional considerations.

The proliferation of designations for non-dialectal variation reflects and is part of this inconsistency in defining varieties. In addition to 'style', the terms 'register' and 'code' are most prominently used. But one of the most influential linguists on the subject of functionally based variation simply refers to 'ways of speaking' (Hymes 1964; 1967). And Quirk *et al.* (1973, pp. 20–32), in what is widely accepted as the current definitive discussion of English grammar, use only 'variety' as a designation. 'Register' arose among British linguists (e.g. Reid 1956; Halliday *et al.* 1964; Spencer and Gregory 1964) as a cover term for 'the linguistic features which are typically associated with a configuration of situational features' (Halliday and Hasan 1976, p. 22), or characterized as a term 'needed when we want to account for what people do with their language' (Halliday *et al.* 1964, p. 87). It originally referred mainly to lexical distinctions and was meant to distinguish dialects from varieties with a different functional basis: dialects were defined according to the user and register according to the use to which the variety was put.[3] Such statements do not restrict register to sub-dialectal variation: it is appropriate for *any* variety distinguished according to use. In practice, however, it has been applied mainly to variation within a dialect. Yet still other uses of register are even more restricted, referring to the more or less conventionalized linguistic features of certain tasks or settings or groups of speakers, such as 'the register of sports-announcer talk' (Ferguson 1983), or 'the female register' (Crosby and Nyquist 1977), although the occurrence of such features could cut across dialects or even languages. Except for discussions of register in these more restricted senses, few studies actually present the linguistic features of existing registers; instead, most offer the social

[3]Note that this distinction is not accepted in this paper. The dialects speakers know and use not only identify them in regard to social membership in their speech community, but mark classes of speech exchanges, such as the national network television newscast, the blue-collar bar encounter, the ethnic-specific wedding party, etc. Further, while styles/registers are partly a function of use (the parameters of the exchange), they also depend on users in regard to their personal perceptions and motivations – how they construe themselves in relation to the exchange.

factors behind register variation.

'Code' as used by Bernstein (1958) applies to sub-dialectal lexical and syntactic markers which he claims cluster according to socioeconomic class and reflect a specific cognitive orientation to topics and talk exchanges. As used by many other linguists, 'code' has an altogether different meaning; it is a cover term in the same sense as 'linguistic variety'.

In general, American linguists have preferred 'style' as a general term for sub-dialectal variation, even though its common use for 'a distinctive or characteristic manner' may lead to confusion about intended referents. They have not, however, been consistent in how styles are defined. The best-known study for American English, Joos (1961), offers definitions hingeing on the relationship between speaker and addressee which the linguistic features of the style presuppose. Joo's scheme will be used in this paper. He distinguishes five basic styles: frozen, formal, consultative, casual and intimate. His definitions are intuitively satisfying, if fanciful and vague. Thus, for example, the two defining features of his 'middle' style – consultative style – are (1) the speaker supplies background information and does not assume he/she can be understood without it, and (2) the addressee participates continuously. 'Because of these two features, consultative style is our norm for coming to terms with strangers – people who speak our language but whose personal stock of information may be different' (Joos 1961, p. 23).

Joos provides no more real details for the other styles. Casual style is marked negatively by an absence of background information and positively by ellipsis and slang. 'Besides . . . ellipsis and slang, casual style is marked by an arbitrary list of formulas, all very stable, which are learned individually and used to identify the style for the hearer's convenience' (Joos 1961, p. 27). Intimate style is marked by extraction and jargon. 'Both are stable once the intimate group (normally a pair) has been formed' (Joos 1961, p. 30). The crucial difference between consultative style and formal style is that participation drops out. It is marked by detachment and cohesion and is designed to inform, 'something which is necessarily ancillary in consultation, incidental in casual discourse, absent in intimacy' (Joos 1961, p. 35–6). 'Frozen style is for people who are to remain strangers' (Joos 1961, p. 41). This style lacks two things: participation and intonation (because it is always written), but it gains one thing: reflection, since the reader can re-read.

In addition, a few studies of syntactic and lexical variation in 'fragments' of stylistic systems exist. Ervin-Tripp (1976a) discusses the different structures of directives and, earlier, (Ervin-Tripp 1973) looked at terms of address in American English. Her purpose, however, is not so much to differentiate styles as to show that alternative forms for 'saying the same thing' do exist and to argue that their differential use is triggered by social factors, most crucially the social identities of speaker and addressee. In discussing politeness phenomena, Brown and Levinson (1978) deal with stylistic variants, but their goal is not to assign them to or group them as distinct styles.

Thus, the state of affairs surrounding non-dialectal variation within a language is marked by confusion of terminology and lack of any generally accepted comprehensive differentiation of available styles. Yet, the present study is possible just because its subject is *shifts* in styles, not the styles themselves. Because the recognition of socially significant variation is part of any speaker's tacit knowledge about at least his/her native language, speakers can identify instances of switching from one style to another, whether or not the full inventory of linguistic features of the styles has been explicitly characterized.[4]

Style shifting is a change from one style of a language to another within the same conversational turn. It is a form of code switching, the use of any two or more linguistic varieties in the same conversation, whether they are different languages, styles, or dialects. An obvious – even flagrant – example of style shifting occurs in this utterance of Tom Snyder, one of the television interviewers studied by Owsley and Scotton (1981 in press):

> 'Why didn't you just want to continue being a magician? I mean, what the heck, sir, you're all dressed up in a magic suit . . .' (Tom Snyder 15 July 1981)

Snyder's comment involves switching because *what the heck* and *magic suit* represent a casual style, one typically used when the degree of social distance between participants is minimal and the subject is informal. But *what the heck* is juxtaposed with *sir*, a term of address normally used in a formal style where there is a good deal of social distance between speaker and addressee. Further, both are shifts away from the middle, consultative style appropriate for the interview and used for most of it.

Lexical colouring consists of embedding a lexical choice implying a value judgement in an otherwise neutral utterance. Functionally, it is related to style shifting, since both propose a change in the talk exchange. But structurally lexical colouring is different since it does not involve a change in style but rather value-laden lexical choices within the same style as the ongoing exchange. For example, *vending* in the following from Dick Cavett, also studied by Owsley and Scotton, is an example of lexical colouring:

> '. . . ah ah people are forever comparing you to and with, I never know which it is, ah most of the people ah vending humour these days . . .' (Dick Cavett 14 May 1981)

This is so because *vending* implies selling (vs words with more positive connotations, such as *entertaining*) and a particularly low form of it (i.e. *peddling*).

Few studies of shifts between linguistic varieties or of lexical choices have considered style shifting or lexical colouring (but see Fischer 1958). Most have dealt with alternation between languages (e.g. Bouris *et al.* 1979; Chapter 7; or Scotton 1982) or less frequently between dialects (e.g. Blom and Gumperz 1972). One reason may be that it is simply easier to identify switching at these levels. But the main reason may be that stylistic variation has not been theoretically interesting to most linguists. Even dialectal variation for motivations other than region of origin has been a subject of systematic study only since the late 1960s (e.g. Labov 1966; Trudgill 1974). Yet these studies have had a narrow focus: the correlation between linguistic variation and social group membership and its role in explaining the mechanisms and rationale of language change.

Also, dialectal variation has been a favoured subject because of another

---

[4]To test this claim, Owsley and Scotton coded the data for style switching cited here independently of each other. Their analysis showed an inter-coder reliability of 0.90 in identifying style shifts. Further, the analysis of part of the data by another native speaker of American English with no knowledge of the results of the previous analysis, showed a correlation of over 0.90 with Scotton's coding. I wish to thank Dan Lefkowitz for serving as an independent coder.

theoretical bias. Within any language, dialects are the linguistic reflection of the more static features affecting linguistic choices. Most obviously, these are the features identifying speakers as members of specific speech communities. For example, dialects are indexical of the speaker's home ties and socioeconomic class memberships. That the bulk of linguistic variation can be accounted for by such static features has been dominant premise within sociolinguistic theory (e.g. Labov 1972; Fishman 1972).

Stylistic variation also is related to social group membership in that a speaker's stylistic repertoire is a function of social experiences; but styles are used not so much to 'place' a speaker within a speech community as to mark individual talk exchanges according to their degree of formality and the interpersonal relationships involved. In this sense, they are more the reflection of dynamic features. Thus, given the fact interest in variation at all has been narrow (tied to its relevance to language change) and the theoretical premise that the more static features such as social group membership account most crucially for variation, neglect of stylistic variation can be understood.

The basic of stylistic choices

The dynamic factors affecting style choices refer to both the speaker and the talk exchange. In reference to the exchange, the style chosen depends on the parameters of the individual exchange regarding most crucially topic, medium and participants. (Some (e.g. Halliday 1975; Gregory 1967) characterize the context of a speech event as a complex of three dimensions, with register as a cover term. These dimensions are: field, mode and tenor of discourse. Field of discourse refers largely to subject matter; mode refers to medium selected; and tenor depends on relationships among the relevant participants.)

The stylistic variation discussed in this paper is related to that attributed to tenor of discourse, but is motivated by the speaker, not the exchange. Gregory and Carroll (1978, p. 8) recognize two types of tenor: personal and functional. Personal tenor has to do with relative status relationships, such as mother and son, employer and employee. Functional tenor refers to the use to which language is put, such as teaching or persuading. Both types of tenor, however, refer to linguistic variation relating to participant relationships only as a function of the parameters of the exchange, as field and mode of discourse are more obviously.[5]

Another source of stylistic variation, outside the exchange itself, are the personal goals and motivations of speakers, this paper argues. Such claims are in line with the accommodation theory of Giles and associates (e.g. Giles and Powesland 1975), and recent work within conversational analysis (e.g. Gumperz 1982) and network theory (e.g. Romaine 1982). The paper will focus on the speaker's use of stylistic variants to negotiate his/her personal rights and obligations in effect during the exchange, relative to those of the addressee. 'Taking charge' is one such negotiation, encoded by the use of powerful linguistic features, such as style shifting and lexical colouring. (Other basic negotiations

[5]The examples cited by Gregory and Carroll (1978, p. 53) to illustrate functional tenor make clear that it is part of the exchange, not a product of speaker motivations. For example, they say, 'The tenor of persuasion defines the generic structure of 'the ad', as the sermon is designed to exhort and to teach.'

include moves toward solidarity, or the politeness strategies to mitigate 'face threats' discussed by Brown and Levinson (1978) as linguistic universals.)

Style shifting and lexical colouring and a theory of markedness

Style shifting and lexical colouring become powerful because such features represent a type of marked choice. This argument is based on a model of linguistic code choice holding that participants in any talk exchange make and interpret linguistic choices in terms of a theory of markedness (Scotton 1983). All linguistic choices are seen as indexical of a rights and obligations set (RO set) holding between participants. That is, any choice points to a particular inter-personal balance and attempts to negotiate its acceptance. Speakers hold this theory of markedness naturally as part of their communicative competence about the connection between linguistic choices and social relationships. This association is speech-community specific, with speakers knowing what choice is unmarked and which others are marked for a specific exchange, as long as the exchange is conventionalized and therefore covered by norms.[6] For example, in the television interviews studied, the unmarked choice is the consultative style of American English.

Of course far from all exchanges are conventionalized. Very often, situations arise for which norms of behaviour are not established or for which conflicting norms apply, and an unmarked choice is therefore not clear. Both speakers and addressee recognize in such cases that any choice is exploratory, intended as a candidate to become the index of a mutually acceptable relationship – to become the unmarked choice.

Linguistic choices, therefore, take place within a normative framework, but still are not determined, according to this model. A normative framework is posited because a societal consensus must be the basis for interpreting the social meaning of choices, associating each with a rights and obligations relationship and assigning unmarked choices for conventionalized exchanges. But, within the framework, speakers have options. They can make any of a range of choices, constrained only by the relative attractiveness of alternative choices and their outcomes. Thus, this model is related to theories of social behaviour based on costs and rewards (Thibaut and Kelly 1959, for example).

Different styles of a language will be unmarked choices for different types of talk exchanges, of course. For example, while a business executive might reject an idea in an office meeting by saying, *I believe it would be counter-productive to do that*, he/she might perform the same speech act at home with a family member by saying, *Are you kidding*? Or the same request in the same setting may take two quite different stylistic forms at all linguistic levels (phonological, syntactic and lexical) depending on differences in social distance and status relationships between speakers and the same addressee. Ervin-Tripp (1976b, p. 123) cites two different directive forms to a physician in a hospital:

(3a)   Hey, Len, shoot the chart to me, willya?

[6]This model views choices as falling along a continuum and therefore grading into each other as more or less unmarked and marked. Further, the same linguistic choice need be unmarked for all members of the exchange, since unmarked choices depend on the parameters of the exchange – most especially social identities of speaker.

(3b)   Oh, by the way, doctor, could you leave me that chart when you're through?

The role of marked choices

Marked choices in conventionalized relationships, however, rock the social boat, or at least alter its course. They are signals of the speaker's intent to change the relationship with the addressee, in terms of the rights and obligations balance – to dis-identify with the normative balance. Further, by implication, the marked choice is a negotiation to establish a *different* RO set as unmarked. For example, in the following exchange, the utterance, *You've got it!* diverges from consultative style as the unmarked choice present in the rest of the exchange. It is an invitation to make the encounter more personal:

(4)   Setting: Sales office in Kenya for local women's cottage industries. The customer and volunteer are about the same age and recognize each other as fellow Americans by their accents, but they are strangers.

Customer: (finishing instructions for a hand-knit sweater she is ordering): And please be sure to get them to make it, because I definitely will come to get it.

Volunteer: (her non-verbal facial signals indicate she isn't worried): All right.

Customer: But I suppose you don't really care if I come by – I suppose you know you can always sell it to someone else. It's a popular item isn't it?

Volunteer: (smiles approval of recognition of her position): You've got it!

Customer: Where exactly are you from, anyway? I'm from. . . .etc.

Because a marked choice is a move to rescind the expected RO set between speaker and addressee, it generally provokes an emotional response from the addressee; and indeed, the marked choice itself is also an emotional move. In example (4) the speaker's marked choice called for less social distance, a move accepted by the addressee. But some marked choices are expressions of anger, encoding a call for more social distance. In the following example from Scotton (1982, p. 439), the switch to English is indexical of anger and authority and is used as a distancing device:

(5)   Setting: Local Development Committee meeting in rural western Kenya. Luyia variety, the shared mother tongue of all present, has been the medium for the entire meeting up to this point. English is the official language of Kenya, but is usually reserved for more public, urban occasions:

Committee Member: Vamemba veru va County Council shivakhuyinzilira vulahi tawe. Inyinga yi tsikura vagadanga vandu valava-yinzirira nawutsa numu shivakholanga varia tawe. (Luyia: Our Councillors don't serve us effectively. During the election campaign, they deceived people, that they will serve them but now they don't do that.)

Another Member   (A Councillor): If there is anyone who wants to take up this post, he should do so now!

Why style shifting and lexical colouring are powerful features

Style shifts as marked choices are powerful language strategies, attempts to take charge in some way, the television interviewer study suggests.[7] In general, marked choices are powerful for two reasons.

First, as noted above, marked choices always encode personally motivated dis-identifications with the unmarked choice, the expected. Obviously, this is a call for a change. Such a move is powerful because any change, pleasant or not, disrupts an ongoing exchange and leaves its future course uncertain. Related evidence about uncertainty in interpersonal relations leads Berger and Bradac (1982) to argue that uncertainty reduction is a basic drive, with uncertainty defined as 'the inability to structure the environment as to render it predictable' (Berger and Bradac 1982, p. 117).

Conversational turns including style shifts as marked choices lead to uncertainty. For example, a boss who says to a subordinate in anger, *Kindly get your ass in here* underlines his rude request by switching from *kindly*, a form from a formal style associated with extra-polite exchanges, to a casual style. Since each stylistic choice in any exchange is indexical of a certain RO set between participants (all choices being the unmarked indices of some RO set), the addressee becomes uncertain how a speaker making style shifts intends the exchange to proceed. Further, such switching, as in the example, makes the rudeness more insulting: it is as if the superior is 'playing with' the subordinate by invoking various RO sets.[8] As the addressee's uncertainty increases, the potential for the speaker to take more charge overall increases.

Much of the style shifting used by the television interviewers may be explained as intended (at some subconscious level) to have this result, it is hypothesized. Of the six interviewers studied (Tom Brokaw, Dick Cavett, Phil Donahue, Jane Pauley, Tom Snyder and Mike Wallace), those who scored highest overall in using powerful language features were also the ones who used the most style shifting. For example, in the following extract from an interview on police brutality, Phil Donahue switches first to the specialized, more learned forms associated with police reports (i.e. *altercations, inebriated*) and then to a casual style:

(6)   Ah they were the people who were in – ah in altercations in bars, sometimes inebriated, sometimes not, *huh*? And the only way you could really *get to them was to beat'em up, up, huh*? (Phil Donahue 19 May 1981) ('downshifts' to a casual style are underlined in examples (6) through (23))

Tom Snyder's interviews showed the largest number of such switchings back and forth between styles. Many of the subjects rating the interviewers in a subjective evaluation test (based on listening to audio tapes of part of an interview) (Owsley and Scotton 1981; in press) criticized Snyder for 'playing around'. It is possible what they perceived were not only his content shifts but also his style switching:

(7)   *Ya know the fogies that don't* understand the magic and the lure of rock music would say, 'Now why would a young man have to get in shape for a tour in which he plays a guitar basically and sings in front of people?' *Whadya do* to get

---

[7] This does not mean all instances of code shifting are marked choices (See Scotton 1983, p. 122; forthcoming).

[8] Subordinates also use style shifting to insult. A ploy of athletes in objecting to a referee's decision is to frame a negative comment with a politeness form from a formal style such as in *You gotta be blind . . . sir*! (I thank Daniel Lefkowitz for this observation and the example.)

in shape and *whydya* have to do that. (Tom Snyder 16 July 1981) (*the magic and the lure* is an 'up shift' to a quasi-literary, frozen style)

(8)   . . . Could you explain to me the mystique of amplification, when it comes to rock music. I mean we – I – *like I say we got* a small room here *an I mean* you come in here *an stack' em up* to the ceiling . . . (Tom Snyder 16 July 1981) (*the mystique of amplification* is quasi-literary, frozen style)

Another way in which a linguistic shift creates uncertainty for the addressee is by creating ambiguity: the precise motivation for switching away from the unmarked choice and the RO set it stands for is not always clear. In their discussion of uncertainty and personal communication, Berger and Bradac (1982, pp. 8–9) acknowledge the importance to participants of prediction-making activities in interpersonal exchanges (Miller and Steinberg 1975), but also point out the need for participants to be able to explain why others say and do what they do. Marked choices may leave the addressee at a loss to understand what the speaker is trying to do. For example, most of the shifts in the television interviewer study were 'down shifts' to a more casual style, embedded in consultative style, the unmarked choice for the entire exchange. The following extracts illustrate this:

(9)   . . . Maybe you put on more tests, maybe you'll put on more (1 sec. pause) chemistries, more blood counts, more (1 sec. pause) – because you know that in the final analysis Medicare is *gonna* pay a certain percentage of them so you *might'uz well load it up* (1 sec. pause) so that in the long run, particularly with a private hospital – but with any hospital – *you're gonna get* more money from Medicare. (Mike Wallace 9 August 1981)

(10) Donahue: Ah why – why is it – why is it important *to beat up a guy* who's handcuffed? Wh – I don't understand the – sociological explanation for that kind of behavior.
      Interviewee: Ahm, I believe that the – that they did not recognize it as brutality. (2 sec. pause) That it's just their way of doing their job . . .
      Donahue: And if you don't get the upper hand
                   '*right now, buddy*'. . .
      Interviewee: That's right.
      Donahue: *This guy is gonna take you.*
                   (Phil Donahue 24 May 1981)

Such downshifts to casual style may encode a desire for more engagement between participants and less social distance. As Joos (1961, p. 23) points out, 'Casual style [in American English] is for friends, acquaintances, insiders, addressed to a stranger, it serves to make him an insider simply by treating him as an insider.' *But* the same casual style also can trivialize either the topics or the participants of the current exchange, indicating that they are not 'status-ful' or 'serious' enough to warrant 'careful' speech. For example, Tom Snyder's shifts to casual style in the following excerpts seem trivializing:

(11) Also the tails have a lot of *pockets 'n stuff* where *you guys* hide all the things that make the illusions. (Tom Snyder 15 July 1981)

(12) Snyder (to rock star about concerts): . . . where you play a concert that runs two and a half or three hours *you gotta be dog tired when you come off that stage.* (Tom Snyder 16 July 1981)

Whether the down shifts in the following excerpts are trivializing seems less clear since they could also be negotiations to promote more solidarity with the addressee:

(13)   Pauley (to mother of cancer victim): . . . After a year *you were pretty sure she was out of the woods*, after five years you knew it. (Jane Pauley 24 August 1981)

(14)   Pauley (to author of book on dealing with bosses): What about ah the kind of boss *who doesn't yell at you*, really doesn't say anybody . . . (Jane Pauley 23 July 1981)

(15)   Brokaw (discussing shoddy journalism): Shall we just read one excerpt of the *kind of stuff* that he would write? (Tom Brokaw 25 July 1981)

Switching to a more formal style may be a strategy to increase social distance since such a style is often unmarked in relationships in which status differentials are salient. However, again, 'up switches' may trivialize, especially if the formal style seems inappropriate because the content is light. Tom Snyder's switches discussed above (*the mystique of amplification, the magic and lure of rock music*) certainly seem intended to trivialize. So do his references to rock star Tom Petty as *mister* and *Thomas*, especially when he follows them with a casual style:

(16)   Snyder: . . . with *Mr* Tom Petty right here. *Thomas*? (applause) You've had some *tough luck* on the tours. . . . (Tom Snyder 16 July 1981)

Again, there are examples in which the motivation seems less clear, but trivialization is a possibility. Note Pauley's use of *disengage*, Cavett's use of *compulsion*:

(17)   Pauley (talking about embarrassing moments for teenagers): . . . how do you *disengage* the straw from the coke you've been drinking from your nose? (Jane Pauley 21 September 1981)

(18)   Cavett (talking about his own reference to his ankle injury): What do you suppose, what strange *compulsion* made me try to explain . . . (Dick Cavett 21 May 1981)

These examples show how switching as a marked choice breaks the rhythm of the interaction. It is a powerful language feature because it deviates from the expected and because its motivations may not be clear, therefore leaving the addressee off balance and unable either to predict the RO set in effect for the rest of the exchange or to explain the speaker's precise motivations.

Second, style switching as a marked choice is a powerful language strategy simply by calling for a change. Negotiating a re-direction of the exchange can be seen as a claim of superior position on the speaker's part because initiators of the use of socially significant linguistic forms are usually superiors. The linguistic universal concerning power and solidarity expressions proposed by Hudson (1980, p. 125) supports this claim: ' . . . wherever power and solidarity are reflected in the same range of forms . . . the form which expresses high solidarity also expresses greater power on the part of the speaker and vice versa.' This is so, Hudson argues, because, as Brown and Ford (1964, pp. 236–7) point out, the superior tends to use the high-solidarity form first. (They have in mind the use of first names, or of the equivalent of French *tu* in languages which mark number in second-person pronouns, as initially from a superior to a subordinate.)

Style shifting asserts superiority for the speaker in two related ways:

(a)   It may present a pattern of shifting as the index of the speaker's perception of his/her own identity as *different* from that of other participants. There are conventionalized exchanges in which shifting may itself be the unmarked choice for all participants. This is the case between bilingual peers who both use switching to signal their mutually dual identities (Scotton 1982, pp. 435–6 forthcoming. But in the television interview, a single style is unmarked (more or less Joo's consultative style). Certainly, that a pattern of switching is *not* the unmarked choice is evidence from the fact that only the interviewers do the switching.

A pattern of switching asserts that the speaker has at least two salient identities in the current exchange, those associated as unmarked choices with two different rights and obligations balances. In presenting this pattern of switching as unmarked for him/her personally (especially in the face of only one style choice by other participants), the speaker is boasting symbolically of the *range* of his/her identities. For example:

(19) Wallace: . . . They were planning on using a quarter million low interest loan to expand. Until they realized *they'd been had.* (Mike Wallace 19 September 1981)

This assertion of being at ease in two styles is a form of threatening other participants who use only one style because such switching claims a range of experience beyond what is unmarked, what is 'required' For some television, interviewers, a range of experience having attraction and even prestige is that associated with the working class, the underworld, or anyone who knows how 'to be tough'.[9] In another culture, switching to a linguistic variety with other associations may be more prestigious, but the overall motivation and effect is the same: the asserting of identities other participants cannot claim.[10]

The responses of interviewees indicate that they find the pattern of switching unacceptable. Almost uniformly, interviewees persisted in the unmarked middle style. Further, some interviewees even 'edited' the shifts of certain interviewers by repeating in a more consultative style what the interviewer had just said. For example:

(20) Interviewee: They see brutality, they work with it, real and imagined, and it becomes an everyday occurrence for them (1 sec. pause). And this is the way they perceive the world.
Donahue: *Us and them.*
Interviewee: We and they. That's right.

Such examples of editing are especially frequent in the Mike Wallace interviews. Wallace did not come out first as the most frequent user of switching, so it was not the sheer barrage of switching which probably motivated the interviewees to edit him. Rather, the editing seems related to Wallace's overall purpose. His object often is to 'extract' from interviewees information which is either self-damaging or at least unsavoury. The interviewee's reluctance to accommodate to Wallace, *even* insofar as letting Wallace's own utterness stand, can be seen as a form of dis-accommodation. (see Giles and Powesland 1975 on accommodation theory):

[9]In relation to this, see Trudgill (1972) on the covert prestige accorded to non-standard dialects.
[10]See Scotton (1982, p. 437) for an example showing that code switching, in an exchange when the unmarked choice is clear, is viewed as a posturing of power. The example comes from western Kenya.

(21)   Wallace: That's *quite a charge*.
       Interviewee: Yes, it's a strong statement. (Mike Wallace 9 August 1981)

(22)   Wallace: . . . had paid their money *up front*,
       Interviewee: paid their money.
       Wallace: They had promised that there was *a darn good* chance,
       Interviewee: very good chance they'd get the money. (Mike Wallace 19 September 1981)

(23)   Wallace: So the incentive is *to load it up*.
       Interviewee: The incentive is to provide more services and services of a more highly technical nature. Yes sir. (Mike Wallace 9 August 1981)

(b) The fact these downshifts characterize the interviewers' contributions, *not* those of the addressees, also is additional evidence from a related point of view that downshifts are negotiations of power (at least in this type of exchange). That using casual style is a call for solidarity has been established. As Joos (1961, p. 23) puts it, ' . . . addressed to a stranger, [casual style] serves to make him an insider simply by treating him as an insider.' But when two strangers meet, who initiates the move toward solidarity? Initiating shifts can be seen as latent statements that the shifter is more powerful since the prerogative to move toward solidarity belongs to the superior, it is hypothesized. Thus, in the television interview, if the interviewer attempts a negotiation of solidarity by shifting to casual style and the addressee reciprocates, indicating he/she accepts the negotiation, the addressee *also* is accepting a one-down relationship in terms of status, it would follow. Therefore, this also may be a reason why the interviewees 'edit' shifts to casual styles. While the interviewer is a well known personality, the interviewee *also* may be a luminary in his/her own field – and that field happens to be the subject of the interview. Such interviewees may find the interviewer's extension of solidarity as not necessarily his/her prerogative. Other guests, such as some of those Mike Wallace interrogates in exchanges involving wrong-doing, may not be competing stars. These persons, however, also may not want a solidarity relationship with Wallace, especially one acknowledging his superior position. They also have cause to 'edit' the exchange back to the consultative level.[11]

Lexical colouring as evaluative language

Lexical colouring cannot be distinguished totally from shifts in style. It is different, however, in that it need not involve a change in stylistic level. Further, while shifting *may* be evaluative of content, lexical colouring is always this. Still, lexical colouring and style shifting as a marked choice are similar because they both deviate from the expected, the unmarked, choice. In addition, lexical colouring is a powerful language feature because it is a tool to control the

[11]Of Wallace's interviewees, the only one who deviated at all from consultative style was a victim, *not* a possible wrong-doer. This person accommodated to Wallace's downshift at one point:

Wallace: You paid by check or by cash.
Interviewee: Cash
Wallace: Lota money.
Interviewee: Lota money.

interaction by passing judgement on its content.

For example, in using the word *propped* Dick Cavett is setting up a negative evaluation of television in the following excerpt:

(24) Cavett: But ah, wha – what's doing it, is it television, for one thing, that kids sit propped in front of the set and they're//
       Interviewee: It ah has to be mainly what it is. (Dick Cavett 2, May 1981)

While it is of course entirely possible for the addressee to contradict a case of lexical colouring, opposition requires more energy than assent, as well as the necessary virtuosity to demur articulately at a moment's notice.

Mike Wallace also passes negative judgements by using *episode* in (25) and *to the tune of* in (26):

(25) Wallace: He also reviewed six hundred pages of doctors' and nurses', and lab records that constituted the medical history of this entire episode. (Mike Wallace 9 August 1981)
(26) Wallace: From March of '74 to January of '77 you paid Cleveland Turr off to the tune of nineteen thousand dollars . . . (Mike Wallace 5 July 1981)

Phil Donahue trivializes his interviewee's contribution by using *little* and *mini*:

(27) Donahue: . . . what is your – give us just your little mini-analysis here . . . (Phil Donahue 24 May 1981)

And in the final example, the use of *tilt* (with its connotation of breaking the rules, since the word 'tilt' appears on pinball machines when the player makes an illegal move) indicates that Tom Brokaw is not really asking for information so much as making an evaluation. The fact the question is negatively phrased also is a factor.

(28) Brokaw: Doesn't that tilt everything right now in favor of people who are well financed and conservative . . . (Tom Brokaw 23 September 1981)

Conclusion

This paper has tried to meet several goals. First, to provide background information, it has discussed the basis of definitions of sub-dialectal variation. Second and related to this, it has argued the importance of dynamic factors in accounting for linguistic variation. This insistence is part of a relatively recent shift away from depending only on correlations of variation with situational factors to explain the basis of variation. Variation has been viewed here not only as a function of static, situational factors (e.g. topic, relative status of participants, etc.) but also as a function of those dynamic factors involving the speaker's individual goals regarding relationships holding within a specific talk exchange.

Third, the paper has considered style shifting as a marked choice within a markedness framework (Scotton 1983). Of relevance here is the claim that in conventionalized exchanges all linguistic choices are understood as more or less unmarked or marked. When marked choices are made, they represent individual speakers' attempts to move away from the existing or expected rights and obligations balance between participants pointed to by the unmarked choice.

Fourth, the paper has argued that the overall function of style shifting as a marked choice is to enhance the speaker's power position within the exchange relative to that of addressees. As such. style shifting, along with lexical colouring, are seen as powerful language features. It has been suggested that style shifting is a move to augment the speaker's power in three ways: (a) by increasing uncertainty about the speaker's aims, thereby 'throwing off' the addressee; (b) by establishing multiple identities for the speaker by displaying a range of styles, thereby presenting an intimidating and hence powerful image; and (c) by assuming the role of a superior by initiating the use of socially significant variants encoding solidarity. Using lexical colouring is an attempt to gain power in an exchange because such features make evaluations of content, the paper claims.

The overall discussion presented here leads to the following more general hypothesis about style shifting and its interactional intentions and effects:

(1) Situational exigencies impinge upon the impact or perception of style shifts. That is, such factors as the relative status of participants affect the success of marked choices as negotiations for different relationships in an exchange.

(2) In any conventionalized exchange, shifts away from the unmarked choice raise the level of addressee uncertainty.

(2a) In any conventionalized exchange, the level of addressee uncertainty and inability to provide an explanation for a speaker's behaviour increases when the speaker shifts to a marked choice.

(3) In any conventionalized exchange, choices of varieties deviating from the expected are seen as powerful strategies intended to change the rights and obligations balance within the exchange.

(3a) Upward or downward shifts away from the unmarked choice in a conventionalized exchange may be seen as trivializing the addressee or topic under discussion.

(3b) Style shifting increases the addressee's perception of the speaker as a multi-faceted personality and powerful in this sense.

(4) In any exchange, conventionalized or not, a speaker initiating moves using individual variants or entire varieties encoding solidarity is perceived as making a negotiation of power by assuming the role of the superior.

While the research reported in this paper has suggested these hypotheses, future studies will be needed to test them adequately. Most obviously, studies must devise systematic ways of considering the conversational turns which follow style shifting and lexical colouring in order to test their effects more objectively.[12] This paper, however, has attempted to suggest how such linguistic choices as style shifting and lexical colouring may be used to negotiate an interactional position.

[12]Erickson *et al*. (1978) and Bradac *et al*. (1981) deal, of course, with different evaluations of fictional courtroom case defendants and witnesses, based on whether their speech contained certain 'powerful' vs 'powerless' features. However, these studies do not consider how linguistic choices are used to negotiate relative interactional positions.

References

BERGER, C.R. and BRADAC, J.J. 1982: *Language and social knowledge, uncertainty in interpersonal relations*. London: Edward Arnold.

BERNSTEIN, B. 1958: Some sociological determinants of perception, an inquiry into sub-cultural differences. *British Journal of Sociology* **9**, 159–74. Reprinted in Fishman, J.A., editor, 1968: *Readings in the sociology of languages*. (The Hague: Mouton) 223–39.

BLOM, J.P. and GUMPERZ, J.J. 1972: Social meaning in linguistic structures: code-switching in Norway. In Gumperz, J.J. and Hymes, D., editors, *Directions in Sociolinguistics* (New York: Holt, Rinehart and Winston) 407–34.

BOURHIS, R., GILES, H., LEYEN, J., and TAJFEL, H. 1979: Psycholinguistic distinctiveness: language divergence in Belgium. In Giles, H. and St. Clair, R., editors, *Language and social psychology* (Oxford: Blackwell) 158–85.

BRADAC, J. J., HEMPHILL, M.R., and TARDY, C.H., 1981: Language on trial: effects of 'powerful' and 'powerless' speech upon judgements of victims and villains. *Western Journal of Speech Communication* **45**, 327–41.

CROSBY, F. and NYQUIST, L. 1977: The female register: an empirical study of Lakoff's hypotheses. *Language in Society* **6**, 313–322.

BROWN, P. and LEVINSON, S., 1978: Universals in language usage: politeness phenomena. In Goody, E., editor *Questions and politeness* (London: Cambridge University Press) 256–89.

BROWN, R. and FORD. M., 1964: Address in American English. In Hymes, D., editor, *Language in culture and society* (New York: Harper & Row) 234–44. Originally in *Journal of Abnormal and Social Psychology* **62**, 375–85 (1961).

ERICKSON, B., LIND, E. A., JOHNSON, B.C, and O'BARR, W., 1978: Speech style and impression formation in a court setting: the effects of 'powerful' and 'powerless' speech. *Journal of Experimental and Social Psychology* **14**, 266–79.

ERVIN-TRIPP, S. 1973: The structure of communicative choice. In Ervin-Tripp, S., editor, *Language acquisition and communicative choice* (Stanford: Stanford University Press) 302–73.

——. 1976a: Is Sybil there? The structure of some American English directives. *Language in Society* **5**, 25–66.

——. 1976b: Speech acts and social learning. In Basso, K. and Selby, H., editors, *Meaning in anthropology* (Albuquerque: University of New Mexico Press) 123–53.

FERGUSON, C.A. 1983: Sports announcer talk: Syntactic aspects of register variation. *Language in Society* **12**, 153–72.

FISCHER, J.L. 1958: Social influence in the choice of a linguistic variant. *Word* **14**, 47–56. Reprinted in Hymes, D. editor, 1964: *Language in Culture and Society* (New York: Harper & Row) 483–8.

FISHMAN, J.A. 1972: *The sociology of language*. Rowley, Mass: Newbury House.

GILES, H. and POWESLAND P., 1975: *Speech style and social evaluation*. New York: Academic Press.

GREGORY, M. 1967: Aspects of varieties differentiation. *Journal of Linguistics* **3**, 177–98.

GREGORY, M. and CARROLL S., 1978: *Language and situation, Language varieties and their social contexts*. London: Routledge & Kegan Paul.

GUMPERZ, J.J. 1982: *Discourse strategies*. London: Cambridge University Press.

HALLIDAY, M.A.K. 1975: Language as social semiotic: towards a general sociolinguistic theory. In Makkai, A. and Makkai V., editors, *The first lacus forum* (Columbia, SC: Hornbeam Press) 17–46.

HALLIDAY, M.A.K., McINTOSH, A. and STREVENS, P. 1964: *The linguistic sciences and language teaching*. London: Longman.

HALLIDAY, M.A.K. and HASAN, R. 1976: *Cohesion in English*. London: Longman.

HUDSON, R.A. 1980: *Sociolinguistics*. London: Cambridge University Press.

HYMES, D. 1964: Introduction: towards ethnographies of communication. In Gumperz, J.J. and Hymes, D., editors, *The ethnography of communication, American Anthropologist* 66 (6), part II, 1–34.

—— 1967: Models of the interaction of language and social setting. *Journal of Social Issues* 23, 8–28.

—— 1972: Communicative competence. In Pride. J. and Holmes J. editors, *Sociolinguistics* (Harmondsworth: Penguin.) 269–93.

JOOS, M. 1961: *The five clocks*. New York: Harcourt Brace Jovanovich.

LABOV, W. 1966: *The social stratification of English in New York City*. Washington, DC: Center for Applied Linguistics.

—— 1972: *Sociolinguistic patterns*. Philadelphia: University of Pennsylvania Press.

MILLER, G.R. and STEINBERG, M. 1975: *Between people: A new analysis of interpersonal communication*. Chicago: Science Research Associates.

OWSLEY, H. and SCOTTON, C.M. 1981: What's my line? Conversational expression of power by television interviewers. Paper presented, Linguistic Society of American Annual Meeting.

—— In press: The conversational expression of power by television interviewers. *Journal of Social Psychology*.

QUIRK, R., GREENBAUM, S., LEECH, G., and SVARTVIK, J, 1973: *A grammar of contempory English*. London: Longman.

REID, T.B.W. 1956: Linguistics, structuralism, philology. *Archivum Linguisticum* 8.

ROMAINE, S., editor, 1982: *Sociolinguistic variation in speech communities*. London: Edward Arnold.

SCOTTON, C.M. 1982: The possibility of code-switching: motivation for maintaining multilingualism. *Anthropological Linguistics* 24, 432–44.

—— 1983: The negotiation of identities in conversation: A theory of markedness and code choice. *International Journal of the Sociology of Language* 44, 115–36.

—— forthcoming: Code switching as indexical of social negotiations.

SPENCER, J. and GREGORY M. 1964: An approach to the study of style. In Enkvist, N. Spencer, J., and Gregory, M., editors, *Linguistics and style*, (London: Oxford University Press).

THIBAUT, J. and KELLEY, H.H., 1959: *The social psychology of groups*. New York: John Wiley.

TRUDGILL, P. 1972: Sex, covert prestige and linguistic change in the urban British English of Norwich. *Language in Society* 1, 179–96.
—— 1974: *The social differentiation of English in Norwich*. London: Cambridge University Press.

7
The sequential nature of language choice in cross-cultural communication[1]

Richard Y. Bourhis

Language plays a key role in the process of interpersonal and cross-cultural communication. Two important research traditions have emerged to account for the dynamic of language usage in cross-cultural communication. The sociolinguistic tradition has focused on how members of speech communities use contrasting registers, accents and languages to communicate 'appropriately' according to pre-established language norms and rules (Gumperz and Hymes 1972). The speech accommodation approach, first developed by Giles (1973), seeks to account for the dynamics of language usage by focusing on speaker's moods, motives, attitudes and group loyalties. These two approaches to language in social interaction will be briefly contrasted in the first two sections of this chapter. Section three presents a discussion of recent efforts designed to integrate the sociolinguistic and accommodation approaches within a common empirical framework which capitalizes on a sequential analysis of language choice in cross-cultural communication. The chapter concludes by proposing some novel conceptual and practical notions which could guide future research on the dynamic of language choice in multilingual settings.

The sociolinguistic approach

Sociolinguistics has long recognized that interest in language as a clue to understanding communication lies not just in an investigation of the literal meaning associated with the *verbal content* of messages, but also with the *style* in which messages are rendered (Gumperz and Hymes 1972; Fishman 1972). Sociolinguistics has developed the notion of speech repertoire to account for the fact that speakers often have more than one speech style at their disposal for communicative purposes. Speakers can adopt the formal or specialized register of their profession when at work (e.g. in the courtroom or hospital) and revert back to a more colloquial style when chatting with friends and family members at home. Similarly, bilingual speakers can switch language depending on the linguistic skills of their interlocutor, the topic of conversation or the role relationship they find themselves in. In sociolinguistics the use of two or more speech varieties in a conversation is known as code switching. Traditionally, sociolinguists have viewed code switching as being determined by normative demands related to the topic, setting and purpose of the conversation as well as

[1] I wish to acknowledge the fruitful discussions I have had with André de Palma concerning various aspects of this chapter.

by various characteristics of the interlocutors such as their age, role, linguistic competence, social class and ethnicity. The traditional sociolinguistic approach has usually 'explained' code-switching behaviour in terms of norms and rules which dictate how individuals should communicate with each other in specific situations and cultural settings.

Although it is reasonable to expect that much code switching can be attributed to social norms and rules, such behaviour may also occur in the 'absence of' or 'despite' the existence of social norms and rules. Indeed, one recent critique of the traditional sociolinguistice approach is that it tends to view speakers as 'sociolinguistic automatons' whose code-switching behaviour is completely determined by sociolinguistic rules and sociocultural norms. Bourhis (1979), Giles (1977) and Scotton (1983) have argued that the traditional sociolinguistic notions of rules and norms are not sufficient to account for the dynamics of speech behaviour in interpersonal and cross-cultural encounters.

Using a social psychological approach, Giles, Taylor and Bourhis (1973) developed a model of interpersonal speech accommodation which sought to account for code-switching behaviour by considering as central the speaker's motives, attitudes and group loyalties. Unlike the traditional sociolinguistic approach (Grice 1975) the interpersonal accommodation approach does not assume that interlocutors wish to communicate as effectively as possible in all circumstances. Furthermore, the accommodation approach does not assume that language rules and norms are sufficient to account for the dynamics of language usage in interpersonal communication. Instead the accommodation approach focuses on the *motivational* bases of code-switching behaviour in communication.

Speech accommodation theory

The notion of interpersonal accommodation first emerged from the observation that in conversations between people who have just met, there is a tendency for interlocutors to become more alike in their pronunciations (Giles 1973), vocal intensities (Natalé 1975), talk and silence patterns (Cappella and Planalp 1981), pause and utterance lengths (Jaffe and Feldstein 1970) speech rates (Webb 1972), etc. In many of these cases it was found that speakers were not necessarily aware of the fact that they were modifying aspects of their speech behaviour to match that of their interlocutor. According to Speech Accommodation Theory (SAT) the above phenomenon known as *speech convergence* can reflect speaker's conscious or unconscious need for social approval from others. Notions from similarity attraction (Byrne 1969), social exchange (Homan 1961), causal attribution (Kelly 1973) and cognitive uncertainty (Berger and Calabrese 1975) have been used to account for the phenomenon of speech convergence in numerous types of interpersonal (Street and Giles 1982) and cross-cultural encounters (Giles, Bourhis and Taylor 1977). However, empirically it seems that the above formulations have been most successful in accounting for code switching occurring during cross-cultural encounters and it is for this reason that much of this chapter will be devoted to cross-cultural aspects of accommodation theory. Let us begin by examining the role of some of the above social psychological processes in accounting for the phenomenon of speech convergence in cross-cultural communication.

Basically, Similarity Attraction theory (Byrne 1969) suggests that the more similar our attitudes and beliefs are to certain in-group or out-group others, the more likely we will be attracted to them. Through speech convergence, linguistic dissimilarities between two speakers can be attenuated. Thus, increased inter-personal similarity on a linguistic dimension can increase mutual liking (Giles *et al.* 1973), intelligibility (Triandis 1960) and predictability (Berger and Calabrese 1975). Language, dialect or accent convergence may be an efficient strategy for facilitating inter-ethnic encounters where linguistic dissimilarities may other-wise be an important stumbling block for effective cross-cultural communica-tion and ethnic harmony (Bourhis 1979). This was demonstrated in study carried out in Montreal by Giles *et al.* (1973). In this study it was found that bilingual Quebec Anglophone (QA) students perceived Quebec Francophone (QF) bilinguals more favourably when the latter converged to English than when they maintained French. Moreover, the QA students were more likely to communicate in *French* with the QF interlocutor if the latter had previously converged to *English* than if he had maintained his communication only in French. Since both the QA and QF communicated in each other's weaker lan-guage (the QA used French while the QF used English), this study showed that mutual language convergence could be used as a strategy to promote ethnic harmony even at the possible cost of communicative effectiveness.

Social Exchange theory, as formulated by Homans (1961), may also help account for the phenomenon of speech convergence. Most succinctly, Social Exchange theory proposes that before one engages in an action one weighs up its potential rewards and costs. Much research has shown that individuals have a tendency to engage in behaviours which reap rewards and avoid behaviours that result in negative or unpleasant outcomes. From this perspective one could expect speech convergence to occur only when it entails more potential rewards than costs. During inter-ethnic encounters rewards for converging to the out-group language could include being better perceived or accepted by the out-group interlocutor, while potential costs may include linguistic effort, the possible loss of in-group identity and possible rejection by in-group peers for having spoken in the out-group speech style. So far studies in a number of cultural settings have shown that in cross-cultural encounters people react more favourably to out-group speakers who converge towards them than to out-group speakers who do not (Bourhis and Giles 1976; Giles *et al.* 1973; Giles and Smith 1979; Harris and Baudin 1973).

In addition, studies in numerous cultural settings have shown that speakers who use prestigious accents, dialects or languages are more favourably perceived on dimensions of competence, self-confidence, and intelligence than speakers who use less prestigious, non-standard speech styles (Giles and Powesland 1975; Ryan and Giles 1982). Furthermore, messages voiced in a standard prestigious speech style are often perceived to be more persuasive, of better quality and more likely to elicit co-operation than messages voiced in a non-standard speech style (Bourhis and Giles 1976). Thus, still according to Social Exchange theory, one would expect some definite social rewards for switches to prestige speech styles and possible disadvantages for switches to less prestigious speech styles. Nevertheless, as will be seen later, convergence to a prestige speech style in the wrong cultural setting or situation may sometimes elicit negative responses (Genesee and Bourhis 1982).

Favourable reactions to speech convergence may also depend on how the intent of the convergence is attributed. Results of studies on Causal Attribution theory (Heider 1958; Kelly 1973) have shown that people attribute others' behaviour not only in terms of their immediate outcome but also by considering th actor's effort, abilities, intentions and the influence of external circumstances. Similar processes may influence the perception of a convergent speech act especially in cross-cultural encounters (Jaspars and Hewstone 1982). For example, a study by Simard *et al*. (1976) in Quebec has shown that when Quebec francophone (QF) listeners attributed Quebec Anglophone (QA) convergence to French as being due to a genuine desire to communicate, convergence was perceived very positively. However when convergence to French was perceived as the product of external pressures in the situation, QFs' reactions to the switch were not as favourable. Thus, evaluative and behavioural reactions to speech convergence in cross-cultural encounters may depend on how the intent of this strategy is attributed by the interlocutors.

However, anecdotal evidence and empirical evidence has also shown that not all encounters favour speech convergence. A speaker may choose to dissociate himself from his interlocutor by deliberately maintaining or using a speech style that differs from that of his interlocutor. Such strategies are most evident in encounters between speakers of contrasting ethnolinguistic groups whose accent, dialect or language serve as important cues to group membership. These linguistic strategies are known as *speech maintenance* and *speech divergence* and may be used by speakers because they personally dislike their interlocutor or because they wish to maintain or assert their group identity (Bourhis 1979). In the case of inter-ethnic encounters, consideration of Tajfel's social identity theory (Tajfel 1978, 1981, 1982) suggests that one can expect speech maintenance and speech divergence to be more frequently occurring speech strategies than one could account for strictly on the basis of the social psychological theories examined so far (Giles *et al*. 1977). Tajfels' research (1981) has shown that the mere act of categorizing individuals as in-group and out-group members is sufficient to trigger in-group favouritism responses whereby individuals favour members of their own group over out-groups. Furthermore, laboratory work using the minimal group paradigm (Tajfel 1978) has repeatedly shown that group members consistently choose to sacrifice absolute in-group profit for the sake of accentuating in their favour differentials between their own group and salient out-groups. On the basis of such results obtained in both laboratory and field studies Tajfel proposed that group members do strive to maintain and assert their positive social identity when in the presence of salient out-group others.

In cross-cultural encounters, Tajfel's theory suggest that speakers who value their group membership highly would have a strong desire to make themselves distinctive on a valued dimension *vis-à-vis* salient out-groups. Since a speaker's language, dialect or accent can be an important and valued dimension of ethnic identity, one could expect speech divergence and sometimes speech maintenance to be important strategies for asserting positive group distinctiveness during inter-ethnic encounters (Giles *et al*. 1977). This has been found to be the case in studies carried out in different cultural settings including Wales, Belgium and Quebec. In Wales, a study by Bourhis and Giles (1977) conducted in a language-laboratory setting showed that Welsh subjects who valued their national language and group membership highly diverged linguistically by accentuating their Welsh accent in their English when responding to a threatening English out-group interlocutor. In contrast, Welsh respondents who did not value their group membership as highly were found to converge to the out-group interlocutor in these circumstances.

Language maintenance was demonstrated in a series of Quebec field studies (Bourhis 1984a) in which it was found that overall, 30 per cent of the Quebec Anglophone (QA) pedestrians sampled in the study maintained English in their responses to a plea for directions voiced in French by a Quebec Francophone (QF) interlocutor. These language-maintenance responses were obtained even though the QA respondents had sufficient linguistic skills to utter a few words of French in their replies to the QF interlocutor. There were indications from these respondents' behaviours that indeed, English language maintenance was being used by QAs as a dissociative response aimed against the QF interlocutor.

More dramatically, the strategy of language divergence was demonstrated in a language-laboratory study carried out in Belgium (Bourhis *et al.* 1979). In this study, trilingual Flemish informants responded to a series of neutral and threatening questions voiced by a Francophone out-group speaker. In the initial speaker turns of the dialogues it was found that Flemish informants converged to English in response to emotionally neutral questions voiced in English by the Francophone confederate. In the next sequence of speaker turns the Francophone confederate provoked the Flemish respondents by asking in English ethnically threatening questions concerning the disadvantages of the Flemish language relative to French as a medium of international communication in Brussels. In this threatening situation all Flemish respondents not only disagreed with the verbal content of the Francophone confederate's statements but a third of the Flemish respondents also symbolized their disagreement through language divergence by voicing their reply in Flemish rather than in the ethnically neutral English language. In the third sequence of speaker turns the Francophone confederate emphasized his position regarding the superiority of French over Flemish by voicing his message in the French language (divergence) rather than in the ethnically neutral English language. It is under these circumstances that the majority of the Flemish respondents not only vehemently disagreed with their interlocutor's statements but voiced their counter-arguments by diverging from their interlocutor through the use of the Flemish language.

Results from respondents' self-reports of how they felt during different phases of the dialogue confirmed that language divergence is a linguistic strategy that can be used to assert in-group identity and out-group rejection during threatening inter-ethnic encounters. Indeed, Flemish respondents disagreed with the Francophone confederate more, were less prepared to help him and considered him more provocative and insulting as the dialogue sequence moved from the neutral phase to the two ethnically threatening parts of the conversation. In addition, the Flemish respondents felt that the fact that their interlocutor was an out-group Francophone interlocutor affected them more in the two threat phases than in the neutral phase of the dialogue. Finally the respondents felt like emphasizing their Flemish group identity more in the two threatening phases of the dialogue than in the neutral phase of the conversation (Bourhis *et al.* 1979).

An important point of this research is that speakers will adopt different language-switching strategies within the same conversation depending on how they feel towards their interlocutor from one speaker turn to the next, and depending on each of the language strategies adopted by their interlocutor during the conversation. In addition to showing that language divergence can be used as a strategy of ethnic dissociation from threatening outgroups this study also shows that divergence can take on many forms. The Flemish respondents not only diverged linguistically by switching from English to Flemish but also displayed content differentiation by vehemently disagreeing with the verbal content of the Francophone's statements and by making disparaging remarks in Flemish against the Francophone interlocutor while the latter was still formulating his questions (Bourhis *et al*. 1979).

These and other results suggest that convergence, maintenance and divergence may be expressed through more than one channel of communication at the same time including paralinguistic aspects of speech (e.g. pitch, speech rate, talk/silence), verbal aspects of speech (e.g. syntax, lexicon and content) and speech sytles (e.g. accent, dialect and language). Furthermore, contrasting strategies may occur simultaneously in the same utterance but in different aspects of speech reflecting both conscious and less conscious motivations speakers may have towards each other (Bourhis and Giles 1977). Indeed, a speaker may feel obliged to defer to a high-status interlocutor by using a certain form of address due to powerful social norms, but may betray or symbolize his dislike of the interlocutor by diverging on speech style or paralinguistic aspects of speech. Such discrepancies may reflect important shifts in the mood of cross-cultural encounters between speakers of rival ethnolinguistic groups or in strictly inter-individual terms may betray subtle changes in the psychological climate of interpersonal encounters.

Convergence, divergence and maintenance may be used more consciously in some channels of communication than others. For instance, speech divergence occuring in the form of an actual language switch would be a more overt, conscious and potent form of disassociation than if it occured on more subtle aspects of speech such as pitch, intonation pattern or talk duration. As regards cross-cultural encounters, language switching may indeed be the most obvious and dramatic channel of communication on which code switching can occur. Relative to switches occurring in other channels of communication language switches are perhaps the easiest ones to monitor by naive perceivers and as such offer an ideal medium in which to investigate further the dynamics of speech usage in social interaction. Furthermore, though accommodation theory evolved as an attempt to account for the dynamics of language switching in the *initial* phases of social encounters it seems timely to explore the usefulness of this approach in accounting for language-switching strategies that evolve in the course of longer, more sustained dialogue sequences. As such the study of the dynamics of language switching during both initial and sustained inter-ethnic encounters offers an *ideal* opportunity to investigate basic issues related to the sequential nature of speech.

Towards an integrative approach

So far in the empirical literature, the dynamics of language usage in cross-cultural communication has been studied mainly from *only* one of the above two perspectives at a time. By focusing on social norms and rules the traditional sociolinguistic approach has tended to downplay or ignore the importance of social psychological factors such as interlocutor's motives, beliefs and perceptions. In turn, most of the empirical work using the social psychological approach has only studied language strategies in settings which lacked clear situational or socio-cultural norms which could interact with the process of interpersonal accommodation (Giles *et al*. 1973; Bourhis *et al*. 1979; Bourhis 1984a). What is needed now is an approach which could take into consideration not only the existence of social norms and rules but also account for how speakers perceive and internalize these norms depending on their psychological needs, motivations and beliefs (Bourhis 1979). An integration of the accommodation and sociolinguistic approach would need to account for how sociolinguistic norms and rules are obeyed or broken depending on how they interact with speaker's motives, feelings and attitudes in the course of conversations. For instance, in a cross-cultural encounter, a speaker may converge not only because he personally likes his interlocutor but also because he believes he *should* by virtue of his role positions, and also because as a subordinate-group member in this particular cultural setting, he should converge towards dominant-group speakers.

Although a first attempt has been made to integrate at a theoretical level aspects of the sociolinguistic and interpersonal accommodation approaches (Bourhis 1979) the tenability of adopting such an integrated view at the empirical level has only just begun in a study by Genesee and Bourhis (1982). Interestingly enough, the results obtained by Genesee and Bourhis (1982) suggest that a *sequential analysis* of language-switching strategies in cross-cultural encounters may be an ideal approach to better elucidate the relative role of language norms and motivational factors in determining language usage in social interaction. Since the study by Genesee and Bourhis (1982) represents a first attempt to integrate the sociolinguistic approach with the interpersonal accommodation approach within a common empirical framework it is worthwhile to discuss in some detail the results obtained in this research.

Genesee and Bourhis (1982) employed the segmented dialogue technique developed by Bourhis *et al*. (1975). In this procedure listeners must rate the personality of two speakers engaged in a dialogue heard on a tape recording. This experimental procedure is very much akin to the real-life situation in which we overhear a conversation between two speakers in a store or restaurant and cannot help but form an impression of these speakers based on what they say, how they speak, and which language they use. The conversational setting chosen for this study was that of a client/clerk encounter in a downtown Montreal retail shop.

The traditional residential, social and economic segregation of Quebec Francophones (QFs) and Quebec Anglophones (QAs) in Montreal has meant that client/clerk encounters in downtown Montreal are perhaps the most likely casual setting in which QFs and QAs have a chance to interact in everyday life. Montreal client/clerk encounters are also interesting because a language law known as Bill 101 not only asserts that French is the only official language of Quebec but also stipulates that all Quebec consumers of goods and services have a right to be informed and served in the French language (Bourhis 1984b; 1984c).

In the present research QF and QA listeners were asked to form their impressions of a QF and QA speaker heard on tape in the role of a client or clerk in a Montreal retail store. In study 1A a *QF* salesman was portrayed serving a *QA* customer while in study 2A a *QA* salesman was portrayed serving a *QF* customer. The verbal content of the dialogues in these first two studies was always the same. Each dialogue sequence consisted of three speaker turns: Turn 1 = salesman speaks; Turn 2 = customer speaks; Turn 3 = salesman speaks. In each dialogue the salesman began the conversation in his native language, but subsequent replies by the customer and salesman were systematically varied in different combinations of French and English language switches reflecting common patterns of language choices heard in downtown Montreal stores.

It was expected that the listeners' reactions to the French/English language choices in the client/clerk encounters portrayed in the scenarios would depend on a complex interaction of four factors. These four factors are situational language norms, language status, interpersonal accommodation and in-group favouritism. The following are competing expectations based on each of these factors.

In public business transactions the *situational norm* which states that the 'customer is always right' suggests that whereas a customer is free to choose whichever language he/she prefers, the salesman is expected to adapt to the customer's language. Indeed survey studies in Montreal (Bourhis 1983) have shown that QF and QA respondents expect salespersons to use English with QA customers and French with QF customers. In line with this situational language norm it was expected that the customer depicted in the scenarios would be evaluated similarly whether he used English or French. Also in accordance with this situational language norm, it was expected that the salesman would be downgraded if he maintained use of his native language when replying to the customer. However it was expected that the salesman would not necessarily be upgraded for complying with the situational norm by replying in the customer's native language.

As regards the *language status* factor, it could be expected that both listener groups would evaluate the use of English more favourably than the use of French. This follows from the preferential status that English has traditionally enjoyed as the language of business and advancement in Quebec (d'Anglejan 1984). However the popularity of Bill 101 amongst QFs leads to the expectation that this group would favour the use of French over English in our scenarios (Bourhis 1984b). Furthermore, self-reports of increased French usage by QAs obtained in surveys by Bourhis (1983) suggests that QAs may also favour French usage in our scenarios.

Motivations in favour of *interpersonal accommodation* suggest that language convergence between the clerk and the client would be evaluated positively relative to maintenance or divergence regardless of whether the convergence was in favour of French or English. Alternatively, language maintenance by in-group speakers may be evaluated positively as an assertion of group pride and loyalty by both QF and QA listerners given that language issues have become so controversial in Quebec recently (Bourhis 1984b).

On the basis of the notion of *in-group favouritism* (Tajfel 1982), one could expect both QF and QA monolinguals not only to favour representative speakers of their own group but also to favour the use of their own-group language over that of the out-group language in the dialogues.

Additional details concerning the procedures used in Study 1A and Study 2A can now be provided. Both groups of QA and QF listeners were made up of senior high-school students attending their respective in-group language schools in Montreal. An average of 200 subjects participated in each of four studies: in each case 100 were QAs, 100 were QFs. Each listener group was equated for sex composition, age and socioeconomic background.

Study 1A consisted of four separate tape-recorded dialogues between the QF salesman and the QA client. The four language-switching sequences used in study 1A are represented in Table 7.1. These four sequences allowed us to investigate listeners' perceptions of a QA client who *maintained* English in response to a QF salesman (dialogues 1 and 2) in contrast to their perceptions of a QA client who *converged* to French with a QF salesman (dialogues 3 and 4). These dialogues also allowed an examination of listeners' perceptions of a QF who either *maintained* French in turn 3 (dialogues 1 and 3) or *converged* to English (dialogues 2 and 4) in response to a QA client who earlier had either maintained English or converged to French.

Table 7.1   Dialogue sequences in Study 1A

Speaker turns:	1	2	3
Speaker role:[1]	S	C	S
Speaker ethnicity:[2]	QF	QA	QF
Language use[3] in:			
dialogue 1:	F	E	F
dialogue 2:	F	E	E
dialogue 3:	F	F	F
dialogue 4:	F	F	E

[1]Speaker role: S = salesman, C = customer
[2]Speaker ethnicity: QF = Quebec Francophone, QA = Quebec Anglophone
[3]Language use: F = French, E = English

Four subgroups of QA listeners and QF listeners each heard *one* of the four dialogue tape recordings. Using a 9-point rating scale listeners rated their impressions of the client and clerk after they heard each actor speak in their turn. To control for voice quality the same two actors played the client/clerk roles in both studies. A native French-speaking Canadian male played the QF in both roles and a native English-speaking Canadian male played the QA in both roles. The two actors were competent in both languages and were chosen for their ability to play their roles realistically and comfortably thus producing plausible dialogues that were rendered in an amiable and calm tone of voice. The QF was always recognized as a QF even when he spoke English because he had a noticeable French accent when speaking English. Likewise the QA was recognized as such even when he spoke French since he had a noticeable English accent when speaking French. The questionnaire and procedures were carried out in the respondents' native language by experimenters of the listeners' own ethnic background. Since results from both studies are reported in detail in Genesee and Bourhis (1982), only the major findings obtained in each study will be discussed in this chapter.

How did the two groups of listeners rate the QF salesman when they first heard him in Turn 1 of study 1A? Results showed that QF listeners rated the QF salesman to be more considerate, kind and honest than did the Anglophone listeners. Conversely results showed that QA respondents rated the QA customer in Turn 2 to be more friendly, considerate and honest than did the QF listeners. Thus both QF and QA listeners displayed in-group favouritism by rating speakers of their own group more favourably than speakers of the out-group.

Was the QF salesman perceived differently depending on whether he maintained French or converged to English in his reply (Turn 3) to the QA customer? The two groups of listeners did downgrade the QF salesman when he violated the situational norm by maintaining French in his reply to the QA client. Indeed, the QF salesman was rated to be less considerate, friendly, kind, honest, competent and intelligent when he failed to switch to English in his reply to the Anglophone customer. These results were obtained regardless of the language used by the QA customer indicating, as the situational norm would imply, that 'the client is always right' and has the freedom to use the language of his choice in addressing the salesman. However, important differences in the reactions of the two listener groups towards violation of the situational norm did emerge in the results. Most noteworthy was the finding that the QA students were less tolerant of French maintenance by the QF clerk than were the QF students.

Finally, interpersonal accommodation played some part in the results since the two groups rated the QA client to feel more pleased and comfortable when his French or English language choice was matched by the salesman's language of reply than when it was not.

To sum up, while both Anglophone and Francophone students downgraded the salesman who violated the situational norm, QA students were more critical of this violation than were the QF students. The possibility remains that Anglophone students may have been using the situational norm to promote the use of English as an in-group favouritism response rather than in support of the situational norm *per se*. Study 2A was designed to explore this possibility by assigning the salesman role to the QA and the customer role to the QF. If in-group favouritism was the basis of the QA students' reactions, then one could expect this group to continue favouring English usage even when the roles are reversed with the situational norm now working in favour of French usage for the QF customer.

The four dialogues used in Study 2A between and QA salesman and the QF client were made up of the language-switching sequences depicted in Table 7.2. The procedures used to obtain listeners' evaluations of the dialogues in Study 2A were exactly the same as those used in Study 1A.

Unlike results obtained in Study 1A, QF and QA listeners did not rate speakers of their own group more favourably than out-group speakers. However, a strong preference in favour of English usage was evident from the Anglophone group who rated the QF client more favourably when he converged to English than when he maintained French. These results were obtained even though as a client the QF had the freedom of choice to use either French or English, as had been the case for the QA client in study 1A and for whom language choices had no such evaluative consequences. These results suggest that

Table 7.2   Dialogue sequences in Study 2A

Speaker turns:	1	2	3
Speaker role:[1]	S	C	S
Speaker ethnicity:[2]	QA	QF	QA
Language use[3] in:			
dialogue 1:	E	F	E
dialogue 2:	E	F	F
dialogue 3:	E	E	E
dialogue 4:	E	E	F

[1]Speaker role: S = salesman, C = customer
[2]Speaker ethnicity: QF = Quebec Francophone, QA = Quebec Anglophone
[3]Language use: F = French, E = English

rather than responding to the situational norm *per se*, QA listeners were displaying in-group favouritism by being biased in favour of English rather than French usage in the dialogues. In contrast, QFs did rate the client equally regardless of his language choices in both studies, whether the client was depicted as a QF or as a QA.

As in Study 1A, violation of the situational norm was downgraded by listeners in Study 2A. The QA salesman was downgraded equally by the two groups of students when he failed to converge to the native language of the client by maintaining English. However the two groups of listeners did rate the QA salesman more favourably when he converged to French with the QF client. It seems that as a member of the traditionally high-status group the QA salesman was rewarded for converging linguistically to the traditionally low-status QF interlocutor. In Study 1A no such rewards accrued for the traditionally low-status QF salesman converging to the language of the traditionally high-status QA client. These patterns of results clearly show that the traditional status disparity between the English and French language in Quebec did have an impact on listeners' reactions to the dialogues (Bourhis 1984b). Finally, the two groups showed their awareness of the situational norm in favour of the QF client since they rated the QF client to be more pleased and comfortable when the QA clerk converged to French than when he maintained English.

In summary, as hypothesized, the listener's evaluations of the dialogue sequence did depend on a dynamic interaction of factors including situational norms, language status, interpersonal accommodation and in-group favouritism. An investigation of this dynamic interaction would have been impossible without adopting a sequential analysis of conversational flow. Listeners' evaluations of the dialogue speakers were most influenced by normative expectations since in both studies the salesman was downgraded for violating the situational norm. These results suggested that in a tense intergroup setting such as Montreal, closely adhering to the situational norm was perhaps the safest way of conducting a potentially conflictual cross-cultural encounter between members of traditionally rival ethnolinguistic groups.

Though adhering to the situational norm may be the safest strategy to adopt at the onset of potentially hostile inter-ethnic encounters, speakers may adopt non-normative language strategies later on in the conversation depending on their affective reactions to the interlocutor, the goals they have for the future

progress of the conversation, and depending on whether or not speakers wish to
assert their group identity in the inter-ethnic encounter. It is also reasonable to
expect that language choices made in the first few speaker turns of a conversation
will have an impact on the evaluation of language choices adopted in subsequent speaker turns of a cross-cultural encounter.

As an initial attempt to explore the above issues, evaluative reactions to four
speaker turns rather than three were investigated in part B of each of the above
two studies (Genesee and Bourhis 1982). The procedures and types of subjects
used in Studies 1B and 2B were exactly the same as those used in Studies 1A and
2A. However, the extension of the stimulus dialogues to four speaker turns
allowed an investigation of evaluation reactions to the *customer's* language
choices across *two* speaker turns rather than just one as was the case in Studies
1A and 2A. Table 7.3 describes the language strategies adopted by the QA
customer in Study 1B.

Table 7.3 Dialogue sequences in Study 1B

Speaker turns:	1	2	3	4
Speaker role:[1]	S	C	S	C
Speaker ethnicity:[2]	QF	QA	QF	QA
Language use[3] in:				
dialogue 1:	F	E	F	E
dialogue 2:	F	E	F	F
dialogue 3:	F	F	E	E
dialogue 4:	F	F	E	F

[1]Speaker role: S = salesman, C = customer
[2]Speaker ethnicity: QF = Quebec Francophone, QA = Quebec Anglophone
[3]Language use: F = French, E = English

These four dialogues allowed us to examine change in evaluative reactions to
a QA customer who in Turn 4 *maintained* English compared to a QA customer
who *converged* to French following either mutual language *maintenance* by
both customer and salesman in Turns 2 and 3 (dialogues 1 and 2) or following
mutual language *convergence* in Turn 2 and 3 (dialogues 3 and 4). Only the
evaluative reactions to the customer's language choices need be discussed here.

How did the two groups of listeners rate the customer's language choices
in Turn 4 following either mutual maintenance or mutual convergence in the
preceding speaker turns? Results showed that following mutual language
convergence (dialogues 3 and 4), perceptions of the QA customer did not
change in Turn 4 regardless of whether the customer used English or French.
Do such results simply reflect the power of the situational norm which grants
the customer freedom of choice since the 'customer is always right'? Results
from dialogues 1 and 2 suggest that this was not the case. Instead, results
support predictions based on interpersonal accommodation since after mutual
language maintenance, the customer's language choice in Turn 4 did have an
impact on the listener's perceptions of him. Following mutual language maintenance in dialogues 1 and 2, the two groups of listeners perceived the QA
customer to be significantly more considerate, more kind and more friendly
when he *converged* to French in Turn 4 (dialogue 2), but significantly less con-

siderate, less kind and less friendly when he *maintained* English (dialogue 1).

The aim of Study 2B was to determine if the above patterns of results would hold up in scenarios where the customer was depicted as a traditionally low-status QF rather than as a high-status QA. Table 7.4 summarizes the four dialogues created in Study 2B.

Table 7.4 Dialogue sequences in Study 2B

Speaker turns:	1	2	3	4
Speaker role:[1]	S	C	S	C
Speaker ethnicity:[2]	QA	QF	QA	QF
Language use[3] in:				
dialogue 1:	E	F	E	F
dialogue 2:	E	F	E	E
dialogue 3:	E	E	F	F
dialogue 4:	E	E	F	E

[1]Speaker role: S = salesman, C = customer
[2]Speaker ethnicity: QF = Quebec Francophone, QA = Quebec Anglophone
[3]Language use: F = French, E = English

Results obtained in Study 2B corroborated the findings obtained in Study 1B. Following mutual language convergence (dialogues 3 and 4), the customer's language choice in Turn 4 had little impact on the evaluative reactions of the listeners. The QF customer was perceived equally regardless of whether he spoke French or English in Turn 4.

However, the customer's language choice in Turn 4 did have an impact on listener's evaluations if it was preceded by mutual language maintenance in the previous speaker turns (ie. dialogues 1 and 2). Following mutual language maintenance the QF customer was rated unfavourably when he maintained French in Turn 4 while he was perceived more favourably when he converged to English. These results and others confirm that interpersonal accommodation rather than situational norms played the major role in determining listeners' responses to the dialogues by speaker Turn 4 of the conversation.

These results demonstrate that indeed language choices made in the first few speaker turns of a cross-cultural encounter can have a dramatic impact on the evaluation of language choices made in subsequent speaker turns of a conversation. When both interlocutors maintained their respective in-group language at the onset of the cross-cultural encounter, the subsequent language choices of the customer in Turn 4 did become evaluatively quite costly. This occurred despite the situational norm working in favour of freedom of language choice for the customer. In contrast, when speakers showed their 'good will' and 'respect' through mutual language convergence early in the conversation (turns 1 to 3), subsequent language choices (Turn 4) seemed emptied of their divisive ideological content and had little impact on listeners' evaluations.

However, the above point is mitigated by another important finding obtained in Study 2B. Regardless of previous language choices at the onset of the dialogue, results also showed that Anglophone listeners seemed biased in favour of English usage *per se* since they rated the QF customer more favourably after Turn 4 when he converged to English. QF listeners also seemed biased in favour of in-group language usage since they rated the QF customers more favourably when he maintained French in Turn 4 while they downgraded the QF customer when he converged to English. In this latter case it appears that the QF customer was perceived as somewhat of a cultural traitor for failing to maintain French in his response to the QA salesman. Conversely, the QF customer was rewarded evaluatively by his QF peers for showing in-group loyalty by maintaining French in his reply to the QA salesman in Turn 4. In both these cases, the results show that individual language choices can reflect intergroup processes in which language serves both as an important badge of group identity and as a tool to symbolize ethnic group loyalty during inter-ethnic encounters (Bourhis 1977).

Taken together, the results of both studies in Montreal have shown that listener's evaluation of the dialogues depended upon a complex and dynamic interaction of factors including situational norms, language status, in-group favouritism and interpersonal accommodation. The most important finding in this research is that the basis of evaluation of the speaker's language choices did shift in the course of the conversation. Whereas the speaker's language choices were evaluated mostly in terms of situational norms in the initial phases of the conversation, subsequent language choices in Turn 4 were rated more in terms of interpersonal accommodation. In a bilingual setting characterized by inter-group conflict such as Montreal, closely adhering to situational norms at the onset of inter-ethnic encounters is a safe way of conducting potentially tense conversation with an out-group speaker (Bourhis 1984b).

Though cross-cultural encounters that proceed exactly according to situational language norms may feel securizing to the interlocutors, such an outcome may leave interactants in the dark about the real attitudes and motives of the individual speakers concerned. Later on in the conversation both speakers may seek more personal information about the interlocutors. One might therefore expect interpretation of the interaction to shift from an emphasis on adherence to situational norms to include non-normative language behaviour which is likely to yield more information about the true attitudes and intentions of the interlocutors. Results from the present study showed that indeed such a shift in emphasis was perceived by our listeners especially by speaker Turn 4 of our dialogue.

Results also revealed that the impact of *not* adhering to the situational language norm did depend upon language choices that occurred in the preceding speaker turns. As Genesee and Bourhis (1982) pointed out: 'Early use of inter-personal language convergence, although perhaps communicatively ineffective since one or both interlocutors is using his/her weaker language, is likely to be beneficial in the long run because it signals interpersonal liking or cooperation and, thereby neutralizes the intergroup implications of subsequent language choices' (p. 24).

Thus, non-normative language convergence can turn a potentially conflictual inter-ethnic encounter into a harmonious encounter defined mostly in inter-individual terms. In contrast, though early use of language maintenance seems communicatively effective since both interlocutors use their native language, it remains that in our studies this strategy was seen as socially ineffective since it violated the situational norm and was seen to signal a mixture of mutual dislike and the assertion of ethnic group distinctiveness. Indeed, dissociative language choices that clash with situational norms early in an encounter can serve as

powerful signals that one or both interlocutors wishes to redefine the status/
power position associated with each other's role and status. As postulated by
Bourhis (1979) language maintenance can also have a long-term negative social
impact since it enhances the intergroup significance of subsequent language
choices thus creating a linguistic duel fought through each language choice of
the conversation. However it remains that mutual language maintenance at the
onset of inter-ethnic encounters may have the advantage of immediately
situating the position of each speaker on the social map thus setting the stage for
a more candid inter-ethnic exchange. Indeed, during an inter-ethnic encounter
speakers may first diverge linguistically to assert their group identity but later
switch to a common language which is perceived to maximize communicative
effectiveness.

A framework for future research

The above findings could not have been obtained without adopting a *sequential
analysis* of language choices in cross-cultural communication. The segmented
dialogue technique (Bourhis *et al.* 1975) is an ideal tool to study evaluative
reactions to virtually any permutation of language-switching strategies of theoretical interest. The segmented dialogue technique also allows a detailed investigation of evaluative reactions to language choices at each speaker turn of a
conversation. Though the present study examined reactions to dialogue
sequences of up to four speaker turns, future studies could be designed to
investigate dialogue sequences of five, six or perhaps eight speaker turns. In
addition, the technique is flexible enough to allow the study of language-
switching sequences which may be quite rare in field settings but which are
interesting theoretically. Since the status, roles and ethnicity of the stimulus
interlocutors can be varied at will, evaluative reactions to the same language-
switching sequences can be explored systematically depending on the characteristics of the stimulus interlocutors and on the cultural setting in which the
dialogues are depicted.

   While the present findings provided useful clues concerning evaluative reactions to language-switching strategies, one cannot presume that our conclusions
could directly account for the motivational bases of actual language usage in
real-life face-to-face encounters. Field observation studies along with field
experiments such as those already carried out in Belgium (Bourhis *et al.* 1979),
Wales (Bourhis and Giles 1977) and Quebec (Bourhis 1984a) should be designed
to test the hypotheses generated from the segmented dialogue studies conducted
so far. Field observation studies monitoring language choices across longer
strings of speaker turns than those discussed so far could yield data of the type
presented in Table 7.5.

   For the sake of continuity, the hypothetical data presented in Table 7.5 refer
to a Montreal salesman/client encounter in which the salesman is depicted as a
QF while the client is depicted as a QA. These data could be generated by recording spontaneously occurring salesman/client dialogues in numerous retail
stores situated in a bilingual city such as Montreal. A minimum number of
speaker turns could be recorded for each dialogue sample in this sort of study.
By clearly specifying the setting, role, ethnicity and status of each interlocutor
involved in the dialogue sequence, the present approach has the advantage of

Table 7.5   Hypothetical lauguage use sequences in Montreal client/clerk encounters.

Speaker turns	1	2	3	4	5	6	7	8	9	10	11
Speaker role[1]	S	C	S	C	S	C	S	C	S	C	S
Speaker ethnicity[2]	QF	QA	QF	QA	QF	QA	QF	QA	QF	QA	QF
Language use[3] in:											
Example 1	F	E	E	E	E	E	E	E	E	E	E
Example 2	F	F	E	F	E	F	E	F	E	F	E
Example 3	F	E	E	F	F	E	E	F	F	E	E
Example 4	F	F	E	E	F	E	F	E	F	E	F
Example 5	F	E	F	E	F	E	F	E	F	E	F

[1]Speaker role: S = salesman, C = customer
[2]Speaker ethnicity: QF = Quebec Francophone; QA = Quebec Anglophone
[3]Language use: F = French; E = English

forcing the researcher to analyse language switching from both a *normative* and *motivational* perspectives at the same time.

How could the sequence of language choices presented in each example of Table 7.5 be conveniently summarized? On first inspection Example 1 represents an instance in which English clearly emerged as the dominant language of use while Example 5 represents a case in which the final total use of French and English competed to a 50–50 draw. Labelling language choices in terms of convergence, maintenance and divergence beyond the initial speaker turns of an encounter such as those depicted in Table 7.5 can lead to confusion even if we assume perfectly sequential turn taking on the part of the interlocutors. A more convenient way of summarizing the language choices made by each interlocutor of this and other speaker turn sequences would be to adopt the following nomenclature of language strategies.

Language strategy A ---- match in out-group language
Language strategy B ---- match in in-group language
Language strategy C ---- mismatch in out-group language
Language strategy D ---- mismatch in in-group language

The first important premise of this nomenclature is that each speaker's language choices are strongly influenced by the previous language choices of their interlocutor (cf. Bourhis *et al*. 1979; Bourhis and Giles, 1977; Giles *et al*. 1973). The second important premise of this approach is that speakers' language choices are also strongly influenced by their knowledge of their interlocutor's native language (Bourhis 1979). Arguably the above nomenclature has some heuristic value since it clearly differentiates between language choices that match the interlocutors' *native* language from those which match the interlocutor's immediately *preceding* language choice.

A strong case of convergence is represented by Strategy A in which the speaker not only matches his interlocutor's previous language choice but also does so by adopting his interlocutor's native language. Strategy B refers to a situation in which the speaker converges by matching his interlocutor's previous language choice but does so by maintaining his own native language. Strategy C represents a situation in which a speaker mismatches his interlocutor's previous language choice but nevertheless does so by adopting his interlocutor's native language. Strategy D represents a case in which a speaker diverges not only by mismatching his interlocutors' previous language choice but does so by maintaining his own-group native language. These four strategies can be pictured as forming a language accommodation continuum with Strategy A at one pole being most clearly identified as a liking or associative response while Strategy D at the opposite pole can be identified as the most psychologically dissociative of the strategies. Strategies B and C can be pictured as occupying an intermediary position on this continuum. The motivational and communicative impact of each of these strategies can be best assessed when understood in the context of the language-switching sequence in which they are embedded. We can now turn our attention to each of these strategies by considering the language-switching sequences presented in Table 7.5.

The percentage score of each language strategy adopted by each speaker in the 5 examples enumerated in Table 7.5 is presented in Table 7.5. The summary scores presented in Table 7.5 should be consulted when attending to the discussion of the hypothetical languages sequences depicted in Table 7.6.

The behaviour of the QF salesman in Example 1 of Table 7.6 can be summarized by stating that in five out of his five possible speaker turns, the QF adopted type A language strategy (100 per cent). In this sequence we can see that the salesman systematically converged to both the native language of his interlocutor and to his previous language choices. This strong form of convergence may indicate that the salesman not only acknowledges the language rights of his interlocutor as a client but also likes his interlocutor as an individual.

In contrast we find that the QA speaker adopted type B strategy (80 per cent) in four of the possible speaker turns available to him. Perhaps by virtue of his client role and the traditional prestige of English in Montreal, a QA customer could afford to adopt a very consistent strategy of English language maintenance with QF salesmen. Indeed numerous studies have shown that in Montreal, traditional language-switching norms have meant that whereas QAs have usually maintained English while interacting with QFs, the latter have usually had to switch to English while interacting with QA interlocutors (Bourhis 1983). However, recent field studies conducted with pedestrians in Downtown Montreal (Bourhis 1984b) have shown that these trends are changing in favour of French usage, though results also showed that some QAs maintained English with QFs not because they lacked the linguistic skills to use French but because they wished to dissociate themselves ethnically from QF interlocutors.

Example 2 in Table 7.5 represents another interesting configuration of possible language choices in Montreal client/clerk encounters. In this case we find the QF salesman adopting Strategy C in 100 per cent of the speaker turns available to him while the QA client adopted Strategy C in 80 per cent of his turns. This mutual use of Strategy C indicates that both speakers are converging to their interlocutor's *native language* while systematically mismatching each other's previous language choices. While the language choice of the QF salesman could be viewed as being determined by the situational language norm, the same norm granted the client freedom of language choice. By converging to their interlocutor's native language these speakers are making a sustained effort in favour of the out-group language, perhaps as an attempt to prove their mutual respect and liking as contrasting group members. Indeed, Giles *et al.* (1973)

Table 7.6 Summary scores for language strategies depicted in Table 7.5

	Language strategies[1] used by QF salesmen				Language strategies used by QA clients			
	A	B	C	D	A	B	C	D
Example 1	100%[2] (3,5,7,9,11)[3]					80% (4,6,8,10)	80% (4,6,8,10)	20% (2)
Example 2			100% (3,5,7,9,11)		20% (2)			
Example 3	60% (3,7,11)	40% (5,9)					40% (4,8)	60% (6,8)
Example 4			20% (3)	80% (5,7,9,11)	20% (2)	20% (4)		60% (6,8,10)
Example 5				100% (3,5,7,9,11)				100% (2,4,6,8,10)
Average use in % of each strategy across 5 examples	32%	8%	24%	36%	8%	20%	24%	48%

[1] Language strategies: A = match in out-group language
B = match in in-group language
C = mismatch in out-group language
D = mismatch in in-group language

[2] Speaker Turn 1 is not included in the percentage score since in this case it is considered the baseline language choice which begins the conversational sequence. For the purpose of our discussion we assume that the salesman makes no attempt to guess the native language of his client from non-verbal cues and that this first language choice is evaluatively neutral. Of course there are real-life settings in which the language choice of a first speaker turn would not at all be evaluatively neutral.

[3] Numbers in parentheses refer to the speaker turn in which the particular language strategy was adopted.

obtained this pattern of mutual convergence in the three speaker turn sequences they monitored in their Montreal study with QA and QF bilingual undergraduate students. However, it remains that the mismatching of the interlocutor's previous language choices could be perceived as a dissociative strategy perhaps reflecting each speaker's view that their interlocutor's efforts in the second language are too pitiful to be worth acknowledging through language matching.

Example 3 provides an interesting case whereby one of the speakers in the conversation systematically matches all the previous language choices of his interlocutor. By adopting Strategy A in 3 speaker turns and Strategy B in 2 turns we find the QF salesman matching the previous language choice of his client in 100 per cent of his possible speaker turns. From this example, the situational language norm could be interpreted to mean that a salesman should match each preceding language choice of his client rather than simply converge to the native language of his interlocutor. Future empirical work should help determine under what circumstances matching all the previous language choices of one's interlocutor is a more 'associative' response than simply converging to the native language of one's interlocutor. Finally, the situational norm in favour of freedom of language choice for the client is evident when one considers that the QA could afford to mismatch his interlocutor's language choices in 100 per cent of the cases by adopting Strategy C twice and Strategy D three times.

The first four speaker turns of Example 4 represent the language choices presented in dialogue 3 of the Genesee and Bourhis (1982) Study 1B. Results from this study showed that the good will and respect conveyed through mutual language convergence in the first three speaker turns of the encounter neutralized the evaluative impact of subsequent language choices in Turn four. The language choices represented in Example 4 portray a situation in which mutual language convergence at the onset of the encounter is followed by mutual in-group language maintenance in all the subsequent speaker turns of the encounter. As can be seen in Table 7.5, both speakers began the conversation by converging toward their interlocutor's native language. The QA client did this first by adopting Strategy A, while the QF salesman immediately reciprocated by adopting Strategy C. However in the subsequent speaker turns we find both the QF and QA maintaining their respective in-group language (Strategies B and D) in 80 per cent of the remaining speaker turns. In other circumstances these latter strategies could symbolize an extreme form of ethnic dissociation but not in this case since speakers first expressed mutual 'respect' through mutual convergence at the onset of the dialogue. This language-switching sequence could gain increasing popularity with bilinguals in a setting such as Montreal since it allows speakers to communicate easily in their native language without triggering ethnic tensions harmful to communicative effectiveness.

Finally, Example 5 represents a case in which both speakers maintain their respective in-group language regardless of existing situational norms and the preceding language choice of their interlocutor. With both interlocutors adopting Strategy D in 100 per cent of the available speaker turns, one can expect ethnic dissociation to be at its maximum with communicative effectiveness being seriously hampered.

If Table 7.5 represented an actual corpus of data obtained from field observations of five actual client/clerk encounters, Table 7.6 could serve as the summary sheet for this data base. As can be seen in Table 7.6, one can calculate for each speaker role the average use of each strategy across the five client/clerk encounters surveyed in the hypothetical study. The actual final scores obtained for each language strategy presented in Table 7.6 are not useful to discuss here since they were based on hypothetical examples designed to illustrate the wide diversity of language-switching sequences likely to emerge in naturally occurring client/clerk encounters. However, given a representative data base, such scores could not only neatly summarize speaker's language strategies in such role relationships but could be used to determine the likelihood for any speaker in these roles to adopt each of these strategies in other client/clerk encounters. Of course as in Genesee and Bourhis (1982) it would be necessary to monitor the language strategies adopted when the speaker roles are reversed so that the salesman is a QA and the client is a QF. Taken together, total scores from each of these studies could reveal a great deal about how language norms and motivational factors combine to account for language choices in cross-cultural encounters.

To explore further the dynamics of language switching in cross-cultural communication, other types of role relationships could also be investigated such as employer/employee relations, high/low status relations and relations between equal-status peers. In addition to reflecting role-position differences, summary scores could also reveal ethnic differences in language-choice strategies across a broad range of role relationships. Such differences should reflect status and power differentials which exist between speakers of contrasting ethnolinguistic groups in different cultural settings. From such studies one could also build probability estimates of in-group/out-group language use given the speakers' role positions, ethnicity, motivations, as well as language norms and previous language use patterns in the conversation. Such baseline estimates could also be used to identify language-choice strategies which reflect personality and attitudinal characteristics of individual speakers.

Though an extension of the present framework seems most suited to an analysis of reciprocal and non-reciprocal use of terms of address and polite forms, other channels of communication including paralinguistics and verbal aspects of speech could also be explored using the present methodological and conceptual approach. The main aim of the present chapter has been to present a framework which could better account for how language norms and motivational factors combine to affect language choice in cross-cultural communication. We have seen that a sequential approach to language behaviour can contribute to a better understanding of the dynamics of language choice in multilingual settings from both the accommodation and sociolinguistic perspective. It is perhaps through a sequential analysis of language behaviour that the above two perspective may be best integrated within a common empirical and conceptual framework.

References

D'ANGLEJAN, A. 1984: Language planning in Quebec: An historical overview and future trends. In Bourhis R.Y., editor, *Conflict and language planning* in Quebec. (Clevedon, UK: Multilingual Matters).

BERGER, C.and CALABRESE, R. 1975: Some explorations in initial interactions and beyond. *Human Communication Research* 1, 99–112.

BOURHIS, R.Y. 1977: *The language of loyalty and treason*. Paper presented at the 34th International Communication Association Convention, Berlin.

—— 1979: Language in ethnic interaction: A social psychological approach. In Giles, H. and St Jacques, B., editors, *Language and ethnic relations* (Oxford: Pergamon Press).

—— 1983: Language attitudes and self-reports of French-English language usage in Quebec. *Journal of Multilingual and Multicultural Development* 4, 163–79.

—— 1984a: Cross-cultural communication in Montreal: Two field studies since Bill 101. *International Journal of the Sociology of Language* 46, 33–47.

—— 1984b:The charter of the French language and cross-cultural communication in Montreal. In Bourhis, R.Y., editor, *Conflict and language planning in Quebec* (Clevedon, UK: Multilingual Matters).

—— 1984c: Language policies in multilingual settings. In Bourhis, R.Y., editor, *Conflict and language planning in Quebec.* (Clevedon, UK: Multilingual Matters).

BOURHIS, R.Y. and GILES, H. 1976: The language of co-operation in Wales. *Language Sciences* 42, 13–16.

—— 1977: The language of intergroup distinctiveness. In Giles, H., editor, *Language, ethnicity and intergroup relations* (London: Academic Press).

BOURHIS, R.Y., GILES, H. and LAMBERT, W. 1975: Social consequences of accommodating one's style of speech: A cross-national investigation. *International Journal of the Sociology of Language* 6, 53–71.

BOURHIS, R.Y., GILES, H., LEYENS, J.-P. and TAJFEL, H. 1979: Psycholinguistic distinctiveness: Language divergence in Belgium. In Giles, H. and St Clair, R., editors, *Language and social psychology* (Oxford: Blackwell).

BYRNE, D. 1969: Attitudes and attraction. In Berkowitz, L., editor, *Advances in experimental social psychology* (New York: Academic Press).

CAPPELLA, J.N. and PLANALP, S. 1981: Talk and silence sequences in informal conversations III: Interspeaker influence. *Human Communication Research* 7, 117–32.

FISHMAN, J.A. 1972: *The sociology of language*. Rowley, Mass.: Newbury House.

GENESEE, R. and BOURHIS, R.Y. 1982: The social psychological significance of code switching in cross-cultural communication. *Journal of Language and Social Psychology* 1, 1–27.

GILES, H.1973: Accent mobility: A model and some data. *Anthropological Linguistic* 15, 87–105.

—— 1977: Social psychology and applied linguistics: Towards an integrative approach. *ITL Review of Applied Linguistics* 35, 27–42.

GILES, H., BOURHIS, R.Y. and TAYLOR, D. 1977: Towards a theory of language in ethnic group relations. In Giles, H., editor, *Language, ethnicity and intergroup relations* (London: Academic Press).

GILES, H. and POWESLAND, P. 1975: *Speech style and social evaluation*. London: Academic Press.

GILES, H. and SMITH, P. 1979: Accommodation theory: Optimal levels of convergence. In Giles, H. and St Clair, R., editors, *Language and social psychology* (Oxford: Blackwell).

GILES, H., TAYLOR, D. and BOURHIS, R.Y. 1973: Towards a theory of inter-personal accommodation through Language: Some Canadian data. *Language in Society* **2**, 177-92.

GRICE, H.P. 1975: Logic and conversation. In Cole, P. and Morgan, J., editors, *Syntax and semantics: Speech Acts* (New York: Academic Press).

GUMPERZ, J.J. and HYMES, D., editors, 1972: *Directions in sociolinguistics* New York: Holt, Rinehard and Winston.

HEIDER, P. 1958: *The psychology of interpersonal relations*. New York: Wiley.

HOMANS, G.C. 1961: *Social behaviour: Its elementary form* New York: Harcourt, Brace and World.

JAFFE, J. and FELDSTEIN, S. 1970: *Rhythms of dialogue* New York: Academic Press.

JASPARS, J. and HEWSTONE, M. 1982: Cross-cultural interaction, social attribution, and inter-Group relations. In Bochner, S., editor, *Cultures in contact* (Oxford: Pergamon Press).

KELLY, H.H. 1973: The process of causal attribution. *American Psychologist* **28**, 107-28.

NATALÉ, M. 1975: Convergence of mean vocal intensity in dyadic communication as a function of social desirability. *Journal of Personality and Social Psychology* **32**, 790-804.

RYAN, E.B. and GILES, H. editors, 1982: *Attitudes towards language variation* London: Edward Arnold.

SCOTTON, C.M. 1983: The negotiation of identities in conversation: a theory of markedness and code choice. *International Journal of the Sociology of Language* **44**, 115-36.

SIMARD, L., TAYLOR, D. and GILES, H. 1976: Attribution processes and inter-personal accommodation in a bilingual setting. *Language and Speech* **19**, 374-87.

STREET, R. and GILES, H. 1982: Speech Accommodation Theory. In Roloff, M. and Berger, C., editors, *Social cognition and communication* (Beverly Hills, Cal.: Sage).

TAJFEL, H., editor, 1978: *Differentiation between social groups* London: Academic Press.

—— 1981: *Human groups and social categories* Cambridge: Cambridge University Press.

—— editor, 1982: *Social identity and intergroup relations* Cambridge: Cambridge University Press.

TRIANDIS, H.C. 1960: Cognitive similarity and communication in a dyad. *Human Relations* **13**, 175-83.

WEBB, J.T. 1972: Interview synchrony: An investigation of two speech-rate measures in the automated standardized interview. In Siegman, A.W. and Pope, B., editors, *Studies in dyadic communication* (Oxford: Pergamon Press).

8
A functional approach to self-disclosure

Kathryn Dindia

Self-disclosure has been approached as a personality trait and a process variable (cf. Cozby, 1973; Pearce and Sharp, 1973). As a personality trait, self-disclosure has been studied in relation to family patterns; sex, race and cultural factors; mental health; and other personality traits. As a process variable, reciprocity of self-disclosure has been studied; as well as self-disclosure and social exchange/penetration processes; self-disclosure and liking, social approval and dependency; and disclosure as a function of the personality of the interactants (Cozby 1973). Although the process approach is clearly an improvement in the study of self-disclosure, it is limited in that it studies self-disclosure without reference to other behaviours. While research on other nonverbal and verbal behaviours has proceeded in a parallel fashion, no attempt has been made to integrate self-disclosure and nonverbal behaviours into a rich description of interpersonal interactions (Altman and Taylor 1973). A complete description of the role of self-disclosure in interpersonal relationships would require focus on the functional relationships between self-disclosure and other verbal and nonverbal behaviours.

This chapter explores self-disclosure from a functional perspective. A functional approach assumes that self-disclosure may serve several functions. It also assumes that more than one behaviour (including verbal and nonverbal behaviours) may serve the same function. Specifically, this chapter discusses the role of self-disclosure, and other related behaviours, in fulfilling the specific communication function of expressing and regulating intimacy. A functional perspective also emphasizes the actual versus intended results of behaviour (Dance and Larson 1976), and immediate observable influences on interpersonal behaviour rather than the original causes of behaviour (Burgoon and Saine 1977). Consequently, this chapter focuses on mutual influence processes observable in social interaction, specifically the relationship between self-disclosure and other behaviours that function to express and regulate intimacy. The implication of a functional approach to explaining exchange processes is that a functional base will lead to a pattern of exchange (Patterson 1982). Several patterns of exchange have been postulated with respect to self-disclosure and other 'intimacy' behaviours, specifically, reciprocity or mutual positive influence, and compensation or mutual negative influence.

This chapter focuses on evidence regarding reciprocity and compensation with respect to self-disclosure and other intimacy-serving behaviours. Specifically, four bodies of research will be reviewed, the evidence concerning the effect of A's self-disclosure on B's self-disclosure, the effect of A's self-disclosure on B's other verbal and nonverbal intimacy behaviours, the effect of A's intimacy behaviours on B's self-disclosure and the effect of A's self-disclosure on A's other intimacy behaviours. Finally, I will try to speculate about how the regular patterns of influence identified with respect to self-disclosure may be explained.

A functional approach is employed because while many studies have addressed both verbal and nonverbal communication behaviours in relation to self-disclosure, the research is fragmented, lacks focus and offers few defensible conclusions (Cline 1982). Conceptualizing self-disclosure from a functional perspective provides a useful framework within which self-disclosure can be examined in relation to a number of other verbal and nonverbal 'intimacy' behaviours.

The functions of self-disclosure

Derlega and Grzelak (1979) identified five functions of self-disclosure. The first three functions are self-expression, self-clarification and social validation. The fourth function of self-disclosure is relationship development. Here self-disclosure is viewed as an information exchange process, which is possibly governed by social exchange theories and/or norms of reciprocity. As pointed out by Derlega and Grzelak, we usually think of self-disclosure as functioning in terms of relationship development, but it also serves to maintain or break down relationships (cf. Baxter 1979). Thus, the label I will use to refer to this function is 'regulating intimacy', making the assumption that regulating the level of the relationship is synonomous with regulating the level of intimacy between the interactants. The fifth function of self-disclosure is social control, the selective use of personal information to control outcomes in social relationships.

Patterson (1982) identified five functions of social involvement behaviours: providing information, regulating interaction, expressing intimacy, social control and service-task. One social involvement behaviour is self-disclosure or verbal intimacy. Patterson's 'expressing intimacy' function is similar to Derlega and Grzelak's 'relationship development' function. Patterson (1982) defined intimacy as a bipolar dimension reflecting the degree of union with or openness to another person. Because this chapter concerns the broader function of affiliation and resource exchange, it will combine Derlega and Grzelak's relationship development function and Patterson's expressing intimacy function and focus on self-disclosure in service of expressing and regulating intimacy.

Reciprocity of self-disclosure

The hypothesis that predominates in the literature on self-disclosure is the reciprocity hypothesis. Jourard originated the idea that self-disclosure is reciprocal. He chose the term 'the dyadic effect' to represent the idea that 'disclosure begets disclosure' (Jourard 1971, p. 66). Reciprocity is conceptually defined as mutual positive influence, (e.g. Cappella 1981; Dindia 1982; Gottman 1979); A's self-disclosure has a positive effect on B's self-disclosure and B's self-disclosure has a positive effect on A's self-disclosure. Although the study of reciprocity of self-disclosure is not a functional approach to self-disclosure it does provide information on how self-disclosure functions in social interaction. The reciprocity hypothesis has been tested in a number of studies (see Cozby 1973; Chelune, *et al.* 1979; Cappella 1981; Cline 1982; and Dindia 1982 for reviews of the literature). In general the results of these studies have been interpreted as evidence of reciprocity of self-disclosure. However Dindia (1982) pointed out that none of these studies provide evidence of mutual positive influence. Instead, they provide evidence that, in general, intrasubjective and intersubjective perceptions of self-disclosure in family and social relationships are positively related, objective observations of dyadic partners' and small group members' self-disclosure are positively related, an experimenter's self-disclosure has a positive effect on a subject's reported intention to self-disclose, and an experimenter's self-disclosure has a positive effect on a subject's actual self-disclosure. These results have, nonetheless, been interpreted as evidence of reciprocity of self-disclosure.

Several theories have been advanced to explain reciprocity of self-disclosure and several studies have been designed to test competing theoretical explanations (cf. Chelune *et al.* 1979). Limitations of the reciprocity hypothesis have been discussed theoretically (Altman 1973) and tested empirically (cf. Chelune *et al.* 1979).

Self-disclosure and expressing/regulating intimacy

This body of research assumes that openness or intimacy may occur through a system of verbal and nonverbal behaviours and that these modes of communication may operate in an integrated and systematic fashion, compensating for one another, substituting for one another, amplifying one another and occurring in different combinations (Altman 1975). They are alternative means of expressing and/or regulating intimacy. This approach proposes that intimacy is multi-determined, any one or more of these behaviours can be altered to affect a change in total intimacy (Patterson 1973).

Cappella (1981) identified a set of behavioural indicators of affiliation which he labelled expressive behaviours. This set includes Argyle and Dean's (1965) intimacy cues, Mehrabians's nonverbal immediacy cues (1969) and Patterson's social involvement cues (1973, 1976). This list includes verbal intimacy or self-disclosure, proximity, gaze, lean, trunk and body orientation, touch, generalized body motion (including object and body-focused gestures), smiling and laughter, speech duration, and latencies of flight, speech and blocking. Three theories: Equilibrium theory (Argyle and Dean 1965), Arousal-Labelling theory (Patterson 1973) and Discrepancy-Arousal theory (Cappella and Greene

1982) have been proposed to explain mutual influence patterns, both reciprocity and compensation, with respect to expressive behaviours (see Anderson 1983; Cappella and Greene 1982; and Street and Giles 1982 for a comparison and contrast of these theories).

The difference between these theories and the theories advanced to explain reciprocity of self-disclosure is that these theories were proposed to explain multiple behaviours related to intimacy, whereas the theories designed to explain reciprocity of self-disclosure pertain to a single behaviour, self-disclosure. These three theoretical orientations assume that a class of related behaviours, one of which is verbal intimacy or self-disclosure, functions to express intimacy. In social interaction, reciprocity or compensation for one behaviour can occur in another behaviour. Reciprocity of self-disclosure implies that reciprocity occurs in a single mode. The studies designed to test the reciprocity hypothesis focused on a single behaviour, and whether or not reciprocation occurred with respect to that behaviour alone. The studies designed to test Equilibrium, Arousal-Labelling and Discrepancy-Arousal theories often employ multiple behaviours.

This section reviews the research which studies self-disclosure in conjunction with other intimacy behaviours. The purpose of this section is to determine whether reciprocation or compensation occurs with respect to self-disclosure and other intimacy behaviours. If openness or intimacy is expressed through several verbal and nonverbal behaviours, then one or another of these behaviours may be used to reciprocate or compensate for self-disclosure, and vice versa.

The effect of intimacy behaviours on self-disclosure

This section will explore the effect of A's intimacy behaviours (e.g. gaze, touch, distance) on B's self-disclosure. Table 8.1 summarizes the results of these studies indicating whether a subject reciprocated or compensated for the increase or decrease in gaze, touch, distance, etc., by changes in self-disclosure. With the exception of one study (Edelman and Hampson 1981) these studies employ an interview procedure. Included in the review are studies in which it is reasonable to assume that the dependent variable is a measure of self-disclosure. Not included are studies in which the dependent variable is 'duration of response' when the response is not assumed or likely to be self-disclosure. Although duration of response is thought to be an expressive behaviour (Cappella 1981), it is conceptually unrelated to duration of self-disclosure.

Gaze

Three studies examined the effect of an experimenter's gaze on the intimacy or duration of a subject's response. Jourard and Friedman (1970) found that constant gaze versus no gaze had no effect on the duration of subjects' responses to a question designed to elicit self-disclosure. Kleinke, Staneski and Berger (1975) interviewed males with a female interviewer and examined the effect of the interviewer's gaze on subjects' duration of response. The results indicated that the subjects made briefer statements in response to no gaze compared with intermittent and constant gaze. Thus, subjects accommodated to (i.e. reciprocated) the experimenter's gaze with duration of self-disclosure.

Table 8.1 Effects of intimacy behaviours on self-disclosure

Study	Variables				
	gaze	touch	distance	intrusion	goal blocking
Edelman and Hampson, 1981			0		
Ellsworth and Ross, 1975	+ (females) − (males)				
Skotko and Langmeyer 1977			0 (females: duration and # of biographic/demographic statements) + (females: intimacy and # of affective statements) − (males: all four measures) − (females with male E) 0 (all other sex compositions)		
Hansen and Schuldt, 1982	0				
Jourard and Friedman, 1970 Study #1		0 (touch vs. no touch)			
Jourard and Friedman, 1970 Study #2		+ (touch and self-disclosure)			
Johnson and Dabbs, 1976			−		
Dietch and House, 1975			−		
Schulz and Barefood, 1974		0	0		
Carr and Dabbs, 1974			0		
Hazelwood and Schuldt, 1977			+ / −		
Stone and Morden, 1976					
Kleinke, Staneski and Berger, 1975	+				
Sundstom, 1975				0	0
Greenberg and Firestone, 1977			+ / − 0	− (intrusion and goal blocking)	
Lassen, 1973				0	
Rogers, Rearden and Hellner, 1981					
Lecomte, Bernstein and Dumont, 1981			+ / − (affective statements in second third of interview) 0 (cognitive self-disclosure)		

+ = reciprocity   + / − = curviliniar effect
− = compensation   0 = null results

Finally, Ellsworth and Ross (1975) examined the effect of interviewer gaze, no gaze and averting gaze when subject becomes personal on intimacy of subjects' responses. Constant gaze and looking at subject only when he says something personal increased the intimacy of subjects' responses in female dyads but decreased the intimacy of subjects' responses in male dyads. Thus, females accommodated while males compensated for interviewer gaze with the intimacy of their self-disclosure.

The effect of gaze on self-disclosure is inconsistent. In a review of the effect of gaze on nonverbal behaviours, Cappella (1981) concluded that subjects compensated for gaze with changes in verbal duration. However, in more than half of the studies reviewed, the dependent measure, duration of response, was an operationalization of verbalization not self-disclosure. Although subjects may compensate for gaze by changes in verbal duration, there is no consistent evidence that they compensate for gaze by amount of self-disclosure as measured by the duration of a response that is assumed to be self-disclosure.

Touch

Two studies examined the effect of an interviewer's touch on subjects' duration of self-disclosure. Jourard and Friedman (1970) manipulated the touch and self-disclosure of a male interviewer. Touch had no effect on duration of subjects' (males and females combined) self-disclosure. However, when the interviewer touched and self-disclosed to the subject, the subject's response was longer than for touch or self-disclosure alone. In a replication, Hazlewood and Schuldt (1977) found that touch did not affect males' duration of response. The contradictory results make it difficult to draw any conclusions concerning whether subjects reciprocate or compensate for touch by changes in self-disclosure.

Distance

In all the studies reviewed, distance is a standing feature of social interaction (Argyle and Kendon 1967). The interviewer does not move closer or further away during the interaction. Consequently, reciprocal or compensatory responses to physical distance are not responses to another individual's behaviour, *per se*, but to the intimacy level created by the seating arrangement.

Only one study found evidence that subjects reciprocated or accommodated to physical distance. Skotko and Langmeyer (1977) found that females in same-sex dyads increased intimacy and number of affective statements as physical distance decreased. However, there was no effect of distance on females' duration and number of biographic/demographic statements.

Several studies found that subjects compensated for physical distance by the duration of their self-disclosure (Dietch and House 1975; Hazelwood and Schuldt 1977; Schulz and Barefoot 1974). Skotko and Langmeyer (1977) found that males in same-sex dyads compensated for distance in all of the four measures of self-disclosures described in the preceding paragraph. Hansen and Schuldt (1982) found that female subjects talked more with a male interviewer at 6 feet in response to medium and high-intimacy questions and talked least when it was a high-intimacy question at 3 feet.

Several studies found evidence of a curvilinear effect. Stone and Morden (1976) found that female subjects had longer utterances with a female interviewer about high-intimacy topics at 5 feet than 2 or 9 feet. However, as pointed out by Rogers, Rearden and Hellner (1981) in two-thirds of the interviews high-intimacy topics were discussed in the final segment of the interview. Lassen (1973) found that psychiatric patients in an initial psychiatric interview reported that they were more open at 6 feet than 3 or 9 feet. Lecomte, Bernstein and Dumont (1981) found that clients disclosed more affective statements at 4.17 feet in the second third of a counselling interview than at 2.5 or 6.67 feet. There was no effect of distance on cognitive self-disclosure.

In addition to the null results already presented, Carr and Dabbs (1975) found that distance had no effect on the duration and rate of subjects' self-disclosure. Rogers, Readen and Hellner (1981) in a replication of Stone and Morden, found no effect of distance on mean duration of response. Edelman and Hampson (1981) found no effect of distance on amount of self-disclosure.

At first there seems to be no discernable pattern to these results. However, by examining the number of distances employed and the actual distances used the results become interpretable. Hall (1969) described four distance levels: intimate distance (up to 18 inches), personal distance (1.5–4 feet), social distance (4–12 feet) and public distance (12 feet and beyond). Hall stated that there is an optimum distance for interaction and distances greater than or less than this distance cause anxiety and discomfort and defensive reactions may result.

Suppose for a minute that distance has a curvilinear effect on self-disclosure. The studies which employed two distances generally employed distances between 2 and 3 feet (personal distance) and 5 and 6 feet (social distance). Because the distances employed are, according to Hall, from adjacent levels on his continuum, we would expect a linear effect. Because they were instances of personal and social distances and because the interactants are generally strangers we would also expect the linear effect to be characterized by compensation as opposed to accommodation. If these studies had employed a third distance, public distance, they might have found evidence of a curvilinear effect with subjects refusing to self-disclose at close and far distances. Alternatively, if the two distances employed were from non-adjacent categories on Hall's continuum we would not be surprised to find no effect if in fact a curvilinear effect existed. The distances employed in the Carr and Dabbs study were 1.5 and 8 feet, or intimate and social distance. The lack of significant differences may be due to the fact that the distances employed were not adjacent distances on Hall's continuum, such as intimate and personal or personal and social. If these researchers had employed a third, intermediate distance, a personal distance, they may have also detected a curvilinear effect. Studies which employ only two distances limit the possible results to no effect, reciprocity or compensation. A curvilinear effect cannot be detected in these studies.

The studies that employed three distances generally found evidence of a curvilinear effect (Stone and Morden 1976; Lassen 1973; Lecomte, Berstein and Dumont 1981). Johnson and Dabbs (1976) found that subjects talked longer at 3 and 4.5 feet than at 1.5 feet for low and medium-intimacy topics. When the topic was highly intimate they talked briefly regardless of distance. Perhaps this finding is also related to a curvilinear effect. In fact, duration of response at 4.5 feet was less (although not significant) than at 3 feet, indicating that had a further distance been employed it may have demonstrated a curvilinear effect on self-disclosure.

Skotko and Langmeyer (1977) found females reciprocated while males compensated. However, there were several instances of equivalence in the 2 and 4 feet conditions and differences between these conditions and the 10 foot condition. According to Hall (1969), both 2 and 4 feet are personal distances (although 2 feet is described as personal-close and 4 feet as personal-far). perhaps this is why the results for these distances were equivalent. If the researchers had employed a third, intimate distance (6–18 inches) they might have found a curvilinear effect. However, the shapes of the curves would be different for males and females. The curve would be U-shaped for males and an inverted U for females. This result also would be explainable if males and females have different optimum levels for distance. In this study males reported feeling physically closer at all distances. Perhaps males were too close at 2 and 4 feet and approximated their optimal level for distance at 10 feet while females approached their optimum level at 2 and 4 feet and were too far at 10 feet. However, the self-report measures also indicated that both males and females felt most tense at 2 feet and least tense at 4 feet.

Previous reviews of the effects of distance have generally supported the claim that increases in proximity lead to compensation in other intimacy behaviours (Cappella 1981). This review of the effect of distance on self-disclosure also found evidence that subjects compensate for distance. However, the compensatory results may be due to the fact that these studies employ two rather than three distances. This review found evidence that can best be interpreted as indicating a curvilinear effect.

Multiple independent variables

Two studies manipulated several variables simultaneously in a single treatment condition to discover the overall effect of the combination on subjects' self-disclosure. Sundstrom (1975) manipulated 'intrusion' (physical contact, eye contact, body lean and distance) and 'goal blocking' (interruptions, no gaze except during interruptions and no backchannels). No main effects were found but, reportedly, intrusion coupled with goal blocking had a negative affect on subjects' reported willingness to engage in intimate self-disclosure. This combination is difficult to comprehend because it supposedly incorporated intruding on the other person's space with high eye contact and blocking the other person's goals with no gaze except during interruptions. The combination had no effect on reported willingness to engage in breadth of self-disclosure. Greenberg and Firestone (1977) manipulated intrusion and found that it inhibited duration of self-disclosure but had no effect on subjects' perceptions of how revealing they had been. These studies offer limited evidence that subjects compensate for a combination of intimacy behaviours by changes in self-disclosure.

Summary

In general, it can be concluded that distance affects subjects' self-disclosure. The existing results for distance on self-disclosure are best characterized by a curvilinear effect. Subjects tend to respond to close and far distances with low levels of self-disclosure. Another way to state this is that they compensate for close distances and accommodate to far distances. Unfortunately, these results are not explainable by reference to any of the theories proposed to explain mutual influence processes with respect to intimacy behaviours.

Equilibrium theory (Argyle and Dean 1965) hypothesizes that excessive intimacy will be compensated for as the interactant seeks to restore the previously established level of intimacy. Reductions in intimacy are also compensated for with greater intimacy to restore the previous level of equilibrium. Arousal-labelling theory (Patterson 1973) predicts compensation when behaviour change produces arousal change which is labelled negatively and reciprocity when behaviour change produces arousal change which is labelled positively. Whether arousal change is labelled negatively or positively depends on cognitive factors such as situational cues, past experiences or the relationship between the interactants. Thus, A may reciprocate or compensate for B's behaviour. Discrepancy-arousal theory (Cappella and Greene 1982) proposes that the discrepancy between person A's expectation of person B's behaviour and B's behaviour leads to arousal. If the arousal is moderate, positive affect will result followed by reciprocity, if the arousal is high, then negative affect will result, followed by compensation.

Equilibrium theory only predicts compensation and therefore cannot explain a curvilinear effect. Arousal-labelling theory predicts compensation when arousal is labelled negatively and reciprocity when arousal is labelled positively. It is possible that subjects label arousal stimulated by close distances as positive and arousal stimulated by far distances as negative. This would be in contrast to Hall's prediction that there is an optimum level of distance, presumably in the social-distance range for strangers, and that deviations from this optimum level, either positive or negative, stimulate arousal which is experienced negatively. Discrepancy-arousal theory predicts reciprocation when discrepancy in actual and desired distance is minimal and compensation when the discrepancy in actual and desired distance is maximum. Assuming that Hall is correct in that moderate levels of distance are desirable, this theory would account for the curvilinear results. However, Hall's distance categories or his predictions regarding them may not be correct. The most parsimonious explanation of the results is Hall's prediction which simply states that deviations from the desired level are experienced negatively and lead to defensiveness. Again, assuming that intermediate distances are optimum, this would account for the fact that self-disclosure is low at close and far distances and high at intermediate distances.

Because of the few studies and inconsistent results it is impossible to determine whether gaze and/or touch have similar effects on self-disclosure. It appears that a combination of intimacy behaviours may have a compensatory effect on self-disclosure. However, further research employing three or more levels of the independent variable may demonstrate that the effect is actually curvilinear. Future research needs to explore the multivariate effect of several intimacy variables on self-disclosure. It also needs to employ more than two levels of the independent variables to determine if the results are linear or curvilinear. More studies need to be done examining the effect of other intimacy variables on self-disclosure.

The effect of self-disclosure on intimacy behaviours

A review of the literature indicated that there are no studies which examine the effect of A's self-disclosure on B's behaviour other than the effect of A's self-disclosure on B's self-disclosure. No studies manipulated the experimenter's self-disclosure and measured the effect on subjects' gaze, touch, smiling, etc. Several studies have examined the effect of an experimenter's self-disclosure on the duration of subjects' response (cf. Jourard and Friedman, 1970; Jourard and Jaffee, 1970). However, in all these studies, duration of response is a measure of amount (and sometimes intimacy) of self-disclosure. It is assumed, correctly or incorrectly, that the subject's response is self-disclosure. Consequently, these studies are included in reviews of reciprocity of self-disclosure which were summarized in the first part of this paper, and are not included here.

The effect of topic intimacy on intimacy behaviours

Several studies have manipulated the intimacy level of topics subjects are requested to discuss. While not being the same as self-disclosure, these studies assume that topic intimacy prescribes a subject's self-disclosure and thus are relevant. In most of these studies an experimenter or confederate interviews a subject and the experimenter does not engage in any self-disclosure, he or she merely asks more or less intimate questions. In a few studies (Anderson 1976; Edelman and Hampson 1981; Amerikaner 1980) pairs of strangers are requested to take turns discussing topics which vary in intimacy. These studies ask the question, will subjects accommodate to or compensate for the intimacy level at which they are requested to self-disclose? These studies assume that the subject actually discloses at the level of intimacy he or she is requested to disclose and test to see if the same subject accommodates to or compensates for the intimacy level of his or her own self disclosure.

The results of these studies are not relevant to reciprocation or compensation between individuals because they do not provide information about the effect of A's behaviour on B's behaviour. Consequently, none of the theories alluded to thus far apply to these studies because these theories are designed to explain and predict reciprocity or compensation between individuals. However, the results of these studies do provide information concerning accommodation or compensation within an individual. This information is valuable because it can provide evidence of the functional similarity of these behaviours. If these behaviours are systematically related to each other, this would provide evidence that these behaviours function as a system of behaviours which communicate intimacy and can accommodate to, compensate for, substitute for or amplify each other.

These studies employ a variety of topics. Four studies employed topics which were scaled for intimacy from Jourard's questionnaire (Jourard and Friedman 1970; Jourard and Jaffe 1970; Johnson and Dabbs 1976; Hansen and Schuldt 1982). Schulz and Barefoot (1974) employed topics from Taylor and Altman's (1966) intimacy-scaled stimuli. Stone and Morden's (1976) and Rogers, Rearden and Hellner's (1981) subjects were asked to discuss academic, social and personal concerns. Carr and Dabbs's (1974) high-intimacy topics were:

favourite sexual fantasy, first sexual encounter and most exciting sexual experience. Low-intimacy topics were marriage plans, anger-provoking situations and hobbies. Exline *et al.*'s (1965) high-intimacy topics were questions about fears, desires, needs, impulses, etc. Their low-intimacy topics were questions about recreational interests, preferred movies, books, sports, etc. Edelman and Hampson (1981) stated that their topics were independently rated prior to the study and gave no further elaboration. Anderson (1976) and Amerikaner (1980) did not provide any information regarding the topics employed. However, in Amerikaner, the disclosure intimacy levels were based on codings of the statements made by subjects rather than the intimacy of the topics being discussed.

Silence

An examination of the results in Table 8.2 shows that intimate topics increased silence in one study (Exline, Gray and Schuette 1965). In another study intimate topics increased latencies but pauses were not affected (Schulz and Barefoot 1974). Schulz and Barefoot acknowledge that the increased latencies may be due to topic difficulty. This may also be true for Exline *et al.*'s results. It is difficult to draw the conclusion that subjects compensate for topic intimacy by a change in amount of silence based on the results of two studies when topic difficulty may have been the cause.

Gaze

The effect of topic intimacy on gaze and mutual gaze has been assessed in a number of studies. Edelman and Hampson (1981) had pairs of strangers interact and found that as the intimacy of topic increased, looking at partner while talking and while listening decreased. Amerikaner (1980) had pairs of strangers interact and found that, in general, subjects reduced their duration of looking at their partner when engaging in high-intimacy disclosure. Frequency of looking at their partner was relatively independent of subjects' self-disclosure. Schulz and Barefoot (1974) found that as topic intimacy increased, returning the interviewer's gaze while talking decreased. Topic intimacy had no effect on looking while listening. Exline *et al.* (1965) found that intimacy of topic decreased returning the experimenter's gaze while talking but did not affect returning the experimenter's gaze while listening or during silence. Anderson (1976) and Edelman and Hampson (1981) studied mutual gaze in pairs of strangers. Anderson found a curvilinear relationship, eye contact increased from low to medium intimacy and decreased from medium to high intimacy. Edelman and Hampson found that mutual gaze decreased and mutual avoidance of gaze increased as topic intimacy increased. Thus, there is considerable evidence that subjects compensate for the intimacy of their response by changes in the duration of their gaze, returning the gaze of their partner and mutual gaze. The effect for mutual gaze suggests that the partner's gaze is also affected by the intimacy of subject's response.

Body motion

Edelman and Hampson (1981) found that body motion increased while talking

Table 8.2 Effects of topic intimacy on intimacy behaviours

Study	Variables					
	duration	silence	gaze	smiling	body motion	speech disturbances
Amerikaner, 1980	−		− (duration of looking at partner) 0 (frequency of looking at partner) +/−			
Anderson, 1976						
Carr and Dabbs, 1975						
Edelman and Hampson, 1982	0 (# of words) 0		− (while talking) − (while listening) − (mutual gaze) + (mutual gaze avoidance) − (return E gaze while talking) 0 (return E gaze while listening) 0 (return E gaze during silence)	+ (while talking) + (while listening)	+ (while talking) + (while listening) + mutual body motion	
Exline, Gray and Schuette, 1965	+	−				
Hansen and Schuldt, 1982	− (females with male E) − (all other sex compositions)					
Johnson and Dabbs, 1976	−					
Jourard and Friedman, 1970	0					
Jourard and Jaffe, 1970	0 (in direction of +)					
Rogers, Readon and Hellner, 1981	0					
Schulz and Barefoot, 1974	+	0 (pauses) − (latencies)	− (while talking) 0 (while listening)	0	0 (manipulative gestures)	
Stone and Mordon, 1976	+				0 (demonstrative gestures)	

+ = reciprocity or accommodation
− = compensation
+/− = curvilinear effect
0 = null results

and listening as intimacy of topic increased. Mutual or syncronized body motion also increased as topic intimacy increased. Edelman and Hampson attributed both these results to increased embarrassment because reported embarrassment was positively related to topic intimacy. It has also been suggested that generalized body motion is a behavioural indicator of affiliation (Cappella 1981). If body motion in this study functions in terms of expressing embarrassment, subjects are compensating for the intimacy of their response, if intimacy, subjects are accommodating. Schulz and Barefoot (1974) studied manipulative gestures (self-adaptors) and demonstrative gestures (all other gestures) and found that neither were affected by topic intimacy.

Speech disturbances

Only one study (Edelman and Hampson, 1981) studied the effect of topic intimacy on speech disturbances. Edelman and Hampson found that speech disturbances increased as topic intimacy increased for pairs of strangers. They attributed this to embarrassment.

Smiling

Edelman and Hampson (1981) studied smiling and found that smiling while talking and listening increased as topic intimacy increased. They also attributed this to embarrassment. Others (cf. Argyle and Dean, 1965; Patterson 1976; Cappella 1981) have suggested that this behaviour functions to express affiliation. Schultz and Barefoot (1974) found that smiles were not affected by topic intimacy.

Duration of self-disclosure

In all of these studies the response is assumed to be self-disclosure. Duration of response is employed as a measure of amount (and sometimes intimacy) of self-disclosure. Schulz and Barefoot (1974) and Exline *et al.* (1965) found that duration increased as topic intimacy increased. Hansen and Schuldt (1982) found that female subjects with a male experimenter talked least in response to questions of high intimacy at 3 feet. There was no effect for other sex combinations of experimenter and subject. Three studies found null results (Jourard and Friedman 1970, Edelman and Hampson 1981; Jourard and Jaffee 1970). The last study found non-significant results but they were in the direction of reciprocation. Stone and Morden (1976) found no main effect for topic intimacy but a significant interaction between topic and distance. Female subjects talked more about high-intimacy topics at the intermediate distance. Edelman and Hampson (1982) also studied the number of words in a subject's response and similarly found no effect of topic intimacy.

It is difficult to discern the effect of topic intimacy on duration of self-disclosure. An almost equal number of studies found accommodation, compensation and no effect. I examined whether the mixed results appeared to be systematically related to differences in topics used, an interview procedure versus a conversation, or sex differences, and found that this did not appear to be the case. In some studies, the increased duration may be due to topic difficulty. In fact, Schulz and Barefoot (1974) attributed their results to the possibility of topic difficulty. In other studies the decrease in duration may be due to an overly intimate, but nongeneralizable, experimental manipulation (for example, Carr and Dabb's 'sex' topics). I also compared the results of the studies that employed two intimacy levels with the results of the studies that employed three intimacy levels and did not find a pattern of results that would be indicative of a curvilinear effect. It is unlikely that a consistent curvilinear effect would have been found had all the studies employed low, medium and high-intimacy topics.

Subjects did not consistently change the duration of their response as a result of topic intimacy. This may be due to a false assumption that duration of response is a valid measure of quantity or quality of self-disclosure. It is based on the assumption that the entire response consists of self-disclosure. Because the content of the response is never checked (with the exception of Amerikaner) it is not known if this assumption is true. While it is possible that individuals compensate in some situations and accommodate in others, the contradictory results may be due to the dependent measure being irrelevant to self-disclosure. However, Cappella (1981) has indicated that verbalization (also measured by duration of response) is also an expressive behaviour. Consequently, duration of response, regardless of whether it is an operationalization of self-disclosure or verbalization, should have been related to topic intimacy.

Summary

An individual may compensate for or accommodate to his or her intimacy of self-disclosure by another intimacy behaviour. If a subject is requested to disclose at too high a level for the situation or relationship, he or she can compensate for his or her intimate self-disclosure by making it brief, reducing gaze, etc. He or she can accommodate to the intimacy of his or her self-disclosure by discussing at length, increasing gaze, proximity, touch, etc. The results of these studies offer contradictory evidence concerning the accommodation or compensation of a subject's response to the intimacy level at which he or she is requested to discuss. The results indicate that subjects compensate for topic intimacy by gaze. The results for other verbal and nonverbal behaviours were mixed and/or inconclusive. Cappella (1981) concluded in a similar review that subjects compensate for topic intimacy with speech latencies, gaze and possibly smiling. However, I think that topic difficulty may account for changes in speech latencies. This review only found two studies that examined the effect of topic intimacy on smiling and only one of them found that subjects accommodated to topic intimacy with smiling. However, smiling may have been functioning as a discomfort cue rather than an intimacy cue in this study.

The results suggest that verbal intimacy and gaze are a system of related behaviours and that changes in gaze compensate for changes in intimacy of self-disclosure. When a subject is asked to self-disclose at a level of intimacy which is inappropriate for the relationship and the situation, he or she will compensate for his or her verbal intimacy by increasing or decreasing his or her gaze. The results also indicate that topic intimacy affects mutual gaze implying that there is also an effect of intimacy of self-disclosure on the partner and the dyad.

However, the results of these studies must be interpreted with caution. These studies are based on a tenuable assumption. With the exception of Amerikaner (1980) none of these studies employed a test of the effectiveness of the topic-intimacy manipulation. There is no evidence that subjects really disclosed at the requested level of intimacy. We do not know how intimate the subjects' self-disclosure was, whether the manipulation (request for self-disclosure) was successful. In fact, subjects may compensate for high-intimacy topics by lowering their level of verbal intimacy below the level requested. The rival hypothesis for the studies which found null results is that self-disclosure, across experimental conditions, was not different.

Conclusions

It is difficult to draw more than a few concrete conclusions from these reviews of literature. First, there is evidence presented by Dindia (1982) and summarized in this chapter that dyadic partners', small group members' and members of family and social relationships's self-disclosure is positively related and that an experimenter's self-disclosure has a positive effect on a subject's self-disclosure. Second, there is some evidence that distance from an experimenter has a curvilinear effect on a subject's self-disclosure. Third, there is evidence that the intimacy of a topic a subject is requested to discuss has a negative effect on the same subject's gaze. There is no evidence concerning the effect of A's self-disclosure on B's intimacy behaviours other than self-disclosure.

From these results it has been tentatively concluded that self-disclosure is reciprocal, that a subject compensates for the intimacy of his or her own self-disclosure by changes in gaze and that a subject will compensate for close distances and accommodate to far distances by his or her self-disclosure. The results and the interpretations of the results are in agreement with other reviews. Reciprocity of self-disclosure was considered a robust conclusion by Cappella (1981) as was the effect of proximity on proximity, latency, gaze, body orientation and speech. We can add to the list the effect of proximity on self-disclosure. However, Cappella concluded that distance had a linear effect on these variables whereas I concluded that distance has a curvilinear effect on self-disclosure. Cappella also tentatively concluded that topic intimacy has an effect on latency, gaze and speech duration. This review found considerable evidence that topic intimacy affects gaze. The results for speech latencies were attributed to topic difficulty. The results for duration of self-disclosure were inconclusive.

The evidence also suggests that self-disclosure is an intimacy cue that functions as part of a system of intimacy cues and is related to at least two other intimacy cues, distance and gaze. A subject can compensate for the level of his or her self-disclosure (or at least the level of intimacy he or she is requested to disclose at) by changes in his or her gaze. A subject can also adjust to the distance between himself or herself and his or her partner by his or her level of self-disclosure.

However, there is also evidence that distance and self-disclosure are not functionally equivalent. The effect of distance on self-disclosure was not the same as the effect of self-disclosure on self-disclosure and not the effect one would predict by applying the reciprocity hypothesis. Subjects reciprocated self-disclosure but compensated for close distances and reciprocated (or accommodated to) far distances. The contradictory effects of experimenter self-disclosure and distance on a subject's self-disclosure cannot be explained by the same theory. The reciprocity hypothesis is not generalizable to the effect of distance on self-disclosure. Subjects disclose more when the experimenter self-discloses but they do not disclose more when the experimenter is physically close. Two studies manipulated self-disclosure and distance (Johnson and Dabbs 1976; Hazelwood and Schuldt 1977) and found no interaction of the effect of an experimenter's self-disclosure and distance on a subject's self-disclosure. Subjects continued to disclose less at closer distances regardless of the experimenter's self-disclosure. Subjects continued to disclose more in response to an experimenter's self-disclosure regardless of distance. This evidence indicates that these variables operate independently of each other. According to a functional approach to expressing and regulating intimacy, if these behaviours are functioning as a system of interrelated behaviours, they should have an interactive effect on self-disclosure. Nonetheless close distance and intimate self-disclosure do not appear to have the same effect on another person's behaviour.

The results for the effect of topic intimacy on a subject's gaze and an experimenter's self-disclosure on a subject's self-disclosure are more systematic. In fact, it may be because self-disclosure is not an isolated behaviour but part of a system of interrelated intimacy cues that reciprocity of self-disclosure is possible. The research on reciprocity indicated that, in general, B will reciprocate even very high levels of A's self-disclosure. Perhaps this is possible because B can reciprocate self-disclosure and still maintain an optimum level of intimacy by compensating for the intimacy of his or her self-disclosure by averting his or her gaze. Although this is entirely speculative, it would explain why there are results supporting two seemingly incompatible predictions, reciprocity of self-disclosure and compensation for topic intimacy with gaze. A subject can reciprocate self-disclosure and still maintain an optimum level of intimacy by averting gaze.

Because there is also evidence that topic intimacy affects mutual gaze, a plausible interpretation is that the intimacy of A's self-disclosure affects both A's and B's behaviour such that both partners compensate for the intimacy of self-disclosure with mutual gaze. This speculation requires evidence concerning the effect of A's self-disclosure on A and B's concurrent and lagged behaviour.

All of the interpretations of the results and the speculations regarding these results must be qualified due to the nature of the evidence on which they are based. Several authors (cf. Cappella 1981; Dindia 1982; Gottman 1970) have discussed the limitations of drawing inferences about mutual influence processes from correlational and experimental evidence. Concurrent and sequential patterns of behaviours, within and between individuals, on a dyad by dyad basis, need to be observed and tested to provide more conclusive evidence regarding reciprocity and compensation of intimacy behaviours.

Little is known about the relationship of self-disclosure to other verbal and nonverbal intimacy behaviours. There is a need to study self-disclosure in relationship to other intimacy behaviours to understand its role in expressing and/or regulating intimacy. Some authors have argued that self-disclosure is *the* variable in relationship development, others have argued that it is a central process in the development of relationships, while others have argued that it

158   *Kathryn Dindia*

functions as part of a system of intimacy behaviours to develop relationships. The extent to which any of these claims is true is unknown. The extent to which self-disclosure and other intimacy behaviours are functionally equivalent, in other words, the extent to which self-disclosure can compensate for, substitute for, accommodate to or amplify other intimacy behaviours, and vice versa, is unknown. Only by approaching self-disclosure from a functional perspective can the relative influence of self-disclosure and its relationship to other intimacy behaviours in the process of expressing and regulating intimacy be determined.

References

ALTMAN, I. 1973: Reciprocity of interpersonal exchange. *Journal for the Theory of Social Behavior* **3**, 249–61.

ALTMAN, I.A. 1975: *The Environment and Social Behavior*. Monterey, Cal: Brooks/Cole.

ALTMAN, I. and TAYLOR, D.A. 1973: *Social penetration*. New York: Holt, Rinehart & Winston.

AMERIKANER, M. 1980: Self-disclosure: A study of verbal and coverbal intimacy. *Journal of Psychology* **104**, 221–31.

ANDERSON, D.R. 1976: Eye contact, topic intimacy, and equilibrium theory. *Journal of Social Psychology* **100**, 313–14.

ANDERSON, P.A. 1983: *Nonverbal immediacy in interpersonal communication*. Paper presented at the International Communication Association Convention, Dallas.

ARGYLE M. and DEAN, J. 1965: Eye contact, distance and affiliation. *Sociometry* **28**, 290–304.

ARGYLE, M. and KENDON, A. 1967: The experimental analysis of social performance. In Berkowitz, L. *Advances in experimental social psychology, Vol. 3*. (New York: Academic Press) 55–91.

BAXTER, L.A. 1979: Self-disclosure as a relationship disengagement strategy: An exploratory investigation. *Human Communication Research* **5**, 215–22.

BURGOON, J.K. and SAINE, T. 1978: *The unspoken dialogue: an introduction to nonverbal communication*. Boston: Houghton Mifflin.

CAPELLA, J.N. 1981: Mutual influence in expressive behavior: Adult-adult and infant-adult dyadic interaction. *Psychological Bulletin* **89**, 101–32.

CAPPELLA, J.N. and GREENE, J.O. 1982: A discrepancy-arousal explanation of mutual influence in expressive behavior for adult and infant-adult interaction. *Communication Monographs* **49**, 80–114.

CARR, S.J. and DABBS, J.M. 1974: The effects of lighting, distance and intimacy of topic of verbal and visual behavior. *Sociometry* **37**, 592–600.

CHELUNE, G.J. and ASSOCIATES, editors, 1979: *Self-disclosure: Origins, patterns, and implications of openness in interpersonal relationships*. San Francisco: Jossey-Bass.

CLINE, R.J. 1982: *Revealing and relating: A review of self-disclosure theory and research*. Paper presented at the International Communication Association Convention, Boston.

COZBY, P.C. 1973: Self-disclosure: A literature review. *Psychological Bulletin* **79**, 73–91.

DANCE, F.E.X. and LARSON, C.E. 1976: *The functions of human communication:*

A theoretical approach. New York: Holt, Rinehart & Winston.

DINDIA, K. 1982: Reciprocity of self-disclosure: A sequential analysis. In Burgoon, M., editor, *Communication Yearbook VI*, (Beverly Hills, Cal. Sage Publications) 506–30.

DERLEGA, V.J. and GRZELAK, J. 1979: Appropriateness of self-disclosure in Chelune, G.J., editors, *Self-disclosure: Origins, patterns, and implications of openness in interpersonal relationships*. (San Francisco: Jossey-Bass) 151–76.

DIETCH, J. and HOUSE, J. 1975: Affiliative conflict and individual differences in self-disclosure. *Representative Research in Social Psychology* 6, 69–75.

EDELMAN, R.J. and HAMPSON, S.E. 1981: Embarrassment in dyadic interaction. *Social Behavior and Personality* 9, 171–7.

ELLSWORTH, P. and ROSS, L. 1975: Intimacy in response to direct gaze. *Journal of Experimental Social Psychology* 11, 592–613.

EXLINE, R.V., GRAY, D. and SCHUETTE, D. 1965: Visual Behavior in a dyad as affected by interview content and sex of respondent. *Journal of Personality and Social Psychology* 1, 201–9.

GOTTMAN, J.M. 1979: *Marital interaction: Experimental investigations*. New York: Academic Press.

GREENBERG, C.I., and FIRESTONE I.J. 1977: Compensatory responses to crowding: Effects of personal space intrusion and privacy reduction. *Journal of Personality and Social Psychology* 35, 637–44.

HALL, E.T. 1969: *The hidden dimension*. Garden City, New York: Doubleday.

HANSEN, J.E. and SCHULDT, W.J. 1982: Physical distance, sex and intimacy in self-disclosure. *Psychological Reports* 51, 3–6.

HAZELWOOD, M.G., and SCHULDT, J.S. 1977: Effects of physical and phenomenological distance on self-disclosure. *Perceptual and Motor Skills* 45, 805–6.

JOHNSON, C.F. and DABBS, J.M. 1976: Self-disclosure in dyads as a function of distance and the subject-experimenter relationship. *Sociometry* 39, 257–63.

JOURARD, S.M. 1971: Self-disclosure: *The experimental investigation of the transparent self*. New York: Wiley.

JOURARD, S.M. and FRIEDMAN, R. 1970: Experimenter-subject distance and self-disclosure. *Journal of Personality and Social Psychology* 15, 278–82.

JOURARD, S.M. and JAFFE, P.E. 1970: Influence of an interviewer's disclosure on the self-disclosing behaviour of interviewees. *Journal of Counseling Psychology* 17, 252–7.

KLEINKE, C.L. STANESKI, R.A. and BERGER, D.E. 1975: Evaluation of an interviewer as a function of interviewer gaze, reinforcement of subject gaze, and interviewer attractiveness. *Journal of Personality and Social Psychology* 31, 115–22.

LASSEN, D. 1973: Effect of proximity on anxiety and communication in the initial psychiatric interview. *Journal of Abnormal Psychology* 81, 226–32.

LECOMTE, C., BERNSTEIN, B.L. and DUMONT, F. 1981: Counseling interactions as a function of spatial environmental conditions. *Journal of Counseling Psychology* 28, 536–9.

MEHRABIAN, A. 1969: Some referents and measures of nonverbal behavior. *Behavior Research Methods and Instrumentation* 1, 203–7.

PATTERSON, M.L. 1973: Compensation and nonverbal immediacy behaviors: A review. *Sociometry* **36**, 237–53.

—— 1976: An arousal model of interpersonal intimacy. *Psychological Review* **83**, 235–45.

—— 1982: A sequential functional model of nonverbal exchange. *Psychological Review* **89**, 231–49.

PEARCE, W.B. and SHARP, S.M. 1973: Self-disclosing communication. *Journal of Communication* **23**, 409–25.

ROGERS, P., REARDEN, J.J. and HELLNER, W. 1981: Effects of distance from interviewer and intimacy of topic on verbal productivity and anxiety. *Psychological Reports* **49**, 303–7.

SCHULZ, R. and BAREFOOT, J. 1974: Nonverbal responsiveness and affiliative conflict theory. *British Journal of Social and Clinical Psychology* **13**, 237–43.

SKOTKO, V.P. and LANGMEYER, D. 1977: The effects of interaction distance and gender on self-disclosure in the dyad. *Sociometry* **40**, 178–82.

STONE, G.L. and MORDEN, C.J. 1976: Effect of distance on verbal productivity. *Journal of Counseling Psychology* **23**, 486–8.

STREET, R.L. and GILES, H. 1982: Speech accommodation theory: a social cognitive approach to language and speech behaviour. In Roloff, M. and Berger, C., editors, *Social cognition and communication*, (Beverly Hills, Cal. Sage Publications) 193–226.

SUNDSTROM, E. 1975: An experimental study of crowding: Effects of room size, intrustion, and goal blocking on nonverbal behavior, self-disclosure, and self-reported stress. *Journal of Personality and Social Psychology* **32**, 645–54.

TAYLOR, D.A. and ALTMAN, I. 1966: Intimacy-scaled stimuli for use in studies of interpersonal relations. *Psychological Reports* **19**, 729–30.

9

Conversational profit-seeking: interaction as social exchange

Michael E. Roloff and Douglas E. Campion

Quisquis magna dedit, voluit sibi magna remitt.

Whoever makes great presents, expects great presents in return.

Marcus Velerius 43-104 AD

Take gifts with a sigh: most men give to be paid.

John Boyle O'Reilly 1844-1890

Although separated by history and culture, the sentiment expressed in the quotations is the same: when one receives a valued commodity from another, one incurs an obligation to return a resource to the giver. While most recognize this rule as controlling economic exchanges, current instances of marital contracts and palimony suits suggest that it also is a pervasive phenomenon in interpersonal relationships. Consistent with this view, a number of scholars interested in marriage and the family have argued that interpersonal relationships might be appropriately viewed as exchange relationships and consequently, may conform to predictions made by the social exchange theories (e.g. Nye 1978; 1979; Scanzoni 1972; 1979). Similarly, a book recently appeared which extended five of the social exchange theories into the closely allied area of interpersonal communication (Roloff 1981). The social exchange theories are composed of three parts: underlying theoretical base, model of decision making, and descriptions of exchange patterns (see Roloff 1981). This chapter will be most concerned with the analysis of exchange patterns or the relationship between the resources given by one partner and returned by the other.

We will extend upon the social exchange theories by casting interaction as an exchange process. Our basic argument will be that an interaction is partly composed of exchanges of symbolic resources. As such, an interaction is a means by which individuals acquire supplies of resources needed to control their environment. Because interactions contain exchanges, we posit that the norm of reciprocity frequently mentioned as a controlling factor in the exchange of concrete resources (e.g. Gouldner 1960) can also be observed in an interaction and provides an explanation for the type of exchange pattern evidenced within. In essence, individuals have learned that unless each party to an exchange attains some level of resource it is unlikely that future interactions will result. Consequently, exchange partners will be motivated to reciprocate when provided with a resource. Specifically, we posit that when evaluating an interaction, a judge will examine the degree to which exchanges are transacted (i.e., a resource given to the interaction partner causes that person to return a resource) and the degree to which the exchanges are roughly equivalent (i.e., in those transacted, is there an appropriate match between types, value, and conveyance of the resources exchanged). Our position will be presented in four sections: (1) interaction as a social exchange process; (2) perspectives on the norm of reciprocity; (3) reciprocity in interactions; and (4) directions for research.

Interaction as a social exchange process

Our conception of interaction as an exchange process hinges on two interrelated constructs: interaction and symbolic exchange. *We define an interaction as a sequence of dyadic communication behaviours partly composed of symbolic exchanges.* In other words, from a set of relatively continuous verbal and nonverbal behaviours, one should be able to observe resources, some of which are linked together as exchanges. We see several implications arising from this definition.

From our perspective once an interaction has begun, it continues in a relatively uninterrupted fashion until some endpoint is reached. In other words, it is bounded. It may begin with transmission of a resource and ends when any of four things happens: (1) an external barrier is reached (e.g. run out of time, interrupted by someone not part of the interaction); (2) one or both partners have achieved a sufficient amount of resource; (3) one or both partners have exhausted their own supplies of resources in the exchange; or (4) one or both partners find each other reluctant to exchange resources. Obviously, we are not positing a strict temporal range for interactions. Since any of the four barriers might be reached at any time after the initial resource is given, some interactions may be very short while others are quite lengthy.

We also note that interactions vary as to the number of exchanges of which they are composed. When exchanging relatively simple instructions, an interaction may be quite short, involving a single exchange. If two 'long lost' friends are reacquainted, the interaction should not only be longer but composed of many exchanges. In fact, they may find that a single interaction (or set of exchanges) is insufficient to communicate all of the important details of their lives apart. Consequently, they make a commitment (often ignored) to 'get together' again in the near future to continue their conversation.

Finally, the resources observed in an interaction may be linked in ways other than exchanges. In some cases, a resource is offered by one party but nothing is returned by the other (i.e., the exchange is initiated but not transacted). In addition, alternative linkages may exist between resources. Foa and Foa (1974) identified what they termed 'five paradigms of interaction'. First, the relational partners may give one another resources (i.e., A gives to B, and then B gives to A). This corresponds to what we consider an exchange. Second, the relational partners may attempt to deny one another resources (i.e., A takes a resource from B, and then B takes a resource from A). This pattern may be observed in an argument wherein both parties insult one another (i.e., deny each other status). Third, one party may provide restitution to his or her victim (i.e., A takes from B, and A then gives to B). Fourth, one relational partner may be unconditionally benevolent toward the other (i.e., A takes from B, and then B gives to A). Finally, one relational partner may act in a selfish manner toward the other (i.e., A gives to B, and then B takes from A). While the preceding five linkages involve one partner taking or giving resources, we posit one last type of linkage found within interactions. We define this linkage as a solicitation in which one party seeks to negotiate the exchange of a resource. Instead of directly providing the resource, a person may seek assurance that the other party wants the resource and will be willing to transact the exchange. Consequently, the solicitation sequence involves negotiation over an exchange. Thus, even though resources may be observed in an interaction, only a portion of them may be linked in an exchange and exchanges may be separated by other linkages within the interaction.

We define a social exchange as linked behaviours through which relational partners voluntarily provide one another resources. Symbolic exchanges are a subset of social exchanges in which intangible resources are provided. Again, we wish to draw several implications from these definitions.

First, exchange behaviours are linked through feelings of obligation. When accepting a resource from another, feelings of obligation (Blau 1964) or indebtedness (Greenberg 1980) are often stimulated. As these feelings increase in magnitude; the probability that a resource will be returned increases and upon its acceptance, feelings of obligation will decrease. Thus, if felt obligation does not reach sufficient magnitude, an initiated exchange will not be transacted.

Second, in symbolic exchanges, the existence of a resource is typically inferred from the verbal and nonverbal behaviour of the partner rather than from the physical traits of an object. In other words, symbolic resources exist within the interpretation of a partner's communication behaviours. Foa and Foa (1974) have provided insight into the exact nature of these resources. They focus on six: love, status, services, information, goods and money. Of those six, love, status, and information are symbolic resources. Love is an expression of affection. Information arises from a person's knowledge base and may constitute instructions or advice, and status involves the evaluation of a person's traits or abilities. Longabaugh (1963) similarly described three resources exchanged in interactions: information, control and support. Control and support are similar to status and love respectively, while information is identical in both perspectives.

While research seems to verify the existence of these three fundamental symbolic resources (see Foa and Foa 1974) there is little research or theory providing the linkage between a specific communication behaviour and a resource category. Indeed, exchange theorists seem more concerned with the resource categories than the behaviours from which they are inferred. It is possible, however to speculate about what behaviours are usually associated with a given resource category. It seems reasonable that information is primarily inferred from linguistic cues. This is not meant to exclude nonverbal cues from this resource category but only suggest that the primary stimuli are found in spoken language. Love and status are probably inferred primarily from nonverbal stimuli. Evidence in support of this hunch arises from Argyle's (1975) review of research related to the transmission of interpersonal attitudes. He argues that two attitudes are often communicated in interaction: friendliness/hostility and dominance/submissiveness. These two attitudes roughly correspond to Foa and Foa's conception of love and status respectively. Argyle has noted that friendliness is often communicated via the following nonverbal channels: (1) bodily contact such as touching, stroking; (2) normal to close proximity; (3) if mutual gaze, direct body orientation or side by side with intimates; (4) frequent eye gaze coupled with smiling; (5) leaning forward with open arms and legs; (6) smiles, and (7) soft tone of voice. Dominance is often communicated via four nonverbal channels: (1) less direct body orientation; (2) less eye gaze; (3) more relaxed posture, head tilted back and hands on hips, and (4) loud and assertive tone of voice.

While the previous listing of behaviours is useful, we do not wish to imply that it represents a definitive answer. Indeed, it raises additional questions. Simply because there may be linguistic or nonverbal cues associated with resource categories does not mean that exchange partners perceive and react to each. For example, a researcher in studying interaction may attempt to operationalize information on the basis of some linguistic unit such as a sentence or thought unit. While it is possible to do so, one should not make the assumption that every thought unit is perceived to be an offer of a resource by the interactants. Similarly, it may not be the case that every smile or direct body orientation is perceived to be love or dominance. It seems to us that resource categories are typically inferred by interactants on the basis of clusters of behaviour rather than discrete actions. If only because of the information processing demands of contending with the myriads of verbal and nonverbal cues emitted in an interaction, exchange partners may 'chunk' incoming stimuli together when determining what is given. This of course, implies that microscopic analyses of interaction behaviour may be at odds with what we speculate is a more macro judgement on the part of the interactants. We repeat, however, that our analysis is speculative and empirical evidence is very much needed.

Our *third* implication is that exchanges can involve transfers and spreading of resources. Cartwright (1965) has noted that a number of different types of resource distributions can be observed. Two of these are transfers and spreading. In a transfer, the giver loses the resource and the receiver gains it. When an exchange is initiated, one should find a deficit in the giver's supply of a resource and a credit in the receiver's. Spreading is a situation in which the giver of a resource provides a resource to the receiver, but the giver does not lose the resource that is provided. With spreading, one should find that the receiver's supply of a resource should increase with the initiation but the giver's supply would not decrease and, in some cases, may even increase.

While the exchange of goods and money typically are transfers, symbolic resources may be exchanged through transfers or spreading. Blau (1964) has argued that when a person bestows status upon another, he or she subordinates him or herself thereby reducing his or her own status. A compliment may imply that another has superior or equal possessions or abilities to oneself resulting in a loss of status. It is also plausible that an expression of love may also result in less affection for self. If one is 'in love' with a cruel person, a self-perception may arise that one is attracted to 'bad people'. One may come to dislike oneself for caring for such an uncaring person. Finally, information may involve a transfer when for some reason the giver no longer possesses the information after the initiation of the exchange. That would seem to be the case when one transmits written or mechanical forms of communication (one gives away a book or record) or when one forgets information once it is transmitted to another.

Spreading may also occur with the three resources. Indeed, research conducted by Foa (1966) suggests that when people initiate exchanges of symbolic resources their supplies can even increase. Foa discovered that when people are 'in love' with someone they often increase their own supply of love through increases in self-satisfaction. Similarly, a parent may actually increase his or her supply of status through complimenting his or her child. The statement, 'you are an honest child', implies both that the child has desirable traits and that the parent instilled those traits through socialization and hence is a good parent. Finally, the supply of information may increase as a result of reinterpreting or thinking about the information as it is transmitted. In other words, simply communicating may cause the giver to acquire new insights into the information, thereby expanding the knowledge base.

Finally, a given act may be perceived as carrying multiple resources. Foa and Foa (1974) have noted that the six resources in their model tend to cluster into patterns. Those resources clustering closer together may be observed within a given behaviour. For example, a person who compliments another's cooking may be perceived as providing all three symbolic resources. The compliments bestow status on the cook. If the exchange partners are courting or have established a satisfying semi-permanent relationship, the compliment may be interpreted as a sign of affection. Finally, the compliment provides information about how the giver feels about certain foods and cooking styles. Thus, a given act within an exchange may have many different interpretations.

Because we believe that the outcomes of an exchange can impact upon the total interaction, it is important that we discover what guides an exchange. If we can understand how people evaluate exchanges, we can move closer to understanding how exchange difficulties will influence interactions. Most social exchange theorists point to the norm of reciprocity as a critical guide and basis of evaluation of exchanges (e.g. Homans 1974; Blau 1964; Thibaut and Kelley 1959). Consequently, an understanding of that norm should provide insight into interactions as well as exchanges.

Perspectives on the norm of reciprocity

The norm of reciprocity has as a construct played a central role in thinking in disciplines such as anthropology, sociology and social psychology. Since we believe that it plays a critical role in interaction, it is important that we note how it has been conceptualized. We will present four sets of theory and research related to the norm of reciprocity. We will examine Gouldner's (1960) analysis as a comparison point. We do not wish to reify his thinking but note that his analysis is frequently cited as embodying the thrust of the norm. We will then examine three alternatives which to some degree have related the norm of reciprocity to interaction: Resource Theory; Reciprocity Therapy; and Self-Disclosure Reciprocity.

Gouldner (1960): the norm of reciprocity

Gouldner (1960, p. 171) argues that the norm of reciprocity minimally prescribes two things: '(1) people should help those who have helped them, and (2) people should not injure those who have helped them.' While he drew a number of implications from these prescriptions, we will focus on eight which seem important to interaction.

First, the obligation arising from the norm of reciprocity is bounded by certain conditions. A person's indebtedness is a function of four things: (1) the receiver's need for the resource at the time of its receipt; (2) the quantity of resource possessed by the giver when the exchange was initiated; (3) the motives of the giver; and (4) external forces placed upon the giver to provide resources. Thus, the acceptance of a resource does not imply an unlimited obligation to the giver. In some circumstances, a person may lack sufficient obligation to even acknowledge the receipt of a resource.

Second, the norm of reciprocity operates differently in alternative social systems. Indeed, Befu (1980) has argued that the norm is translated into more specific cultural rules of exchange which permit some range of individual exchange strategies. It is plausible that cultural exchange rules may differ across societies and that individual strategies may differ within a culture. Thereby we expect that reciprocity will also be influenced by the nature of the relationship between exchange partners. Clark and Mills (1979) discovered that immediate reciprocation of a benefit or requests for reciprocation created less attraction when partners expected a relationship based upon need rather than equity. In a follow-up, Clark (1981) reported that observers of a relationship inferred closer friendship between relational partners when they exchanged noncomparable resources than when they exchanged identical resources. From the viewpoint of observers, the exchange of comparable rather than noncomparable resources constituted the repayment of debt rather than meeting the other's needs.

Third, the norm of reciprocity suggests that returns should be roughly equivalent to those given. In other words, a person might be expected to return a resource of similar but not identical value to what was received. Gouldner noted that this allowance permits the repayment of debts through several resources and also leaves the relational partners somewhat uncertain as to whether the debt has really been repaid. Thus, it provides greater flexibility to the repayment process but at the same time introduces ambiguity.

Fourth, the judgement of rough equivalence inherently resides in the exchange partners. It is possible that the relational partners may differ in their judgements about exchanged resources and hence the degree to which the norm has been met. Further, Gouldner noted that the judgements of the actors may differ from the 'objective' judgements of outside observers.

Fifth, two forms of reciprocity might exist: heteromorphic and homomorphic. Heteromorphic reciprocity specifies that a returned resource may be different in form but equal in value to the resource that was received. Homomorphic reciprocity prescribes that a resource of an identical type to that received must be returned. The former would allow an exchange of love for status as long as the value of each was equal; the latter would only permit the exchange of love for love or status for status regardless of value. Gouldner argued that homomorphic reciprocity is most frequently observed in conflict situations controlled by the 'negative norm of reciprocity' (i.e., an eye for an eye).

Sixth, the norm of reciprocity does not require an *immediate* return of a resource. Partners may delay repayment for some time and may even transact exchanges before an earlier initiation is completed. In fact, Gouldner argues that exchange partners may desire longer time periods before returns are made. These delays allow the indebted partner time to accumulate sufficient resource to repay the debt and during the interim, ensures a positive relationship between giver and receiver. Similarly, Blau (1964, p. 99) wrote, 'Generally, posthaste reciprocation of favours, which implies a refusal to stay indebted for a while and hence an insistence on a more businesslike relationship, is condemned as improper . . . social bonds are fortified by remaining obligated to others as well as by trusting them to discharge their obligations for considerable time.' Thus, a rapid repayment of debt might challenge the underlying basis for a relationship, since it implies a desire to be independent of the partner.

Seventh, the norm of reciprocity may exist in both a manifest and latent form. Gouldner argued that people may reciprocate benefits in an exchange without being aware they are doing so. In other words, the norm may operate below the level of awareness until it is violated or one expects that it might be violated.

Finally, the norm of reciprocity is enforced through social sanctions. A person who is cavalier about his or her obligations can expect to be punished by his or her relational partners just as the victims of nonreciprocation can justifiably seek retribution from those who have received benefits but have not reciprocated.

Thus, the norm of reciprocity dictates that a person should return benefits to some degree comparable in form and/or value to those received from another. Until that return is made, the receiver of a benefit is obligated to be kind and avoid being cruel to the giver. Because the norm is general in nature, the exchange partners play a pivotal role in determining when and how an exchange should be transacted.

Foa and Foa's (1974) resource theory

As is implied by its name, the primary focus of this theory is upon the resources observed within an exchange. A resource is defined as 'any commodity – material or symbolic – which is transmitted through interpersonal behaviour, (Foa and Foa 1974, p. 36). Resources are inferred from the behaviours and objects observed within an exchange. As noted earlier, Foa and Foa (1974) hypothesize and research (Turner *et al.* 1971) has discovered six resource categories: love, status, services, information, goods and money. The analysis of how these resources are exchanged stems from two propositions: '(1) Every interpersonal behaviour consists of giving and/or taking away one or more resource;' and '(2) Behaviours that involve closely allied resources occur more frequently than behaviours that involve less closely related resources' (Foa and Foa. 1976, p. 106). While a number of important implications have been drawn from these propositions (see Foa 1971; Foa and Foa 1972; 1974; 1976; 1980 for a complete explication of their theory), we will only focus on those important to interaction.

Foa and Foa argue that exchange partners translate their behaviours into resource categories. In other words, resource theory stresses the importance of the interpretation of acts rather than the actual properties of acts themselves. From this perspective, attaching meaning to exchange behaviours is the process of interpreting the observed behaviours from the perspective of one or more of the resource categories. Consequently, their taxonomy of resources reflects cognitive structures used to attach meaning to actions rather than a listing of specific behavioural types.

Often exchange partners may reach different conclusions about the meaning of resources observed in an exchange. For example, the exchange partners may differ as to the resources observed within an exchange. This difference may be due to mismapping or mismatching. When mismapping, the exchange partners assign a given action to different resource categories (e.g. one person views a compliment as an expression of status while the other interprets it as an expression of love). Mismatching occurs when relational partners vary in the degree of differentiation they see between resource categories. One relational partner may see status and love as being so similar that any expression of status also entails an expression of love. The other partner may see the same two resource categories as being sufficiently different such that the expression of one has no bearing upon the expression of the other. Consequently, relational partners may leave an exchange or interaction with different perceptions of the events.

While people vary in the degree to which they see the resources as being differentiated, individuals seem to evaluate the resource categories along two dimensions: concreteness and particularism. Turner *et al.* (1971) reported that the resources may be ranked in the following way according to the degree to which they are perceived to be concrete: (1) goods and services; (2) money and love; and (3) information and status. In addition, the resources vary in the degree to which they are perceived to acquire their value from the particular exchange partner (particularistic) or are valuable regardless of the provider (universalistic). The rank order from most particularistic to universalistic is: (1) love; (2) services and status; (3) goods and information; and (4) money. It should be noted, however, that recent research by Brinberg and Castell (1982) found strong support for the ranking on the concreteness dimension but only moderate support for the ranking on the particularistic dimension (love and money were perceived to be more similar in particularism than they initially hypothesized).

Once an exchange has been initiated and a behaviour placed into a given resource category or categories by the recipient, an attempt will be made to return either the same or a similar resource. By 'similar' Foa and Foa mean that a resource similar in the degree of particularism and concreteness may be substituted. For example, having received love, one may return one of two similar resources (status or services), or two less similar resources (information or goods) but would rarely return the most dissimilar resource (money).

This implication approximates what Gouldner (1960) referred to as homomorphic reciprocity. This does not mean that Foa and Foa discount heteromorphic reciprocity but simply do not include it in their model. In fact, the two types may be somewhat related. Beach and Carter (1976) discovered that people attach the greatest worth to a returned resource that falls into the same resource category to that which was given. In addition, this implication is also consistent with Gouldner's (1960) notion of rough equivalence. The recipient of information may return a different piece of information or even a similar but not identical resource and still not violate the norm of reciprocity.

Research seems to support this implication. Turner *et al.* (1971) reported that while partners reported preferences for in-kind resource exchanges, they were also willing to accept similar resources (for example, love, status and information could be appropriately exchanged for one another). It should be noted, however, that while Brinberg and Castell (1982) also report similar results, Beach and Carter (1976) found inconsistent support for the relationship between similarity of resource category and preference for exchange. When collapsing across all of the resource categories (thereby ignoring specific types), one finds that the in-kind and similar resource exchanges are more preferred than the exchange of dissimilar resources. However, when examining each specific resource category separately, the patterns were only partly consistent with the predictions of the theory. Of importance to interaction though, their findings suggest that love, status and information could be appropriately exchanged with one another but inappropriately exchanged for goods and money.

Finally, a person's evaluation of an interaction will be affected by the perceived appropriateness of the content of the resources exchanged. If dissimilar resources are exchanged, satisfaction should be lower than if identical or similar resources are provided. Indeed, Teichman (1971) discovered that relational partners evaluated their interactions more positively when they received love in exchange for love, status, or information than when they received money for those three resources. Consistent with the theory, money reciprocation produced higher levels of satisfaction when made for the receipt of money or goods than for love, information or status.

Thus, resource theory encompasses many of the same notion suggested by Gouldner. Beyond conjecture, empirical research suggests that homomorphic reciprocity guides social exchanges. However, despite its apparent usefulness for analysing interactions, most of the research arising from this perspective has used only limited interaction situations. Individuals have been (a) given questionnaires in which they judge the appropriateness of the resource exchange in hypothetical situations, (b) allowed to communicate by passing cards through barriers, or (c) confronted with a confederate who provides them with a resource and then given the opportunity to reciprocate through some limited number of options. None of the research has investigated the resource exchange arising within the natural, unconstrained interaction between two people.

Reciprocity therapy

We use the term 'reciprocity therapy' to refer to a set of clinical techniques used to alleviate marital and familial discord. Included in this set are Stuart's Operant-Interpersonal Therapy (1969; 1975), Azrin *et al.*'s Reciprocity Counselling (1973), and Weiss *et al.*'s Oregon Approach (1973). While these techniques are based in several theoretical perspectives (e.g. reinforcement theory, social exchange theory, social learning theory), each views the establishment of reciprocal exchanges as an important factor in creating a satisfying married and family life.

These theorists focus primarily upon what Gouldner (1960) referred to as heteromorphic reciprocity. In other words, the focus is upon providing resources of roughly equivalent value (measured dichotomously as having positive or negative value, or as pleasures or displeasures), rather than roughly equivalent form. For example, Patterson and Reid (1979, p. 139) refer to reciprocity as 'an equity in the giving and receiving of positive and aversive consequences which occur in most social interaction. . . . This would require that over a series of interactions, two persons reinforce or punish each other for approximately the same proportion of behaviour.'

It is assumed that individuals acquire the propensity to exchange through learning. As we noted earlier, exchanging is but one of several behavioural sequences occurring within an interaction. In some cases, behaving independently of or aggressively toward a relational partner may accrue greater profits (at least in the short run) than exchanging resources. Consequently, a person must learn through experience, socialization or therapy that exchanging is a more profitable behavioural sequence. Indeed, Molm and Wiggins (1979) discovered that relational partners were more likely to establish stable exchange patterns if they received reinforcements from the experimenter for exchanging rather than working as individuals (i.e., they were operantly conditioned to exchange).

Violations of reciprocity are assumed to be a major source of marital and familial dissatisfaction. A number of studies indicate that distressed and non-distressed families differ in their resource exchange. Alexander (1973) discovered that stable families communicated in such a manner that the number of supportive statements (e.g. empathic understanding) made by a parent to a child was significantly correlated with the number of similar statements made by the child to the parent. The same correlation was not significant for disintegrating families. Disintegrating families communicated in such a manner that significant correlations were observed between defensive statements (e.g. dogmatic or superiority statements).

Two studies have focused on the volume of positive and negative statements made in distressed and non-distressed marriages. Vincent *et al.* (1975) and Birchler *et al.* (1975) both discovered that distressed marrieds sent a larger proportion of negative statements and smaller proportions of positive statements to their spouses than did non-distressed marrieds.

It should be noted however, that these data have been subject to criticism (see Gottman *et al.* 1976; Gottman *et al.* 1977). Two major challenges have been levelled as to whether the results really demonstrate the presence or absence of reciprocity. First, Gottman *et al.* (1976) have argued that the results may have changed had the prior research asked the marrieds to code their own interactions rather than relying upon outside observers to code them. In other words, outside observers may have miscoded or simply missed some of the rewards viewed by the actors in the interactions. This argument seems reasonable given that Gouldner (1960) had argued that the norm of reciprocity might be perceived differently by the actors in the exchange and 'objective' outside observers. In fact, when Gottman *et al.* (1976) had marrieds code their own interactions into positive and negative statements, they discovered something previously unrecognized in research. Distressed and non-distressed couples did not differ significantly in the number of messages that were meant to be interpreted as positive. They differed in that distressed marrieds tended to interpret positively intended messages as being negative in tone. Thus, a spouse in a distressed marriage may send a message which he or she intended to be positive and have it reacted to in a negative manner since the partner misperceived its valence. Hence, reciprocity may be violated due to misperceptions.

The second criticism made of previous research is that the data are not analysed in a fashion that adequately tests for reciprocity. Gottman *et al.* (1977) correctly argue that the norm of reciprocity assumes that the value of a resource to be returned is contingent upon the value of the resource received. Since previous research merely reports the frequency of positive and negative behaviours or the correlation between the frequencies of behaviours, the contingency aspect is overlooked. In fact, the observed increased frequency of positive behaviours in non-distressed marriages may reflect what Gottman *et al.* (1976) refer to as a bank account model rather than a reciprocity model. The bank account model is one in which spouses provide each other with large numbers of positive statements which are not contingent upon each other's behaviours. Spouses in non-distressed marriages appear to some degree to be unconditionally benevolent toward each other.

Gottman *et al.* (1976) offer an alternative method of testing for reciprocity. They argue that reciprocity is evidenced when the conditional probability that a given spouse will make a positive statement after receiving a positive statement from his or her spouse should be significantly greater than the nonconditional probability that the given spouse will make a positive statement. This implies that the diagonal elements of a first-order Markov matrix of conditional probabilities should be significantly greater than the nonconditional probabilities of positive statements. Using this approach, Gottman *et al.* (1976) discovered in only one of two reported studies that non-distressed and distressed marrieds differed in reciprocal exchanges within interactions. Further, Gottman *et al.* (1976) reported that differences in reciprocity of affective resources between distressed and non-distressed marrieds only partly distinguished them. Thus, Gottman *et al.* (1977) concluded that reciprocity models are not as useful as assumed and have to be revised.

It should be noted, however, that Gottman's approach differs from that proposed by Gouldner (1960) and some of the theorists interested in reciprocity therapy. By focusing upon the diagonals of the first-order Markov matrix, the researchers are implicitly imposing a time order on the test of reciprocity. Specifically, they assume that reciprocity requires that a positive statement be preceded immediately by a positive statement. Even if the coding is done on an event rather than a time basis, the assumption is still that reciprocity occurs when there is a high relationship between a consequent statement and the statement just preceding it. Gouldner (1960) assumes an unspecified time obligation. Similarly, Stuart (1969, p. 625) noted, 'Whenever one partner to a reciprocal interaction unilaterally rewards the other, he does so with the confidence that he will be compensated in kind in the future. For example, if the husband agrees to entertain his wife's parents for a weekend, he does so with the expectation that his wife will accompany him on a weekend fishing trip at some time in the future.' Thus, these theorists do not assume that resources must be immediately returned or that resource exchanges may not transpire after another exchange has been initiated and before it is finally transacted.

In addition, it is not clear that the bank account model is really inconsistent with reciprocity. Spouses may be accumulating credits in the relationship which they can use to support their demands for reciprocity in the future. Blau (1964) has noted that often powerful people will overwhelm less powerful individuals with resources they cannot repay, and because of the demands of the norm of reciprocity, the high-power person can keep the less powerful person in a subservient position indefinitely. Thus, providing seemingly noncontingent resources now may mask an incurred obligation which one must repay in the future.

Finally, these theorists assume the restoration of reciprocity will increase marital and familial satisfaction. It is beyond the scope of this paper to review the evaluation research associated with these therapies. However, in a review of such research, Jacobson and Martin (1976) noted that the therapies do seem to improve marital satisfaction but also advocated that further research be done. It should also be noted that these therapies are actually packages of techniques including some which are not related to reciprocity. Consequently, it is difficult to evaluate the degree to which any improvement is due to the restoration of reciprocity.

Thus, reciprocity therapy is the most applied of the approaches. It differs from Gouldner's (1960) analysis in that it relies heavily upon reinforcements as a stimulus for the norm of reciprocity and Gottman *et al.*'s (1976) measures of reciprocity imply a more stringent temporal requirement.

Self-disclosure reciprocity

The norm of reciprocity is one of several constructs used to explain a pattern of self-disclosure called the dyadic effect (see Chaikin and Derlega 1976; Archer 1979; Taylor 1979). Jourard (1971, p. 66) described this pattern in the following way: 'In ordinary social relationships, disclosure is a reciprocal phenomenon. Participants in dialogue disclose their thoughts, feelings, actions, etc., to the other and are disclosed to in return. I called this reciprocity the 'dyadic effect': disclosure begets disclosure.' It is not our goal to review all of the self-disclosure literature (see Cozby 1973; Chaikin and Derlega 1976; or Dindia 1982; Chapter 8 for such reviews), but instead to draw implications about the norm of reciprocity emerging from selected research related to self-disclosure.

Self-disclosure reciprocity had been conceptualized either as a homomorphic reciprocity or a combination of homomorphic and heteromorphic. For example, Dindia (1982, p. 506) defines reciprocal self-disclosure as though it is homomorphic: 'Reciprocity of self-disclosure is defined conceptually as mutually contingent self-disclosure. This means that A's self-disclosure to B causes B's self-disclosure to A, and vice versa.' Thus, resources of identical types are exchanged. However, others have argued that there is a tendency to match the same level of value (measured as the degree of intimacy) within the self-disclosures. Chaikin and Derlega (1974, p. 118) write: '. . . a subject tends to reciprocate the same level of intimacy to the discloser that has been revealed to him.' In one sense, homomorphic reciprocity is a more liberal definition since a person need only make a self-descriptive statement (regardless of intimacy level) to fulfil the obligation of having received one. When looking at the two in combination, the receiver must be concerned with not only returning a self-disclosive statement but one which which matches the intimacy level of the stimulus.

Regardless of reciprocity type, rough equivalence of disclosure seems to be acceptable. For example, while homomorphic reciprocity suggests that self-disclosure should be returned in kind, research by Ehrlich and Graeven (1971) indicated that while subjects did reciprocate information at the same level of intimacy as received, they did not reciprocate in the same topic area. In addition, Berg and Archer (1980) found that expressing concern for a self-disclosing communicator was judged to be a more appropriate response than the return of any level of self-disclosure. Thus, the recipient of a self-disclosing statement may self-disclose in return but about a different topic or may even shift resource type in a manner predicted by Foa and Foa (1974). When looking at the match of intimacy levels, the same rough equivalence is evident. Three studies have reported that while self-disclosures at higher levels of intimacy prompt more intimate returns than low-intimacy disclosures, subjects do not exactly match the degree of intimacy of the stimulus (Cozby 1972; Derlega *et al.* 1973; Levin and Gergen 1969). Generally, communicators return self-disclosing statements that are somewhat less intimate than the stimulus disclosures.

Self-disclosure reciprocity specifies no time order for the return of a disclosure. This point is made in Altman's (1974, p. 250) discussion of the dyadic effect: '. . . the dyadic effect is assumed to be a time-bound process in which people mutually regulate their disclosure to one another, at some agreed upon pace. But, little more is said about temporal aspects of reciprocity. The rate at which it occurs, how it ebbs and flows, factors which accelerate or retard reciprocity of exchange are not discussed in detail.' Thus, even though receipt of self-disclosure requires some return within a given time frame, we have little notion of what that time frame might be.

Self-disclosure reciprocity is influenced by a number of different conditions. Won-Doornink (1979) discovered that reciprocal self-disclosures varied by both intimacy level and stage of relationship (i.e., a negative linear relationship was observed between the stage of relational development and the reciprocation of non-intimate self-disclosure whereas a curvilinear relationship existed between the stage of relational development and the reciprocation of intimate self-disclosures). In addition, Archer and Berg (1978) noted that when the obligation to return a self-disclosing fact threatens a receiver's decision freedom, a person may choose to avoid reciprocating. Finally, Berg and Archer (1982) have discovered that different forms of self-disclosure are reciprocated depending upon the interaction goals of the participants. When subjects are trying to form impressions of each other and exchange information, they tend to reciprocate descriptive disclosures. On the other hand, when attempting to make themselves attractive, reciprocation of evaluative intimacy tends to be found. Topical reciprocity was most frequently observed in situations in which information exchange or impression formation are not highly salient.

Actors may differ in their assessments of the degree to which they reciprocated self-disclosures. A number of studies have found higher correlations between a person's own assessment of the degree of reciprocity that occurred between self and partner than between the self-reports of each partner's self-disclosures (e.g. Pearce *et al.* 1974; Rubin *et al.* 1980; Rubin and Shenker 1978; Dindia 1983). Thus, independently of one another, the partners perceive they have reciprocated self-disclosures, whereas the assessments of each differ from one another.

In addition, the judgements of actors about their own levels of reciprocity may differ from the judgements of outside observers. Specifically, actors may perceive they have reciprocated (even if they differ between themselves as to the amount) while a statistical analysis of observer judgements indicates no reciprocity. Dindia (1983) had dyads engage in conversations. Outside observers of the conversation coded the frequency of self-descriptive statements and these codes were subjected to lag sequential analysis (i.e., testing the probability that a self-disclosure by A produced a self-disclosure by B the first utterance after A's self-disclosure, or the second, or the third, or so on). When testing for the existence of reciprocity at one to five lags from the stimulus disclosure, no significant reciprocity was observed. However, when each subject was asked to indicate the degree to which he or she and his or her partner disclosed, statistically significant and moderately large correlations were observed. Thus, partners felt they had reciprocated self-disclosures but the statistical analysis of observer judgements demonstrated none within a given time frame. It should be noted, however, that Dindia's statistical analysis makes assumptions inconsistent with Gouldner's (1960) conception of the norm of reciprocity. As we have noted throughout, the norm of reciprocity does not specify that a return be made at a given time (i.e., it does not specify that the return should be made within five utterances) nor does the norm specify that the return should always be made at the same point in a given sequence of behaviours (i.e., consistently returned on the first or whichever opportunity after receipt). It is plausible that the actors saw returns occurring at various lags throughout the conversation while statistical analysis would miss them.

Thus, research on self-disclosure has identified what appears to be a norm of reciprocity operating within an interaction. However, the perception of the norm varies somewhat among the interactants and in comparison with the sequential analysis of judges.

Reciprocity in interactions

Our discussion of reciprocity in interactions will be presented in two sections. In the first section, we will formulate a definition of the norm of reciprocity based upon the various theoretical and research perspectives outlined in the preceding pages. We will also explicate what we see to be some of the important ramifications of that definition. The second section will consist of the description of a methodology used for the study of reciprocity in interpersonal communication and some preliminary results of a study designed, in part, to evaluate the efficacy of that methodology.

Definition of the norm of reciprocity

Based upon the perspectives reviewed, *we define the norm of reciprocity as the shared expectation that the recipient of a resource is obligated to and at some time will return to the giver a resource roughly equivalent to that which was received.* As was the case with previous definitions, this formulation carries several implications with it.

First, the assessment as to whether the norm has been satisfied within a given interaction involves a form of social cognition. That is, in employing the norm of reciprocity, interactants utilize '. . . the cognitive structures and processes underlying social judgement and social behaviour' (Higgins *et al.* 1981, p. ix). The norm thus provides a *control* mechanism for social interaction in that it outlines a generalized prescription for the 'give and take' of conversation. In addition, it serves as a standard for *evaluating* interaction; an individual's satisfaction with an interaction will depend upon the degree to which he or she and his or her partner conformed to the expectations outlined by the norm.

. While the norm of reciprocity is a standard by which performances may be created or evaluated, we do not mean that it intrudes constantly into our consciousness. Instead, once people have learned to reciprocate, judgements about reciprocity become automatic and in most cases operate with limited awareness (see Langer. 1978). It seems unlikely that a person, after having received a piece of information, will always consciously think about his or her obligation to return a roughly equivalent resource. The person formulates a roughly equivalent resource without necessarily thinking about doing so. If a conversation has become scripted (see Schank and Abelson 1977), then reciprocated exchanges will likely have been incorporated into the sequence alleviating the necessity of mindfully judging reciprocation. However, when the norm is violated or one is uncertain about the conversation, judgements about reciprocity may be mindful.

Second, there exist at least two methods of empirically evaluating the extent to which an interaction is characterized by reciprocity. We will label these judgements *phenomenological reciprocity* and *statistical reciprocity*. Phenomenological reciprocity is said to exist when the interactant or an observer of the interaction draws a causal linkage between the resources that are given and those that are received in the interaction. By the phrase 'causal linkage' we mean that the judge makes an attribution of intent on the part of a partner. He or she sees the return of a resource as having been prompted by *and* intended to be a response to the proffer of a resource. The judgement of that linkage resides entirely within the perceiver and, if asked, we believe that he or she can describe the linkage with some degree of accuracy.

Statistical reciprocity is said to exist when a significant probabilistic association is observed between the occurrence of resource giving on the part of the two interactants. Although, as in research conducted by Dindia (1983) and Gottman (1979), outside judges are asked to code the occurrence of resource offers within an interaction, for statistical reciprocity those judges are *not* asked to describe or even to look for any linkages between those offers. Instead, a statistical procedure such as lag sequential analysis is employed to assess the probability that the offer of a resource by one interactant is followed by the offer of a resource by the other interactant.

Because both statistical reciprocity and phenomenological reciprocity rely fundamentally on observer judgements of resource offers, it is possible that the two forms of evaluation may produce equivalent results. However, we feel it is more likely that the procedures will produce different findings. For example, statistical reciprocity may be found where neither the interactants themselves, nor outside observers would have claimed a causal linkage existed between resource offers. No less illustrative for its extremity, a scenario which could produce such a contradiction is that of two mentally disturbed persons, both simultaneously conducting schizophrenic soliloquies (see Longabaugh *et al*. 1966) while seated in the same room. Adopting a convention frequently used in studies of self-disclosure, we could have observers of this 'conversation' code the occurrence of self-descriptive or self-referent utterances. It is extremely unlikely that those observers would make any attribution of intent regarding either of the interactants' self-references being a response to that of the other, and thus no phenomenological reciprocity would be found. However, if self-references occur frequently enough and at consistent intervals in both monologues, it is possible that a lag sequential analysis would imply the existence of statistical reciprocity. The inverse of this contradiction is also possible: statistical analysis may reveal no reciprocity where the interactants would have judged it to exist. Lag sequential analysis tests the probability of the co-occurrence of resource offers at prescribed, fixed lags. The phenomenological procedure, however, is less restrictive in that it allows the *judges* to specify the number of utterances which occur between the offer and the return of a resource. Thus significant phenomenological reciprocity may be observed with variable lags, while in the same interaction statistical reciprocity would appear non-significant at each of several fixed lags.

Third, the norm of reciprocity is functional. Because the expectation regarding the exchange of roughly equivalent resources need not be negotiated *de novo* with every new interactant, the norm allows even strangers to communicate with one another with the understanding that they will leave the interaction with approximately the same resource 'balance' with which they entered. In addition, as mentioned previously, because interactants are able to conform to the norm of reciprocity without consciously having to evaluate each and every exchange, individuals are able to conserve a great deal of cognitive energy – energy which can instead be devoted to ensuring that the interaction, itself, proceeds logically and fluently. The norm is functional, also, in that it virtually assures the availability of needed resources. An individual in search of information can increase his or her chances of obtaining it by bestowing status or affection on another, thus creating a feeling of indebtedness or obligation.

Fourth, several criteria may be used by interactants in making the judgement as to whether the resources exchanged are roughly equivalent. Those criteria include, but are not restricted to, the following four standards. First, and most basic, is the judgement that an exchange has been transacted. That is to say, the minimal requirement for rough equivalence of resources (and thus for reciprocity) is that an interactant perceive that his or her offer of a resource has prompted his or her partner to respond with the offer of some (*any*) resource in return. This minimal requirement is similar to what Davis and Perkowitz (1979) termed responsiveness in a conversation. It is a sign that one's partner at least acknowledges that a resource was given. Second, the interactants may appraise the resources on the basis of a subjective standard of value. Unfortunately, there is no international 'gold standard' for symbolic resources and, consequently, the perceived value of two resources may vary according to each individual's past experience with the particular resources, their current utility to the individual, and other factors which combine to form the subjective standard he or she employs in the appraisal. Third, the judgement of the rough equivalence of resources may be affected by the similarity of resource categories involved in the exchange. This criterion follows directly from the claim made by Foa and Foa (1974) that interactants attempt to exchange resources which are of approximately the same valence on the particularism and concreteness dimensions. Finally, resources are more likely to be judged roughly equivalent if they share the same mode of conveyance. For example, as a response to a resource offered via nonverbal channels, a nonverbally transmitted resource would more likely be judged roughly equivalent than would a verbally transmitted resource. Although no direct test has been made of this standard, research indicates that positive and negative nonverbal cues tend to be reciprocated in the same mode (Rosenfeld 1966; 1967).

Fifth, judges may differ in their assessment of the norm. A few of the preceding implications have alluded to this point, but we feel it is important enough to justify more explicit consideration. Besides the different conclusions we noted which may arise from the use of phenomenological as opposed to statistical reciprocity as an empirical guideline, at least two other variables may differentially influence raters' judgements of the extent to which interactants exhibit reciprocity. As we have already indicated, aspects unique to a person's exchange history and current needs may have an impact upon his or her appraisal of the value of a resource. Thus, for example, a starving man and a gourmet chef may make diametrically opposed assessments of the value of directions to the nearest McDonald's, though when given to each, the information is intrinsically the same. Because their judgements will affect the value of the resources they choose to return, the person providing the directions may have difficulty concluding that *both* individuals' responses are roughly equivalent in value to the resource he or she provided (and to each other). In a study conducted by Beach and Carter (1976), the subjective nature of resource appraisal was shown to have an impact on judgements of reciprocity in that interactants were consistently found to rate the resource they returned as more valuable than that which they received.

In addition to differences in the subjective standards judges employ in appraising resources, actor–observer differences may result in a lack of correspondence between ratings of conformity to the norm. We expect, for example, that even as a result of their proximity to each other and the salience each has in the perceptual field of the other, the interactants will be more likely than will outside observers to interpret the nonverbal nuances of gestures, facial expression, voice intonation, and such as conveying resources in addition to those transmitted verbally.

The study of reciprocity

Our exploratory investigation of phenomenological reciprocity required that participants in the study each attend two different sessions. In the first session, two participants were introduced and asked to spend five minutes discussing with each other a topic which had been selected for its relevance to the sample of interactants. The conversation was videotaped. After interacting, the participants were separated and asked to complete a questionnaire designed to assess their feelings about the interaction and the extent to which they felt they had given and received each of seveal symbolic resources.

One week later, the members of each dyad returned separately for the second session, to view and analyse the videotape of their conversation. Before viewing the recording, the experimenter read the following paragraph aloud as the participant followed along on a typewritten copy:

We are interested in your perceptions of the conversation you had last week. We want to replay the conversation for you and have you make some judgements about it. In particular, we want you to look for specific exchanges between yourself and the other student. An exchange is defined as one person (either yourself or your partner) providing a resource to another who in turn transacts or completes the exchange by giving something in return. An exchange begins when one party gives the other some resource and it is not over until something is returned from the other. You should note that sometimes no exchange ever occurs. For example, one person gives the other something and the receiver gives nothing in return.

Before proceeding, the experimenter then answered whatever questions the participant may have had about the instructions.

Given this format, it was possible for the participant to observe the initiation of an exchange *before* he or she had sufficient information to judge that the previous exchange had or had not been transacted. In such cases, the participant was instructed to set aside the coding form for the earlier exchange and begin one for the intervening exchange. Each form was completed as the participant made the relevant judgements regarding the transaction of each exchange. Although such occurrences were rare, this procedure thus allowed for the possibility of overlapping exchanges.

The videotape was then played a first time through without interruption both to remind the participant of the interchange he or she had had a week earlier with his or her partner and to give the participant an opportunity to anticipate the offer and return of resources during the second viewing. Before playing the tape a second time, however, the participant was instructed to say 'stop' each time he or she saw an exchange beginning (i.e., the offer of a resource by either interactant) and again if and when he or she saw that exchange transacted (i.e., the return of a resource). With each call from the participant, the experimenter put the video tape player in the 'pause' mode to allow the participant to complete an exchange coding form containing several questions about that particular exchange.

The exchange coding form consisted of eight items: (1) Who initiated the exchange? (Self or Partner); (2) What resource(s) was (were) initially given by [the person who initiated the exchange]? (Liking or Friendship, Information, Status, or 'Other'); (3) How valuable was that resource? (Not Valuable, Somewhat, Quite, or Extremely Valuable); (4) How was the resource transmitted? (Verbally, Nonverbally, or Both); (5) Did the receiver transact the exchange by giving something in return? (Yes or No), [IF *YES*:] (6) What resource(s) was (were) returned? (Same response format as question 2); (7) How valuable was the resource? (Same response format as question 3); (8) How was it transmitted? (Same response format as question 4). A new coding form was used for each offer of a resource whether or not that offer elicited the return of a resource. After coding every exchange he or she saw in the five-minute segment of video tape, the participant was debriefed.

We wish to make explicit that we do not assume a one-to-one correspondence between the 'after-the-fact' judgements of subjects and their judgements during the conversation. While we expect later judgements will reflect some degree of residue from the interaction, other influences may also be operative. For example, the observation of self may induce self-evaluation through objective self-awareness (Duval and Wicklund 1972). Because of the difficulty of assessing cognition during the interaction, we cannot determine the extent to which these judgements are correlated with those made during the conversation.

The sample group observed in this investigation consisted of 88 undergraduate volunteers who had been recruited from introductory classes in communication studies at Northwestern University. Using the procedures just described, we were able to record 44 dyadic interactions and obtain exchange judgements from 82 of the participants (six participants failed to return for the coding session).

The assessment of the reliability of these judgements was made difficult by both practical and theoretical problems. At the core of determining reliability is insuring that individuals are judging the same time or action units. Because the taping equipment used at the time of this study did not have a reliable counter for assessing time units, we were unable to examine the number of judgements made within a given time frame. In addition, none of the approaches to reciprocity or social exchange specify the exact action units which convey a given resource. This problem was compounded given that the resources may be transmitted via both verbal and nonverbal communication. If, for example, one divided the interaction according to thought units, one would miss any resource conveyed partially or entirely through nonverbal communication. Similarly, if one unitized the interaction according to some nonverbal stimulus (e.g. smiles), the linguistic aspects of resources would not be judged.

In order to provide some assessment of reliability we obtained equipment which would allow us to determine the time at which the judge saw a resource provided and had two independent coders make judgements about ten randomly selected tapes utilizing the same instrument and instruction as the subjects. Because we feel that it is premature to arbitrarily choose a given action unit, we instead chose to look at the reliability of the judgements across time. Our first set of analyses looked at the correlation between the judgements of our two coders during the entire interaction, the first and second halves ($2\frac{1}{2}$ minutes each). When examining the judgements as to how frequently resources were *offered* by a given interactant during a given time unit, all correlations between the judgements were significant ($p \le .05$). The correlations focused on the judgements of behaviour of the interactant sitting on the right in each interaction were as follow: .95 for the total interaction; .95 for the first half and .65 the last half of the interaction. The same correlations for the communicator sitting on the left were as follows: .73 for the total interaction; .65 for the first half and .93 for the last half of the interaction.

The correlations between judgements about the number of times a given interactant *returned* a resource were also significant. The correlations for the interactant on the right were as follows: .83 for the total interaction; .75 for the first half and .79 for the last half of the interaction. The same correlations for the person sitting on the left were as follows: .99 during the total interaction; .85 during the first half and .86 during the second half of the interaction.

Having determined significant relationships between the coder's judgements as to the frequency with which offers and returns were made over time, we then examined the relationship between the coder's judgements as to the characteristics of the resources offered and returned. We will again report the correlations between judgements during the two halves of the interaction and for the interaction as a whole. When examining judgements as to the type of resource provided, both of our coders concurred that no offers or returns of affection were observed in the sampled interactions. Significant correlations ($p < .05$) were observed between judgements about the frequency with which information was offered (interactant on the right: r = .57 for the first half, r = .93 for the last half, and .68 for the total; interactant on the left: .93 for the first half, .67 for the last half, and .96 overall). Similar significant correlations (p < .05) were evidenced for judgements about the return of information (interactant on the right: r = .83 for the first half, r = .96 for the last half, and r = .98 overall; interactant on the left: r = .80 for the first half, r = .89 for the last half, and r = .73 overall). So little variation occurred in the judgements of one of our coders about the frequency with which status appeared, correlation coefficients could not be computed. However, the percent of agreements are relatively high for offers (interactant on right: 90 per cent for the first half, 93 per cent for the second half and 90 per cent overall; interactant on the left: 83 per cent for the first half; 73 per cent for the last half and 74 per cent overall) and returns (interactant on the right: 87 per cent for the first half; 77 per cent for the last half, and 78 per cent overall; interactant on the left: 83 per cent for the first half, 73 per cent for the last half, and 76 per cent overall).

In order to examine the reliability of judgements related to the value of resources, we examined each code on the four-point scale separately (e.g. the frequency with which resources having a value of 1 were offered). Insufficient variation in the use of code 1 (the lowest value) make it impossible to compute a correlation. However, the percentage of agreement for this code was relatively high for offers (interactant on the right: 83 per cent for the first half, 73 per cent of the last half, and 76 per cent overall; person on the left: 73 per cent for the first half, 77 per cent for the last half, and 72 per cent overall) and returns (interactant on the right: 83 per cent for the first half, 67 per cent for the last half and 74 per cent overall; interactant on the left: 73 per cent for the first half, 90 per cent for the last half, and 78 per cent overall). Correlations for the frequency with which resources of value 2 (moderate value) were exchanged were all significant (p < .05) for both offers (interactant on the right: r = .56 for the first half, r = .87 for the last half, and r = .72 overall; interactant on the left: r = .88 for the first half, r = .79 for the last half, and .90 overall) and returns (interactant on the right: r = .70 for the first half, r = .87 for the last half, and r = .89 for the total; for the interactant on the left: r = .71 for the first half, .95 for the last half, and .73 overall). Insufficient variation occurred for the value code three (moderately high value) in order for a correlation to be computed. However, the percentages are relatively high for offers (interactant on the right: 90 per cent for the first half, 97 per cent for the second half, and 92 per cent for the total; interactant on the left: 87 per cent for the first half, 87 per cent for the second half, and 84 per cent overall) and returns (person on the right: 93 per cent for the first half, 87 per cent for the second half and 88 per cent overall; person on the left: 83 per cent for the first half; 93 per cent for the second half; and 86 per cent overall). Both coders concurred that no resources of the highest value (4) were provided or returned.

Finally, the reliability for judgements as to the channel of conveyance were computed. Both coders agreed that no resources were provided via nonverbal channels in the sampled interactions. Significant correlations (p < .05) were observed between coder judgements about the frequency with which verbally conveyed resources were offered (interactant on the right: r = .70 for the first half, r = .93 for the second half and r = .73 for the overall; interactant on the left: r = .92 for the first half, r = .72 for the second half and .97 overall) and returns (interactant on the right: r = .85 for the first half, r = .86 for the second half, and r = .98 overall; interactant on the left: r = .84 for the first half, r = .87 for the last half, and r = .71 overall).

While the instrument has some obvious areas in which it is in need of improvement, we feel that the judgements were sufficiently reliable to report our results in a preliminary fashion. We note that we are continuing to refine the instrument and are currently calculating test–retest stability of judgement. We present a preliminary, descriptive analysis of these data in an effort to demonstrate the most basic manner in which interactants can be seen to perceive themselves as conforming to the norm of reciprocity. The results will be outlined in four general sections, each corresponding to one of the standards previously defined as being employed in the judgement of reciprocity: (1) transaction of the exchange, (2) relative value of the resource exchanged, (3) similarity of the resources exchanged, and (4) similarity of the channel of conveyance.

We posited that the first, most fundamental criterion for reciprocity is that the exchange be transacted (i.e., that something be returned in response to an offer). Operationally, the extent of adherence to this standard is defined simply as that proportion of resource offers which the interactant judged to have elicited the return of a resource from the recipient. Our sample perceived a high percentage of offers being reciprocated regardless of whether they were self-reciprocated ($\overline{X}$ = 84%, s.d. = 26.7) or other-reciprocated ($\overline{X}$ = 92%, s.d. = 14.9). Together these results indicate that at the most basic level, a substantial degree of reciprocity is perceived by the interactants.

The second criterion for reciprocity is the rough equivalence of the values of the resource offered and the resource returned in a given exchange. This criterion was operationally defined as follows: the offered resource and the returned resource are said to be of roughly equivalent value if the following relationship holds.

$$|V_o - V_r| \leq 1$$

where V_o is the value of the resource offered and V_r is the value of the resource returned, both rated on the four-point scale on the exchange coding form. On this basis, the interactants' judgements revealed that a substantial portion of exchanges were reciprocated in value regardless of whether self-reciprocated ($\overline{X}$ = 96%, s.d. = 10) or other-reciprocated ($\overline{X}$ = 96%, s.d. = 14). In addition, we also note the proportion of transacted exchanges in which a resource of the exact value of that which was given was returned. On the average, our subjects perceived that they reciprocated with a resource of exact value in 67 per cent (s.d. = 30) of the exchanges and that their partners reciprocated with a resource of exact value in 71 per cent (s.d. = 31) of the cases. In addition, we also computed a chi square between the judgements of the value of what was offered and the value of what was returned. The chi square for self-reciprocation was highly significant (chi square = 248.15, p. < .001) as was the same analysis for other-reciprocation (chi square = 247.95, p. < .001) Given a potential maximum of .87, the contingency coefficient for self-reciprocation was .67 and for other-reciprocation .66.

The third standard for assessing conformity to the norm of reciprocity is the similarity of the resource exchanged. We have acknowledged both in the conceptual formulation and in the phrasing of the questions on the coding form that it is possible for multiple resources to be transmitted simultaneously. Given that assertion, an offer and a return were said to be roughly equivalent with respect to similarity if the return was judged to include at least one of the resources offered. For example, if only information was seen to be offered, information must minimally have been judged to be part of the return regardless of other resources provided. In addition, rough equivalence of resource type must meet Foa and Foa's requirement that at least a similar resource be returned. This meant, for example, that status could be returned for love but information could not. Our subjects saw rough equivalence in the exchange of love, status, and/or information in an equally high percentage of cases regardless of who was the reciprocator $\overline{X}$ = 99%, no computable variance). Exact equivalence required that the reciprocator return the same resources as provided. On the average, subjects viewed themselves as returning the exact resource(s) as given in 58 per cent (s.d. = 38) of the exchanges and perceived their partners to do the same in 62 per cent s.d. = 35) of the cases. Chi square analyses between the type of resource given and returned were again computed and were significant (for self-reciprocation, chi square = 121.17, p. < .001; for other-reciprocation, chi square = 152.65, p. < .001). With an upper limit of .92, the contingency coefficient for self-reciprocation was .58 and for other-reciprocation .61

Our last criterion concerned reciprocation of resources via similar channels. Operationally, rough equivalence of conveyance modes was defined in a manner analogous to the definition used for resource categories. An exchange was roughly equivalent if the resource returned was judged to have been transmitted via at least one of the channels judged as having been used in the transmission of the resource initially offered. For example, if one interactant saw a resource offered verbally, the return must be done at least partially through the verbal channel. On the average, subjects saw a large percentage of exchanges as being roughly equivalent regardless of whether self-reciprocated ($\overline{X}$ = 92%, s.d. = 20) or other-reciprocated ($\overline{X}$ = 95%, s.d. = 13). As with the other standards, exact equivalence required that the same channel be used. On the average, subjects saw themselves as reciprocating through the same channels through which they received in 58 per cent (s.d. = 35) of the exchanges and their partners in 70 per cent (s.d. = 31) of the cases. Again, chi square analyses were significant. The chi square between the channels used in self-reciprocation was 29.28 (p. < .001) and for other-reciprocation 51.26 (p. < .001). With an upper limit of .82, the contingency coefficient for self-reciprocations was .30 and for other-reciprocation .37.

Our preliminary analysis of reciprocity judgements suggest that communicators characterize their interactions as possessing significant levels of reciprocity. Regardless of whether one is judging one's own returns or one's partner's, high degrees of rough equivalence and relatively high degrees of exact equivalance are observed in interactions.

Directions for research

While our preliminary investigation was limited in scope, the rather substantial degree of reciprocity perceived by the interactants suggests that future research may be quite rewarding. We see three avenues for future investigation: methodological issues, conditions affecting the form of reciprocity, and the relationship between reciprocity and satisfaction.

Methodological issues

We previously noted that we are currently working on increasing the reliability of the instrument. In addition, we feel that it is necessary to expand the nature of the stimulus being judged. Specifically, we are concerned that reciprocity judgements made about a videotaped interaction might differ from the same judgements made about the interactant's recall of the conversation. It is likely that the interactants will recall the conversation in much less detail than is afforded by the observation of the videotape. It also seems reasonable that the videotape will afford a better perspective of one's own behaviour in the interaction than would recollection. Consequently, we are currently comparing reciprocity judgements about the videotaped interaction with those made about the reconstruction from memory of the dialogue and nonverbal cues. If you will, we are asking: is it videotape or is it memory?

An additional methodological issue concerns the instructions we provided to subjects making the reciprocity judgements. Because we were committed to studying phenomenological reciprocity, we wanted the judgements to be as uncontaminated as possible. On the other hand, we found it difficult to provide instructions to the subjects which would allow them to make reliable judgements which at the same time did not in part mention some aspect of reciprocity. We felt that our blind for the conversation did not sensitize the subjects to reciprocity but the instructions used prior to making the judgements about the videotape might have. We are currently working on developing a set of instructions which provide sufficient detail so that naive subjects can make the judgements in a reliable fashion but are not forced to see reciprocity where none exists.

Our final methodological issue also has a theoretical component. We feel that it is important to determine the conditions under which differences occur between phenomenological judgements of reciprocity and statistical determinations of such. Although the investigation presented here could not demonstrate such differences, we believe that it is likely that research will discover them. We see at least two explanations of such potential divergences. The first suggests that people are motivated to see reciprocity where none exists. This approach implies that people distort reality, perhaps in an attempt to convince themselves that they are the kind of persons who discharge their obligations or that their current relationship is actually a fair one when it really isn't. This suggests a 'self-serving bias' is at the core of such differences. The second approach is a more cognitive explanation. It simply states that phenomenological judgements are made in a fashion different than statistical results. We dealt with this issue earlier, when noting that the assumptions of statistical techniques such as lag sequential analysis are at variance with the conceptualization of reciprocity made by many theorists. It is possible that statistical techniques which make different assumptions may produce results that are similar to human judgements. Unlike the first approach, this one suggests that both phenomenological and statistical judgements are correct within their assumptions but the assumptions differ.

Conditions affecting reciprocity

As previously noted, most of the perspectives on reciprocity acknowledge that it is influenced by specific conditions. In other words, we may find situations where the forms of reciprocity differ.

For example, the type of relationship in which the interaction is embedded may influence the form of reciprocity. Hinde (1979) has argued that relationships are composed of interactions. Consequently, an interaction may be influenced by the general nature of other interactions which are combined with it in the relationship. This perspective suggests several hypotheses about how reciprocity might be influenced by the nature of the relationship. To the degree that the partners anticipate future interactions (i.e., see their relationship as longer-term), the less pressure they should feel to reciprocate in the current interaction. In other words, relational partners may be able to leave a given interaction with felt obligation since the possibility to reciprocate in the future exists. However, interactants who perceive that the relationship and the interaction end at the same time may be under greater pressure to reduce their obligation in the existing interaction.

This general effect of anticipated interaction may be modified somewhat by the affective nature of the relationship. It is possible that two individuals who dislike one another may feel *less pressure* to reciprocate under conditions of *low anticipated interaction* than under conditions of high anticipated interaction. In superficial encounters with a disliked other, one may feel less pressure to reciprocate since the chance of future retaliation is less and the evaluation of the other matters little. However, one might still reciprocate with a disliked other in order to prevent falling into that person's debt in the long-term relationship. The interactions are kept on a businesslike level.

The relationship may also affect the form of reciprocity through relational rules. Elsewhere, it has been noted that relationships may be defined as mutual agreement, implicit or explicit, to interact in order to maximize rewards (Roloff 1976). This implies that some general rule exists which defines how related resources might be distributed. Such a rule might focus on equity (Walster *et al*. 1978), equality (Sampson 1975), need (Deutsch 1975), status (Berger *et al*. 1972) or some combination of rules (Leventhal 1976). These rules imply differences in the time required to return a resource. For example, in a relationship based upon need, strict requirements of immediate reciprocity may be absent. Since the partners provide one another resources when needed, no expectation exists that the needy partner can make returns immediately. In a relationship based upon equity or even equality, partners may have a greater anticipation that returns will be made much faster since a person's obligation is a function of the value of the resource provided (according to equity) and the desire to maintain an equal partnership.

Satisfaction

While the existence of reciprocity is interesting in and of itself, the primary contribution of such a concept lies in how it is related to certain outcomes. We see the degree of reciprocated exchanges as being a partial determinant of relational and interactional satisfaction. Given that we have approached relationships, interactions and symbolic exchanges as interrelated constructs, it seems reasonable that satisfaction with one should have 'ripple effect' on the others. Indeed, research indicates that relational difficulties can carry over into other areas of the relationship (Sternberg and Beier 1977) and conflicting relational partners may avoid interacting with one another (Birchler *et al.* 1975). On the other hand, if one perceives that he or she can have pleasant interactions or exchanges with another then one might find the other to be an attractive relational partner (Davis 1981). While in general we would expect the absence of reciprocity in exchanges will influence satisfaction with the interaction and relationship, we note that other variables may influence the strength of this relationship. For example, if anticipated interaction exists, then violations of reciprocity in a given interaction may be compensated for later and little relational dissatisfaction may be felt.

Thus, we view the study of reciprocal exchanges of resources to be a potentially fruitful area of inquiry. While the lack of research has forced our analysis to be overly speculative in parts, we are actively pursuing questions which we believe will demonstrate the utility (or lack there of) of the social exchange approach.

References

ALEXANDER, J.F. 1973: Defensive and supportive communications in family systems. *Journal of Marriage and the Family* 35, 613–17.

ALTMAN, I. 1973: Reciprocity of interpersonal exchange. *Journal for the Theory of Social Behaviour* 3, 249–61.

ARCHER, R.L. 1979: Role of personality and the social situation. In G.J. Chelune, and Associates, editors, *Self-disclosure: Origins, patterns, and implications of openness in interpersonal relationships* (San Francisco: Jossey-Bass) 28–58.

ARCHER, R.L. and BERG, J.H. 1978: Disclosure reciprocity and its limits: A reactance analysis. *Journal of Experimental and Social Psychology* 14, 527–40.

ARGYLE, M. 1977: *Bodily communication*. New York: International Universities Press.

AZRIN, N. H., NASTER, B. J. and JONES, R. 1973: Reciprocity counseling: A rapid learning-based procedure for marital counseling. *Behaviour Research and Therapy* 11, 365–82.

BEACH, L.R. and CARTER W. B. 1976: Appropriate and equitable repayment of social debts. *Organizational Behaviour and Human Performance* 16, 280–93.

BEFU, H. 1980: Structural and motivational approaches to social exchange. In Gergen, K., Greenberg, M. and Willis, R., editors, *Social exchange: Advances in theory and research* (New York: Plenum) 197–214.

BERG, J. H. and ARCHER, R. L. 1980: Disclosure or concern: A second look at liking for the norm breaker. *Journal of Personality* 48, 245–57.

—— 1982: Responses to self-disclosure and interaction goals. *Journal of Experimental Social Psychology* 18, 501–12.

BERGER, J., ZELDITCH, M., ANDERSON, B. and COHEN, B. 1972: Structural aspects of distributive justice: A status value formulation. In Berger, J., Zelditch, M. and Anderson, B., editors, *Sociological theories in progress, volume 2*

(Boston: Houghton Mifflin).

BIRCHLER, G. R., WEISS, R. L. and VINCENT, J. P. 1975: Multimethod analysis of social reinforcement exchange between maritally distressed and nondistressed spouse and stranger dyads. *Journal of Personality and Social Psychology* 2, 349–60.

BLAU, P. 1964: *Exchange and power in social life.* (New York: John Wiley & Sons.

BRINBERG, D. and CASTELL, P. 1982: A resource exchange theory approach to interpersonal interactions: A test of Foa's theory. *Journal of Personality and Social Psychology* 43, 260–9.

CARTWRIGHT, D. 1965: Influence, leadership, control. In March, J. G., editor, *Handbook of organizations* (Chicago: Rand McNally & Company) 1–47.

CHAIKIN, A. L. and DERLEGA, V. J. 1974: Liking for the norm-breaker in self-disclosure. *Journal of Personality* 42, 117–29.

—— 1976: Self-disclosure. In Thibaut, J., Spence, J. and Carson, R., editors, *Contemporary topics in social psychology* (Morristown, NJ: General Learning Press) 169–210.

CLARK, M. S. 1981: Noncomparability of benefits given and received: A cue to the existence of friendship. *Social Psychology Quarterly* 44, 375–81.

CLARK, M. S. and MILLS, J. 1979: Interpersonal attraction in exchange and communal relationships. *Journal of Personality and Social Psychology* 37, 12–24.

COHEN, R. S. and CHRISTENSEN, A. 1980: Further examination of demand characteristics in marital interaction. *Journal of Consulting and Clinical Psychology* 48, 121–3.

COZBY, C. 1972: Self-disclosure, reciprocity and liking. *Sociometry* 35, 151–60.

COZBY, P.C. 1973: Self-disclosure: A literature review. *Psychological Bulletin* 79, 73–91.

DAVIS, D. 1981: Implications for interaction versus effectance as mediators of the similarity-attraction relationship. *Journal of Experimental Social Psychology* 17, 96–116.

DAVIS, D. and PERKOWITZ, W. 1979: Consequences of responsiveness in dyadic Interaction: Effects of probability of response and proportion of content-related responses on interpersonal attraction. *Journal of Personality and Social Psychology* 37, 534–50.

DERLEGA, V. J., CHAIKEN, A. L. and HERNDON, J. 1973: Are demand characteristics responsible for disclosure reciprocity? Unpublished manuscript, Old Dominion University.

DEUTSCH, M. 1975: Equity, equality, and need: What determines which value will be used as the basis of distributive justice? *Journal of Social Sciences* 31, 137–49.

DINDIA, K. 1982: Reciprocity of self-disclosure: A sequential analysis. In Burgoon, M., editor, *Communication Yearbook VI* (Beverly Hills Cal.: Sage Publications) 506–28.

—— 1983: *Reciprocity of self-disclosure: Limitations and illusions.* Paper presented at the 33rd Annual Conference of the International Communication Association.

DUVAL, S. and WICKLUND, R. 1972: *A theory of objective self-awareness.* New

York: Academic Press.

EHRLICH, H. J. and GRAVEN, D. B. 1971: Reciprocal self-disclosure in a dyad. *Journal of Experimental Social Psychology* 7, 389–400.

FOA, E. B. and FOA, U. G. 1976: Resource theory of social exchange. In Thibaut, J., Spence, J. and Carson, R., editors, *Contemporary topics in social psychology* (Morristown, NJ: General Learning Press) 99–131.

—— 1980: Resource theory: Interpersonal behaviour as exchange. In Gergen, K., Greenberg, M. and Willis, R., editors, *Social exchange: Advances in theory and research* (New York: Plenum Press) 77–102.

FOA, U. G. 1966: Perception of behaviour in reciprocal roles: The ringex model. *Psychological Monographs: General and Applied* 80, 1–22.

—— 1971: Interpersonal and economic resources. *Science* 171 345–51.

FOA, U. G. and FOA, E. B. 1972: Resource exchange: Toward a structural theory of interpersonal communication. In Siegman, A. and Pope, B., editors, *Studies in dyadic communication* (New York: Pergamon Press) 291–325.

—— 1974: *Societal structures of the mind.* Springfield, Ill.: Charles C. Thomas.

GOTTMAN, J. M. 1979: *Marital interaction: Experimental investigations.* New York: Academic Press.

GOTTMAN, J., MARKMAN, H. and NOTARIUS, C. 1977: The topography of marital conflict: A sequential analysis of verbal and nonverbal behaviour. *Journal of Marriage and the Family* 39, 461–477.

GOTTMAN, J., NOTARIUS, C., MARKMAN, H., BANK, S., YOPPI, B. and RUBIN, M. E. 1976: Behaviour exchange theory and marital decision making. *Journal of Personality and Social Psychology* 34, 14–23.

GOULDNER, A. W. 1960: The norm of reciprocity A preliminary statement. *American Sociological Review* 25, 161–78.

GREENBERG, M. 1980: A theory of indebtedness. In Gergen, K., Greenberg, M., and Willis, R., editors, *Social exchange: Advances in theory and research* (New York: Plenum Press) 3–26.

HIGGINS, E. T., HERMAN, C. P. and ZANNA, M. P. 1981: *Social cognition: The Ontario symposium, volume 1.* Hillsdale, NJ: Lawrence Erlbaum Associates.

HINDE. R. 1979: *Towards understanding relationships.* New York: Academic Press.

HOMANS, G. C. 1974: *Social Behaviour: Its Elementary Forms.* New York: Harcourt Brace Jovanovich, Inc.

JACOBSON, N. S. and MARTIN, B. 1976: Behavioural marriage therapy: Current status. *Psychological Bulletin* 83, 540–56.

JOURARD, S. M. 1971: *Self-disclosure: An experimental analysis of the transparent self.* New York: John Wiley & Sons.

LANGER, E. 1978: Rethinking the role of thought in social interaction. In Harvey J., Ickes, W. and Kidd, R., editors, *New directions in attribution research, vol. 2* (Hillsdale, NJ: Lawrence Erlbaum Associates) 35–58.

LEVENTHAL, G. 1976: Fairness in social relationships. In Thibaut, J., Spence, J. and Carson, R., editors, *Contemporary topics in social psychology* (Morristown, NJ: General Learning Press) 211–39.

LEVIN, F. M. and GERGEN, K. J. 1969: *Revealingness, ingratiation, and the disclosure of self.* Paper presented at the 77th Annual Meeting of the American Psychological Association.

LONGABAUGH, R. 1963: A category system for coding interpersonal behaviour as social exchange. *Sociometry* **26**, 319–44.

LONGABAUGH, R., ELDRED, S. H., BELL, N. W. and SHERMAN, L. J. 1966: The interactional world of the chronic schizophrenic patient. *Psychiatry* 78–99

MOLM, L., and WIGGINS, J. 1979: A behavioural analysis of the dynamics of social exchange in the dyad. *Social Forces* **57**, 1157–79.

NYE, F. I. 1978: Is choice and exchange theory the key? *Journal of Marriage and the Family* **40**, 219–32.

—— 1979: Choice, exchange, and the family, In Burr, W. R., Hill, R., Nye, F. I. and Reiss, R., editors, *Contemporary theories about the family, volume 2* (New York: The Free Press) 1–41.

PATTERSON, G. R. and REID, J. B. 1970: Reciprocity and coercion: Two facets of social systems. In Neuringer, C. and Michael, J. L., editors, *Behaviour Modification in Clinical Psychology* (New York: Appleton-Century-Crofts) 133–77.

PATTERSON, G. R., HOPS, H. and WEISS, R. L. 1973: A social learning approach to reducing rates of marital conflict. In Stuart, R., Liberman, R. and Wilder, S., editors, *Advances in Behaviour Therapy* (New York: Academic Press).

PEARCE, W. B., WRIGHT, P. H., SHARP, S. M. and SLAMA, K. M. 1974: Affection and reciprocity in self-disclosing communication. *Human Communication Research* **1**, 5–15.

ROLOFF, M. E. 1976: Communication strategies, relationships, and relational changes. In Miller, G. R., editor, *Explorations in interpersonal communication* (Beverly Hills, Cal.: Sage Publications) 173–95.

—— 1981: *Interpersonal communication: The social exchange approach* Beverly Hills, Cal: Sage Publications.

ROSENFELD, H. 1966: Instrumental affiliative functions of facial and gestural expressions. *Journal of Personality and Social Psychology* **4**, 65–72.

—— 1967: Non-verbal reciprocation of approval: An experimental analysis. *Journal of Experimental Psychology* **3**, 102–11.

RUBIN, Z. and SCHENKER, S. 1978: Friendship, proximity, and self-disclosure. *Journal of Personality* **46**, 1–22.

RUBIN, Z., HILL, C. T., PEPLAU, L. A. and DUNKELSCHETTER, C. 1980: Self-disclosure in dating couples: Sex roles and the ethic of openness. *Journal of Marriage and the Family* **42**, 305–17.

SAMPSON, E. E. 1975: On justice as equality. *Journal of Social Issues* **31**, 45–64.

SCANZONI, J. 1972: *Sexual bargaining: Power politics in the American marriage.* Englewood Cliffs, NJ: Prentice Hall.

—— 1979: Social processes and power in families. In Burr, W. R., Hill, R., Nye, F. I. and Reiss, I., editors, *Contemporary theories about the family, volume 1* (New York: The Free Press) 295–316.

SCHANK, R. and ABELSON, R. 1977: *Scripts, plans, goals and understanding: An inquiry into human knowledge structures.* Hillsdale, NJ: Lawrence Erlbaum Associates.

STERNBERG, D. and BEIER, E. 1977: Changing patterns of conflict. *Journal of Communication* **27**, 97–9.

STUART, R. B. 1969: Operant-interpersonal treatment for marital discord. *Journal of Consulting and Clinical Psychology* **33**, 675–82.

—— 1975: Behavioural remedies for marital ills: A guide to the use of operant-interpersonal techniques. In Gurman, A. S. and Rice, D. G., editors, *Couples in conflict* (New York: Jason Aronson) 241–57.

TAYLOR, D. A. 1979: Motivational bases. In Chelune G. J. and Associates, editors, *Self-disclosure: origins, patterns, and implications of openness in interpersonal relationships* (San Francisco: Jossey-Bass) 110–50.

TEICHMAN, Y. 1971: *Satisfaction from interpersonal relations following resource exchange.* Unpublished Doctoral Dissertation, Columbia, Missouri: University of Missouri.

THIBAUT, J. W. and KELLEY, H. H. 1959: *The social psychology of groups.* New York: John Wiley and Sons.

TURNER, J. L., FOA, E. B. and FOA, U. G. 1971: Interpersonal reinforcers: Classification, interrelationship, and some differential properties. *Journal of Personality and Social Psychology* **19**, 168–80.

VINCENT, J. P., WEISS, R. L. and BIRCHLER, G. R. 1975: A behavioural analysis of problem solving in distressed and nondistressed married and stranger dyads. *Behaviour Therapy* **6**, 475–87.

WALSTER, E., WALSTER, G. and BERSCHEID, E. 1978: *Equity: theory and research.* Boston: Allyn & Bacon.

WEISS, R. L., HOPS, H. and PATTERSON, G. R. 1973: A framework for conceptualizing marital conflict: A technology for altering it, some data for evaluating it. In Hamerlynck, L., Handy, L. C. and Mash, E., editors. *Behaviour change: Methodology, concepts and practice* (Champaign, Ill: Research Press) 309–42.

WON-DOORNINK, M. J. 1979: On getting to know you: The association between the stage of a relationship and reciprocity of self-disclosure. *Journal of Experimental Social Psychology* **15**, 229–41.

10

The evolution of a functional model of nonverbal exchange: a personal perspective

Miles L. Patterson

The goal of this chapter is to provide a kind of historical perspective on the development of a functional model of nonverbal exchange. An understanding and appreciation of the functional model may be facilitated by analysing changing theoretical viewpoints over time. Because I have been involved in some of those developments this discussion will no doubt be somewhat biased by my own experience. On the other hand, because of that involvement I hope to be able to identify some of the continuities that underlie the evolution of theory in this area. There is little disagreement about the prime movers in the development of theory of nonverbal exchange. Argyle and Dean (1965) clearly hold that honour and this discussion of theory development appropriately starts with them.

Equilibrium theory

Argyle and Dean's (1965) equilibrium model of interpersonal intimacy was the first structured theoretical approach to the dynamics of nonverbal exchange. Equilibrium theory was important, however, not only for its specific content, but also for the general perspective it provided on the analysis of nonverbal behaviour. In contrast to the then prevailing tendency of focusing on isolated behaviours or channels, equilibrium theory stressed the interdependence present across different behaviours or channels. In particular, Argyle and Dean proposed that interpersonal intimacy was manifested as the joint product of several behaviours including distance, gaze, smiling, verbal intimacy, and possibly other behaviours. A similar appreciation for cooordinated *patterns* of nonverbal behaviour was also present in Hall's (1963, 1966) proxemic analysis and in Mehrabian's (1969) 'immediacy' construct. The direction that these researchers provided in emphasizing patterns of nonverbal behaviour was critical in promoting an understanding of nonverbal behaviour and social interaction.

In terms of its substantive content, equilibrium theory proposes a homeostatic regulation of the intimacy that is behaviourally expressed between individuals. Basic to that process is the assumption that an appropriate or comfortable level of interpersonal intimacy can be specified for any interaction. Practically, this means that the behavioural intimacy will tend to match the 'true' underlying intimacy appropriate between individuals in a given situation. As the expressed intimacy (manifested in terms of distance, gaze, smiling, and other behaviours) diverges from the appropriate underlying level of intimacy, there will be increased pressure to restore the appropriate level of expressed intimacy. That is, at least one individual will adjust his or her behaviour to compensate for deviations from the appropriate level of intimacy. In that way, an equilibrium or homeostasis may be achieved in the behavioural intimacy.

Although comfortable levels of intimacy vary across people and situations, the predicted process of compensation should always operate in a similar fashion. Specifically, when there is a mismatch between the underlying intimacy level and the behavioural level of intimacy directional compensatory adjustments will be made in one or more behaviours. Thus, too much behavioural intimacy by one person might result in the other person moving away, decreasing gaze or smiling less, whereas too little behavioural intimacy might result in the other person moving closer or gazing and smiling more.

As multivariate research on nonverbal behaviour became more common in the late 1960s and early 1970s it became possible to evaluate the validity of the compensation process proposed in equilibrium theory. That was the purpose of my 1973 review paper in *Sociometry*. Across almost 20 studies reviewed, strong support for the compensation process was found. In most of the experimental studies, interpersonal distance was manipulated and behavioural adjustments were monitored in gaze, lean or body orientation. Typically, closer approaches by an experimenter or confederate precipitated decreased gaze, leaning away or a less direct body orientation – reactions that were consistent with the adjustments predicted by equilibrium theory. More recently, Cappella (1981) has also documented further empirical support for equilibrium theory.

Even though the empirical support for equilibrium theory was substantial, an important limitation of the theory was evident in that early review, namely, that the intimacy behaviours also serve functions in addition to the expression of intimacy (Patterson 1973). Argyle and Dean recognized and admitted that limitation in describing their model, but the implications of such an observation are considerable. Practically, to the extent that gaze, distance or other nonverbal behaviours contribute to functions such as coordinating conversational turns or providing evaluative feedback, the dynamics of nonverbal exchange may not be guided by the process of compensation. In addition, the results from a few studies indicated that matching or reciprocation of intimacy can occur in response to increased intimacy (e.g. Breed 1972; Chapman 1975; Jourard and Friedman 1970). Such findings are in direct opposition to the predictions of equilibrium theory. This latter circumstance prompted me to consider an alternate explanation for nonverbal that eventually led to the arousal-labelling model.

Arousal-labelling model

Although equilibrium theory proposed an interesting, yet simple, mechanism that could account for the results of many studies, its failure to account for reciprocal or matching results was a significant weakness of the theory. In reviewing this circumstance, it seemed to me that the compensation process described by equilibrium theory was a useful, though probably incomplete, explanatory mechanism. Consequently, I tried to build on equilibrium theory in developing a more comprehensive explanation for varied patterns of nonverbal exchange. The research on nonverbal intimacy and arousal suggested an important link in determining the contrasting patterns of reaction. Specifically, a number of studies had shown that increased intimacy can precipitate arousal (Gale *et al.* 1972; Kleinke and Pohlen 1971; McBride *et al.* 1965; Nichols and Champness 1971). In addition, the labelling or self-attribution process proposed by Schachter and Singer (1962) provided a mechanism that could mediate compensatory and reciprocal reactions to another person's change in intimacy. Although Schachter and Singer proposed that the self-labelled affect was initiated by an increase in arousal, it seemed possible that a noticeable increase or *decrease* in arousal might precipitate the self-labelling process. That is, arousal *change* may be a critical mediating event. An illustration of the dynamics of the model can be seen in Figure 10.1. As A initiates a change in behavioural intimacy, one can follow the course of B's reaction to A. If the change in behavioural intimacy is *not* sufficiently large, B will experience no change in arousal, which will, in turn, require no self-labelling. The absence of any change in emotion or affect provides no motivation for behavioural adjustment. This particular track described situations in which relatively small changes in intimacy necessitate no behavioural adjustment of the partner. When A's change in behavioural intimacy is sufficiently large, arousal change results which triggers the self-labelling process. If the arousal change is negatively labelled, a compensatory reaction would be predicted. If the arousal change is positively labelled, a reciprocal change would be predicted. The compensation track is, of course, consistent with equilibrium theory. However, it extends equilibrium theory by specifying the arousal change – labelling process as the critical mediating event. The reciprocation track is unique to the arousal-labelling model and offers increased explanatory power beyond that of equilibrium theory.

Since the publication of the arousal-labelling model, several studies have provided at least moderate support for the model (Coutts *et al.* 1980; Foot *et al.* 1977a; Foot *et al.* 1977b; Schaeffer and Patterson 1980; Storms and Thomas 1977; Whitcher and Fisher 1979). Basically, these studies found that *positive* affect following a partner's increased intimacy typically produced more favourable impressions and/or a reciprocation of that intimacy. In contrast, *negative* affect following a partner's increased intimacy typically produced unfavourable impressions and/or compensation for that intimacy. Research from our own laboratory, however, has not been so supportive of the theory. Specifically, our results showed little support for arousal change serving as a necessary mediator. In summary, the results of these studies suggest that specific patterns of nonverbal behaviour do not have consistent effects on arousal and behavioural reactions. One factor that may influence the impact of a particular behavioural pattern is the meaning of that pattern.

First, in a study of nonverbal involvement and crowding (Patterson *et al.* 1979), we manipulated involvement by placing chairs in either a circular or L-shaped arrangement. As hypothesized, subjects in the circular·arrangement (high involvement) rated the room more negatively than those in the L-shaped arrangement (low involvement). There was no evidence, however, for increased arousal mediating the more negative reactions. Specifically, both self-rating and task performance (anagram-type problems) measures of arousal were unaffected by the involvement manipulation. In a second study, two relatively high-involvement patterns (discrete touch plus 50 per cent gaze and 80 per cent gaze alone) were manipulated in a confederate–subject interaction in a 'waiting

B's REACTION

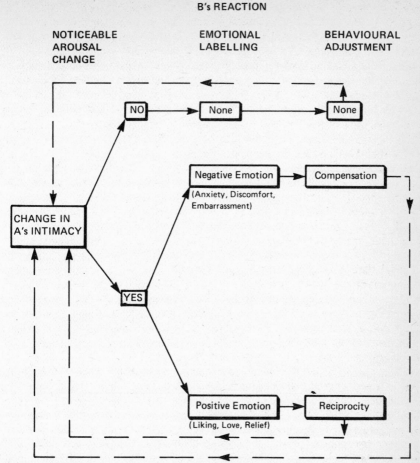

Figure 10.1 An arousal-labelling model of nonverbal intimacy. From Patterson (1976) An arousal model of interpersonal intimacy, *Psychological Review* 83, 235–45, copyright 1976 by the American Psychological Association, reprinted by permission of the author.

period' (Patterson *et al.* 1981). Only the touch plus 50 per cent gaze condition produced evidence for increased arousal, and then only when it occurred in the middle (but not at the beginning) of the waiting period. Apparently, the same or comparable levels of involvement in this study had a different impact depending on the order and the context in which they appeared. Finally, in a study that factorially manipulated level of nonverbal involvement, expectancy, and sex composition of subject–confederate pairs, no effect of confederate involvement level was found on either the subject's arousal response or his or her behavioural adjustment (Ickes *et al.* 1982). Although the results of the Ickes *et al.* study did not support the predictions of the arousal-labelling model, the clear expectancy effects on nonverbal behaviour found in that study are consistent with the functional perspective that will be discussed in the next section.

The issue of the meaning of a given behavioural pattern is one that Ellsworth

(1977) has stressed. Specifically, she proposed that the first stage in reacting to another person's behaviour may be an evaluation of the meaning of that behaviour. In such a case, the cognitive activity may be primary and arousal change merely the consequence of that activity. Of course, that sequence is exactly opposite the arousal-labelling sequence proposed in my model. It might be noted here that even the existing research that apparently supports the arousal-labelling model does not permit a determination of the sequencing of the arousal and labelling components. That is, the presence of arousal change and differential affect may be the result of either an arousal-labelling sequence or labelling-arousal sequence. In fact, if the labelling or attribution stage is primary, arousal may be completely unnecessary as a mediator.

The mixed empirical support for the model and the difficulty in determining the sequence of mediating events are important concerns for the arousal-labelling model. However, a more important limitation of the model lies in its basic reactive nature. That is, the model is focused only on explaining reactive adjustments to another person's momentary change in nonverbal involvement. Furthermore, such adjustments are presumed to be an 'automatic' consequence of the valence of one's mediating affect. Although I did not mean to imply that all nonverbal exchange could be explained by a series of interdependent reactions between interactants, it might be easy to draw that inference from the model. In any case, it is clear that this model does not address the initiation of behavioural sequences or the motivation for reactive adjustments. Even if the arousal-labelling model predicted reactive adjustments accurately, it would still be deficient in not addressing either the initiation of behavioural sequences or the role of motivation.

Although it is probably fair to say that the arousal-labelling model represented a useful alternative to equilibrium theory, I became interested in trying to develop an alternate approach that did not rely solely on reactive mechanisms. It seemed to me an adequate explanation of nonverbal exchange, one that encompassed both purposeful and automatic adjustments, was not likely to result from minor changes in the arousal-labelling model. In considering an alternate approach, I became intrigued by the two issues described earlier, namely, the initiation of behavioural sequences and the role of motivation in nonverbal exchange. It appeared to me that a comprehensive explanation of nonverbal exchange required that these two issues be central in any theoretical framework. The pursuit of reasons for either initiating a behavioural sequence or simply reacting to the behaviour of another person leads to a focus on the purpose or meaning of an interactive exchange. One very useful way of analysing the purpose or meaning of an interaction is in terms of its function. Fortunately, other researchers have provided some direction in analysing the functions of nonverbal behaviour (e.g. Argyle 1972; Ekman and Friesen 1969; Harrison 1973; and Kendon 1967). Although there are differences among these various functional classifications, the commonalities are substantial. For example, most discussions identify (a) communication, (b) regulating interaction, and (c) expressing intimacy as basic functions of nonverbal behaviour. My judgement was that an analysis of the functions of nonverbal behaviour could not only provide insight into the meaning of different behavioural patterns, but also provide a way of resolving apparent inconsistencies in the results from various studies of nonverbal exchange. The development of the functional perspective into a theory of nonverbal exchange is discussed in the next section.

A sequential functional model

Basic assumptions

Several basic assumptions underlie the dynamics of the sequential functional model and making them explicit should facilitate a description of the model. First, this model attempts to describe and analyse interactive behaviour in terms of the level of interpersonal involvement in that interaction. That is, the functional approach is focused on describing and analysing different functional bases that influence the levels of involvement initiated by interactants. Second, it is assumed that the level of nonverbal involvement is the product of behaviours such as (a) distance, (b) gaze, (c) touch, (d) body orientation, (e) lean, (f) facial expressiveness, (g) talking duration, (h) interruptions, (i) postural openness, (j) relational gestures, (k) head nods, and (l) paralinguistic cues. These behaviours combine in some unknown weighted fashion to identify the momentary behavioural involvement present between two individuals. Third, this approach to nonverbal behaviour stresses the related and patterned nature of interactive behaviour in contrast to a channel approach that describes and analyses behaviours in isolation. Fourth, a clear distinction should be made between the overt behavioural construct of involvement and the various covert constructs that describe the underlying functions served by behaviour. Finally, implicit in this last distinction is the assumption that different patterns of behaviour can serve the same function, and identical patterns of behaviour can serve different functions. Thus, although it is recognized that some behaviours, e.g. emblems (Ekman and Friesen 1969), can carry very specific meanings, the meaning of most interactive behaviour is substantially determined by the context of the interaction and the relationship between the interactants.

Functional categories

The classification of functions in this model includes the following categories: (1) informational function, (2) regulating interaction, (3) expressing intimacy, (4) social control, and (5) the service-task function. The informational and regulatory functions may be seen as orthogonal to the last three functions. In particular, providing information and regulating interaction may be seen as descriptions of isolated behaviours, e.g. a specific smile or a distinct head nod, whereas expressing intimacy, social control and the task-service function describe the more general overall patterns of behaviour. Thus, the last three functions are especially relevant for understanding the extended course of an interaction.

Although all behaviours may be judged as being at least potentially informative, it is useful to distinguish those behaviours that are critical for regulating interaction. For example, behaviours such as a change in gaze direction, a head nod, or a forward lean can facilitate fluid turn taking in conversations. An important distinction may also be suggested in the description of informative behaviours. Specifically, informative behaviours that are goal-oriented or purposeful will be described as *communicative*, whereas informative behaviours that are spontaneous and not goal-oriented will be described as *indicative*. The contrast between communicative and indicative behaviours is one that is critical for making attributions about an actor's behaviour. Behaviours that are judged indicative would be seen as accurately representing an actor's true disposition or feelings. Behaviours that are judged communicative would be seen as managed in order to achieve a particular purpose and may not represent an actor's true feelings.

An evaluation of the molar functions of an exchange is particularly useful for understanding the initiation and development of interactions. The first of three molar functions is the *intimacy* function. A great deal of the research on nonverbal exchange has been developed from an intimacy perspective. In fact, both equilibrium theory and the arousal-labelling model are intimacy-based explanations of nonverbal exchange. Generally, intimacy might be described as a bipolar dimension that reflects the degree of union with or openness toward another individual. Usually, that intimacy may be seen as the product of either greater liking or love for another person or a greater commitment to that person. In general, it might be expected that the intimacy function would be dominant when an interaction occurs between acquaintances, friends or family members in a setting that is not a highly evaluative one. Thus, an actor's affective evaluation of the other person should be the major determinant of his or her level of nonverbal involvement. In that situation, behavioural involvement with an interaction partner should flow with relative spontaneity from the underlying level of perceived intimacy toward the person.

The second molar function is that of *social control*. The social-control function involves the use of nonverbal behaviour to influence the reactions of others. Such influence might include managing one's behaviour to achieve goals such as changing a partner's attitude and behaviour on a particular topic or simply managing one's behaviour to create a more favourable impression. Thus, a moderately close approach, similing and a high level of gaze might serve to make a message more persuasive. Alternately, a moderately high level of involvement might be managed so that other people would view the actor more favourably. With the exception of discussions by Goffman (e.g. 1967, 1972) and Henley (1973, 1977), the processes represented by the social-control function have received relatively little attention in research on nonverbal behaviour. In contrast to the indicative character of behaviour serving the intimacy function, behaviour serving the social-control function is typically communicative. Thus, behaviour serving the social-control function is more deliberate and managed than is behaviour serving the intimacy function. Presumably, the actor monitors the effectiveness of his or her behavioural routine and the incentive to continue or extend a social-control pattern is diminished as the actor's goals are achieved.

The last molar function is the *service-task* function. This function describes the situational or activity constraints that determine levels of nonverbal involvement. Thus, the levels of involvement resulting from this function do not reflect the nature of the personal relationship between individuals, but do reflect the nature of the service or task constraints. For example, some services require that touch be initiated by the professional in filling the needs of the client or customer (Heslin 1974). Included among such professionals are physicians, dentists, barbers and tailors. In some cases where the touch might be considered very intimate, the circumstances surrounding the professional's activity may be very formal and structured. For example, the circumstances under which an obstetrical exam is given are probably much more formal and stylized than are those governing an eye exam. In that way the legitimacy and meaning of the intimate touch are clarified and the nature of the physician–patient relationship is reinforced. In many cases the structure of various service relationships may be specific enough that the exchange takes the form of a predictable, orderly sequence or script (Abelson 1981).

Service exchanges are governed by the need to provide particular services, whereas task exchanges are governed by the need to foster and complete specific task goals. Task requirements (cf. Poole, Chapter 11; Putnam, Chapter 12) might either promote higher levels of involvement (e.g. sitting close together so that materials may be shared) or promote lower levels of involvement (e.g. moving away from others so that a demanding cognitive task might be completed). It should be emphasized that patterns of involvement resulting from specific service or task goals are typically impersonal. On the other hand, an individual might use the guise of particular service or task demands as an excuse for managing involvement with another person. For example, a woman might suddenly become intensely involved in her work so that she can discourage the approach of the office bore. Although such a behavioural routine might be described as social control, the actor prefers to have the intruder think that her behaviour is task focused.

Dynamic relationships

Although the contrasting functional categories are at the basis of this model, those functions exert their directing influence in a larger context of related sequential events. The details of those sequential relationships are available elsewhere (see Patterson 1982b, 1983), but an overview of those processes may be informative. Figure 10.2 provides an illustration of the sequential relationships proposed in the model. The first stage of the model identifies the influence of factors antecedent to the interaction. These antecedent influences can be classified into the general categories of (1) personal, (2) experiential, and (3) relational–situational factors.

The personal factors include those individual or group characteristics that contribute to variability in nonverbal involvement. For example, Hall (1966, 1968) has described the differences in the closeness and intensity of interaction as a function of culture. Hall noted that Arab, southern Mediterranean, and Latin American people exhibit higher levels of involvement than British or northern European people. Next, gender seems related to different patterns of nonverbal involvement. In general, females seem to prefer higher levels of nonverbal involvement. This tendency may be seen in females (1) interacting at closer distances (Aiello and Aiello 1974; Patterson and Schaeffer 1977), (2) exhibiting higher levels of gaze (Dabbs *et al.* 1980; Exline 1963; Exline *et al.* 1965; Libby 1970), and (3) engaging in touch more often (Jourard 1966). Personality is another important individual difference factor. The research on personality correlates of nonverbal involvement is extensive. Among the more promising dimensions predicting differential involvement are social

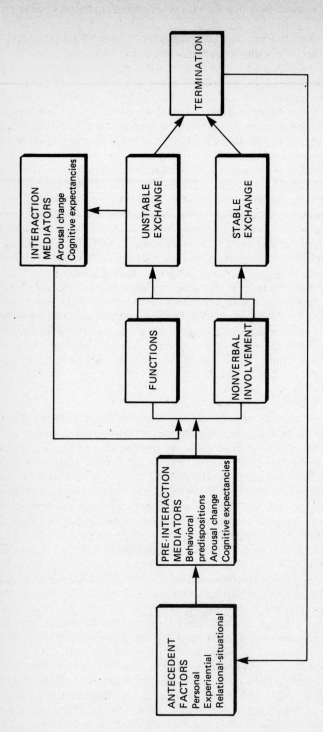

Figure 10.2 A sequential functional model of nonverbal exchange. From Patterson and Heslin, R., *Nonverbal behaviour and social psychology*, reproduced by permission of Plenum Publishing Corp.

approach–avoidance, internal–external locus of control, field dependence–independence, and self-monitoring (Patterson 1982a).

The experiential factors refer to the influence of recent and/or similar experiences on later interactions. Experiential influences might be the product of learning and reinforcement. That is, well learned and reinforced behavioural patterns are more likely to be repeated than those that are not well learned and not reinforced. Alternately, new involvement patterns may be constrained by recent levels of involvement. Thus, under- or over-stimulation from recent past behaviour may lead to a kind of compensatory adjustment. For example, recent high levels of involvement may predispose an individual to seek out less involving interactions.

The relational and situational factors are grouped in a common category because they often interact with one another in specifying a particular influence on nonverbal involvement. In other words, the influence of the type of relationship between individuals is often moderated by the nature of the setting. Thus, the way one acts towards a spouse, friend or boss depends on whatever that exchange occurs at home, at work, out in a restaurant or in a church. The considerable research on relationships and nonverbal involvement permits some generalizations on that dimension alone, but there is relatively little on the influence of the situation on nonverbal involvement. Representative of the former is the trend for those in more intimate relationships to stand at closer distances (Patterson 1978a), engage in more eye contact (Rubin 1970), and touch more frequently (Jourard 1966) than those in less intimate relationships.

The influence of the antecedent factors on the course of an impending interaction is assumed to be a product of more covert processes. These processes are described in the second stage of the model. However, the mediating mechanisms exercise their influence both in anticipation of the interaction and later during the interaction itself. The mediators proposed here include behavioural predispositions, cognitive assessment and potential arousal change. Behavioural predispositions refer to those habitual patterns of nonverbal behaviour that reflect stable individual characteristics. It is assumed that these predispositions are usually more or less 'automatic' and often not well represented cognitively. In particular, behavioural predispositions may commonly mediate the influence of the personal factors on nonverbal involvement. That is, the involvement differences described earlier as a function of culture, sex or personality apparently represent relatively stable preferences requiring little or no cognitive reflection.

A second mediator is that of arousal change. Because there is utility in considering the role of decreases, as well as increases, in arousal, the term 'arousal change' seems appropriate (Patterson 1978b). In fact, in circumstances in which a person is fearful, anxious or distressed, a comforting hug or touch may decrease arousal and alleviate some of the negative affect (Whitcher and Fisher 1979).

The last mediator of cognitive–affective expectancies involves the formation of any kind of evaluative cognition, from simple affective judgements to more complex patterns of cognitions. Representative of the former are affective reactions or preferences that are primary responses to stimuli, separate from cognitions about the same stimuli (Zajonc 1980). More complex cognitive processes may focus on either self–other or setting–activity characteristics. These processes may be especially important in the formation of interpersonal expectancies. In general, it is assumed that an expectancy causes the actor to behave in a fashion that elicits confirming reactions from the target person.

As the interaction is initiated, the converging effects of the preinteraction mediators have constrained the level of involvement and structured the potential functions of the interaction. The course of the subsequent nonverbal exchange is then determined primarily by the relative intensity of each person's nonverbal involvement and by the degree of correspondence between their perceived functions. When the initiated level of involvement is either extreme or inappropriate, then increased arousal and a negative cognitive evaluation are likely. The result is a condition of instability that requires compensatory adjustments (Patterson 1976). Similarly, greater disparity between the interactants in their functional expectancies should also create instability and increase the likelihood of compensatory behaviour.

Although the involvement levels and perceived functions are viewed as separate elements in this model, their impact on one another is assumed to be substantial. When functional expectancies are particularly explicit, they can determine the level and pattern of nonverbal involvement. Thus, script-like expectancies of meeting a long-absent loved one versus meeting a personnel manager about a new job lead to contrasting patterns of nonverbal involvement. If the actual involvement level of one person is discrepant from that characteristic of the other's functional expectancies, the latter person is likely to re-evaluate the underlying function of the interaction and adjust involvement accordingly.

An example may be informative. Let us take the case of a young, newly hired, female attorney meeting the male senior partner in the law firm over lunch. The gender differences (classified under the personal factors) would probably lead to relatively different behavioural predispositions. Specifically, the woman may typically prefer higher levels of involvement than her older boss. Those contrasting behavioural predispositions are, of course, affected by the relational–situational determinants. If the young woman perceives the relationship as an egalitarian one and the setting as informal, but the older boss does not, then there is considerable opportunity for differences in the initiation of interaction. Specifically, the young attorney's behavioural involvement might be determined more by a behavioural predisposition (i.e., a relatively high involvement level) that is appropriate between friendly peers. In contrast, the boss perceives the interaction to be a formal exchange between a superior and subordinate that ought to be relatively restrained. The differences in the perceived functions and, more directly, the initial involvement levels should lead to some recognition of the instability of the exchange. That instability should trigger the cognitive–affective processes that mediate the behavioural adjustments and functional attributions. In this example, the young attorney would probably recognize the behavioural reserve of her boss and realize that he judged the interaction to be a more formal one than she had. Because she has far more to lose than the boss does, it is more likely that her behaviour, not his, would change. Presumably, her behavioural change would lead to a more stable interaction and continued employment.

Evaluating a functional perspective

The functional model described here represents one approach to describe and analyse nonverbal exchange in a relatively comprehensive fashion. Obviously, there are other approaches that accomplish such a description and analysis. In addition, there are other forms that a functional model may take. My own experience in building (and dismantling) theoretical models leaves me very cautious in becoming too satisfied with any particular model. I hope that there is legitimacy to the specific theoretical processes discussed here, but that is not a matter for me to judge. Rather, I would like to address the relative strengths and weaknesses of a functional perspective in general.

There are at least two general advantages of a functional perspective that may be identified. First, a functional perspective stresses the reasons or purposes underlying specific behavioural patterns. The distinction between reasons and causes is a controversial one which I will conveniently avoid here (see Buss 1978, 1979; Harvey and Tucker 1979; Kruglanski 1979). However, some assessment of the reason or purpose behind a particular behavioural pattern may help us to understand the individual's motivation in initiating a particular behaviour pattern. Such an understanding would seem necessary in going beyond a simple reactive explanation for nonverbal exchange. Other models including equilibrium theory, my own arousal-labelling model, and Cappella and Greene's (1982) discrepancy arousal model have emphasized reactive rather than purposeful behaviours. Obviously, the relatively spontaneous reactive adjustments predicted by those models do occur often. It might be suggested that those reactive adjustments serve to complement the broad, coordinated patterns emphasized in the functional model.

A second general advantage of a functional approach is its compatibility with a multivariate analysis of nonverbal behaviour. Much of the empirical research on nonverbal behaviour has been channel-oriented. That is, studies often focus on a single 'critical' channel such as gaze or distance and ignore other related meaningful behaviours. A functional approach emphasizes the coordinated and patterned nature of behaviour across channels. Furthermore, isolated behaviours may substitute for one another in serving the same function. For example, a smile, a gaze or a gentle touch may all communicate affection and the response to each of them may be identical. Finally, understanding the significance of even relatively isolated sequences often requires knowledge of the broader behavioural context. Obviously, that is possible only when a multivariate analysis is used.

Potential problems with this functional approach can also be identified. First, the sense of the term 'function' is somewhat different in describing the molecular functions than in describing the molar functions. I have suggested that an identification of the molecular functions (information vs interaction regulation) might be made on an 'objective' basis, whereas the critical determination of the molar functions is a matter of the actor's perception. I realize that such a distinction reduces the commonality across the different functions, but the contrast does have some utility. The second concern is a related one, namely, inferences about the molar functions are often tentative. Practically, the important determinant is the actor's *perceived* function of the interaction. In most circumstances such perceptions are not available to observers, although the actor may be aware of those judgements. Of course, the issue of the validity of verbal reports of mental processes (Nisbett and Wilson 1977) is relevant here, but that should not discourage attempts to study such processes. In addition to self-reports, inferences about the functional bases of interactions might be made by observing consistencies in behaviour over time, both within and across actors. Nevertheless, identifying the functions of an interaction is a difficult undertaking and one that is subject to error. A third, and related, concern is that many exchanges may serve more than one function. In such instances, the description and prediction of interactive behaviour become more complex. This circumstance, however, may reflect the real complexity of interactive behaviour, and not necessarily a weakness in the functional perspective.

In conclusion, a functional approach provides a means for describing and analysing the underlying purposes of nonverbal exchange. Such an approach becomes an alternative to mechanistic reactive explanations of nonverbal exchange. In addition, the functional perspective is consistent with a multivariate analysis of nonverbal exchange. That is, a functional perspective stresses the equivalence of different behaviours in serving the same or similar functions. In effect, a functional approach provides a broad theoretical rationale for multivariate research on nonverbal exchange. At the same time, the specific functional analyses that are required in research are often tentative and vulnerable to error. Finally, the classification of functions of given exchanges are made more difficult when multiple functions are represented in an interaction and, unfortunately, that may be a common occurrence. Independent of these evaluative comments, the utility of a functional approach and this model in particular may be judged in terms of the research generated by this model in the years to come.

References

ABELSON, R. P. 1981: Psychological status of the script concept. *American Psychologist* 36, 715–29.

AIELLO, J. R. and AIELLO, T.D. 1974: The development of personal space: Proxemic behaviour of children 6 through 16. *Human Ecology* 2, 177–89.

ARGYLE, M. 1972: Non-verbal communication in human social interaction. In Hinde, R.A., editor, *Non-verbal communication* (Cambridge: Cambridge University Press).

ARGYLE, M. and DEAN, J. 1965: Eye-contact, distance and affiliation. *Sociometry* 28, 289–304.

BREED, G. 1972: The effect of intimacy: Reciprocity or retreat? *British Journal of Social and Clinical Psychology* 11, 135–42.

BUSS, A.R. 1978: Causes and reason in attribution theory: A conceptual critique. *Journal of Personality and Social Psychology* 36, 1311–21.

—— 1979: On the relationship between causes and reasons. *Journal of Personality and Social Psychology* 37, 1458–61.

CAPPELLA, J.N. 1981: Mutual influence in expressive behaviour: Adult–adult and infant–adult dyadic interaction. *Psychological Bulletin* 89, 101–32.

CAPPELLA, J.N. and GREENE, J.O. 1982: A discrepancy-arousal explanation of mutual influence in expressive behaviour for adult and infant–adult interaction. *Communication Monographs* **49**, 89–114.

CHAPMAN, A.J. 1975: Eye contact, physical proximity and laughter: A re-examination of the equilibrium model of social intimacy. *Social Behaviour and Personality* **3**, 143–55.

COUTTS, L.M., SCHNEIDER, F.W. and MONTGOMERY, S. 1980: An investigation of the arousal model of interpersonal intimacy. *Journal of Experimental Social Psychology* **16**, 545–61.

DABBS, J.M., Jr., EVANS, M.S., HOPPER, C.H. and PERVIS, J.A. 1980: Self-monitors in conversation: What do they monitor. *Journal of Personality and Social Psychology* **39**, 278–84.

EKMAN, P. and FRIESEN, W.V. 1969: The repertoire of nonverbal behaviour: Categories, origins, usage and codings. *Semiotica* **1**, 49–97.

ELLSWORTH, P.C. 1977: *Some questions about the role of arousal in the interpretation of direct gaze.* Paper presented at the annual meeting of the American Psychological Association, San Francisco.

EXLINE, R.V. 1963: Explorations in the process of person perception: Visual interaction in relation to competition, sex, and need for affiliation. *Journal of Personality* **31**, 1–20.

EXLINE, R., GRAY, D. and SCHUETTE, D. 1965: Visual behaviour in a dyad as affected by interview content and sex of respondent. *Journal of Personality and Social Psychology* **1**, 201–9.

FOOT, H.C., CHAPMAN, A.J. and SMITH, J.R. 1977a: Friendship and social responsiveness in boys and girls. *Journal of Personality and Social Psychology* **35**, 401–11.

FOOT, H.C., SMITH, J.R. and CHAPMAN, A.J. 1977b: Individual differences in children's responsiveness in humour situations. In Chapman, A.J. and Foot, H.C., editors, *It's a funny thing, humour* (London: Pergamon).

GALE, A., LUCAS, B., NISSIM, R. and HARPHAM, B. 1972: Some EEG correlates of face-to-face contact. *British Journal of Social and Clinical Psychology* **11**, 326–32.

GOFFMAN, E. 1967: *Interaction ritual.* Garden City, NY: Anchor.

—— 1972: *Relations in public.* New York: Harper Colophon.

HALL, E.T. 1963: A system for the notation of proxemic behaviour. *American Anthropologist* **65**, 1003–26.

—— 1966: *The hidden dimension.* New York: Doubleday.

—— 1968: Proxemics. *Current Anthropology* **9**, 83–108.

HARRISON, R.P. 1973: Nonverbal communication. In Pool, I.S., Schramm, W., Maccoby, N. Fry, F., Parker, E., and Fern, J.L., editors, *Handbook of communication* (Chicago: Rand McNally).

HARVEY, J.H. and TUCKER, J.A. 1979: On problems with the cause-reason distinction in attribution theory. *Journal of Personality and Social Psychology* **37**, 1441–6.

HENLEY, N.M. 1973: Status and sex: Some touching observations. *Bulletin of the Psychonomic Society* **2**, 91–3.

—— 1977: *Body politics: Power, sex, and nonverbal communication.* Englewood Cliffs, NJ: Prentice-Hall.

HESLIN, R. 1974: *Steps toward a taxonomy of touching.* Paper presented at the annual meeting of the Midwestern Psychological Association, Chicago.

ICKES, W., PATTERSON, M.L., RAJECKI, D.W. and TANFORD, S. 1982: Behavioural and cognitive consequences of reciprocal versus compensatory responses to pre-interaction expectancies. *Social Cognition* 1, 160–90.

JOURARD, S.M. 1966: An exploratory study of body-accessibility. *British Journal of Social and Clinical Psychology* 5, 221–31.

JOURARD, S.M. and FRIEDMAN, R. 1970: Experimenter–subject 'distance' and self-disclosure. *Journal of Personality and Social Psychology* 15, 278–82.

KENDON, A. 1967: Some functions of gaze-direction in social interaction. *Acta Psychologica* 26, 22–63.

KLEINKE, C.L. and POHLEN, P.D. 1971: Affective and emotional responses as a function of other person's gaze and cooperativeness in a two-person game. *Journal of Personality and Social Psychology* 17, 308–13.

KRUGLANSKI, A.W. 1979: Causal attribution, teleological explanation: On radical particularism in attribution theory. *Journal of Personality and Social Psychology* 37, 1447–57.

LIBBY, W.L. 1970: Eye contact and direction of looking as stable individual differences. *Journal of Experimental Research in Personality* 4, 303–12.

MCBRIDE, G., KING, M. and JAMES, J.W. 1965: Social proximity effects of galvanic skin responses in adult humans. *Journal of Psychology* 61, 153–7.

MEHRABIAN, A. 1969: Some referents and measures of nonverbal behaviour. *Behaviour Research Methods and Instrumentation* 1, 203–7.

NICHOLS, K.A. and CHAMPNESS, B.G. 1971: Eye gaze and the GSR. *Journal of Experimental Social Psychology* 7, 623–6.

NISBETT, R.E. and WILSON, T.D. 1977: Telling more than we can know: Verbal reports on mental processes. *Psychological Review* 84, 231–59.

PATTERSON, M.L. 1973: Compensation in nonverbal immediacy behaviours: A review. *Sociometry* 36, 237–52.

—— 1978a: The role of space in social interaction. In Siegman, A. and Feldstein, S., editors, *Nonverbal behaviour and communication.* (Hillsdale, NJ: Erlbaum).

—— 1978b: Arousal change and cognitive labelling: Pursuing the mediators of intimacy exchange. *Environmental Psychology and Nonverbal Behaviour* 3, 17–22.

—— 1982a: Personality and nonverbal involvement: A functional analysis. In Ickes, W. and Knowles, E.S., editors, *Personality, roles, and social behaviour* (New York: Springer-Verlag).

—— 1982b: A sequential functional model of nonverbal exchange. *Psychological Review* 89, 231–49.

—— 1983: *Nonverbal behaviour: A functional perspective.* New York: Springer-Verlag.

PATTERSON, M.L., JORDAN, A., HOGAN, M.B., and FRERKER, D. 1981: Effects of nonverbal intimacy on arousal and behavioural adjustment. *Journal of Nonverbal Behaviour* 5, 184–98.

PATTERSON, M.L., ROTH, C.P. and SCHENK, C. 1979: Seating arrangement, activity, and sex differences in small group crowding. *Personality and Social Psychology Bulletin* 5, 100–3.

PATTERSON, M.L. and SCHAEFFER, R.E. 1977: Effects of size and sex composition on interaction distance, participation, and satisfaction in small groups. *Small Group Behaviour* 8, 433–42.

RUBIN, A. 1970: Measurement of romantic love. *Journal of Personality and*

Social Psychology **16**, 265-73.

SCHACHTER, S. and SINGER, J.E. 1962: Cognitive, social and physiological determinants of emotional state. *Psychological Review* **69**, 379-99.

SCHAEFFER, G.H. and PATTERSON, M.L. 1980: Intimacy, arousal, and small group crowding. *Journal of Personality and Social Psychology* **38**, 283-90.

STORMS, M.D. and THOMAS, G.C. 1977: Reactions to physical closeness. *Journal of Personality and Social Psychology* **35**, 412-18.

WHITCHER, S.J. and FISHER, J.D. 1979: Multidimensional reaction to therapeutic touch in a hospital setting. *Journal of Personality and Social Psychology* **37**, 87-96.

ZAJONC, R.B. 1980: Feeling and thinking: Preferences need no inferences. *American Psychologist* **35**, 151-75.

11

Tasks and interaction sequences: a theory of coherence in group decision-making interaction

Marshall Scott Poole

The tasks people engage in are a critical determinant of their interaction sequences. The nature of the task sets the basic requirements for effective action and patterns what individuals can do as they interact. Notwithstanding their importance, the effects of tasks on interaction sequences are not well understood. While there is a large body of literature relating tasks to outcome variables, such as effectiveness, satisfaction, or organizational structure, we have very little knowledge of the effects on tasks on interaction or on how interaction mediates the effects of tasks on outcomes (Hackman and Morris 1975). This paper attempts to spell out some of the relationships between task and interaction.

We will concentrate on a particular type of task in a particular context. We focus on groups because they are basic (many social theorists have called the small group the building block of society), because they are important (many consequential decisions in government and business are made by groups), and because they are interesting (group behaviour is considerably more complex than the dyadic case). The task in question is decision-making, which includes behaviours otherwise called negotiation, problem-solving or creativity. Decision-making represents only a small portion of group behaviour, but it is perhaps the most important behaviour groups undertake. As well as being significant in its own right, decision-making sets the course for other group activities.

This essay consists of three sections. The first discusses several conceptions of the task construct and raises issues regarding how tasks enter into group work. The second section summarizes the theories and findings on group-activity sequences and how tasks and other contingency factors shape them. In this section we conclude that present theories of decision-making sequences do not acknowledge the role of microinteractional processes sufficiently. The third section presents a theoretical framework to account for how group decision sequences are constituted in group interaction. We will argue that this theory, which is grounded in recent work on the theory of structuration, provides a more useful explanation of group decision sequences than do the classical phasic theories of decision development.

Tasks

There is considerable evidence for the importance of task in the explanation of group behaviour and effectiveness. Hackman and Morris (1975), for example, report that task differences alone can account for over 50 per cent of the variance in interaction patterns for various 'intellective' tasks. Studies by Chapple and Sayles (1961) and Van de Ven and Delbecq (1974) show that the internal structure and composition of groups within organizations is dependent on the nature of the tasks they form around. Poole (1978) suggests that task type determines the degree of synergy or 'assembly bonus' groups can achieve. These studies represent only a fraction of the work on this topic, but they clearly illustrate the broad spectrum of task effects: tasks influence group interaction, group structures, group composition and group performance outcomes.

Despite its acknowledged importance, there is no consensus on how the task construct should be defined or conceptualized. There are numerous tasks typologies, ranging from Steiner's (1972) division of tasks by coordination requirements to Shaw's (1973) seven task dimensions. Fleischman (1982), building on the work of Hackman (1969), distinguishes several approaches for defining tasks: (1) behaviour description, which describes what people actually do while performing a task (e.g. handling objects, analysing data); (2) specification of behaviour requirements for tasks achievement (e.g. problem solving, scanning); (3) specification of ability requirements for task achievement (e.g. spatial abilities); and (4) description of task characteristics (e.g. goals, instructions).

Comparison of these schemes calls to mind the blind men's descriptions of the elephant: each focuses on a single aspect of a complex whole and each yields a somewhat distorted view. Perhaps the principal value of the multitudinous task schemes are the dilemmas and choices they pose, oppositions which must be transcended for a coherent theory of task to emerge. In particular, they highlight three critical features of decision-making tasks.

First, in defining a decision task it is necessary to specify *both* its formal structure *and* its particular content. Most task typologies focus on formal properties of tasks, such as task difficulty or goal clarity. These are important properties, because they specify general parameters governing group effort – for example, if goals are unclear the group must spend time in defining them and coordinating members' work. However, if we are to trace the effects of tasks on group interaction with any degree of precision, we must also consider the content of the task, that is, the steps required by the particular decision and the nature of the issues involved. McKenzie (1976), for example, has analysed tasks in terms of a series of 'milestones', states groups must achieve to accomplish their goals; for example in solving a math puzzle, the milestones include a state where all members understand the problem, a state where one member solves it, and a state where that member convinces the others that his/her solution is correct. These milestones differ according to the particular issues the group must deal with and according to the subtasks involved in working out the decision. Issues and subtasks determine the specific episodes that occur in group discussions and therefore they must be included along with formal properties for precise explanation of group interaction.

Second, the group's representation of its task mediates the effect of 'objective' task features on group interaction. It is not task requirements *per se*, but members' *perceptions* of task requirements that guide the group's work. Tasks defined by an outside party are typically redefined in the light of member's understanding of the instructions, their knowledge about the task, their past experience with the task, and their attitudes toward work. This process gives rise to what Abric (1971) has termed the group's task representation, which can be defined as:

> . . . the theory or system of hypotheses individuals work out regarding the nature of the task, its objective, the means to employ to carry out the task, and the behaviour conducive to effectiveness. To the extent that this representation is shared by the whole group, it determines a collective representation of the given facts of the environment, that is, a social representation of the task. (p. 313)

An experiment by Abric showed that performance on two experimental tasks depended on the groups' task representation. When groups construed a task as requiring 'problem-solving' they performed differently and evolved different communication structures than when they were led to represent the same task as requiring 'creativity'. Task representations are the product of the group's attempt to structure its environment in an understandable way and, as such, serve as a proximate influence on group behaviour, mediating objective task characteristics.

Related to this is the third point: tasks should be considered not only as constraints but also as resources for group activity. Traditional research has construed task as a constraint on group behaviour and organization. Effective performance on a highly difficult task, for example, has been shown to require a different type of group structure than does execution of routine tasks. However, tasks also serve as resources for organizing group activities. Members who represent their task as problem-solving organize their activities around problem diagnosis and solution-finding. Their interaction is characterized by 'problem' talk and they use a 'rational' standard to resolve disagreements. On the other hand, members whose task representation is 'routine-approval-and-disposal' organize their activities around expeditions decision-making. Their interaction centres on disposing of the agenda and disagreements are often resolved by informal bargaining and tradeoffs. In both cases the group's task representation sets boundaries on acceptable interaction styles and behaviour strategies. It serves as a resource that enables members to coordinate their activities and sets a general direction for the group. Groups do not react to tasks in a passive manner; they actively work with the task and use it as an organizing principle.

Models of group activity

Research on how groups actually make decisions has focused primarily on the phases or stages they pass through to arrive at a decision. A phase is defined as a period of unified and coherent activity that fulfils some function necessary for completion of the group's task – for example, in the orientation phase of Bales and Strodtbeck's (1951) model members define the problem, decide how to attack it, and share relevant information. The description of each phase normally consists of two parts: (1) A definition of the general tenor of interaction in the phase, which derives from the particular issues or problems the group must face during the phase. This definition is qualitatively unique for each phase and forms the basis for the explanations of group interaction advanced by phasic theories. (2) In addition, there is an operational definition of the phase in terms of the specific activities members engage in during the phase. These activities are usually operationalized with interaction coding procedures and the codings are used as tags that indicate when a group is in a given phase. In orientation, for example, the group faces the problems of defining its task, sharing information, and establishing a working relationship among members. Bales and Strodtbeck (1951) argued that periods of orientation would be characterized by high levels of information giving and low levels of disagreement, expression of opinions and solution suggestions. Using a different coding scheme Fisher (1970) operationalized orientation as a period characterized by acts and interacts (two-act sequences) expressing ambiguity, offering clarification, and advancing tentative evaluations of the problem.

Phasic theories chart group activities as a series of such phases and attempt to explain the evolution of group interaction patterns with an account of why phases occur in a particular order. For instance, Bales and Strodtbeck (1951), advance a three-stage sequence for group problem-solving: (1) orientation; (2) an evaluation phase, which is marked by the expression of opinions about the problem and a high degree of conflict; and (3) a control phase, in which members work out a unified course of action. The phases occur in this particular order because each phase is a functional prerequisite for those that follow: the orientation phase is necessary to proceed to the evaluation phase and both orientation and evaluation are required for a successful joint action.

What sort of explanation for interaction sequences do these models give? Phasic theories do not attempt to explain or predict specific sequences. Instead, they offer explanations of the *types* of interaction patterns that generally occur during specific periods of discussion. Knowing a group's phasic progression allows the researcher to account for the appearance of certain forms of interaction and to rule out other forms during various stages of the decision process. In the orientation phase, for example, we would expect to find acts and interacts that provide clarification, define the problem, suggest procedures, and express tentative opinions and solutions, and voting or confirmation behaviours. This says nothing about the exact sequences that occur during a particular orientation phase; instead, it tells us the general tenor we may expect during orientation and the types of acts that should occur within a bounded time frame. For some phases this permits fairly precise delineation of expected sequences, while for others the situation is more ambiguous. For example, the integration phase (Bales 1953; Poole 1981; 1983a) exhibits a fairly small number of possible sequences, mostly centred on joking and self-congratulation; as a result it is possible to specify likely interaction sequences with some confidence. This is not the case for the conflict phase (Fisher 1970; Poole 1981; 1983a), which may unfold through a wide variety of moves and countermoves.

This explanation of interaction sequences clearly does not have the power or precision of sequential interaction models advanced for dyads (e.g. Jaffe and Feldstein 1970; McLaughlin *et al.* 1983). However, it is probably the best that can be expected for group interaction. Groups involve multiple actors, and a sequence between two or three members is often interrupted by an interjection between a fourth and fifth. Usually several lines of thought are developing simultaneously in group discussions, and this makes such interjections and topic shifts common (Berg 1967). Short of decomposing the group into dyads (and then we are no longer studying a group), the best that can be hoped for is the prediction of short sequences – interacts and double interacts (three-act segments) – and delineation of the types of acts and patterns that generally occur within bounded time frames.

As we have noted, the key issue for phasic models is the explanation of *why* phases occur in the order in which they do. Two genres of explanations have been advanced, and both offer important insights regarding the relationship of tasks and group interaction.

The most influential theories have characterized group decision-making as a *unitary sequence*, with all groups passing through a uniform, graded sequence of phases en route to a decision. Bales and Strodtbeck (1951) present the archetypal unitary sequence model in their progression from orientation to evaluation to control. Subsequent researchers (Tuckman 1965; Fisher 1970; Mabry 1975) have advanced more detailed unitary models and considerable experimental evidence has been amassed in support of the unitary formulation (see LaCoursiere 1980). In general, unitary sequence theories explain group behaviour in terms of necessary structural conditions that require a certain set of phases to occur in a definite temporal order, such as Bales and Strodtbeck's logical sequence of problems, Fisher's four-step conflict resolution sequence or Mabry's pattern variable cycle.

Unitary sequence models are appealing because they offer a parsimonious explanation of group decision activity that rests on both logical and normative foundations. They not only conform to classical descriptions of logical thought processes (Dewey 1910), but also permit us to give clear, straightforward advice to 'real-world' decision-makers. However, appeal does not necessarily entail accuracy. Recent research strongly suggests that unitary sequence models present an oversimplified account of decision behaviour (Poole 1981; 1983a; 1983b). Instead of a set unitary sequence, this research supports a *multiple sequence* theory which incorporates between-group variations in the occurrence, ordering and number of developmental stages. For example, one group may follow the traditional orientation: evaluation: control sequence, while another may take a more complex route, such as orientation: evaluation: orientation: control: evaluation: control. The multiple sequence model implies a contingency theory to explain the occurrence of different sequences: the group will take different paths depending on the ensemble of conditions holding at various points in the decision process. Among the contingency variables advanced to explain these differences are task characteristics and the nature of relationships in the group (Poole 1983b).

Several findings support the validity of the multiple sequence model. Poole (1981) and Chandler (1981) compared unitary and multiple sequence models directly and both rejected the unitary sequence in favour of the more complex alternative. These and other studies of multiple sequences (Mintzberg *et al.* 1976; Segal 1982; Hirokawa 1983) indicate that phases can occur in many possible orders, depending on various factors. One important factor is the group's task: studies of phasic development in negotiative decision-making have shown an ordering of phases quite different from that obtained for problem-solving (Putnam and Jones 1982). Mintzberg *et al.* (1976) suggest that degree of environmental uncertainty and the degree of consensus on values govern the complexity of decision paths.

In general, the multiple-sequence model has garnered more support in recent research than has its unitary counterpart. However, as noted above, the unitary sequence model is both parsimonious and powerful and it has also received its share of support. How does the unitary-sequence model fit with the newer multiple-sequence approach? A study by Poole (1983a) suggests that the unitary models spell out an important class of determinants operating in the contingency theory, namely, the necessary structural requirements of the decision-making task. Dewey's problem-solving sequence, adapted by Bales and Strodtbeck, is probably the most widely accepted of these. Fisher's (1970) conflict management sequence (orientation: conflict: emergence: reinforcement) is also promising. Both schemes attempt to set out minimal necessary activity structures for group convergence and action and, as such, advance generative mechanisms to explain the sequence of group activities. Although their authors equate logical order with temporal order, there is no reason this is empirically necessary. The schemes certainly represent paths of least resistance for group work, but various contingencies, such as conflict or task difficulty, may prevent groups from following them and diversify phasic progressions. These patterns are a critical aspect of the explanation of activity sequence, just not the *sole* explanation.

Poole (1983b) has advanced a contingency theory of decision development that incorporates both structural requirements and contingency variables. Structural requirements include recognition of the need for a decision, definition of the decision problem, problem diagnosis, search for and generation of solutions, solution evaluation and adaptation, and implementation planning. In many cases some of these prerequisities will already be met; for example, members may already have a shared sense of the problem. The set of unmet prerequisites forms the problem structure the group has to address; those prerequisites which are met will be dealt with only cursorily in the group's work.

Poole's theory also incorporates two contingency variables, task and the group's working relationships. Task is defined in terms of two dimensions, difficulty and coordination requirements; working relationships are composed of three, the degree of member involvement in the group, the degree of member consensus on leadership and status relationships, and whether members have evolved procedural norms to guide their decision-making.

Together, structural requirements and contingency factors determine which phases occur and the order in which they occur. Poole develops a number of propositions to specify these influences, for example:

Proposition 1.　The group will engage in those [phases] that correspond to the missing components of the task completion structure.

Proposition 1a.　The order of [phases] will correspond to the logical priority of the missing task components.

Proposition 3a. High task difficulty will result in more problem definition and diagnosis and more recycling through these than will low-difficulty tasks. It will also result in more orientation and process comments.

A network of 20 propositions delineates the properties developmental sequences should exhibit under various conditions and offers an explanation for how group interaction patterns evolve in response to different contingencies.

Two comments are in order here. First, as these propositions indicate, structural requirements dictate the basic form or logic of the phasic sequence and contingency factors result in departures from this form. Contingencies complicate the normative or logical progression from stimulus to decision. Second, like all phasic theories, Poole's contingency theory is cast at the macro-level: it focuses on extended blocks of group activity rather than on specific, micro-level interaction sequences members may engage in during these blocks. Hence, there are limits as to what this and other phasic theories can tell us about particular interaction sequences.

Tasks, group interaction and group activity

The importance of microanalysis

Because phasic theorists paint with broad strokes, they have not capitalized on the potential of microanalysis. They take a one-dimensional view which regards interaction sequences as useful indicators of broader phases of group activity, but ignores their role as an active force in the development of group decisions. This results in a serious problem for phasic research:

Without reference to microlevel processes a complete explanation of decision development is impossible. Contingency theories promise extremely effective prediction and explanation of group developmental sequences. However, knowing the order of a group's phases does not tell us *how* the sequence developed as it did. Existing accounts of logical requirements and the effects of contingency variables on group activities give us some penetration of this question, but they still leave open the mechanism through which these factors operate. An adequate explanation must lay out the generative mechanism whereby causes have their effects (Harre and Madden 1975). And any generative mechanism for the explanation of group activity must be tied to an account of *members'* activity and interaction, because this is the only means by which any group activity can be carried out. It is not satisfactory simply to assert that the decision structure, the contingency factors and the phases relate to each other. An adequate theory must account for how a decision is constituted in and through interaction, how the contingency factors are mediated by member reactions, and how interaction advances the group toward a decision. And this implies that the theory must centre on two issues hitherto ignored by phasic research: (1) how are coherent phases constituted by group interaction and (2) how does the group manage transitions from phase to phase?

The theory of structuration (Giddens 1979; Bordieu 1977; McPhee and Poole 1981; Poole *et al.* 1982) provides the broader framework for this discussion. It is specifically concerned with the relationship of structures and human action and introduces several distinctions important to an understanding of tasks and interaction. Basic to the theory is the distinction between system and structure. *Structures* are rules and resources people use in interaction. *Systems* are observable outcomes of the applications of structures, 'regularized relations of interdependence between individuals and groups' (Giddens 1979, p. 66). In our case the group's decision-making behaviour can be regarded as a social system. This system can be depicted as a series of activities which reflect members' efforts to solve the problem. The structure behind the system consists of rules and resources, such as the task structure, possible strategies for moving the group toward a decision, (i.e., voting) members' task-related knowledge, and members' relative power in the group. The decision-making system has a pattern because it is structured: Members use rules and resources to create and maintain the decision process; the path the decision takes can be explained in terms of how members use these structures and the constraints structures place on what members can do.

But it is not simply a matter of members using structure to accomplish a decision. Structures have a dual nature: They are both the medium and outcome of action. They are its medium because structures provide the rules and resources people must draw on to interact. They are its outcome because rules and resources only exist through being applied and acknowledged in interaction – they have no reality independent of the social practices they constitute (Taylor 1971). Thus *structuration* – the production and reproduction of social systems via the application of generative rules and resources – operates in a recursive fashion: the very rules and resources interactors use are produced and recreated in the ongoing interaction. This implies that structure is not necessarily deeper or more fundamental than system, as some argue (Bordieu 1977; Clegg 1975; Cicourel 1974). The play of human creativity in the interaction system can introduce structural changes that are reproduced and thereby become abiding structural features. System and structures codetermine each other.

An explanation of the structuration of group decisions will provide the generative mechanism lacking in phasic studies. In order to capture fully the nature of the structurational process this explanation must make both causal and interpretive moves. At the most basic level the explanation must reconstruct the decision system as it is apprehended and experienced by group members. Member's constructions, their negotiations and their practical reasoning are crucial features of an action system, because they guide how members work within the system. This interpretive reconstruction is not sufficient, however; members' activities are also conditioned by causal forces, which may limit their freedom in ways they do not know or understand. For example, it is well established that members with high status outside the group (e.g. physicians) have more influence over decisions than those with low external status; the nature of American social structure conditions the decision process, even though members may not be aware of its effects. In order to understand the structuration of decisions we must focus not only on members' frame of reference and practical activities, but also on how structural features condition and constrain these activities, *and* on how members' actions mediate and reproduce these very structural features.

Coherency in task interaction

The agenda set in the preceding section focuses on two issues, both related to how a group generates a decision: (1) how are coherent phases constituted in group interaction and (2) how does the group manage transitions from phase to phase? Implicit in these questions are two assumptions. First, the questions assume that phases – reasonably unified activity periods – are the fundamental unit of interest in the analysis of group decision behaviour. Second, we assume that members have some notion of 'coherency' that enables them to understand a period of group activity as a unified whole and to take actions aimed at maintaining the coherency of this period. Parallel with Reichman's (1978) study of conversational coherency, the framework advanced here attempts to clarify the process by which members structure coherent decisions.

Our framework focuses on two aspects of structure in group decision-making: members' task representations and the rules and resources they can use to generate the activities implicated in these representations. We will discuss each in turn and then try to spell out their relationship to each other and to group decision activity.

Task representations

A task representation is a theory regarding 'the nature of the task, its objective, the means to employ to carry out the task, and the behaviours conducive to effectiveness' (Abric 1971, p. 313). The structure of this representation for decision-making tasks consists of two interdependent parts: A theory of the formal requirements of decision-making and an 'agenda' of the particular issues that must be dealt with in the decision before the group. Inclusion of both formal and content-based properties is warranted both by the nature of human cognition and by the instrumental requirements of task activity. Research on comprehension and memory suggests that both formal schemes and content-based classifications are involved in cognitive representations of texts and activities (Reiser and Black 1982). Since members' memory is in part the 'carrier' of the groups' task representation, the structure of task representations and cognitive representations should parallel one another. On the instru-mental level, as we noted above, formal task properties alone are insufficient to generate group activity sequences; sequences are also oriented by the group's attempts to resolve certain content issues specific to the particular task at hand.

The formal aspect of the task representation consists of a 'decision logic', a construct that enlarges upon the structural requirements identified by phasic research. A decision logic is a scheme depicting how a decision should be made, the strategy for decision in a particular situation. Perhaps the best known decision logic is the rational model, which assumes that the goal of decision-making is the best possible decision and presumes that the way to get this is means–ends analysis. Decision logics are not necessarily the same for every case: they may vary from decision to decision and group to group. Sometimes members explicitly formulate a logic at the beginning of the decision process; more often they use various schemes in conjunction with the particular issues involved – to generate a sense of required steps as the group proceeds. In observation of various groups I have discerned at least four decision logics (see also Meyer 1984):

(1) *Assumed consensus* – Members assume that they agree on basic values and on the nature of their problem or task. Their orientation is to find a solution as

quickly as possible and work it out in detail. The steps this orientation implies are (a) share information, (b) select a solution, and (c) work out implementation.

(2) *Political* – Members assume that decision-making is a process of winning adherents for their own preferred alternative. Their primary criterion is political acceptability, and originality or effectiveness take secondary status. Their orientation is to fasten onto their own preference early, win adherents, and shoot down other positions. This may require them to hide their own preferences until other positions are destroyed. The steps implied are (a) get preferred solutions on table, (b) build cases against other solutions, (c) get the group to converge on the preferred solutions by compromising or persuading, and (d) adopt and work out implementation of the solution.

(3) *Rational* – This orientation aims at making the best possible decision in the technical sense. It employs rational standards and means–ends analysis and implies a sequence like the following: (a) problem definition, (b) problem analysis, (c) solution search, (d) solution evaluation and selection, and (e) implementation.

(4) *Reactive* – Members may have no expectations. They look to others for cues and 'ad hoc' their way through the decision. (These members cannot be said to have a task representation; they form a 'null set' for our purposes.)

Decision logics are essentially 'logics-in-use'. They may reflect cultural norms or metaphors: the rational orientation implicitly incorporates an economic metaphor (Simon 1960), while the metaphor for the political orientation may well be 'cutting a deal' (Lindblom 1959).

In addition to the decision logic, the group's decision is structured by a content-based agenda of issues specific to the decision being made. For example, consider a group of managers meeting to decide on the purchase of a small computer who might consider several issues: relative cost, ease of operation, maintenance demands, need for staff retraining, and whether the friendship between one manager and a particular computer salesperson represents a problem. Sometimes this agenda will be set formally at the beginning of the decision; more often it is partially specified and additional issues arise as the group works. Issues can be arranged in a hierarchy of relevance, in which more fundamental or preliminary issues must be resolved before later ones are addressed.

Together, the group's decision logic and the issues nested within it define a task representation structure that prescribes an ordering of decision-making activities. For example, if the computer selection group's orientation was 'assumed consensus' the following structure might emerge:

(1a) Sharing information on performance.
(1b) Sharing information on price.
(1c) Sharing information on maintenance.
(1d) Sharing information on manager–salesperson friendship.
(2a) Deciding whether manager–salesperson friendship is important.
(2b) Deciding on which computer to buy.
(3a) Planning how to make purchase.
(3b) Planning retraining of staff.

This structure defines a plan (a set of milestones, in MacKenzie's terminology) for the decision-making session.

Task structures exist at two distinct levels in group discussions. On one plane they exist in member's heads as implicit theories of how a decision should be made. Because they are individualized, member's task representations may disagree; there can be as many task representations in a group as there are members. The individual's task representation supplies him or her with a strategy for conduct in the session. This strategy may be proactive (as in the case of the rational decision logic) or it may be reactive and relatively passive (as in the case of the reactive decision logic).

On an entirely different plane, there exists a *collective* task representation, of the same form as an individual task representation, but commonly held and publicly displayed in the group's interaction. This collective task representation is a property of the group's discourse; it is instantiated and developed through such devices as explicit and implicit goal statements, agendas, and 'process-related' comments. It formulates what the group has done and is doing, and entails with various degrees of stringency future steps and issues. Because it exists in discourse and is a social product, a collective task representation unfolds and evolves as the discussion proceeds. Sometimes a collective representation is entirely laid out as a plan or agenda, while in other cases it is only partially realized and may only imply the *group's* next step and no more. In still other cases it may be an object of contention. A group's collective task representation can be identified through analysis of its discourse; methods developed by Goguin and Linde (1979) to map planning discourse show promise for this purpose.

Collective task representations are determined in part by individual representations, but they are neither an average of individual views nor simply a substitute term for agreement among individual representations. There is a clear difference between this conception of collective task representation, which is discourse-based and objectifiable, and Abric's (1971) definition, which refers to a perception shared by group members. Several lines of research support the existence of collective task representations. Meyer (1984) identified several shared, public 'theories of decision-making' in his analysis of deliberations over hospital equipment purchases. Davis (1973) reports extensive evidence for the existence of social decision schemes, normative decision procedures holding for large populations of groups. Finally, the structural requirements identified in phasic research can be construed as 'stock' task representations.

Other things being equal, a group's decision path should be generated by its collective task representation. The utterances within each step have coherency (form a phase) because of a common relationship to the task structure. Any pair of utterances are related either by being part of the same step or by the relationship between their respective steps. This notion of task structure draws upon and parallels work on 'focus spaces' (Grosz 1977) and 'context spaces' (Reichman 1978) in analyses of conversational coherence. Various linguistic devices, to be discussed in the next section, are used to show that utterances are part of the same space, to make connections between separate spaces, and to manage transitions from one space to another.

Even though the collective task representation should generate group activities, observed progressions will not be this simple, for two reasons. First, exogenous contingency variables, such as the nature of the group's task, may constrain the group's ability to work out a decision. For instance, when the group's task representation does not correspond to objective task features (e.g. if the task is very difficult and requires creative problem-solving, but the group's representation has it as a fairly easy and routine decision), the group is likely to experience difficulties and travel a more complex path than the representation implies (Abric 1971). Second, there may be disagreements among members over the correct task representation. Such disagreements will complicate the group's development considerably and the procedural struggle may result in a considerable departure from the previous collective representative or even in a period of undirected, incoherent activity. Resolution of such disagreements depends partly on the other relevant structural feature, the available rules and resources for generating coherent activity periods. These are the subject of the next section.

Rules and resources for managing coherency

To accomplish a coherent decision, members must draw upon two classes of rules and resources: (1) Those necessary to carry out decision-making behaviours, such as proposing solutions and calling for a vote; and (2) Those related to what we will call *discussion-management tactics*, moves that create connections between utterances and make transitions from one step to another. This discussion focuses on the second class.

At least three classes of discussion-management tactics can be distinguished (see Table 11.1). First, there are elementary devices for linkage and separation of conversational elements. Elementary devices are integrated into the sentences they relate to and can be divided into two types; semantic (e.g. reference) and syntactic (e.g. conjunction). Second are *alignment moves*, tactics designed to avoid or remedy misunderstandings and problems in conversations. Unlike elementary devices, alignment moves generally stand alone, separate from the sentences or episodes they relate. Third, there are *structuring moves*. Like alignment moves, structuring moves attempt to remedy potential or actual problems in the discussion; unlike alignment moves, which are linguistic devices, structuring moves rely on extralinguistic resources, such as a member's capacity to reward or punish the group or the member's expertise. Structuring moves implicitly or explicitly bring power to bear in the discussion.

The three classes of tactics represent different complexes of rules and resources members can bring to bear in a discussion. Elementary devices and alignment moves rest primarily on structural properties of the language itself, while structuring moves rely on linguistic structures and extralinguistic resources. All three classes can be and are used in conjunction, but as we move up the hierarchy from elementary devices to alignment moves to structuring moves, differences in level of response emerge. In particular, each successive level of the hierarchy is designed to address more serious problems with coordination than the former one addresses, each involves a more overt intervention than the former one, and with each successive level, we observe an increasing probability of opposition to the move.

Task structure, coherency moves, and decision sequences

The linkage of task structure and coherency moves in interaction provides a

11.1 Examples of three classes of discussion-management tactics

---

I *Elementary devices (see particularly Halliday and Hasan 1976)*
  1 Reference to previous statement: e.g. use of pronouns, repetition of concept in previous sentence; this move can also be used to signal transitions when reference focus changes (McCutchen and Perfetti 1982; Vucinich 1977).
  2 Comparison: analysis of the attributes of two or more objects (McCutchen and Parfetti 1982).
  3 Lexical ties: paraphrases, semantic overlaps (McCutchen and Perfetti 1982).
  4 Event-related ties: ellipsis, implied repetitions (McCutchen and Perfetti 1982; Vucinich 1977).
  5 Conjunctions: single words signalling continuity or shift, such as also, yet, because, though, anyway (McCutchen and Perfetti 1982). Reichman (1978) terms these 'cluewords.'
  6 Causal relationships (Vucinich 1977).

II *Alignment moves (Ragan 1983)*
  1 Motive talk: statements that legitimize potentially inappropriate acts (Mills 1940).
  2 Disclaimers: statements that prospectively interpret and rectify possible problematic events (Hewitt and Stokes 1975).
  3 Side sequences: statements constituting a meta-communication break in the conversation (Jefferson 1972).
  4 Formulations: statements that express what is being done in the conversation ('I see we're coming to agreement') (Garfinkel and Sacks 1970).
  5 Meta-talk: statements that question problematic utterances and initiate repairs (Schiffrin 1980).
  6 Accounts: justifications and excuses exonerating a breach of conversational norms (Scott and Lyman 1968).

III *Structuring moves*
  1 Quid pro quo: One member offers a concession to the group in exchange for the group's undertaking his/her plan of action ('Look, I gave in on item 1; let me have some say in how we're gonna do this.') (Wilmot and Wilmot 1978).
  2 Procedural messages: comments which state agendas, lists of activities, group goals, means of dividing labour, or topics the group should address.
  3 Fractionation: breaking the decision into a series of issues, each of which can be addressed separately (Fisher 1971).

---

generative mechanism for decision development. This explanation has two aspects, an account of how task representations govern members' activity (particularly their use of coherency tactics) and an account of how coherency tactics themselves structure group activity sequences. The first aspect explores the operation of global factors in producing coherent decision activity, while the second refers to effects of local factors (Tracy, Chapter 2).

At the outset we assume that members prefer to employ elementary devices over alignment moves or structuring moves and that they prefer alignment moves over structuring moves. This assumption is based on a notion of economy in interaction: members follow the principle of least disruption in regard to their choice of discussion-management tactics. Effects of habit or the desire for power may cause members to favour more disruptive interventions, but initially this assumption seems to reflect the empirical occurrence of the tactics in group discussions.

The generative mechanism for decision development at the global level operates as follows: Member's activities are guided by their task representations. These representations arise from an interaction of their own presuppositions and experiences and objective features of the task itself. The collective task representation, which governs the path of decision development, is constituted in the course of working on the decision and emerges from the interaction of member's representations. The collective representation serves as a steering mechanism which predisposes members to enact various constellations of task-related behaviours in a distinct sequence, giving rise to observed phases.

The constellations of behaviours and the transitions between them are given coherence via the tactics discussed in the previous section. Employment of the various classes of tactics is constrained by the degree of consensus in members' task representations. When member representations are in agreement (or nearly so) and the collective representation corresponds to them, phasic coherence and transitions are managed primarily by elementary devices and alignment moves. There are no major points of divergence, so problems in coordinating members consist primarily in resolving differences in the speed with which they move through the phases (Hewes *et al.* 1981). We would expect sequences of alignment moves and occasional structuring moves at phasic transition points. Within the phases we would expect to observe a higher ratio of elementary devices with occasional alignment moves.

When members disagree the group must resolve the divergence, and this complicates the development path considerably. Members may try to take several paths at once or to hybridize paths, and this results in a more complex developmental sequence, characterized by halting, shifting patterns of activity. Disagreement over the shape of the collective representation also implicates different coherency tactics: structuring and alignment moves assume a much more prominent role in the discussion. Transition points between phases will be marked by structuring and alignment moves. There will also be phases of conflict which are primarily composed of these moves, as groups members attempt to work out how the group will proceed.

Group interaction, structured via the processes just discussed, mediates the effect of contingency variables on development sequences. Tasks and normative decision procedures are mediated by the group's collective task representation and the moves available to members for giving coherency to the discussion. However, task, working relationships and normative decision procedures also exert independent influence on the structuring of group decisions in two ways. First, they condition both the form of members' task representations and the degree of consensus members have on them. As we noted above, task representations are constrained by objective task requirements by normative decision models. The degree of consensus over representations is influenced by normative procedures and by working relationships. For some types of decisions a single normative model is dominant (for example, business purchasing decisions are generally subject to economic rationality), but for others (for example, moral judgements) many models are possible, and there is a wide-open field for competing representations. In the same vein, a group with poor working relationships should engender more disagreement over task representations than one with good, well established relationships. Tasks also condition group decision sequences in another way: As we noted above, to the extent that the collective task representation is not commensurate with the objective demands of the task, the group will be ineffective and its development will be complicated. Thus, task representations mediate the effects of contingency factors on decision development, but they are also constrained by those factors in a recursive process of structuration.

There is also a second aspect of the generative mechanism, the microlevel influence of coherency moves themselves on decision sequences. The coherency moves are not simply structural features members use to shape decisions; they also condition the decision process. Particularly at the levels of alignment and structuring moves, coherency tactics have sequential entailments which may turn the discussion in directions not implied by the task representation. The use of certain alignment moves may entail others and the resulting activity pattern may structure the group's decision path 'from the bottom up', as it were, with little relation to the task itself. For example, 'meta-talk', statements questioning problematic utterances, may well initiate a series of accounts and disclaimers that take up a considerable period of time (c.f. Cody and McLaughlin Chapter 3; Morris, Chapter 4), yet do not advance the group toward a decision.

This localized structuring is inherent in the use of coherency devices and operates in interaction with the first moment and the constraints upon it. The collective task representation guides the general direction of discussion, but is not specific enough to guide details. It provides global structure and the group may go off on tangents either when members lose track of the relationship between what they are saying and the general issue or when others fail to see the relationship of utterances to issues and introduce other topics. The coherency devices usually function to keep this from happening at a local, specific level, but they may also lead the group astray by giving the impression of coherence to non-relevant utterances or by introducing side issues related to control of the discussion.

On the structuration of task representations

As we have noted, structures are both the medium *and* outcome of action. In the course of the group's work its task representation itself is structured. In some cases the group's task representation will change radically over the course of the decision, while in others it will remain fairly stable, subject only to small adaptations. In the latter case it remains stable not because it is not subject to structuring, but because some feature of the structuring process is maintaining its stability. For example, in some groups a policy document outlining the nature of the group's problem and what decisions are required might 'freeze' the group's task representation by serving as a continuous point of reference.

Considerations of space prevent us from going into the structuring of task representations in any detail. Work by Volkema (1983), who portrays the problem-solving process as a series of problem redefinitions, is suggestive of one approach to this issue. The important point here is that the contingency variables and the structures themselves – both task representations and available coherency moves – are continually being structured during the decision, and that this must be taken into account in any encompassing theory of decision development.

Summary and conclusion

The theoretical framework developed in this paper rests on the assumption that decisions are actively structured by group members. It evolved in response to a problem in earlier theories of decision development: Although these theories were becoming increasingly sophisticated in their ability to account for observed sequences of group activities, they did not explain *how* these sequences evolved, that is, they did not specify a mechanism that could generate coherent phases and motivate the transitions between phases. The theoretical framework advanced here offers one mechanism that could generate multiple sequences such as those considered in Poole's (1983b) contingency framework. The theory posits that decision sequences are generated via members' use of two structures, task representations and coherency moves, and attempts to specify how these two structures relate to each other in group interaction, as well as how they are constrained by external factors such as the objective task and prevalent decision norms. Between-group differences in developmental sequences can result from at least four distinct dynamics in this framework; (a) for groups where there is initial consensus on a task representation, different groups may have different task representations; (b) in groups where there are disagreements between members' task representations, the activities undertaken to resolve these disagreements will complicate the developmental sequence, resulting in different patterns for different types and degrees of disagreement; (c) when the group's task representation is not commensurate with the objective nature of the task, the group's developmental sequence will diversify as it attempts to cope with this; and (d) localized sequential implications among coherency moves may introduce further idiosyncrasies into developmental sequences, patterns independent of the task itself.

This framework is not intended to replace or supersede contingency theory. Instead it attempts to specify the mechanism by which contingencies have their effects on group activity: Through a process of structuration, the effects of task and other contingency factors are mediated by one or more of four dynamics just summarized.

Nor is the framework completely developed here. To specify how phasic coherency is accomplished would require a much more detailed analysis of task representations than is presented here. A full explanation necessitates an account of how task demands are translated into action and of how participants judge their own and others' remarks as relevant to a representation.

The theory of structuration suggests additional issues that would have to be explored to develop the theory fully. As noted at the end of the previous section, the structuration of contingency variables and structural features must also be considered. In addition, we must consider the role of outside structures, such as economic rationality, in shaping members' task representations. Finally, differences in knowledge and skill among members must be considered. Some members have definite strategic orientations toward decisions, while others take a reactive stance; some members are facile with language while others are not; some have extensive power resources while others do not. These differences enable some members to exert more influence than others over the course of decision development.

The author wishes to thank Dean Hewes, Bob McPhee, Sally Planalp, and Maude Graham for their helpful comments. Of course they are in no way responsible for the final product.

222   *Marshall Scott Poole*

References

ABRIC, J.C. 1971: An experimental study of group creativity: Task representation, group structure, and performance. *European Journal of Social Psychology* 1, 311–26.

BALES, R.F. 1953: The equilibrium problem in small groups. In Parsons, T., Bales, R., and Shils, E., editors, *Working papers in the theory of action* (New York: Free Press).

BALES, R.F. and STRODTBECK, F. 1951: Phases in group problem-solving. *Journal of Abnormal and Social Psychology* 46, 485–95.

BERG, D.M. 1967: A descriptive analysis of the distribution and duration of themes discussed by task-oriented small groups. *Speech Monographs* 34, 172–5.

BORDIEU, P. 1977: *Outline of a theory of practice.* New York: Cambridge University Press.

CHANDLER, T.A. 1981: *Decision-making in small groups: A comparison of two models.* Masters Thesis, Cleveland State University.

CHAPPLE, E. and SAYLES, L. 1961: *The measure of management.* New York: Macmillan.

CICOUREL, A.V. 1974: *Cognitive sociology.* New York: Free Press.

CLEGG, S. 1975: *Power, rule, and domination.* London: Routledge & Kegan Paul.

DEWEY, J. 1910: *How we think.* Boston: D.C. Heath.

FEYERABEND, P. 1970: Against method: Outline of an anarchistic theory of knowledge. In Radner, M. and Winokur, S., editors, *Minnesota studies in the philosophy of science*, vol. IV (Minneapolis: University of Minnesota Press).

FISHER, B.A. 1970: Decision emergence: Phases in group decision-making. *Communication Monographs* 37, 53–66.

FISHER, R. 1971: Fractionating conflict. In Smith, C.G., editor, *Conflict resolution: Contributions of the behavioural sciences* (Notre Dame: University of Notre Dame Press).

FLEISHMAN, E.A. 1982: Systems for describing human tasks. *American Psychologist* 37, 821–34.

GARFINKEL, H., and SACKS, H. 1970: On formal structures of practical actions. In McKinney, J.C. and Tiryakin, E.A., editors, *Theoretical sociology: Perspectives and developments* (New York: Appleton-Century-Crofts), 337–66.

GIDDENS, A. 1979: *Central problems in social theory: Action, structure, and contradiction in social analysis.* Berkeley, Cal.: University of California Press.

GROSZ, B.J. 1977: *The representation and use of focus in dialogue understanding.* Dissertation, University of California, Berkeley).

HACKMAN, J.R. 1968: Effects of task characteristics on group products. *Journal of Experimental Social Psychology* 4, 162–87.

—— 1969: Toward understanding the role of tasks in behavioural research. *Acta Psychologica* 31, 97–128.

HACKMAN, J.R. and MORRIS, C.G. 1975: Group tasks, group interaction process, and group performance effectiveness: A review and proposed integration.

In Berkowitz, L., editor, *Advances in experimental social psychology*, vol. 8, 45–99.

HALIDAY, M.A. K. and HASAN, R. 1976: *Cohesion in English*. London: Longman.

HARRE, R. and MADDEN, H. 1975: *Causal powers*. Totowa, NJ: Rowman & Littlefield.

HEWITT, J. and STOKES, R. 1975: Disclaimers. *American Sociological Review* **40**, 1–11.

HIROKAWA, R.Y. 1980: A comparative analysis of communication patterns within effective and ineffective decision-making groups. *Communication Monographs* **4**, 312–21.

—— 1983: Group communication and problem-solving effectiveness: An investigation of group phases. *Human Communication Research* **9**, 291–305.

JAFFE, J. and FELDSTEIN, S. 1970: *Rhythms of dialogue*. New York: Academic Press.

JEFFERSON, G. 1972: Side sequences. In Sudnow, D., editor, *Studies in social interaction* (New York: Free Press), 294–338.

LACOURSIERE, R. 1980: *The life cycle of groups*. New York: Human Sciences Press.

LINDBLOM, C. 1959: The science of muddling through. *Public Administration Review* **19**, 79–99.

MABRY, E.A. 1975: Exploratory analysis of a developmental model for task-oriented small groups. *Human Communication Research* **2**, 66–74.

MACKENZIE, K. 1976: *A theory of group structures, vol. I*. New York: Gordon & Breach.

MCCUTCHEN, D. and PERFETTI, C. 1982: Coherence and connectedness in the development of discourse production. *Text* **2**, 113–39.

MCPHEE, R.D., and POOLE, M.S. 1981: The theory of structuration as a meta theory for communication research. Department of Speech Communication: University of Illinois.

MENZIES, K. 1982: *Sociological theory in use*. London: Routledge & Kegan Paul.

MEYER, A.D. 1984: Mingling decision-making metaphors. *Academy of Management Review* **9**, 6–17.

MILLS, C.W. 1940: Situated actions and vocabularies of motive. *American Sociological Review* **5**, 266–74.

MINTZBERG, H. RAISINGHANI, D., and THEORET, A. 1976: The structure of 'unstructured' decision processes. *Administrative Science Quarterly* **21**, 246–75.

POOLE, M.S. 1978: Group performance, member competence and synergistic effects. Department of Speech Communication: University of Illinois, 1978.

—— 1981: Decision development in small groups I: A comparison of two models. *Communication Monographs* **48**, 1–24.

—— 1983a: Decision development in small groups II: A study of multiple sequences in group development. *Communication Monographs* **50**, 206–32.

—— 1983b: Decision development in small groups, III: A multiple sequence model of group decision-making. *Communication Monographs* **50**, 321–41.

POOLE, M.S., SEIBOLD, D.R. and MCPHEE, R.D. 1982: *A structurational theory of group decision-making*. Paper presented at the Conference on Small Group Decision-Making, Pennsylvania State University.

PUTNAM, L. and JONES, T. 1982: The role of communication in bargaining. *Human Communication Research* 8, 262–80.

RAGAN, S. 1983: A conversational analysis of alignment talk in job interviews. In Bostrom, R., editor, *Communication Yearbook* 7 (Beverly Hills, Cal.: Sage).

REICHMAN, R. 1978: Conversational coherency. *Cognitive Science* 2, 283–327.

REISER, B., and BLACK, J. 1982: Processing and structural models of comprehension. *Text* 2, 225–52.

SCOTT, M., and LYMAN, S. 1968: Accounts. *American Sociological Review* 32, 46–62.

SEGAL, U.A. 1982: The cyclical nature of decision-making: An exploratory empirical investigation. *Small Group Behaviour* 13, 333–48.

SHAW, M.E. 1973: Scaling group tasks: A method for dimensional analysis: *JSAS Catalog of Selected Documents in Psychology* 3, 8.

SIMON, H.A. 1960: *The new science of management decision*. New York: New York University.

STEINER, I.D. 1972: *Group process and productivity*. New York: Academic Press.

STOKES, R. and HEWITT, J. 1976: Aligning actions. *American Sociological Review* 41, 838–49.

TAYLOR, C. 1971: Interpretation and the sciences of man. *Review of Metaphysics* 25, 1–52.

TUCKMAN, B. 1965: Developmental sequence in small groups. *Psychological Bulletin* 63, 383–99.

VAN DE VEN, A. and DELBECQ, A. 1974: A task contingent model of work unit structure. *Administrative Science Quarterly* 19, 183–97.

VUCINICH, S. 1977: Elements of cohesion between turns in ordinary conversation. *Semiotica* 20, 229–57.

VOLKEMA, R. 1983: Problem formulation in planning and design. *Management Science* 29, 639–52.

WILMOT, J. and WILMOT, W. 1978: *Interpersonal conflict*. Dubuque: Wm. C. Brown.

12

Bargaining as task and process: multiple functions of interaction sequences

Linda L. Putnam

Formal negotiations are becoming a popular form of decision-making and conflict-management in organizations. In the private sector, collective bargaining is a long-standing event in labour–management relations. The popularity of this process has recently spread to the public sector where teachers, police, firemen, and other government employees engage in an annual ritual of discussing salaries, fringe benefits and working conditions. Even though we typically treat bargaining as a formal event, the process of negotiation pervades a number of daily interpersonal and organizational activities, including marital conflicts, sales and marketing, legal transactions, and interdepartmental disputes. Thus bargaining is gradually emerging 'as a major mechanism for conflict resolution in our society' (Rubin and Brown 1975, p. 1).

Bargaining is defined as a 'process whereby two or more parties attempt to settle what each shall give and take or perform and receive, in a transaction between them' (Rubin and Brown 1975, p. 2). This process of give and take in search of a settlement ultimately defines the degree of interdependence between two parties (Walton and McKersie 1965). Five characteristics distinguish bargaining from other problem-solving activities. First, bargaining is classified as a subset of social conflict; hence participants hold or perceive they hold mutually exclusive or incompatible goals based on scarce resources or divergent interests. 'Incompatibility refers to goals or values that are antithetical or diametrically opposed to one another' (Putnam and Jones 1982b: 262). The second characteristic, social interaction, is the means through which bargaining is enacted. Thus, to reach a settlement on issues, participants must engage in some form of social interaction. Thirdly, participants are interdependent in that one party's gain depends on the choices of the other. Each party has the power to constrain or interfere with the goals of the other. Fourthly, compromise occurs through a willingness to exchange proposals and counterproposals that lead to a mutually acceptable solution. This characteristic suggests that each party enters the proceedings with the expectation of reaching a minimally satisfying agreement. Finally, bargaining is strategic and intentional in that parties aim for a calculated advantage over their opponents, but within the boundaries of mutually shared rules (Schelling 1960).

This chapter addresses the role of communication in bargaining. Magenau and Pruitt (1979) contend that bargaining is accomplished through the verbal and nonverbal actions of its participants. Communication leads to a settlement and signals how to proceed through the use of arguments, reasoning, and persuasive appeals embedded in bargaining strategies and tactics. Communication performs other vital functions in the bargaining process; namely it serves as a means of information exchange, a way of coordinating outcomes, and a basis for identifying behavioural patterns and regularities. Since bargaining interaction is both tacit and explicit, communication patterns are particularly important. That is, each verbal and nonverbal message paradoxically conceals while it reveals an individual's true position. Patterns or regularities over time make each person's actions predictable to the other by serving as a form of tacit communication – 'an impromptu code for signalling intentions and responding to each other's signals' (Schelling 1960, p. 84).

This chapter concentrates on interaction sequences in bargaining – patterns and regularities in communicative behaviour that evolve over time. More specifically, it aims to review the research findings on interaction sequences at both the micro- and macro-levels. At the micro-level, interaction sequences determine the nature of conflict cycles, manage information exchanges, recast goals and purposes, and structure bargaining relationships. At the macro-level, interaction sequences comprise phases and cycles that move bargaining sessions toward an eventual resolution. These cycles take on a larger macro-appearance as the end of one bargaining event sets the stage for future encounters.

Bargaining as a task-oriented activity

Interaction sequences evolve from negotiating divergent positions on a particular task. That is, perceptions of the task and the actual task demands influence interaction patterns. Walton and McKersie (1965) distinguish between two types of bargaining tasks: distributive and integrative. Distributive tasks entail a greater amount of perceived or inherent conflict than do integrative tasks. As a 'fixed-sum' agenda item, the total objective value of a distributive issue cannot be altered easily. For example, if the legislature allocates only a certain percentage of its budget for public employee raises, then teachers who insist on a sum greater than their district's fixed amount, stretch the range of a possible settlement. The school district might give the teachers extra dollars, but only at a reduction in teaching staff, summer programmes, or some other expenditure in the budget. Thus distributive bargaining assumes a fixed-sum in the alternatives available for a settlement. The parties involved experience a conflict of interest as each side attempts to maximize its own share; one person's gain is the other person's loss. In this case, compromise is the appropriate mode of conflict management.

Even though some tasks entail more distributive components than do others, the enactment of distributive bargaining hinges on perceptions of the task and the types of bargaining strategies participants employ. Distributive strategies include commitments, demands, arguments through repetition, threats, rejections, denials, and other forms of offensive or defensive communication. In distributive bargaining an individual seeks maximum information from his or her opponent while making minimal disclosures. Thus the distributive bargainer tries to manipulate his or her opponent through the use of aggressive tactics and minimal disclosures.

Integrative tasks allow for expansion of alternatives and an increase in the size of joint gain. This 'variable-sum' bargaining occurs through broadening the pie, creating new alternatives, or developing trade-offs between more and less important items (Pruitt and Lewis 1975). In integrative negotiation, both parties seek accurate information about alternatives and try to remain tentative and flexible in their thinking. The climate resembles problem exploration rather than attack–defend cycles of demands and commitments. Integrative strategies entail openness in information exchange, joint problem exploration, acceptances, concessions, and other-supporting statements. Mixed bargaining refers to tasks that combine distributive and integrative items. One type of mixed bargaining begins with fixed-sum items and then switches to integrative problems; thus integrative negotiation emerges after a period of distributive bargaining. Participants cooperate to enlarge their interdependency, and then compete for high outcomes (Walton and McKersie 1965). In mixed bargaining, cooperation extends beyond simply avoiding mutual disaster, as is often the case with distributive interaction. Rather, mixed bargaining focuses on finding alternatives that will expand mutual gain.

Since distributive and integrative are not only characteristics of the task but also descriptors of the process, it is difficult to separate the two in an actual negotiation. However, Walton and McKersie (1965) contend that the strategies that foster one task are the reverse of the other. Competitive attack–defend strategies make it difficult for each party to see that both sides can win (Pruitt and Lewis 1977). Despite these differences, the process of negotiating ultimately shapes perceptions of particular issues and problems. Hence what begins as a distributive task can evolve into problem-solving bargaining. For example, the teachers' union includes in their contract proposal a section on deduction of union dues. When the administration reads this section, they see the task as distributive – an infringement of managerial rights. Management has no intention of collecting dues for the union. But as the two sides interact, the teachers convince the administration that their proposal is not a change in policy, but merely a clarification of the current procedures, with administrative assistance in the timing and targeting of dues collection. What appears a distributive task with an inherent conflict of interest ends up a problem-solving issue.

Bargaining tasks also differentiate interpersonal from intergroup negotiations, although these differences also become fuzzy. Some bargaining tasks, as Stephenson (1981) points out, are primarily dyadic. The two negotiators represent their own interests rather than answering to other parties. In marital disputes, buying and selling of goods, and employment interviews, at least one party bargains independently. In contrast, intergroup tasks require the negotiator to represent a constituent group. Labour–management negotiations, legal transactions, and international contracts illustrate types of intergroup tasks in which the ultimate settlement resides with a constituent party. But again, the two types of tasks are not neatly distinct. Marital disputes may entail lawyers, sales negotiations involve company practices, and employment offers are restricted by organizational budgets. Moreover in intergroup bargaining, interpersonal relationships between negotiators can dictate bargaining process and outcomes, despite the wishes of representatives. In fact, Douglas (1957) characterizes negotiations as a balance between interpersonal and intergroup forces.

The constraints that representatives place on their negotiators is a topic of concern for boundary-role bargaining as well as intergroup relations. Boundary-role spanning refers to an individual's role of linking organizations to suppliers, customers, public and outside personnel. Individuals in marketing, supply, recruiting, governmental relations, advertising and public relations frequently serve as boundary-role negotiators who represent their respective companies. Although their tasks differ from those in labour–management negotiations, their roles resemble the representative functions of formal bargainers. Adams (1976) argues that boundary-role negotiators with a high degree of constituent trust are more likely to develop closer interpersonal relationships with the other bargainer. Constituent distrust of the boundary-role person, in contrast, increases competitiveness between bargainers and results in tighter intergroup relationships. In effect, even when the task calls for intergroup bargaining, interpersonal relationships of the negotiators shape the bargaining process.

Bargaining process and interaction sequences

Micro-level functions

Although the demands of a particular bargaining task impact on the distributive and integrative nature of negotiations and the interpersonal and intergroup relationships, task is a static variable and negotiations are 'dynamic processes of mutual accommodation' (Schelling 1960: p. 102). Thus even though the task influences process, process also shapes the task. In laboratory research, 'bargaining process' refers to the sequence of moves and counter-moves that culminate in a settlement. In natural settings and simulations of actual bargaining, 'process' centres on interaction sequences – the contiguous messages exchanged between negotiators or between bargaining teams. Although researchers have coded bargaining communication since Landsberger's work in 1955, testing for interaction sequences is a recent development (Putnam and Jones 1982b). Early research concentrates on frequencies of verbal messages that inventories the types of behaviours exchanged but does not reveal patterns and regularities in bargaining behaviour. Work on interaction sequences, in contrast, treats bargaining behaviours as interdependent and interlocked. This interdependency is particularly salient since each party is guided by what he or she thinks the other person will do and since each party can alter, intensify or inhibit the planned behaviour of the other. Interaction sequences in negotiation function to shape conflict cycles, manage information exchanges, recast goals and purposes, and structure relationships.

Conflict cycles. Sequential behaviour between negotiators is an important determinant of conflict escalation or de-escalation. Conflicts escalate through a growth in the number of issues, motives and costs that participants are willing to bear (Deutsch 1973). Escalation develops from conflict cycles characterized by specific attack–defend patterns. Two lines of research illustrate the escalation and de-escalation of conflict cycles. The first and most traditional research restricts communication to moves and countermoves of bargainers. When analysed as a sequence of events, bargaining moves depict a negotiator's position and his or her ability to exert influence (Schelling 1960). Research on moves and countermoves cluster into cooperative–competitive choices and concession making.

Studies on cooperative–competitive choices reveal that cooperative moves are successful only when they are reciprocated (Kelly and Slahelski 1970). If both bargainers begin with a cooperative pattern then one defects to a sequence of competitive moves, negotiators will end up in an escalating conflict. Once a pattern sets in, bargainers predict their opponent's response from it. If a negotiator switches to a competitive sequence, the first bargainer deems his or her opponent as untrustworthy and thus responds with a competitive move (Wilson 1969). Competitive choices engender competitive responses, even when a cooperative player prefers to make cooperative moves. A pattern of 'locking-in' to either cooperative or competitive moves often persists for the remainder of the interaction (Pilisuk and Rapoport 1964).

Bargaining moves, when analysed as sequential patterns, also reveal the magnitude, rate and timing of concessions and the extent to which concessions depend on the opponent's behaviour. If a negotiator follows a series of competitive choices with a cooperative move, this change in behaviour signifies a positive concession. Sequential changes from high competitiveness to cooperativeness induce greater cooperation than does the absence of concessions or the use of negative concessions (Bixenstine and Wilson 1963). Moreover, Druckman *et al.* (1972) report that the rate and magnitude of concessions tend to be reciprocated in kind. In general, research on bargaining moves demonstrates that negotiators reciprocate concessions and competitive behaviours, but when a pattern of cooperative moves develops, one competitive choice can break the cycle and send the interaction into a competitive spiral.

Treating communication as a series of strategic moves heightens the artificiality of bargaining research, obscures the meaning of any one move, and falsely dichotomizes cooperation and competition (Gergen 1969). By focusing on verbal communication as the essence of bargaining, each message contributes to both cooperation and competition, depending on its function in the interaction structure. A second line of research, then, studies sequences of verbal messages as indices of the escalation or de-escalation of conflicts.

Specifically, Donohue (1981a, 1981b) adopted a distributive task to test the rules that governed use of attack, defend and regression tactics. He coded each utterance twice – first, as a response to the previous statement and secondly, as a cue for the following utterance; thus each statement functioned both as a tactic and a strategy for analysing the relative advantage of each participant's gain in a simulated economic negotiation. His study revealed that successful negotiators maintained a strong position by demonstrating diversity in argument, giving more offers, denying faults more frequently, offering more rejections, and changing the topic more frequently than did unsuccessful negotiators. Losers, in contrast, responded with more self- and other-support statements and more concessions than winners did. Analysis of the interaction patterns of negotiators disclosed an action–reaction pattern with extreme attacks balanced by extreme regressive moves. For example, a threat or charge of fault (attacking cues) might be followed by an other-support or disconfirmation message (regression response). This sequence sets up an action–reaction pattern with the softer regression strategies counter-balancing the harder attack cues. Impasse dyads, however, employed this pattern less frequently than did agreement dyads, suggesting that the action–reaction pattern buffers negotiators against a spiraling conflict cycle. Moreover, regression statements, similar to integrative communication, followed other regression comments with a high degree of regularity.

In a similar study, but one that focused on mixed rather than distributive bargaining, Putnam and Jones (1982a) employed Hopmann and Walcott's (1974, 1976) Bargaining Process Analysis II (BPA II) to examine the effects of bargainer role on the development of conflict cycles. The BPA II is a category system comprised of 30 different types of messages clustered into substantive, strategic, persuasive, task, affective and procedural categories. Bargainers interacted for 30 minutes on a simulated grievance case. This study demonstrated that labour and management reciprocated distributive tactics, but labour specialized in offensive manoeuvres while management relied on defensive messages. Types of defensive tactics include self-supporting arguments, retractions, demands and commitments while offensive strategies include such behaviours as attacking arguments, rejections, threats and initiating reactions. Two characteristic patterns emerged from the study. In the first one management initiated a defensive tactic and labour responded with an offensive message or labour initiated an offensive message and management followed with a defensive response. In this offensive–defensive pattern, management might make a self-supporting argument (defensive tactic) and labour might respond with a rejection (offensive statement). If labour initiated an attacking argument first, then management would respond with a defensive behaviour like retraction or demand. The second pattern paralleled an action–reaction sequence with management initiating offensive moves and labour responding with information-giving messages. That is, if management initiated a threat or rejection then labour would follow by providing information. Thus when management moved into labour's characteristic mode of attacking, labour prevented a conflict spiral from developing by making a less volatile response. Both patterns then served as buffers against the escalation of conflict cycles. Similar to Donohue's (1981a, 1981b) research, both sides initiated and followed integrative messages with integrative responses. But in contrast to these agreement dyads, bargainers who reached an impasse demonstrated a tight, highly predictable structure of interaction characterized by reciprocating the other side's tactic. When management initiated a defensive comment, labour followed with a series of defensive moves; when labour initiated a defensive statement, management followed with an offensive remark that developed into a series of offensive attacks. Thus mismanagement of distributive tactics by matching behaviours and escalating one-upmanship characterized the development of a round-robin, conflict cycle.

Even though these two studies differ in the type of bargaining task employed, they uncover similar patterns for the escalation and de-escalation of conflict cycles. Both studies, however, use student negotiators, dyadic designs and simulations with short time limits. In an investigation that relied on natural subjects, Donohue et al. (1984) compared the tactics and strategies used in actual and simulated negotiations. The simulated sessions consisted of teacher-training bargaining that involved a two-day or 15-round negotiation while the naturalistic bargaining consisted of 24 private-sector contract sessions. A comparison of interaction sequences from the two settings revealed that the natural setting contained more attack sequences than did the simulated bargaining. Specifically, in the actual negotiations labour used more attack sequences, presented more proposals, and offered more assertive responses than did management. Management, in turn, used more question extension and more clarification than did labour or managers in the simulation. Overall, the simulation contained more integrative statements and less attack-oriented cues than did the actual negotiations.

These studies demonstrate that interaction sequences are a viable way of understanding the evolution of conflict cycles. Conflict cycles, once they escalate to a point of redefining goals, 'locking-in' to a position, and matching tactics, frequently lead to stalemates, impasses, work stoppages or strikes. Hence it is important for researchers to understand the way bargaining can avoid conflict cycles and can develop integrative techniques. The Donohue (1981a, 1981b) and the Putnam and Jones (1982a) studies suggest that distributive and integrative tactics are intermingled in bargaining interaction. Distributive patterns when buffered with offensive–defensive tactics, attack-regression responses, and reciprocation of integrative remarks do not tend to spiral. However, matching tactics, tightly structured interactions, and one-upmanship manoeuvres typically lead to conflict cycles.

Blake *et al.* (1964) in their field observations of labour–management negotiations describe the way distributive patterns escalate and integrative ones intervene to break a conflict cycle. First, management and labour follow a pattern of attack and counterattack, dwelling on their differences and exaggerating the magnitude of their claims. They begin to shift from distributive to integrative strategies when one group, usually management, seeks similarities in positions or when both teams try to penetrate each other's proposals and test for mutual intentions. Then management requests an explanation from the union, the union takes this as an attack, and returns with a counterattack. Management asks the union for proof of their demands, the union makes firm commitment statements, management denies labour's position, the union counterattacks, and a conflict spiral escalates with emotions peaking as both sides 'lock-in' on issues. In desperation, management returns to cooperation, the union responds in kind, and the last stage of interaction consists of a factual problem-solution discussion. These observations suggest that while distributive and integrative bargaining elicit opposite tactics, the two can and do develop simultaneously. Thus integrative bargaining does not necessarily follow a lengthy period of distributive negotiation. An integrative process cannot develop, however, unless management and labour are willing to abandon, at least temporarily, their respective offensive and defensive postures (Walton and McKersie 1965: p. 152).

Recasting goals and purposes. One outgrowth of a conflict cycle is redefining goals. As a conflict escalates, the aim of winning becomes a goal in itself. Hence a competitive interaction sequence changes the goals of bargaining from reaching a settlement or maximizing one's payoff to making sure the opponent *does not win*. Bargainers focus on scorekeeping rather than on finding alternatives for joint or personal gain. As Katz and Kahn (1978, p. 165) observe, whether in the laboratory, labour–management sessions, management training, or a boys' camp, 'the escalation process not only intensifies conflict over the original issues; it proliferates to other issues . . . if unchecked, this culminates in a perceived need to end the relationship.' Although a number of theorists operate from the belief that goals determine actions, interaction sequences function in a reflexive way to redefine the negotiation process.

Hawes and Smith (1973) argue for a retrospective view of goal definition, one in which communicative behaviours clarify goals rather than goals directing behaviour. Research on interaction sequences and the way bargainers interpret these sequences might yield important findings as to how goals become reshaped during the bargaining process.

Managing information exchanges.   A substantial amount of negotiation time centres on information exchanges. Bargainers use information to ascertain salient issues, to locate areas for trade-offs, and to assign priorities and meanings to demands. In Pruitt's (1981) view, information management is a way of attaining a functional level of coordination between negotiators. Donohue and Diez (1983) examine the role of interaction sequences in the management of bargaining information. Their study employs conversational analysis to determine how negotiators respond to information requests and imperatives and how these responses control the informational environment. Since bargainers aim to gain data about their opponent's position while revealing little knowledge about their own intentions, negotiators must choose how to access and manipulate information exchange (Bacharach and Lawler 1981). In this perspective, 'utterance sequences are viewed as a careful dance in which participants manage the level of ambiguity associated with a particular idea' (Donohue *et al.* 1983:, p. 250). Donohue and Diez (1983) coded utterances from 16 hours of simulated teacher negotiations. The unit of analysis in their study was a double interact – a sequence of three successive utterances initiated by an information request in the form of a question or an imperative. They found that questions were more successful than imperatives in gaining the desired information, in that questions obligated respondents to answer. But responses were often abrupt and short, compelling the questioner to continue requesting information. Use of questions, then, generated a chain-expansion sequence with information requests followed by providing information, a topic expansion request, and then providing more information. Questions served as a test of the opponent's firmness while allowing the questioner to sustain requesting rights, thus controlling the information flow.

In addition to questions and imperatives, Donohue *et al.* (1983) contend that bargainers manage information exchanges through the use of arguments. Research on bargaining arguments might analyse how negotiators disagree, how they delimit the content of their disagreements, and how rules govern the structure of their arguments. Other topics that would be pertinent to research on arguments include turn-taking between bargainers, adjacency pairs, expansion of arguments and advocation of proposals. Interaction sequences, then, serve an information-management function by defining the question–answer exchange, controlling the flow of information and influencing the use of arguments.

Structuring relationships.   One of Walton and McKersie's (1965) subprocesses of bargaining is attitudinal structuring – behaviours aimed at influencing the relationship between negotiators. Attitudinal structuring centres on the socio-emotional dimensions of interaction rather than on the content or the task effects. Bargainers use interaction sequences to develop or to change attitudes through such emotions as friendliness, trust or hostility. In response to the pressures constituents place on their negotiators, attitudinal structuring is typically a subtle outgrowth of control patterns, politeness or distancing. Bednar and Curington (1983), in a re-examination of Bednar and Glauser's (1981) study, used Markov chain analysis to study the content and relationship dimensions in seven negotiation sessions of the Barrington Oil Company. The unit of analysis was an interact in which both the antecedent and the subsequent act comprised one unit. Their study used the BPA II and Ellis's (1979) relational coding system consisting of control bids, deference messages and equivalence attempts. In the sessions that were conducted by a bargainer from the local union, labour directed procedures and attempted to be persuasive while management engaged in task-oriented statements.

A deference–equivalence pattern developed in this phase with management deferring to the union and labour responding with an equivalence remark. But when a representative from the national union took over, the labour negotiator responded to management's deference with dominant, controlling strategies. The researchers concluded, however, that the predominant relational pattern was competitive symmetry – both sides trying to control and direct the interaction. This relational pattern continued throughout the negotiation, even though the content of messages changed from one phase to the next. Moreover, Bednar and Curington's study (1983) did not replicate previous findings on the reciprocity of integrative strategies. Concessions did not follow concessions with a high degree of regularity. Perhaps concessions, in this study, were eventually reciprocated but not in sequential moves. The Bednar and Curington investigation did reveal a dominance–equivalence pattern, similar to the action–reaction sequence in Donohue's (1981a) study and similar to the offensive information giving pattern in the Putnam and Jones (1982a) investigation.

Another way to investigate relational development between bargainers is through discourse analysis. Specifically, researchers could study the phrasing of threats and demands as indices of communication style, the use of polite language and confrontive questions to indicate speaker position, and the use of personal pronouns to reduce or increase the psychological and social distance between negotiators (Donohue *et al.* 1983). The structuring of relationships between bargainers is a significant and neglected area in the work on interaction sequences. Future studies could enhance research on conflict cycles by examining how goal redefinition shapes cooperation and competition, by studying arguments and proposal advocacy as types of integrative and distributive sequences, and by determining the overt and covert ways that bargainers signal relational messages.

Macro-level functions

In micro-level analysis contiguous acts or sets of antecedent and subsequent moves form the basis of sequential interaction. Macro-analytic approaches focus on larger aggregates of communicative behaviour to determine how phases and cycles of bargaining activity develop. Researchers examine interaction sequences to discover phases of bargaining development and stages embedded in an historical context of recurring bargaining events.

Efforts to identify bargaining phases began with Douglas's (1957, 1962) classic field observations and audiotaped recordings of four different private-sector negotiations: the Marathon case, the Crescent City case, the Irving Mining case and the Atlas case. She characterized negotiation as a sequence of phases – a developmental process that cannot be telescoped. Through study and interpretation of bargaining transcripts, she identified three phases: establishing the bargaining range, reconnoitering the bargaining range, and precipitating the decision-reaching crisis. Phase 1 lasted a long time and consisted of a series of lengthy public orations characterized by dogmatic pronouncements, vehement demands and 'spirited' critiques of the other side's position. Even with this high degree of conflict, negotiators exhibited an aura of friendliness and warmth, thus giving the appearance of role-playing conventional procedures. Phase 2 was also long and consisted of tactical manoeuvres and jockeying for position while pressing the other side to capitulate and show signs of tacit agreement. Phase 3 was shorter and consisted of reducing alternatives to a formal agreement. Interaction was characterized by 'yes–no' responses, forced-choice alternatives, and the use of private 'side bar conferences' between negotiators.

Douglas's major contribution, however, came in the testing of observers' abilities to identify bargainer affiliation across phases. She sent copies of transcripts of the Atlas case to nine mediators and negotiators across the country and asked them to identify the speaker and the importance of that speaker's role in four different bargaining sessions. She found that identification of party affiliation became more difficult across bargaining phases. It was especially low in the second stage, but it regained strength in the third one. Stephenson *et al.* (1977) replicated Douglas's (1962) procedures in a phase analysis of three wage disputes and one contract negotiation. They employed the Conference Process Analysis, a category system consisting of four modes of information exchange, nine categories of information types, and seven categories of message reference. Their findings paralleled Douglas for Phases 1 and 2 but showed a gradual decrease in party identification for Phase 3. As the bargaining progressed, negotiators reduced their use of party-affiliation references, reduced the frequency of limitation and rejection statements, increased references to self, and increased their use of procedural and positive statements.

Bednar and Curington (1983) added to this finding by observing that Phase 1 differed from Phases 2 and 3, not in the content areas of communication, but in the relational messages. Phase 1 showed a higher degree of competitive symmetry than appeared in Phases 2 and 3. Davis (1982) employed a different twist to the identification of bargaining phases in the Lewiston teacher negotiation. He asked bargainers to describe the major phases of bargaining by tracking the movement of issues across sessions. Consistent with previous research, bargainers identified three phases: specifying priorities, posturing for positions and exchanging proposals.

Phase analysis studies allow researchers to make comparisons between bargaining stages and unidimensional models of small group development. Morley and Stephenson (1977) claim that negotiation groups begin with vigorous argument that leads to orientation, while small groups start with orientation and move to conflict and evaluation (Bales and Strodtbeck 1951). The opening stages of negotiation are characterized by hard-hitting aggressive tactics; conflict leads to coping with the task. But in small groups, coping with the task leads to conflict (Morley and Stephenson 1977, p. 259). Small groups also exemplify a relational pattern of equivalent symmetry whereas the dominant pattern for negotiation groups is competitive symmetry. Phase analysis in small groups currently demonstrates greater support for a multidimensional rather than a unidimensional model of group development (Poole 1981). This work suggests that bargaining research on interaction phases needs more scrutiny. As Stephenson (1981:, p. 183) argues, 'Not all negotiations are so stage-managed, and perhaps it is inappropriate to conceive of negotiations as being obliged to pass through a *particular* sequence of stages.' Since the atmosphere of negotiation changes from one item to the next, perhaps research on phase development should examine the complete discussion of one item across several sessions rather than assuming that phases evolve in unidimensional steps from one session to the next.

The most neglected area in phase analysis is the study of bargaining as a recurring event. Walton and McKersie (1965) and Douglas (1962) acknowledge the ongoing nature of bargaining relationships, but they spend very little discussion on the impact of historical sequences on bargaining process. Labour–management negotiations are framed within an historical context of previous negotiations; this year's bargaining sets the stage for next year's activities. If an item in a proposed contract is not accepted this year, the union can bring it to the table next year. If the teams experience impasse or a strike, these events colour future negotiations as well as daily work relationships. If the same negotiators meet annually to bargain contracts, they are likely to develop abbreviated codes that govern conflict cycles, information management and relationship expectations. Most research operates in an historical vacuum without attending to the way interaction patterns are similar or different from one year to the next. An exception to this practice is a case study and interaction analysis of arbitration documents in the 1969 and 1980 collective bargaining between the Teacher Assistant Association and the University of Wisconsin-Madison. Keough (1983) analysed interview data and historical documents to identify the structures that influenced collective bargaining and then she applied these structures in an analysis of arguments used in the 1979 arbitration hearings on negotiation rights. She found differences between the university and the teacher assistants' reliance on past negotiations, prerogative arguments and coalition appeals in the arbitration transcripts.

Intra-organizational bargaining

Bargaining history is one contextual variable that can impact on negotiations. Other variables include intra-organizational bargaining and organizational communication prior to, during and following the negotiation. Intra-organizational bargaining refers to the process of reaching consensus within each negotiation group. It includes the relationship between the negotiator and his or her team members, the caucus sessions of team members, and information exchanges between team members and their constituents. Research on intra-organizational bargaining concentrates primarily on the effects of team pressure on negotiator communication and on the interaction patterns between negotiators and team members. Repeated studies in laboratory settings demonstrate that bargainers who represent constituent groups tend to be tougher than non-representatives, especially when the negotiator's actions are visible to his or her team (Chertkoff and Esser 1976; Adams 1976). On the one hand negotiators must struggle with the demands of their team and on the other hand they must maintain a satisfactory relationship with their opponent.

Walton and McKersie (1965) cite examples of interaction patterns that show how negotiators attempt to moderate their team's position through monitoring information disclosures, guiding expectations and controlling emotional reactions. To reach a settlement, bargainers often conform to behavioural directives given by their team while using subtle cues to indicate a willingness to concede. To entice their team members to accept a settlement, negotiators keep issues complicated, exaggerate their levels of achievement and limit opportunities for surveillance of their actions. A critical factor in the success of these tactics is the degree of trust between negotiators and their constituents. In a situation that illustrated a high level of trust, Putnam and Bullis (1983) investigated the way communication in 'side bars' between negotiators and communication between bargainers and their respective teams ultimately defined a bargainer's role. In the 12-hour teacher negotiation that they observed, the bargainers met privately on three separate occasions. The remainder of the bargaining was spent in caucus meetings. A comparison of interaction sequences across these sessions revealed that the union bargainer served primarily as a gatekeeper and manipulator of information while the management negotiator functioned as a facilitator, who accurately reported the issues discussed in side bars and who guided caucus deliberations toward a settlement. High levels of distrust lead to greater surveillance of negotiator's actions, fewer concessions at the table and stronger evidence in support of commitments (Wall 1975). Thus the communication between negotiators and their constituents impacts on interaction sequences at the table.

Only a few studies focus on communication during planning meetings and caucus sessions of negotiation teams. Douglas (1962) transcribed interactions in caucus meetings, but she concentrated on the impact of the mediator on group deliberations. Diez (1983) employed discourse analysis to compare linguistic patterns that emerged in teacher caucus meetings with interaction sequences at the table. Using data collected from three teacher simulations, she coded independent clauses, listenability indices, back-channels, talkovers, utterance lengths, and personal pronouns used by the same participants in two different settings. Caucus session interaction was significantly different from communication at the table in the use of independent clauses, length of utterances and listenability index. Specifically, caucus sessions employed shorter utterances, more talkovers and fewer back-channels than did bargaining communication at the table. Intra-organizational bargaining is a rich untapped domain for communication research. To understand the basis of interaction sequences at the table, researchers must extend their work beyond the bargaining dyad into the intergroup relations that constitute the negotiation event.

Conclusion

Analysis of bargaining interaction is in a state of infancy; hence the conclusions drawn from this review are at best tentative and speculative. For decades bargaining has served as the dominant research paradigm for studying conflict management in general and cooperation–competition in particular. The bulk of these studies employ matrix games and input–output variables that ignore communication processes. Through communication, however, participants identify trades and develop stable, recognizable patterns of movement. These patterns emerge in the form of interaction sequences that escalate or de-escalate conflict spirals, manage information, redefine goals and structure relationships. At this embryonic stage, researchers have gleaned more insights about conflict cycles than about the other three functions. Basically, bargainers reciprocate integrative messages and buffer conflict spirals with action–reaction, attack–defend and attack–information giving patterns. Escalating conflict spirals develop from matching distributive strategies, specifically from both sides adopting a series of either defensive or offensive tactics. The crucial question, addressed by Blake *et al.* (1964), remains open for empirical scrutiny. That is, how do bargainers move from a highly pronounced series of distributive tactics to integrative bargaining?

Research on information management, goal redefinition and relationship structuring is sparse. Bargainers who use question–answer sequences typically develop a chain-expansion form of probing for and controlling information flow. Putnam (1983) is currently conducting research on the way arguments and proposals in negotiations reshape agenda items, thus changing bargaining goals. Studies on relational structuring reveal that bargainers develop a pattern of competitive symmetry, but one that appears complementary with management making deferent statements and labour relying on equivalence or control strategies. At the macro-level, phase analysis of sequential interaction reveals that bargainers establish their positions and engage in intense conflict during Phase 1; then they jockey for positions and search for agreements in Phase 2; and finally they culminate the process through reaching an agreement in Phase 3. Phase researchers, however, seem preoccupied with finding one dominant pattern, rather than with examining multiple models of bargaining development.

Research on interaction sequences is undergoing changes. Specifically, investigators seem disenchanted with procedures and category systems that require coding every utterance. Elaborate and comprehensive schemes like the BPA II, the Conference Process Analysis, and Donohue's cue–response system are unwieldy and suitable for only specific types of study. Since most category systems are atheoretical, they provide only a modicum of explanatory information about research findings. Current studies are isolating particular types of behaviours, for example, question–answers, arguments, proposals and issue development, for analysis of interaction sequences.

Interaction analysis in bargaining currently operates from three broad-based theoretical orientations: game and social exchange theory, process or pragmatic models and language-discourse perspectives. Originating from economic models, game theory aims to discover the logical structure of conflicts. It assumes that conflict decisions are rational, arising from the strategies that participants employ to maximize their own gains and minimize their losses (Rapoport 1965). Game theorists typically focus on the manifest reasons for a conflict, the utilities or values assigned to outcomes, and predetermined alternatives for settlements. Hence, conflict is purely competitive, defined by a fixed-sum game in which the utility and the alternative choices are predetermined. To test game theoretic assumptions, researchers typically employ matrix games where each player simultaneously chooses a competitive or a cooperative option across repeated trials. The research design centres on the perspective of the individual, in particular, on his or her strategies and sequences of moves to maximizing personal gain (Steinfatt and Miller 1974). Social exchange models, as variations of game theory, shift the focus from the logical structure of conflict to the trade-offs that bargainers make. Researchers typically examine the effects of cooperative and competitive orientations on reciprocity of trades, attributions of self and opponent, individual traits of competitors, and types of offers exchanged. Game theory is a very narrow perspective for the study of conflict. Even though research in this area yields insights about the convergence of final choices, game theory oversimplifies alternative outcomes, treats utilities of outcomes as factors that remain constant throughout the negotiation, assumes that fixed-sum conflicts parallel real-choice situations, and typically ignores the social interaction that leads to creating joint settlements.

Donohue's (1981a, 1981b) original work on the rules that govern cue-response sequences combines a game theoretic model with a rule-based approach to communication. His design employs a fixed-sum outcome, predetermined goals to maximize individual gain and the assumption that clear-cut winners and losers emerge from the process. This model parallels traditional economic approaches that characterize studies of the Prisoner's Dilemma and other matrix games. Game theory, while suitable for particular types of bargaining, offers limited insights on the ways goals, issues and values change through interaction sequences (Walton and McKersie 1965).

In game theory models, stability has been an unquestioned assumption; the process of bargaining is typically ignored. The process or pragmatic perspective concentrates on the evolution of bargaining over time. It assumes that bargainers coordinate their behaviours to understand each other and to discover patterns that make their actions predictable to the other. Conflict operates within individual and social systems where the participants share common interests. Strategic behaviour centres on influencing the other person through anticipating how one's own move relates to the other person's behaviour. Thus, conflict is self-reflexive in that the messages exchanged are circular. 'Behaviour precipitates behaviour in a circular response . . . I never fight you; I fight you plus me' (Follett 1940, p. 44). Bargainers then rely on one another to create their environment which, in turn, reflects back on them and constrains their interaction. This constraint also serves as a way of predicting pattern and regularity in bargaining. Interaction over time serves to reduce uncertainty in that a bargainer's choice becomes more limited as he or she adheres to the coordinated pattern that both participants create. In effect, once bargainers develop a system of interaction that allows each to anticipate the other's moves, some behaviours are less likely to occur (Fisher 1978). Moreover, in this perspective, goals, values and outcomes evolve from the coordination system that bargainers create. Hence, exact knowledge of these variables or of the power of negotiators emanates from the conflict itself (Angell 1965).

Putnam and Jones (1982a), Bednar and Curington (1983), and Donohue *et al.* (1984) adhere to a process or pragmatic model of negotiation. In their work, bargaining interaction defines the nature of the conflict, the strategies and tactics employed, and the eventual outcome. Interaction sequences constitute the structure of the bargaining process – one which shapes an eventual agreement or impasse. The process perspective is a refreshing change from traditional game theory models, but it is limited by its narrow and almost exclusive focus on the interpersonal and formal dimensions of bargaining.

The language-discourse approach evident in the work of Donohue and Diez (1983), Donohue *et al.* (1983) and Diez (1983) is less developed than the other two perspectives. It adheres to similar assumptions about interaction sequences, but it lends itself to the study of meanings that bargainers assign to their own and their opponent's messages. For example, politeness and psychological distancing probe beyond a description of acts into the way these acts function in the process. Meanings are revealed through the structure of discourse and through examination of symbols. Conversational analysts break interaction into its constituent parts and scrutinize language behaviours for multiple meanings. For example, research on question and answer sequences focuses on the way the conversational structure indicates power and control relationships between bargainers. An examination of language use might reveal the way bargainers use references to state laws, previous contracts and past grievances to symbolize the parameters for a joint settlement. In an arena characterized by the use of explicit messages to conceal tacit moves, the ability to combine interpretations of actions with description of sequences offers great potential to researchers.

Both the process and the language-discourse perspectives appear tied to formal, interpersonal models of negotiation. To enhance our understanding of interaction sequences in natural settings, we need to incorporate systemic features of the context into our models. We need to examine how bargainers incorporate contextual factors such as bargaining history, state laws and organizational constraints in their interaction. Finally, we need to broaden our focus to tap the intergroup as well as the interpersonal dimensions of negotiation. In particular, we should compare the content and sequences of messages in caucus meetings with the way bargainers enact their roles at the table. We need to study the way team members in caucus meetings talk about interaction at the table and how they use this 'metacommunication' to predict their opponent's behaviour and to formulate settlements. With the rise of formal bargaining in the public sector, researchers have new-found opportunities to observe, record, and analyse negotiations. Although this research is time-consuming, tedious and almost overwhelming, it uncovers rich insights about the process dimension of a very significant and pervasive form of communication – bargaining and negotiation.

References

ADAMS, J.S. 1976: The structure and dynamics of behaviour in organizational boundary roles. In Dunnette, M.D., editor, *Handbook of industrial and organizational psychology* (Chicago: Rand McNally Press) 1175–99.

ANGELL, R.C. 1965: The sociology of human conflict. In McNeil, E.B., editor, *The nature of human conflict* (Englewood Cliffs, NJ: Prentice Hall) 91–115.

BACHARACH, S.B. and LAWLER, E.J. 1981: *Power and politics in organizations* San Francisco: Jossey-Bass.

BALES, R.F. and STRODTBECK, F.L. 1951: Phases in group-problem solving. *Journal of Abnormal and Social Psychology*, **46**, 485–95.

BEDNAR, D.A. and CURINGTON, W.P. 1983: Interaction analysis: A tool for understanding negotiations. *Industrial and Labor Relations Review,* **36**, 389–401.

BEDNAR, D.A. and GLAUSER, M. 1981: Interaction analysis of collective bargaining: The Barrington Oil Company case. In Chung, K.E., editor, *Academy of Management Proceedings '81* (Academy of Management Association) 188–92.

BIXENSTINE, V.E. and WILSON, K.V. 1963: Effects of level of cooperative choice by the other player on choices in a Prisoner's Dilemma game, Part II. *Journal of Abnormal and Social Psychology,* **67**, 139–47.

BLAKE, R.R., SHEPARD, H.A., and MOUTON, J.S. 1964: *Managing intergroup conflict in industry.* Houston, Texas: Gulf Publishing Company.

CHERTKOFF, J.M. and ESSER, J.K. 1976: A review of experiments in explicit bargaining. *Journal of Experimental Social Psychology,* **12**, 464–86.

DAVIS, W.L. 1982: *Communication at the table: A case study of collective bargaining negotiations.* Unpublished doctoral dissertation, Ohio State University.

DEUTSCH, M. 1973: *The resolution of conflict.* New Haven: Yale University Press.

DIEZ, M.E. 1983: *Situated code choice: An empirical examination of two types of bargaining interaction.* Paper presented at the annual convention of the Speech Communication Association, Washington DC, November.

DONOHUE, W.A. 1981a: Analyzing negotiation tactics: Development of a negotiation interact system. *Human Communication Research,* **7**, 273–87.

—— 1981b: Development of a model of rule use in negotiation interaction. *Communication Monographs,* **48**, 106–20.

DONOHUE, W.A. and DIEZ, M.E. 1983: *Information management in negotiation.* Paper presented at the annual convention of the International Communication Association, Dallas, Texas, May.

DONOHUE, W.A., DIEZ, M.E. and HAMILTON, M. 1984: Coding naturalistic negotiation interaction. *Human Communication* Research **10**, 403–25.

DONOHUE, W.A., DIEZ, M.E. and STAHLE, R.B. 1983: New directions in negotiation research. In Bostrom, R.N., editor, *Communication Yearbook* 7 (Beverly Hills, Cal.: Sage Publications) 249–79.

DOUGLAS, A. 1957: The peaceful settlement of industrial and intergroup disputes. *Journal of Conflict Resolution,* **1**, 69–81.

—— 1962: *Industrial peacemaking.* New York: Columbia University Press.

DRUCKMAN, D., ZECHMEISTER, K. and SOLOMON, D. 1972: Determinants of bargaining behaviour in a bilateral monopoly situation: Opponent's concession rate and relative defensibility. *Behavioural Science,* **17**, 514–31.

ELLIS, D.G 1979: Relational control in two group systems. *Communication Monographs,* **46**, 153–66.

FISHER, B.A. 1978: *Perspectives on human communication.* New York: Macmillan.

FOLLETT, M.P. 1940: Constructive conflict. In Metcalf, H.C. and Urwick, L., editors, *Dynamic administration: The collected papers of Mary Parker Follett* (New York: Harper & Brothers).

GERGEN, K.J. 1969: *The psychology of behaviour exchange.* Reading, Mass.: Addison-Wesley.

HAWES, L.C. and SMITH, D.H. 1973: A critique of assumptions underlying the study of communication in conflict. *Quarterly Journal of Speech*, **59**, 423–35.

HOPMANN, P.T. 1974: Bargaining in arms control negotiations: The Seabeds Denuclearization Treaty. *International Organization*, **28**, 313–44.

HOPMANN, P.T. and WALCOTT, C. 1976: The impact of international conflict and debate on bargaining in arms control negotiations: An experimental analysis. *International Interactions*, **2**, 189–206.

KATZ, D. and KAHN, R.L. 1978: *The social psychology of organizations*. New York: John Wiley & Sons.

KELLY, H.H. and SLAHELSKI, A.J. 1970: Errors in perceptions of intentions in a mixed-motive game. *Journal of Experimental Social Psychology*, **6**, 379–400.

KEOUGH, C.M. 1983: *Bargaining communication and arbitration arguments: An analysis of the collective bargaining between the Teacher Assistants' Association and the University of Wisconsin-Madison*. Unpublished masters thesis, Purdue University.

LANDSBERGER, H.A. 1955: Interaction process analysis of the mediation of labor-management disputes. *Journal of Abnormal and Social Psychology*, **51**, 552–8.

MAGENAU, J.M. and PRUITT, D.G. 1979: The social psychology of bargaining. In Stephenson, G.M. and Brotherton, C.J., editors, *Studies on behaviour in organisations: A research symposium* (Athens, Georgia: University of Georgia Press) 101–34.

MORLEY, I.E. and STEPHENSON, G.M. 1977: *The social psychology of bargaining*. London: George Allen & Unwin Ltd.

PILISUK, M. and RAPOPORT, A. 1964: Stepwise disarmament and sudden destruction in a two-person game: A research tool. *Journal of Conflict Resolution*, **8**, 36–49.

POOLE, M.S. 1981: Decision development in small groups 1: A comparison of two models. *Communication Monographs*, **48**, 1–24.

PRUITT, D.G. 1981: *Negotiation behaviour*. New York: Academic Press.

PRUITT, D.G. and LEWIS, S.A. 1975: Development of integrative solutions in bilateral negotiation. *Journal of Personality and Social Psychology*, **31**, 621–33.

—— 1977: The psychology of integrative bargaining. In Druckman, D., editor, *Negotiations: Social psychological perspectives* (Beverly Hills, Cal.: Sage Publications) 161–92.

PUTNAM, L.L. 1983: *An interpretive view of communication and the bargaining process*. Paper presented at the annual convention of the Speech Communication Association, Washington, DC, November.

PUTNAM, L.L. and BULLIS, C. 1983: *Order and mystery in negotiation groups*. Paper presented at the annual convention of the Eastern Communication Association, Ocean City, Maryland, April.

PUTNAM, L.L. and JONES, T.S. 1982a: Reciprocity in negotiations: An analysis of bargaining interaction. *Communication Monographs*, **49**, 171–91.

—— 1982b: The role of communication in bargaining. *Human Communication Research*, **8**, 262–80.

RAPOPORT, A. 1965: Game theory and human conflict. In McNeil, E.B, editor, *The nature of human conflict* (Englewood Cliffs, NJ: Prentice Hall) 195–226.

RUBIN, J.Z. and BROWN, B.R. 1975: *The social psychology of bargaining and negotiation*. New York: Academic Press.

SCHELLING, T.C. 1960: *The strategy of conflict*. Cambridge: Harvard University Press.

STEPHENSON, G.M. 1981: Intergroup bargaining and negotiation. In Turner, J.C. and Giles, H., editors, *Intergroup behaviour* (Chicago: University of Chicago Press) 169–98.

STEINFATT, T. and MILLER, G. 1974: Communication in game theoretic models of conflict. In Miller, G. and Simon, H., editors, *Perspectives on communication in social conflicts* (Englewood Cliffs, NJ: Prentice Hall).

STEPHENSON, G.M., KNIVETON, B.K. and MORLEY, I.E. 1977: Interaction analysis of an industrial wage negotiation. *Journal of Occupational Psychology*, **50**, 231–41.

WALL, J.A. 1975: The effects of constituent trust and representative bargaining visibility on intergroup bargaining. *Organizational Behaviour and Human Performance*, **14**, 244–56.

WALTON, R.E. and McKERSIE, R.B. 1965: *A behavioural theory of labor negotiations*. New York: McGraw-Hill Book Company.

WILSON, W. 1969: Cooperation and cooperativeness of the other player. *Journal of Conflict Resolution*, **13**, 110–17.

13

Sequence and pattern in communicative behaviour: a model and commentary

Richard L. Street, Jr and Joseph N. Cappella

As editors of this volume, we have consciously tried to achieve several purposes and have enlisted the authors of various chapters to assist us in these goals. This book is but one of many written about social interaction and communication. We believe that it offers a unique view of these processes because it emphasizes behavioural patterns and sequences rather than unobservable states or traits possessed by the interactants. But more importantly, all chapters have consciously adopted a functional approach to communication patterns. One of the implications of a functional approach that should by now be obvious to all is that multiple behaviour, verbal, vocal and kinesic, receive attention rather than single behaviours isolated from the others that make up the complex behaviour that interaction is.

To simply study more than a single behaviour is not the only goal of the functional approach to interaction. Rather, the functional approach tries to study together those communicative behaviours that serve similar functions. Thus, part of the task of a functional approach is to enquire into the empirical and logical bases for grouping behaviours in interactional functions. Chapter 1 sought to describe some methods for functional groupings and to hesitatingly offer a set of functional categories. The chapters that follow that introduction take up commonly acknowledged functions such as regulation, coherence, accounting remediation, control, affiliation, information exchange, decision-making and negotiation and carry us through the typical patterns and sequences that operate with those functions. We hope that the utility of the functional approach both for organizing research and for making coherent what can be a bewildering array of behavioural components of interaction is no longer in need of defence.

In this final chapter we take the best current evidence about pattern and sequence in communicative functions and use that empirical knowledge in trying to explain how and why certain patterns and sequences exist. The theories and models that come out of such efforts always seem Rube Goldberg contraptions whose plumbing can only be appreciated by the most remote and ethereal of academicians. We want to make very clear to our audience, both the purely academic and the more pragmatic among you, that we consider the business of theory a very pragmatic and policy-oriented enterprise.

The practical benefits of theoretical excursions are often lost because theories often leave the world of tangible events and data and enter the world of the unobservable. However, it is this world of the unobservable which can offer explanations of how certain events come about. If we do not know how events come about, then the proper and most efficacious way of altering those events is not available to us. In short, an accurate theory is practical because it tells us how to control events. Consider a brief example. A recent controversy in the literature has arisen between Patterson's arousal-labelling (AL) theory (1976) and Cappella and Greene's discrepancy-arousal (DA) theory (1982). The crux of the controversy concerns whether cognitive labelling alters the experience of arousal (arousal-labelling) or whether certain extremes of arousal are experienced as affectively negative regardless of cognitive labelling (discrepancy-arousal). If AL is correct, then the remedy for stress due to overcrowding is cognitive relabelling. If DA is correct, then excessive arousal cannot be corrected by a mere relabelling, rather the source of the stress itself must be treated. The point is simply that lack of information about the process leading from crowding to withdrawal makes treatment ambiguous. Theory building and explanation may appear to be arcane exercises but their fruits are eminently practical.

Empirical bases for theory

Sound theory develops from reliable and comprehensive data. The chapters in this volume have contributed to our understanding of communication by explicating particular and distinctive aspects of social interaction. Our purpose is to propose a model of social interaction which identifies basic processes, has explanatory potential across communication contexts, and incorporates extant research findings and ideas well represented by chapters in this volume. Before turning to that model we wish briefly to overview the findings of the chapters of this volume and other writings on sequence and pattern in communicative behaviour.

Mutual influence processes have been extensively reviewed elsewhere (Cappella 1981, 1983, 1984; Patterson 1973, 1976, 1983) and cannot be repeated here. However, the central findings include: (1) General trends toward reciprocity in vocal behaviours, verbal self-disclosure, gaze behaviours (for neutral and positive social situations), verbal accounts, and many linguistic behaviours (accent, lexical choice, dialect, language choice in bilingual settings); (2) Strong tendencies toward compensatory reactions in response to increases in proximity and question intimacy; (3) The use of gaze, pause, gestures, loudness cues, and grammatical cues in the regulation of turn-taking. Strong findings of mutual influence with cues of verbal dominance and submission must await research directed at this topic.

Two predominant patterns of this mutual influence are reciprocity and compensation. Reciprocity occurs when participants produce similar behaviours, adapt behaviours in similar directions, or respond to partner's behaviours with behaviours of comparable functional value (such as when one romantic partner signals intimacy with a smile and the other responds with touch). Compensation results when participants respond with dissimilar behaviours or adapt them in opposite directions. Reciprocal and compensatory patterns have been observed among loudness (Natale 1975a), utterance duration (Matarazzo and Wiens 1972), pause duration (Jaffe and Feldstein 1970; Natale 1975b), and speech rate (Webb 1972), with kinesic behaviours such as eye gaze (Schneider and Hanswick 1977), proximity (McDowell 1972), nonverbal immediacy

(Sundstrom 1972), and with verbal behaviours including verbal intimacy (Davis 1976, 1977), question intimacy (Schulz and Barefoot 1974), verbal accounts of transgression (McLaughlin, Cody and Rosenstein 1983), and various linguistic features (Giles, Taylor and Bourhis 1973; Giles and Powesland 1975). Reciprocity and compensation are not restricted to adult social interaction only but occur early in the social interaction of infants and children with their adult partners (Cappella 1981; Trevarthen 1977; Tronick, Als and Brazelton 1974). The functional impact of reciprocity and compensation will be discussed later.

The interaction pattern also contributes to the regulation of interaction exchanges. The probability of smooth turns, back channel responses, and successful and unsuccessful interruptions are determined in large measure by the configuration of various vocal and kinesic cues prior to action (Duncan and Fiske 1977; Meltzer, Morris and Hayes 1971; Wiemann, Chapter 5).

Most of the research cited above and summarized in previous work concerns individual behaviours, uncategorized as to function. When functional groupings are employed the empirical results are not profoundly different but the power of a summary statement by functions is far greater than one by individual behaviour.

Before presenting our own explanation of processes accounting for interaction patterns and sequences and their functional relevance for interactants, we will initially overview research on social interaction functions and secondly briefly summarize current theoretical accounts of these processes.

Social interaction functions

Interactants mould behaviour toward the accomplishment of individual or multiple goals which, when juxtaposed with the partner's goals and behaviours, create interaction patterns having some functional relevance for the interactants. While they may be purposive (related to goals and intentions) or may be responses to restore preferred arousal or stimulation levels, these behavioural patterns are often produced at varying degrees of awareness, an issue to be discussed later. Given previous research, common social interaction functions include impression management, coherence, control, intimacy and task.

Impression management entails conscious and subconscious control of behaviour configurations. As Cody and McLaughlin (Chapter 3) and Morris (Chapter 4) have pointed out, participants reconcile perceived transgressions by choosing speech acts, presumably with high levels of awareness, which follow consistent patterns: reproach, relief, evaluation. Vocal and nonverbal behaviours, while typically produced and perceived at low awareness levels, nonetheless reveal purposive intent toward posturing favourable impressions. Bond (1972) reported that subjects, expecting to interact with a 'cold' confederate, acted more warmly (as judged by independent raters) to the 'cold' partner than did those subjects expecting to interact with a 'warm' confederate. Ickes, Patterson, Rajecki and Tanford (1982) reported two experiments supporting this odd finding. In Experiment I, subjects expecting an unfriendly partner smiled *more* than did subjects expecting a friendly partner though the friendly partner was liked more. In Experiment 2, interactants expecting a dissimilar partner revealed *more* nonverbal involvement behaviours (i.e. more smiles, longer gazes, longer turn durations, and more direct body orientation) than did interactants expecting to interact with a similar partner. Patterson (1983; Edinger and Patterson 1983) drew two conclusions from these results: (1) in the friendly and similar conditions, involvement served the intimacy function and was mediated by mutual attraction and (2) in the dislike and dissimilar conditions, higher involvement reflected a social control strategy designed to compensate for a partner's expected non-involvement or to elicit a favourable impression and reciprocal involvement or to minimize the negative features of a potentially hostile or cold interaction.

Acquiring or maintaining *control* over interlocutors or during interaction is generally accomplished by behaviours such as interruptions (Wiemann, Chapter 5), style shifting (Scotton, Chapter 6), loud speech, long floor-holdings, gaze while talking, looking away while listening, non-reciprocal touch, etc. As Patterson (1983) notes, however, there may be different behavioural approaches related to the emergence of dominance (e.g. interruptions, long floor-holdings) and maintenance of dominance (e.g. non-reciprocal touch, indirect body orientations). Persuasion is obviously another example of the control function. Persuaders usually adapt compliance-gaining strategies (Cody *et al.* 1981) or modify vocal and kinesic behaviours (e.g. relatively loud and fast speech, more direct body orientation, eye contact; Mehrabian and Williams 1969) given target characteristics and with varying degrees of awareness. Yet another type of control is evidenced when interactants reciprocate or compensate the expressive behavioural responses of partner in order to establish preferred involvement levels (Cappella and Greene 1982). For example, the arousal generated by the too close approach of another will likely produce a compensatory response (i.e. backing away) to alleviate the anxiety. Of course, such moves are functional for the human organism, though these responses among expressive behaviours are typically produced and received nonconsciously (Cappella 1981).

Trying to maintain *coherence* also reflects conscious and nonconscious behaviours. Obviously one is often aware of strategies (such as slow speech and common lexical items) employed to help students comprehend course material, or to convey an idea to a young child or a foreigner who has difficulty with English. Language choice in multilingual settings also represents conscious choices (Bourhis, Chapter 7) as well as alignment and structuring moves during group discussion (Poole, Chapter II) and bargaining tasks (Putnam, Chapter 10). These situation-specific adaptations appear to complement the global and automatic processes governing topic extensions (Tracy, Chapter 2) and speech matching (Natale 1975a) which can promote communicative effectiveness.

Thus far, we have discussed behaviours which are clearly goal directed. Interactants accomplish these objectives by creatively deriving behavioural strategies or by activating applicable scripts or response sets which guide behaviour selection. *Intimacy*, however, presents an interesting problem because many behaviours indicative of intimacy (e.g. high eye contact, close interpersonal distance, touch) are probably mediated by arousal and by innate needs for security, attachment, etc. Nevertheless, much of the regulation of intimacy is 'negotiated' between participants. The male that approaches too closely or touches too intimately will likely observe compensatory responses such as nonreciprocation, eye gaze avoidance, an increase in interaction distance, or indirect body orientation. Dindia (Chapter 8) suggests that self-disclosure styles serve to establish mutually preferred intimacy levels. For example, to arrive at moderate levels of intimacy, interactants disclose gradually more intimate information generally of a positive nature. To maintain that intimacy level, self-disclosure may actually decrease, be less reciprocal, but still have a positive valence. To move toward high intimacy levels, interactants may disclose more but the disclosure becomes increasingly negative (see also Gilbert 1976).

In short, interactants regulate intimacy levels until (usually) a mutually preferred level is established. Relative to other interaction functions, intimacy behaviours may be easily confused with physiological or innate processes (e.g. interpersonal needs, arousal, sex drive, etc.). However, many behaviours such as distance, gaze, smiles, disclosure, and resource exchange strategically function to regulate preferred intimacy levels.

The *task* functions are instrumental and relatively situation-specific given the task itself, participants, and their objectives. Poole (Chapter 11) and Putnam (Chapter 12) have discussed behavioural sequences and patterns which may be characteristic of group discussion and bargaining negotiations respectively.

One cannot expect a theory to account easily for the above array of empirical findings regarding pattern and sequence. Not only must reciprocity, compensation and maintenance all be explained within the same theory but also the situational, cognitive, personal and relational factors that moderate the relationship between A's and B's behaviours and which are capable of altering reciprocal response patterns to compensatory ones. This is a tall order for an area with a short history of theoretical work. However, recent developments offer promising insights. We now consider these.

Substantive accounts of social interaction processes and outcomes

Our overview of pertinent theoretical models is presented under three categories – arousal models, cognitive models, and functional models.

Arousal models. The arousal models propose that reciprocity and compensation among affiliative and expressive behaviours (e.g. gaze, touch, proximity, body orientation, vocal behaviour, and verbal intimacy) are largely influenced by arousal changes experienced by the human organism. Patterson's (1976) arousal-labelling model holds that changes in a partner's affiliative behaviours (e.g. greater approach or greater avoidance) stimulates arousal changes. If the arousal is labelled positively (i.e. change in affiliative behaviours is acceptable), then the interactant will reciprocate the involvement levels displayed by the partner. If labelled negatively, compensatory responses will result. Thus Patterson (1976) argued that interactants' arousal changes stimulate cognitive assessments of causes of the arousal which in turn generate the interactants' subsequent responses. Though there has been some support for the model, several shortcomings are apparent. First, as Patterson (1983; Chapter 10) later acknowledged, the model cannot account for some findings such as those of Bond (1972) and of Ickes *et al.* (1982). In these studies, subjects expecting to interact with either 'cold' or 'unfriendly' (thus, non-affiliative) partners, actually displayed affiliative responses such as smiles, head nods, more gaze, etc. These findings suggest interactants may 'manage' nonverbal responses toward goals of control and impression management. Second, Cappella (1983; Cappella and Greene 1982) argued that the cognitive processes of labelling arousal positively or negatively would consume more time than the often momentary behavioural adjustments would allow.

Cappella and Greene's (1982) discrepancy-arousal model holds that interactants have expectations for a partner's expressive behaviours (derived either from previous experience or from normative/situational expectancies). The interface between a partner's behaviour and behavioural expectancies for the partner then influences arousal levels in a monotonic fashion. Little discrepancy generates little arousal; moderate discrepancy elicits moderate arousal; and large discrepancies are experienced as highly arousing. Little to moderate arousal in turn is experienced affectively positively and large arousal levels generate negative affect. Positive affect leads to reciprocal responses; negative affect to compensatory responses. As opposed to arousal-labelling, the discrepancy arousal model places some cognitive activity (i.e. expectancies for the partners' behaviour) prior to arousal changes. Cappella and Greene's (1982) literature review provides some support for the model among gaze, verbal intimacy, proximity, and (to some extent) vocal behaviour, especially for parent–infant interactions. A direct test of the model received mixed results (Cappella in press b). Nevertheless, this model too has been criticized for confusing 'expected' behaviours with 'preferred' behaviours, not elaborating on situational influences creating exceptions to the predictions, not clarifying whether arousal per se or arousal changes generate responses, and for not providing interactants' goals with a more significant role (Street and Giles 1982).

Cognitive models. As opposed to arousal explanations, cognitive models of interaction attempt to explain reciprocity and compensation as generated from cognitive processes.

Roloff (1981; Roloff and Campion Chapter 9) has formulated a social-exchange theory approach to social interaction. According to this view, human behaviour is guided by self-interest. Relationships, as defined through interaction, evolve and dissolve around the exchange of perceived rewards and costs (e.g. love, status, time, commitment). While not reiterating the contents of their chapter, we will highlight the exchange patterns espoused by Roloff and Campion. Reciprocated exchanges exist in strict form (love for love), flexible form (love for status), or based on some quantity distribution (equal number of resources distributed between partners). Unreciprocated exchanges do not reflect compensatory patterns but entail the offering of rewards by one interactant without reciprocation by the partner.

The social exchange approach is largely cognitive since its foundation rests upon interactants perception of reward numbers and values. However, the model's application rests principally with the exchange of *symbolic* resources manifested in material exchange and verbal and nonverbal behaviour content. For example, self-disclosure reciprocity is likely largely influenced by social exchange forces (see, e.g., Roloff and Campion Chapter 9; Dindia Chapter 8). Also, this approach appears unable to account for compensation among behaviour responses.

Giles's (1977; Giles and Powesland 1975; Giles and Street in press; Street and Giles 1982) speech accommodation theory (SAT) attempts to account for speech and language adaptations during interaction. Giles has also suggested that SAT may also explain nonverbal behaviour patterns (Giles and Powesland

1975; Giles and Street in press). In a recent update, Street and Giles (1982) have articulated four tenets of SAT. First, interactants will converge speech toward that perceived characteristic of their partner if they (a) desire the partner's approval and the perceived costs of so doing are lower than the rewards anticipated, and/or (b) desire a high level of communication efficiency, and/or (c) perceive social norms not to dictate alternative speech strategies. Second, speech convergence will be positively evaluated by receivers when the convergence is (a) perceived as such psychologically, (b) perceived to be an optimal socio-linguistic distance from them, and (c) attributed to positive intent.

Third, interactants will maintain or diverge speech patterns when they (a) define the encounter in intergroup terms and desire a positive ingroup identity, or (b) wish to dissociate personally from another in an interindividual encounter, or (c) wish to bring another's speech to a personally acceptable level. Fourth, speech maintenance and divergence will be negatively evaluated by recipients when the acts are perceived as psychological divergence but favorably evaluated by recipients who perceive the speech difference to reflect appropriate sociolinguistic distance given interaction role or intergroup differences.

There has been strong support for SAT regarding language choice in multilingual settings, self-disclosures, and among some vocal behaviours such as accent, speech rate and response latencies. However, Cappella (1983; Cappella and Planalp 1981) has criticized SAT on several grounds including that the cognitive processes allegedly regulating speech adaptations are too complex to account for moment-to-moment adjustments and, if the processes are more automatic (see e.g. Giles and Street in press; Street and Giles 1982), SAT has yet to explain how automatic procedures got into memory, why they have one procedural content (e.g. converging for approval) rather than another, or how procedural knowledge translates into action. Also, the explanatory potential of SAT to other interaction behaviours (e.g. gaze, touch, body orientation, posture, etc.) awaits empirical testing.

Functional models. Patterson's (1982, 1983) sequential-functional model of nonverbal exchange is the most developed of theoretical approaches accounting for social interaction functions. This volume (Chapter 10) already contains Patterson's summary of the model and thus we will not discuss it in detail. However, we will point out that the model seeks to reconcile the arousal and cognitive approaches through the notion of 'interaction function'. As noted in Figure 10.2 (p. 198), Patterson proposes that interactants have scripted levels of nonverbal involvement appropriate for particular functions. If there is a match between the participants' perceived function and nonverbal involvement levels, a stable exchange results and reciprocity occurs. If there is a mismatch, then cognitive assessments of the function and/or behaviour result, and arousal change occurs. An unstable exchange will probably lead to compensatory responses (Patterson 1983).

Patterson's model contributes significantly to our understanding of social interaction processes and outcomes, yet it is not without its critics. Giles and Street (in press) have criticized the model as placing too much emphasis on the 'termination' of unstable exchanges, as having a lack of conceptual clarity regarding distinctions between antecedent factors, pre-interactional, and interactional phases, assuming isomorphism between 'perceived' and 'actual' behaviour characteristics, and underplaying the influences of social-motivational forces. We would add two additional reservations concerning the model. First, while arousal changes and cognitive assessments are assumed to influence one another, little analysis of this process is provided. Second, the implication that reciprocity characterizes stable exchanges and compensation typifies unstable exchanges is not without exception. For example, reciprocal behaviour exchanges (e.g. interruptions, loud and fast speech, body orientation) may characterize unstable interactions such as two participants arguing or vying for relational dominance. Comparably, the interaction between a dominant spouse and his/her submissive counterpart displays compensatory behaviour patterns but may be highly stable and to the satisfaction of both participants.

Reconciliation among competing models is hindered in two respects. First, while much research has examined relationships between isolated cognitive or physiological variables (e.g. speech stereotypes, arousal) and individual behaviour (e.g. speech rate, gaze), little empirical attention has yet been provided to the study of functions of multiple behaviours and to the identification of basic processes influencing interaction patterns and outcomes.

Second, two approaches to model building appear to characterize previous theoretical work. One, some researchers have restricted themselves to a particular behavioural domain and produced elegant and parsimonius models of processes influencing these behaviours. Two representative examples are Pattersons's (1976) arousal-labelling model of interpersonal intimacy and Cappella and Greene's (1982) discrepancy-arousal model of expressive behaviours. In addition to their simplicity, these theoretical models allow for specific predictions for testing relationships among model components. Yet, Patterson (1983) and Cappella (1984), as well as others (e.g. Giles and Street in press; Street and Giles, 1982), acknowledge certain inadequacies of these models such as limited empirical support and generalizability. The second set of theories take a quite different approach. Arguing that human behaviour is complex, several theorists have produced extremely complex models of social interaction. Representative of this group include Patterson's (1983; Chapter 10) sequential-functional model of nonverbal exchange, Giles's (1980; Street and Giles 1982) speech accommodation theory and Giles and Street's (in press) communicator characteristics model. These theories have also been criticized, primarily for being too cumbersome and for not allowing specific and testable hypotheses (Cappella 1983; Giles and Street, in press).

We face similar limitations when formulating our own model of social interaction. Thus, our objectives are twofold. First, we will initially provide a framework for synthesizing extant research findings and ideas presented in the volume. Second, we will focus our attention primarily on forces underlying the production of and outcomes accrued from reciprocal and compensatory interaction patterns.

Explaining sequence and pattern in social interaction

In Figure 13.1 we have tried to summarize some of the components and processes that must operate in explaining what we know about the sequences and patterns of social interaction. The model is not intended to supplant the theories currently sparking empirical work (Burgoon 1978; Cappella and Greene 1982;

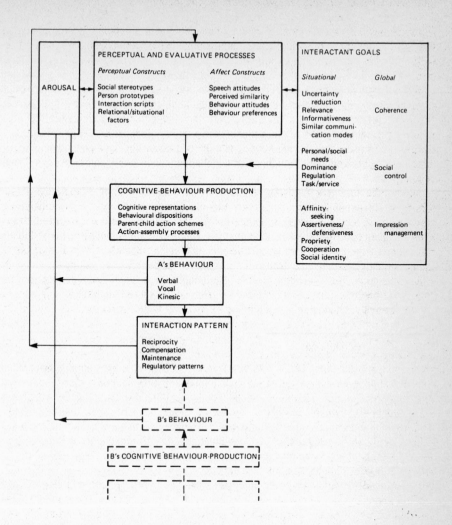

Figure 13.1 A model of social interaction

Patterson 1982; Street and Giles 1982) but rather to bring together those features of an explanation that later theories will need to incorporate more fully. We will discuss the model in terms of its components and links across components.

An overview

Inherent in any social encounter are the *interactant goals*; that is, his or her desires, objectives and purposes for the interaction. These goals may be influenced by, and influence *perceptual and evaluative processes* which include perceptions of the situation, affective responses to others, perceptions of others, and conceptions of self. Evaluative and attributional processes and the interactant's goals mutually activate relevant *cognitive-behaviour production operations* which in turn produce behaviours presumably directed toward achieving the goal(s) given the salient situational information. *Arousal levels* may facilitate or inhibit all these processes. The interactants's own *behaviour* may induce arousal level changes as well as provide information, via self-monitoring, to the perceptual and evaluative processes. The interlocutor's behaviour, as well as the participants' *pattern of conjoint behaviour*, influences arousal levels, evaluative and perceptual processes, and interactant goals.

Components of the model

Interactant goals. As can be seen in Figure 13.1, the interactant goals are classified into two groups, global or cross-situational goals and situation-specific goals. The cross situational goals – coherence, impression management and social control – are distinguished from the situation-specific goals in that the former are frequently, if not entirely, operative during most social encounters while the latter become individually operable given situational exigencies. *Social control* represents the desire to influence others in order to satisfy personal needs and obligations and to enhance self-image (Patterson 1983; Tedeschi 1974; Tedeschi and Norman, in press). While coherence and impression management could conceivably be considered inherent in the social control motivation, we distinguish them because of their distinctive influences on perceptual and behaviour production processes. *Coherence* consists of three primary objectives, connectedness of discourse exchange (Tracy 1982; Chapter 2); uncertainty reduction (Berger and Bradac 1982; Berger and Calabrese 1975; Neisser 1976), and optimal speech formating (Natale 1975a; Street 1983). In short, this motivation reflects an individual's desire for relevance, understanding and communicative efficiency during social interaction. Regarding *impression management*, several theoretical perspectives, such as symbolic interactionism (Mead 1934), social comparison theory (Festinger 1954), and self-presentation theory (Weary and Arkin 1981) hold that self-conceptions are moulded by how people believe others perceive them. Individuals in turn attempt to present themselves in a socially acceptable manner (e.g. friendly, polite) or in ways consistent with their ideal selves (e.g. independent, knowledgeable, Goffman 1959; Smith 1984; Tedeschi and Norman, in press; Weary and Arkin 1981).

The situation-specific goals are as endless as the imaginations of actors. They could include gaining compliance, escalating relational intimacy, remediating a faux pax, being compassionte, etc. We have already elaborated on some of these (Chapter 1) and will later discuss the impact of goals on perceptual and behaviour production processes.

Although our purpose is not to examine in detail the psychology of human motivation, we need to mention two characteristics of interactant goals which have relevance for social interaction. First, social participants have varying degrees of awareness of particular motivations (Freud 1900; Niesser 1976; Nisbett and Ross 1980). Some goals, perhaps more global or routine objectives, may be activated non-consciously (e.g. maintaining coherence) whereas others, perhaps because of their novelty or perceived salience, are enacted more consciously (e.g. impress an employer; Berger and Bradac 1982; Giles and Street, in press; Patterson 1983). Second, an interactant's behaviour or judgements may be influenced by mulitiple goals (e.g. being coherent, appearing competent, instructing a class) or by competing goals (e.g. punishing children and being compassionate, O'Keefe and Delia 1982). For example, Smith's (1984) contingency rules theory holds that interactants have two primary rule structures governing persuasive behaviours. Self-evaluative rules are composed of personal values and self-presentational concerns. Adaptive rules link action to extrinsic goal achievement. Depending on individual motivation and situational factors these rules assume varying degrees of salience and may even be contradictory.

Perceptual and evaluative processes. Perceptual and evaluative processes are comprised of experiential knowledge having informational/attributional contents and affective values. Most theories of cognition hold that this information has an hierarchial and sequential/parallel structure. The hierarchial organization refers to the existence of general categories of knowledge (e.g. eating at a restaurant) which in turn may have smaller categories organizing additional information (e.g. eating at a fancy restaurant). Metaphors labelling the hierarchial structure of knowledge have been coined for semantic knowledge ('frames', Minsky 1975; for a review see Foss and Hakes 1978), person perception ('stereotypes', Hamilton 1979, 'prototypes', Cantor and Mischel 1979), 'interpersonal contructs', O'Keefe and Delia 1982), visual, auditory, and tactile perception ('schema', Neisser 1976), behavioural sequences ('scripts', Schank and Abelson 1977), and making sense of social activity ('frames', Goffman 1974).

The sequential and parallel structure of this knowledge refers to the interrelations within and across perceptual structures (see, e.g., Bock 1982; Johnson-Laird 1983). Once a particular construct is activated, others may have an increased potential for activation (Norman 1981). For example, persons are much more likely to respond more strongly, behaviourally and affectively, when a young child crosses their path when driving down a busy highway than when walking in the park.

Given a particular social encounter, relevant perceptual and affect constructs are activated from the reservoir of experiential knowledge in order to make sense of interaction events, to establish expectations for the interaction, and to guide behavioural sequences. As depicted in Figure 13.1 we have identified some of these cognitive structures which influence participants' responses during interaction.

Perceptual constructs include experiential knowledge which hold information available for attributions about persons and situations (Harvey and Weary, 1984; Sillars 1982). 'Social stereotypes' are schemata containing characteristics of individuals given group affiliations based on ethnicity, age, sex, culture, religion, etc. differences (Hamilton 1979). 'Person prototypes' are similar to stereotypes yet contain information about certain types of persons such as waitresses, dominant others, scholars, etc. (Cantor and Mischel 1979). According to Abelson (1976), 'scripts' are 'a coherent sequence of events expected by the individual, involving him either as a participant or as an observer' (p. 33). Thus, interaction scripts refer to those situational (e.g. setting, occasion, partner) and behavioural (e.g. nonverbal, verbal and vocal) requirements constituting particular forms of interaction such as small talk, public speech, job interview, etc. Of course, interaction scripts may vary in their level of specificity ranging from very well defined (e.g. greeting ritual) to the more ambiguous and creative (e.g. small talk), 'Relational/situational factors' entail behavioural expectancies given previous experiences (e.g. interacting with a friend or a family member) or given a role-relationships between interactants (e.g. interacting with an employee or a teacher).

Certainly stereotypes, prototypes and scripts may contain affective information. However, we separately discuss *affect constructs* (see Figure 13.1) given widespread research attention on receivers' evaluative responses to speech, language and nonverbal behaviours. 'Speech attitudes' refer to receivers' stereotypic judgements of speech/language variants (Giles and Powesland 1975; Ryan and Giles 1982; Williams 1976). Speech attitudes tend to vary along two evaluative dimensions, competence or status (e.g. prestige, intelligence, social standing) and social attractiveness (e.g. trustworthiness, friendly, likeable, kind, etc.). 'Perceived similarity' also appears to mediate affective judgements with receivers preferring cognitive (Duck 1973), vocal (Giles and Powesland 1975; Natale 1975a; Street 1982; 1983; in press), nonverbal (Cappella, in press b; La France 1979; Trout and Rosenfeld 1980), and verbal (Bradac *et al.* 1979) similarity, especially for communication accuracy, persuasion, and social attractiveness related judgements, unless the similarity is on a dimension deemed unattractive by the perceiver (e.g. reticence, Daly *et al.* 1979) or situational or role requirements dictate otherwise (Street and Giles 1982).

'Behaviour preference regions' represents our term which entails dimensions of both language and nonverbal behaviour attitudes as well as perceived similarity. Though arguing for different generative mechanisms, Cappella and Greene (1982) and Street and Giles (1982) proposed that receivers evaluatively respond to interlocutors in terms of a range of preferred behaviour, and that these evaluative reactions guide subsequent behaviour responses. Partners' behaviours may be affectively positive if they are perceived to be relatively similar, appropriately complementary and/or different in a stereotypically favourable direction (Cappella 1983; Street *et al.* 1983). These preferences are mediated by personal factors (e.g. personality, sex, age), experiential history with this or similar partners, and the receiver's own behavioural style. In a subsequent section of this chapter, we will elaborate on some of the evaluative, perceptual and behavioural responses interactants produce when encountering partners having varying verbal, vocal and nonverbal behaviour levels.

Note that in Figure 13.1, we depict perceptual and affect constructs as mutually influencing one another. The relationships between cognitive (or attributional) assessments and evaluative (or affective) responses remain unclear. Some researchers have held that cognitive assessments of behaviour, such as the interface between an interlocutor's behaviour and a priori expectations for that behaviour (Cappella and Greene 1982) or the perception of a partner's message characteristics (Giles and Street, in press; Street and Hopper 1982) or of one's own message choices (Greene and Sparks 1983), precede affective and evaluative responses. Others hold that affect may precede inferential activity (Zajonc 1980), or that a partner's behaviour causes an interactant to experience arousal level changes which in turn are labelled either positively or negatively (Patterson 1976). In a recent discussion of this issue, Patterson (1983; Chapter 10) has argued that affective and cognitive assessments have bidirectional influences on one another.

The relationship between cognition and affect needs clarification since both often operate instantaneously upon judgement and behaviour levels. The process entails some degree of non-concscious automaticity. For example, Street (1982, Street and Brady 1982) reported that receivers were unaware of the preferences for speakers with similar to marginally faster speech rates (see also Nisbett and Wilson 1977). On the other hand, perceptual processing may be brought to consciousness as one assesses novel or highly evaluative situations (Berger and Roloff 1980; Street and Giles 1982).

We can shed little light on these issues except to note that perceptual constructs appear to have both informational and affective components and both mutually influence the other. While future research will need to sort out the details of these processes, we will later discuss the impact of interactants' affective and attributional responses on subsequent behaviour choices.

Cognitive-behaviour production processes. Relative to perceptual processing, cognitive processes controlling behaviour production have received scant empirical and theoretical attention (Norman 1981). As Greene (1984) has recently noted, cognitive models of communication behaviour are limited given the current lack of understanding of cognitive-behaviour production processes. Greene contended that cognitive approaches to social interaction will be productive only when basic cognitive structures, contents and processes are identified and explicated. While many issues remain unresolved, some research has provided insights into components of the cognitive-behaviour production system.

As can be seen in Figure 13.1, we have identified at least four features of cognitive-behaviour production operations: cognitive representations, behaviour dispositions, parent–child behaviour schemas, and action-assembly processes. As was the case with perceptual processes, cognitive structures governing behaviour production processes appear to be hierarchically organized and activated in sequential and parallel fashion (Anderson 1976; Johnson-Laird 1983; Cappella and Street, Chapter 1). Investigators have recently speculated on what constitutes some of these structures and their contents. Giles and Street (in press) proposed that interactants' experiential knowledge contains various 'cognitive representations' of interaction situations and strategies and 'behaviour dispositions' typically producing favourable outcomes. For example, one representation may contain a very specific objective, 'maintain the floor', with its associated behavioural disposition being 'few pauses, moderately loud speech, and counter interruptions'. Another cognitive representation may be more general and less specific. For example, contents of 'appear friendly' might include an open, animated style, self-disclosure, jokes, attentiveness, etc. Giles and Street (in press) add that one to several of these cognitive representations may be activated for any one interaction. Admittedly, Giles and Street's list is speculative and incomplete. Also, the contents of the cognitive representations sometimes appear to be worded as goals (e.g. persuade someone to donate money), strategies (e.g. appear friendly), or situations (e.g. unfamiliar with teleconferencing).

While the separation of the knowledge of strategies to achieve outcomes from the knowledge of behaviour dispositions to accomplish these goals presents an initial effort to identify cognitive-behaviour production structures and contents, increased specificity of the processes linking these representations to behaviours is required. Two recent and promising theoretical efforts have been advanced by Norman (1981) and Greene (1982).

Street and Giles (1982) have posited that Norman's (1981) activation-trigger-schema model (ATS) could explain how conscious or non-conscious purposive action is coordinated among an array of interaction behaviours including syntactic and semantic choices, speech convergence, gesturing, social smiling, etc. The ATS model hypothesizes that behavioural skills and strategies are hierarchically organized in the actor's cognitive system. The actor may have a particular intention (say, create a favourable impression) which in turn activates schemas of situation-specific strategies (e.g. sound intelligent) which in turn activates particular motor and language behaviour schemas such as diverse lexical choices and relatively fast speech rate. Although interactants may be aware of the 'parent' schemas such as the intention and perhaps the strategy, the individual responses elicited from invoking the intention and strategy need not be consciously recognized. This is probably typical of routine or familiar interaction settings. For highly evaluative or unfamiliar settings, interactants may not have a developed system of intention-strategy-behaviour links. Under such situations, we would expect the actor to be more self-conscious and aware of his or her own behaviour (Berger and Bradac 1982; Patterson 1983; Street 1982).

Greene's (1982) action-assembly theory also represents a cognitive account of communication behaviour production. Greene posits that behaviour production is contingent upon a repository of procedural knowledge. The procedural knowledge contains condition-action records (modular entities which influence a limited portion of the behavioural stream) which regulate motor outputs. Associated with each condition-action record is a threshold value for activating the condition-action schema. These activating conditions are a function of interaction goals and perceived situational information relevant to the goal. The ease of assembly of the action records is contingent upon the degree to which the situation, goal and actions are routine, the facilatory or inhibitory effects of arousal, the complexity of the task, and the structural compatibility of eligible behaviours.

Of course, the usefulness of these models awaits empirical attention. Two issues in particular remain problematic. First, what process differences characterize the activation of routine interaction sequences (e.g. greeting rituals, small talk) and what processes influence behaviour production in unfamiliar or highly evaluative settings? For example, whereas the former may entail the activation of habituated action sequences the latter contains more complex operations related to self- and other – monitoring and improvization. Second, how does the production system reconcile inputs from competing goals and motivations? For example, how does a person resolve one desire to be generous (e.g. give money to a friend) with another desire to control (e.g. saying 'no' because of limited finances)?

Behaviour. The behaviour component of our model is simply the actual verbal, vocal and kinesic behaviour produced during social interaction (see Chapter 1).

Interaction pattern. The interaction pattern (e.g. reciprocity and compensation) represents the unique characteristics of the interactants' conjoint behavioural output. We distinguish the 'pattern' of interaction from simply the 'sum' of individual behaviours because of functional significance of the former. In other words, interactants' behaviours are contingent upon partners' behaviours and this interface is the foundation upon which participants perceive, define and negotiate their social relationships. Although individual behaviours can impact upon perceptual and production processes, the dyadic pattern of these behaviours could be of equal importance (Cappella 1984; Giles and Street, in press; Watzlawick *et al*. 1967) and certainly deserve the same attention as mean levels of behaviour. Although the correlation between pattern (e.g. degree of reciprocal gaze) and outcome (e.g. attraction) may be more difficult to obtain than the correlation between A's gaze and B's attraction, it may be equally important (e.g. Noller 1980).

Arousal. Arousal represents the degree of cognitive activation experienced by the individuals (Duffy 1962; Berlyne 1967) and is often indexed by changes in various autonomic behaviours such as heart rate, blood pressure, galvanic skin response, electromyograph and other signs. Evidence that arousal change follows changes in a partner's communicative behaviour is quite strong (Cappella 1983; Patterson 1976).

Significant interrelationships among components of the model

Overview

Our brief description of components of the model suggests that the formulation of models of social interaction is hampered by the sheer quantity of cognitive, individual difference, physiological and behavioural variables influencing processes regulating social interaction. Rather than provide a complete inventory of these factors, we instead focus our discussion on three sets of interrelationships across components of the model: the influence of interaction goals on perceptual-evaluative processes, the perceptual-evaluative processing of interactant behaviours and interaction patterns, and arousal and cognitive mediators of behaviour production and interaction patterns.

Interaction goals and perceptual-evaluative processing of interaction behaviour

The inherent selectivity of perceptual processes is in part a function of particular goals activated by an interactant. Regarding *coherence*, perceivers generally rely on various interpretive strategies to comprehend discourse and other events of the interaction. These include: (1) relevance – the assumption that a partner's remarks are relevant to preceding remarks and to the interaction as a whole (Grice 1975); (2) the et cetera principle – perceivers' willingness to 'fill in' meaning when comprehending discourse (Cicourel 1973); and (3) other taken-for-granted devices employed to make sense out of enigmatic aspects of communicative behaviour (see Hopper 1981 for review). These interpretive strategies facilitate coordination of interaction (McLaughlin 1984) and the meaning of conversational extensions (Tracy 1983; Chapter 2). While the above primarily concern discourse processing, related strategies guide information processing for uncertainty reduction as well.

The *social control* and *impression management* goals affect perceptual processes in a variety of ways. Our discussion focuses on the influences of social stereotypes and person prototypes, maintenance of self-esteem, desire for social rewards, affective orientation and cognitive involvement.

'Social stereotypes' and 'person prototypes' serve two general functions. First, they provide meaningful categories of information about people which serve to reduce uncertainty about and to make sense out of others' behaviours (Cantor and Mischel 1979; Hamilton 1979). Second, stereotypes serve to maintain the receiver's positive in-group identity (Tajfel 1981). Stereotypes and person prototypes can influence stimuli perception by focusing perceivers' attention on particular aspects of a person's behaviour such as dress, sex, and certain verbal/nonverbal behaviours; by creating inferences about target persons which are consistent with the stereotypes (e.g. associating 'black' with 'lazy', see Hamilton 1979; Tajfel 1981); by seeing or hearing message features not actually in the stimulus field (Street and Hopper 1982). For example, relative to white teachers, black teachers are generally able to make more distinctions in perceiving message features of blacks, probably as a function of more experience with such speech (Robinson 1979; Williams 1976). Also, receivers with strong person prototypes may produce behaviour judgements of targets which are somewhat distorted. For example, persons believed to be 'dominant' or having 'high status' may be perceived as talking louder (Scherer 1979) and faster (Thakerar and Giles 1981) respectively than in reality. Williams, Whitehead and Miller (1972) reported that white teachers perceived speech believed coming from a videotape of black children as being more hesitant and nonstandard than when the same speech was dubbed over a videotape of white children playing. Lowery, Snyder and Denney (1976) demonstrated how sex stereotypes can influence person perceptions based on verbal messages. In that study, women were judged more aggressive when uttering a threatening remark to a woman than to a man.

'Desire for social rewards' can also influence perceptual and evaluative judgements. For example, Larsen, Martin and Giles (1977) noted that receivers paid more attention to a speaker's lisp when the speaker had low as opposed to high reward value. 'Maintaining self-esteem' can also bias perception of an interlocutor's message. Bourhis, Giles, Leyens and Tajfel (1979) reported that, when a Francophone speaker threatened the ethnic identity of Flemish listeners, he was rated as sounding more Francophone than when producing low threat messages. Interviewees who have very high self-esteem may overestimate their actual performance effectiveness during job interviews (King and Manaster 1977).

'Positive affective orientations' among interactants (e.g. friends) may result in greater acceptance of behavioural variation or idio-syncratic verbal and nonverbal exchange patterns than among interactants sharing neutral (e.g. stranger) or negative (e.g. disliked others) affective orientations. Among strangers or disliked others, conversants may prefer adherence to normative guidelines for interaction including distance (Burgoon 1983), resource exchange (Roloff and Campion, Chapter 9), nonverbal involvement (Patterson 1983; Chapter 10), and self-disclosure (Dindia, Chapter 8). For example, Nisbett and Ross (1977) reported that American listeners perceived a European speaker more negatively and as having a heavier accent when he interacted in a cold, distant manner than when he was warm and friendly.

Finally, 'cognitive involvement' refers to the extent to which interactants perceive a message, behaviour, or interaction to be of personal importance (Cacioppo and Petty 1982). Petty, Cacioppo and Heesacker (1981) reported that for low-involvement messages to undergraduates (hearing a message that within 10 years the university would require a comprehensive exam in students' major areas of study), rhetorical questions (a stylistic variable) influenced attitude change more than strength of argument. However, for high-involvement messages (e.g. the university would implement the comprehensive exam next year), the reverse held true. These results indicated that receivers may be influenced more by speech style when processing low-salience messages and more by content or argument quality when encountering high-involvement messages. In a related study, Street (in preparation) found that participants' evaluations of partners during fact-finding interviews were related to speech similarity measures and not to speech level per se (e.g. how fast one talked, how long one paused). The reverse held true for observers listening to audio-recordings of the same interviews.

Perceptual and evaluative processing of interactant behaviour and interaction pattern

Receivers appear to have *preference ranges* for interlocutors' vocal, verbal and kinesic behaviour levels (Cappella 1983; Cappella and Greene 1982; Street and Giles 1982). Behaviours falling within these zones are perceived favourably, those falling outside the range are judged unfavourably. The interactant's behavioural style and behavioural expectancies given various types of interaction mediate the width and constitutents of preferences for own and one's partner's behaviour and, subsequently, the interaction pattern.

There are two kinds of relationships between communicative behaviour and outcome that are important for study. One studies the correlations between mean, typical or average behaviours and interpersonal outcomes while the second asks if patterns of mutual influence are associated with significant differences in interpersonal outcomes (Cappella 1984). The study of the associations between individual behaviours and outcomes such as attraction, satisfaction, perceptions of dominance, potency, and the like is actually the study of the interpersonal functions of these behaviours. The study of the association between mutual influence patterns and outcomes is much more subtle and indeed difficult. For example, are dyads who exhibit strong patterns of reciprocity more attracted and satisfied with one another than dyads who exhibit compensatory patterns? To answer this question, behaviours must be coded, patterns described, and correlations to outcomes obtained. Such a process is costly.

Let us first focus on one type of pattern: convergence, reciprocity and matching. As individuals adapt verbal, vocal and kinesic behaviours to those expressed by others, we might expect positive outcomes to obtain as a result of increased similarity of behavioural expression (Byrne 1971), as a result of the perception of interactional responsiveness (Davis and Martin 1978; Davis and Perkowitz 1979), or as a result of more efficient communication (Street and Giles 1982). Indeed, favourable partner evaluations have been associated with similarity among behaviours such as dialect and accent (Giles and Powesland 1975), speech rate (Street 1982; Street and Brady 1982; Street *et al.* 1983), response latency (Putman and Street 1984; Street 1982; in press; Welkowitz and Kuc 1973), self-disclosure (Worthy *et al.* 1969), lexical diversity (Bradac *et al.* 1979), posture (La France 1979), and topical shifts (Planalp and Tracy 1980). Little research has assessed the relationship of other vocal, verbal and kinesic patterns on outcomes. However, Shrout and Fiske (1981) reported a significant positive relationship between a target's nonverbal activity and expressiveness levels (i.e. nod rate, gaze time, smile time, back channel rate) and favourable observer evaluations. Given that these behaviours are frequently characterized by reciprocity (Cappella 1981; Cappella and Greene 1982), it would appear that most interactants prefer relatively expressive partners who tend to match their own expressiveness levels.

In more general terms Warner (1979) has speculated that individuals must adjust their baseline behavioural tempos to those of their partners if there is to be a smooth flowing interaction. Research by Davis (Davis and Martin 1978; Davis and Perkowitz 1979) has been directed at the importance of responsiveness (certainly the defining characteristic of mutual influence) in interpersonal perception. In one study the percentage of responsiveness independent of frequency of response was positively related to attraction. In a later study the number of pleasurable shocks given depended upon how responsive the recipient was and on the level of appropriateness of the response. Excessively responsive actions, beyond normatively established bounds, actually reduced the number of pleasant shocks administered.

The evidence is certainly suggestive: convergence, reciprocity and similarity in behavioural expression tends to produce positive evaluation by fostering effective communication (Giles and Powesland 1975; Natale 1975a; Street 1983), mutually preferred involvement levels (Cappella 1983), and/or reinforces participants' conceptions of themselves and their social behaviour (Giles 1977; Thakerar *et al.* 1982).

The other side of mutual influence that cannot be ignored is compensation, divergence and mismatching. Similarity is not always expected or preferred. Behavioural differences may be appropriate given role, relational or psychological/group differences among interactants. For example, interpersonal and intergroup situations (Bourhis Chapter 7) can arise in which the maintenance or increase of distance and separation from an obnoxious, intrusive, or aggressive other necessitates verbal, vocal and kinesic distancing. Similarly, the protection of personal autonomy, personal freedom, ingroup identity, or group distinctiveness might require compensatory, diverging and mismatched responses. Bourhis (Genesse and Bourhis 1982; Chapter 7) has been investigating this process in intergroup settings with language choice in Quebec. He finds that the evaluation of convergence and divergence in language choice depends upon the role relationship between the interactants and the group affiliation of the judges but compensatory reactions may be just as socially competent and psychologically necessary as reciprocal responses.

Status differences may be reflected in gaze, touch and talk patterns. During interactions between high-low status individuals, high status person typically gaze more while talking and less while listening, touch more (Patterson 1983), may talk more slowly (Thakerar *et al*. 1982), and show less deference (Ragan 1983) than their low status counterparts. A high level of reciprocity among affiliative and supportiveness behaviours may characterize satisfactory marital relationships (Gottman 1982). On the other hand, behaviour differences between married partners can reflect complementary interaction preferences. For example, Hershey and Werner (1975) reported that, among couples, feminist wives spoke for longer periods than their husbands while the reverse held true for couples having a non-feminist wife.

Three additional issues regarding preferences for reciprocal or compensatory patterns warrant acknowledgement. First, the behaviour levels characterizing preferred interaction patterns may vary among interactants. Thus, there are some individual differences among interactants regarding the preferred behaviour levels reciprocated or compensated. For example, Cappella (in press b) argued, and found some support for the claim that high sensation seekers compensate less for close interpersonal distances than low sensation seekers do. Women prefer to interact with one another at closer distances, with more gaze, and with more touching behaviour than is characteristic of interactions among men (Patterson 1983). Middle-aged and elderly adults appear to prefer slower speech than young adults (Sabin, Clemmer, O'Connell and Kowal 1979; Street, Brady and Lee 1984). These are but a few examples of the impact of personality and demographic differences as preferred behaviour levels. Extensive reviews of such issues are available elsewhere (Giles and Street in press; Haas 1979; Harper, Wiens and Matarazzo 1978).

Second, given the array of behaviours produced during interaction, participants may prefer reciprocation of some behaviours (e.g. loudness levels, response latencies) for purposes such as communication effectiveness and compensation of others (e.g. gaze patterns, talk duration) for reasons like maintaining status differences. For example, during interviews, favourability of participants' and observers' evaluations of participants has been linked to *differences* among the interactants' talk durations and speech rates and to *similarities* among the directions of their speech rate adaptations (i.e. slower speech by one partner is followed with slower speech by the other) and among their response latencies (Putman and Street 1984; Street 1982; in press). Similarly, Giles and Smith (1979) reported that a Canadian speaker was perceived most favourably by an English audience when he slowed his speech rate to a level approximating the audience's typical rate by maintained his Canadian accent than when he converged both behaviours. Apparently, speech rate convergence facilitated communication effectiveness and accent maintenance kept appropriate cultural differences intact.

Third, evaluative responses to unusual, novel or normally unacceptable behaviours may be mediated by receivers' accounts of reasons and causes underlying the behaviour. Simard, Taylor and Giles (1976), observing interaction in a French–English bilingual setting, reported that more favourable evaluations and accommodations to the interlocutor's dominant language were more likely if the receivers attributed the interlocutor's accommodation to an effort to communicate effectively than to a situational requirement to do so. Similarly, Sillars (1980) found that attributions about conflict influenced the choice of communication strategies to deal with the conflict. The more situational the conflict, the more openly it was handled. The more permanent the conflict, located in the character of the partner, the more likely that the conflict would be avoided. Stereotypically undesirable behaviours, such as slow speech, may be acceptable, even preferred, if attributed to positive intent such as helping an unfamiliar audience comprehend an unfamiliar topic (Giles, Brown and Thakerar 1981; Street in press).

In sum, whether interactants prefer reciprocity or compensation and on what behavioural dimensions is a function of their own individual preferences and their perceptions of appropriate behaviour patterns given relational and situational parameters.

Interrelationships among interactant goals/arousal and behavioural interaction patterns

Interactant goals. The impact of interactant goals on cognitive-behaviour production can be discussed in two senses: the influences of global motivations and of situation-specific intentions. The global motivations such as coherence, social control and impression management, contribute to consistent behaviour performances across varying contexts. Regarding *coherence*, interactants typically extend conversational remarks by making comments germane to the 'issue' or topic of the interaction as opposed to the specifics of the previous conversational remark (Tracy 1983, Chapter 2). Natale (1975a) has argued that participants match the intensity, duration and frequency of partners' speech characteristics (e.g. rate, pause and utterance durations, vocal intensity, etc.) automatically in order to establish an optimal speech format for communication effectiveness (see also Giles and Powesland 1975; Street 1983).

Regarding *social control* and *impression management* intentions, we have already mentioned the work of Tedeschi (1974; Tedeschi and Norman in press) and of Arkin (1981; Weary and Arkin 1981) on self-presentation. Tedeschi and Norman (in press; see also Tedeschi and Melburg 1984) distinguished between 'tactical' and 'strategic' self-presentation strategies along a defensiveness/ assertiveness continuum. Tactical strategies are moment-to-moment, situation-specific behaviours whereas strategic self-presentational behaviours are cross-situational and frequently operative. Assertive cross-situational strategies include behaviours aimed at enhancing attraction, prestige, status and credibility. Giles and Street (in press) extended this notion to communicative behaviours and proposed that speech convergence, relatively fast speech, social smiles, talkativeness, eye contact, etc. may represent assertive strategic responses. Repeated use of self-protection strategies produce defensive conditions such as phobias, learned helplessness, and drug abuse (Tedeschi and Norman in press). Regarding interaction, these conditions may be manifested by speech divergence, silence and nonverbal behaviours signaling avoidance (Giles and Street in press).

Self-presentation styles appear to vary systematically as a function of certain personal characteristics. Space precludes a discussion of these individual differences. Excellent reviews are available on behavioural patterns as a function of personality (Giles and Street in press; Harper *et al.* 1978; Scherer 1979; Siegman 1978), sex (Giles and Street in press; Haas 1979; Smith 1979), age (Helfrich 1979), socio-economic status (Robinson 1979), and cognitive complexity (O'Keefe and Delia 1982) to name a few.

The existence of relatively stable verbal, vocal and kinesic behaviours among subgroups of individuals and ubiquitous interactant goals of social control and impression management would imply that interactants' behaviours are relatively stable within, and across interactions. Interactants indeed demonstrate consistency among vocal (Cappella 1980, Cappella and Planalp 1981; Jaffe and Feldstein 1970; Street 1983; in press) and nonverbal behaviours such as gaze, distance and touch (Libby 1970; Natale 1976; Patterson 1982), smiling and back channel rates (Duncan and Fiske 1977), and object- and body-focused gestures (Cappella 1984). Even interactions between children and adults show behavioural consistency for children that would not be readily expected (Coates 1978; Jaffe, Stern and Peery 1973; Thomas and Martin 1976; Street 1983). Within individual interactions this consistency can probably be attributed to the establishment of stable (Patterson 1983) and/or preferred (Cappella and Greene 1982) interaction exchanges. Even with changes in partners, interactants' pauses, talk durations, and simultaneous speech patterns (Cappella 1980; Jaffe and Feldstein 1970) and nonverbal behaviours (Duncan and Fiske 1977; Patterson 1982) show noticeable consistency.

These findings are important because they set a baseline against which changes due to situational alterations, partner switches and partner involvement can be measured. Individual communicative behaviours are not completely adaptable but accommodate around some preferred level. Superimposed on relatively stable patterns within interaction are regular fluctuations by partners in response to one another. These fluctuations are generally reciprocal or compensatory in nature and result from efforts to establish optimal interaction modes (Cappella 1983; Natale 1975a), to win the approval of others (Giles and Powesland 1975; Street and Giles 1982), or to achieve psychological distinctiveness (Bourhis, *et al.* 1979, Bourhis, Chapter 7; Giles and Powesland 1975).

As depicted in Figure 13.1, the cognitive-behaviour production system receives inputs from interactant goals and the perceptual-evaluative processing component. Using Greene's (1982) terminology, we could say that these two components establish the activation threshold for relevant procedural scripts. The influence of goals, perceived partners' behaviours and contextual information on communication behaviour production and on subsequent interaction patterns is now considered.

Verbal and nonverbal behaviours which are perceived as appropriate or preferred are reciprocated or complemented, while behaviours deemed unsatisfactory are compensated or diverged. This contention is a general proposition of several social interaction models (Cappella and Greene 1982; Giles 1977; Natale 1975a; Patterson 1983; Street and Giles 1982). Unless role or normative constraints dictate otherwise, interactants who are satisfied with partners' behavioural involvement will reciprocate. This reciprocity facilitates establishment of stable interaction exchanges (Cappella and Greene 1982; Patterson 1983), and has been observed on self-disclosure (Dindia Chapter 8), vocal behaviour (Cappella and Planalp 1981; Street and Giles 1982), and gestural and postural behaviour (La France 1979; La France and Broadbent 1976; Trout and Rosenfeld 1980).

For dyads asymmetrical in power (e.g. employer–employee; counsellor–client), differences in communication behaviour may be appropriate because the behaviours define the role relationship between participants. For example, during counselling interviews, clients typically talk longer and pause more than do counsellors (Matarazzo and Wiens 1972). If the interaction is rather stable, however, the ratio of participants' speech–silence patterns remains relatively stable. If one participant changes the pattern (e.g. the counsellor pauses or talks longer than in previous exchanges), the other participant ofteฅ makes corresponding changes (Matarazzo and Wiens 1972; Natale 1975a; Street in press). Similarly, high status individuals appear to be more directive, touch more, and gaze more while talking than their low status counterparts in high–low status dyads. To establish a complementary pattern, the low status person typically is more deferential, gazes while listening, and does not touch the high status partner.

For behaviours of interactants that are perceived negatively, one of two response types tend to occur. Maintenance of speech and nonverbal behaviour and divergence may be moves toward dissociation or signals of disapproval (Giles 1977). For example, individuals whose ethnic identity has been threatened by another may produce more ethnic speech markers than persons not so threatened (Bourhis and Giles 1977; Bourhis *et al.* 1979). Ethnic identity may also be emphasized in forms of kinesic behaviour divergence (von Raffler-Engel 1980). In short, participants try to distance themselves from others by not accommodating their communication styles. Although the evidence for this claim comes primarily from research in multilingual settings, it seems reasonable to expect similar responses in intracultural encounters. Avoidance behaviour such as indirect body orientations, gazing away, short and rapid speech durations appear divergent in nature.

Some compensatory verbal and nonverbal behaviour adjustments away from a partner's behaviour levels may be moves to balance another's interaction style peculiarity or to get the partner to adjust his/her communicative behaviour to a more preferred level (Cappella 1983; Cappella and Greene 1982). Typical examples include indirect body orientation and gaze avoidance when interpersonal proximity is excessive, slowing speech to calm a panicky child, and backing up when a partner approaches too closely.

Three other perceptual dimensions warrant attention. First, the attribution of intent underlying partners' behaviour impacts upon interactants subsequent behaviour with those partners. Behaviour attributed to positive intent (e.g. being friendly, cooperative, or trying to communicate effectively) elicits reciprocal or compatible responses (Bourhis Chapter 7; Street and Giles 1982). Negative attributions may result in normative or avoidance responses (Burgoon

1983; Street and Giles 1982), or may lead to friendly and cooperative interaction styles (e.g. smiling, gazing) to counteract or alleviate the anticipated negative consequence of interacting with an undesirable other (Patterson 1983).

Second, judgements of partners' traits will also affect communicative choices. Perceived partner characteristics derived from stereotypes (e.g. ethnic minorities, the elderly), prototypes (e.g. extraverts, dominants), and previous interaction experience will influence how one approaches interaction with these persons. While one would expect such judgements to influence *a priori* expectancies for behaviour, they will also dictate strategies for interacting with these interlocutors. For example, a person interacting with a very elderly person is likely to talk more loudly and slowly because of assumed communication difficulties with such partners. Believing someone is domineering may produce behaviour geared toward social control whereas anticipating a friendly other may generate intimacy behaviours. In short, perceptions of partners' traits will influence not only expectancies for behaviour but also conceptions of interaction modes for relating with others. Once the interaction is underway, one would think that preconceptions about others and their behaviours would be confirmed or disconfirmed and subsequently stabilized.

Third, most researchers assume that receivers respond to the *actual* behaviour levels of communicators. For most behaviours, *perceived* behaviour levels indeed correspond closely to actual behaviours. Street (1982; Street and Brady 1982) has reported that perceived speech rates, turn durations, and response latencies of interactants correlated highly with objectively measured levels. In some circumstances, however, perceived and actual behaviours are discrepant given perceptual schemata (e.g. stereotypes, prototypes, strong affective biases) which distort perception of actual behaviour (Street and Hopper 1982). Interactants then may adapt behaviours toward or away from those presumed characteristic of their interlocutors. Thakerar *et al.*'s (1982) study points to the importance of perceived messages influencing interactants' message choices. In high–low status dyads of English nurses, the low-status participant increased speech rate and standardized accent thinking such adjustments were toward the speech of the high-status interlocutor. Likewise, the high-status participant decreased rate and informalized accent for similar reasons. Though both participants believed their speech styles were similar, objective measurement indicated the low-status party actually spoke faster and more formally than the high-status person.

To sum, several models of social interaction are grounded in the view that interaction patterns such as reciprocity and compensation are constructed given the interactants' goals, and perceptions of the situation, partner's behaviour levels, and meaning derived from partners' behaviours (e.g. Giles and Street in press; Patterson 1982, 1983; Street and Giles 1982). The function(s) of the interaction are manifested through the participants' response contingencies. As Patterson (1983; Chapter 10) noted, these response patterns may be fairly stable as interactants share goals and behavioural routines accomplishing these goals. Under such circumstances, reciprocity or mutually preferred complementarity (e.g. gaze and touch behaviour in high–low status dyads) is often the resulting interaction pattern. On the other hand, interactants with incongruous goals or incompatible behavioural routines perceived appropriate for these goals will likely produce unstable exchanges characterized by compensation (e.g. a female avoiding the advance of a male) or by competitive reciprocity (e.g. when two participants increase loudness levels and interruption behaviour to assert dominance over the partner).

Arousal. The arousal-behaviour relationship is perhaps the most neglected and least understood of our model. A substantial amount of research has studied the impact of anxiety, a form of arousal, on speech and nonverbal behaviour. For example, state anxiety appears to be positively related to silence, negatively related to verbal output, positively related to speech disturbances, and related to speech rate in an inverted-U fashion (Murray 1971; Siegman 1978). Nervousness, due to evaluative conditions or uncertainty, typically leads to increases in the number of adaptors (Knapp 1978), self-touches (Ekman 1972), and decreases in lexical diversity and intensity (Bradac 1982).

Though not necessarily concerned with interaction, other research has focused on the influence of arousal on performance. The findings are relatively consistent: (1) performance effectiveness is greatest at moderate levels of arousal and least at extremely high and low arousal levels and (2) arousal tends to facilitate the performance of well learned behaviours and inhibit perfor= mance of novel motor operations (Cottrell 1972; see Shaw 1981 for discussion of mediating factors).

Not only does arousal influence behaviour production but behaviours of the interactants also elicit arousal changes. Though there are no direct, unconfounded findings, indirect evidence suggests that subjects' GSRs have been increased by unusually long latencies (Goldband 1981), verbal content (Smith, Malino and Shagass 1954), and music tempo (Zimny and Weidenfeller 1963). Similarly, closer interpersonal distances, excessive gaze by partners, intimate disclosures and intimate questions from partners, high anxiety topics, partner smiles, and touch typically increased an interactant's experienced arousal as measured on a variety of indices (Cappella 1983).

If arousal and behaviour mutually influence one another; then response matching or mismatching may indicate that participants are experiencing arousal changes which are positively or negatively correlated. Though research on such a proposition awaits, Cappella (1983; Cappella and Greene 1982) reviewed research indicating that interactants' arousal levels often demonstrate covariation and that this covariation appears to be influenced by the inter-actants' affective orientation to partners.

The arousal-behaviour link may also be influenced by cognitive responses mediating the experience of arousal. Patterson's (1976) review of research on intimacy and arousal led to the claim that interactants' experienced arousal changes were cognitively labelled as positive or negative and this label then guided the interactants' subsequent behaviours. However, Cappella and Greene (1982) argued differently. The nature of experienced arousal changes is a function of the partner's behaviours and the interactants' *a priori* expecta-tions or preferences for that behaviour. Street and Giles (1982) criticized this notion by pointing out that Cappella and Greene's model fails to account for arousal levels (which may range from very high to very low) experienced before the interaction with another occurs. The issue of arousal and anticipated inter-action has been addressed by Greene and Sparks (1983). These authors argued, and provided some support for the claim that public speaking anxiety was a function of the speaker's perceived behaviour options for the event. The more perceived behaviour choices, the less the arousal as measured by both self-report and physiological measures of anxiety.

In short, the influences among arousal, cognition and affect are not clear at this point. As Cappella (1983) noted, arousal could be presumed when the organism activates relevant perceptual and motor schema to perform tasks. Thus, arousal increments in listening states can be attributed to attention and comprehension efforts (Kahneman 1973) as well in behaviour responses when activating motor production. However, arousal changes are also likely to occur given the affective value of assorted interaction experiences which have been stored in memory. Thus, recall of an extremely gratifying or horrifying event would stimulate arousal level fluctuations. To sum, arousal increments can facilitate or inhibit performance and perceptual tasks, can lead to response strategies to cope with it when at extreme levels, and is linked to affective experience. Yet the exact nature of these processes is unknown.

Conclusion

Our model of social interaction is but a modest effort to integrate current research findings with recent theoretical positions on interaction processes and sequences. We would immediately criticize this framework as still a bit variable-analytic for our tastes. This characteristic is in part unavoidable given the single-behaviour approach of most previous studies and the limited amount of interaction process research to date.

Given that the functions of social interaction evolve via participants' *response contingencies*, subsequent theoretical and empirical work should address two questions. First, how do interactants construct reciprocal, compensatory or other interaction sequences? One approach to this question would be to examine how communicators' current behaviours were influenced by their own previous behaviours and by partners' behaviours. There is sound conceptual foundations for using current methodological tools such as stochastic modelling (Hewes 1979), structural equation modelling (Cappella 1980), and lag sequential analysis (Sackett *et al*. 1979) Second, what forces undergird the establishment and maintenance of interaction patterns? Two possibilities have been discussed. One, there is strong evidence of mutual influences between the experiences of arousal and behaviours (Cappella and Greene 1982). Yet, relationships between arousal, behaviour and affective responses currently are not well defined. Two, interactants' motivations and cognitive processes affect the production of behaviour and perceptual/ evaluative responses. However, as Greene (1984) has argued, researchers efforts to explicate the relationships between cognition and communication are hindered given confusion regarding what constitues basic cognitive structures and processes.

Obviously, the need exists for much more basic research on interaction processes and outcomes. The authors in this volume have contributed significantly to our understanding of particular facets of communicative sequences. With the exception of Patterson, most have limited themselves to explicating processes pertaining to a specific behavioural domain (e.g. accounts, language choice, turn-yielding cues) for specific functions or purposes (e.g. remediation, untoward behaviour, maintaining coherence, control). Hopefully, theoretical advances in limited domains will stimulate the formulation of more

268   *Richard L. Street, Jr and Joseph N. Cappella*

comprehensive models without loss of parsimony. Such efforts to date – our model, Patterson's (1983) sequential-functional model, Cappella and Greene's (1982) discrepancy-arousal model, Giles and Street's (in press) communicator characteristics model – remain speculative given the dearth of empirical evidence elucidating relationships between interaction patterns and goals, cognition, arousal and outcomes.

References

Abelson, R.P. 1976: Script processing in attitude formation and decision making. In Carroll, J.S. and Payne, J.W., editors, *Cognition and social behaviour* (Hillsdale, NJ: Erlbaum) 33–45.

Anderson, J.R. 1976: *Language, memory and thought.* Hillsdale, NJ: Erlbaum.

Arkin, R.M. 1981: Self-presentation styles. In Tedeschi, J.T., editor, *Impression management theory and social psychological research* (New York: Academic Press).

Berger, C.R. and Bradac, J.J. 1983: *Language and social knowledge: Uncertainty in interpersonal relations.* London: Edward Arnold.

Berger, C.R. and Calabrese, R.J. 1975: Some explorations in initial interaction and beyond: Toward a developmental theory of interpersonal communication. *Human Communication Research*, 1 99–112.

Berger, C.R. and Roloff, M.E. 1980: Social cognition, self-awareness, and interpersonal communication. In Dervin, B. and Voight, M.J., editors, *Progress in communication sciences 2* (Norwood, NJ: Ablex) 1–49.

Berlyne, D.E. 1967: Arousal and reinforcement. In Levine, D., editor, *Nebraska symposium on motivation 15* (Lincoln, N: University of Nebraska Press).

Bock, J.K. 1982: Toward a cognitive psychology of syntax: Information processing contributions to sentence formulation. *Psychological Review*, **89**, 1–47.

Bond, M.H. 1972: Effect of an impression management set on subsequent behaviour. *Journal of Personality and Social Psychology*, **24**, 263–6.

Bourhis, R.Y. and Giles, H. 1977: The language of intergroup distinctiveness. In Giles, H., editor, *Language, ethnicity, and intergroup relations.* (London: Academic Press).

Bourhis, R.Y., Giles, H., Levens, J.P. and Tajfel, H. Psycholingustic distinctiveness: Language divergence in Belgium. In Giles, H. and St Clair, R., editors, *Language and social psychology* (Oxford Blackwell.

Bradac, J.J. 1982: A rose by another name: Attitudinal consequences of lexical variation. In Ryan, E.B. and Giles, H., editors, *Attitudes toward language variation: Social and applied contexts* (London: Edward Arnold), 99–115.

Bradac, J.J., Bowers, J.W. and Courtright, J.A. 1979: Three language variables in communication research: Intensity, immediacy, and diversity. *Human Communication Research*, **5**, 257–69.

Burgoon, J.K. 1978: A communication model of personal space violations: Explication and an initial test. *Human Communication Research*, **4**, 129–42.

—— 1983: Nonverbal violations of expectations. In Wiemann, J.M. and

Harrison, R.P., editors, *Nonverbal interaction* (Beverly Hills, Cal:. Sage) 77–112.

Byrne, D. 1971: *The attraction paradigm*. New York: Academic Press.

Cacioppo, J.T. and Petty, R.E. 1982: Language variables, attitudes, and persuasion. In Ryan, E.B. and Giles, H., editors, *Attitudes toward language variation: Social and applied contexts*. (London: Edward Arnold) 189–207.

Cantor, N. and Mischel, W. 1979: Prototypes in person perception. In Berkowitz, L., editor, *Advances in experimental social psychology 12* (New York: Academic Press) 1–52.

Cappella, J.N. 1980: Talk and silence sequences in informal conversation II. *Human Communication Research*, **6**, 130–45.

—— 1980: Structural equation modeling: An introduction. In Monge, P.E. and Cappella, J.N., editors, *Multivariate techniques in human communication research* (New York: Academic Press) 57–110.

—— 1981: Mutual influence in expressive behaviour: Adult–adult and infant-adult dyadic interaction. *Psychological Bulletin*, **89**, 101–32.

—— 1983: Conversational involvement: Approaching and avoiding others. In Wiemann, J.M. and Harrison, R.P., editors, *Nonverbal interaction* (Beverly Hills, Cal: Sage) 113–48.

—— 1984: The relevance of the microstructure of interaction to relationship change. *Journal of Social and Personal Relationships*, **1**, 239–64.

—— In press a: The management of conversations. In Knapp, M.L. and Miller, G.R., editors, *Handbook of interpersonal communication* (Beverly Hills, Cal: Sage).

—— In press b: The effects of distance and individual differences in arousability on nonverbal involvement: A test of discrepancy-arousal theory. *Journal of Nonverbal Behaviour*.

Cappella, J.N. and Greene, J.O. 1982: A discrepancy-arousal explanation of mutual influence in expressive behaviour for adult–adult and infant–adult interaction. *Communication Monographs*. **49**, 80–114.

Cappella, J.N. and Planalp, S. 1981: Talk and silence sequences in informal conversations. III: Interspeaker influence. *Human Communication Research*, **7**, 117–32.

Cicourel, A.W. 1973: *Cognitive sociology*. Harmondsworth: Penguin Education.

Coates, B. 1978: Consistency of attachment behaviour in the human infant: A multivariate approach. *Child Study Journal*, **8**, 131–48.

Cody, M.J., McLaughlin, M.L. and Schneider, M.J. 1981: The impact of intimacy and relational consequences on the selection of interpersonal persuasion tactics. *Communication Quarterly*, **29**, 91–106.

Cottrell, N.B. 1972: Social facilitation. In McClintock, C.G., editor, *Experimental Social Psychology* (New York: Holt), 185–236.

Daly, J.A., Richmond, V.P. and Leth, S. 1979: Social communicative anxiety and the personnel selection process: Testing the similarity effect in the selection decisions. *Human Communication Research*, **6**, 18–32.

Davis, D. and Martin, H.J. 1978: When pleasure begets pleasure: Recipient responsiveness as a determinant of physical pleasuring between heterosexual dating couples and strangers. *Journal of Personality and*

Social Psychology, **36**, 767–77.

Davis, D. and Perkowitz, W.T. 1979: Consequences of responsiveness in dyadic interaction: Effects of probability of response and proportion of content related responses on interpersonal attraction. *Journal of Personality and Social Psychology*, **37**, 534–50.

Davis, J.D. 1976: Self-disclosure in an acquaintance exercise: Responsibility for level of intimacy. *Journal of Personality and Social Psychology*, **33**, 787–92.

—— 1977: Effects of communication about interpersonal process of the evaluation of self-disclosure in dyads. *Journal of Personality and Social Psychology*, **35**, 31–7.

Duck, S.W. 1973: Personality similarity and friendship choice: Similarity of what, when? *Journal of Personality*, **41**, 543–58.

Duffy, E. 1962: *Activation and behaviour*. New York: John Wiley.

Duncan, S. and Fiske, D.W. 1977: *Face-to-face interaction*. Hillsdale, NJ: Erlbaum.

Edinger, J.A. and Patterson, M.L. 1983: Nonverbal involvement and social control. *Psychological Bulletin*, **93**, 30–56.

Ekman, P. 1972: Universal and cultural differences in facial expressions of emotion. In Cole, J., editor, *Nebraska symposium on motivation 19* (Lincoln, NE: University of Nebraska).

Festinger, L. 1954: A theory of social comparison processes. *Human Relations*, **7**, 117–40.

Foss, D.J. and Hakes, D.T. 1978: *Psycholinguistics*. Englewood Cliffs, NJ: Prentice-Hall.

Freud, S. 1900: *The interpretation of dreams*. Reprinted in Brill, A.A., editor, *Basic writings of Sigmund Freud* (New York: Modern Library, 1938).

Genesee, F. and Bourhis, R.Y. 1982: The social psychological significance of code switching in cross-cultural communication. *Journal of Language and Social Psychology*, **1**, 1–28.

Gilbert, S.J. 1976: Empirical and theoretical extensions of self-disclosure. In Miller, G.R., editor, *Explorations in interpersonal communication*, (Beverly Hills, Cal: Sage) 197–216.

Giles, H. 1977: Social psychology and applied linguistics: Towards an integrative approach. *ITL: Review of Applied Linguistics*, **33**, 27–42.

—— 1980: Accommodation theory: Some new directions. In de Silva, S., editor, *Aspects of linguistic behaviour* (York: University of York Press).

Giles, H. Brown, B.L. Thakerar, V.N. 1981: The effects of speech rate, context, and accent on the attribution of a speaker's personality characteristics. Unpublished ms. University of Bristol.

Giles, H. and Powesland, P.F, 1975: *Speech style and social evaluation*. London: Academic Press.

Giles, H. and Smith, P.M. 1979: Accommodation theory: Optimal levels of convergence. In Giles, H. and St Clair, R.N., editors. *Language and social psychology* (Oxford: Blackwell), 45–65.

Giles, H. and Street, R.L., Jr In press: Communicator characteristics and behaviour: A review, generalizations, and model. In Knapp, M.L. and Miller, G.R., editors. *Handbook of interpersonal communication* (Beverly Hills, Cal: Sage).

Giles, H., Taylor, D.M. and Bourhis, R.Y. 1973: Towards a theory of inter-personal accommodation through language: Some Canadian data. *Language in Society*, **2**, 177–92.

Goffman, E. 1959. *The presentation of self in everyday life*. Garden City, NY: Doubleday.

—— 1974: *Frame analysis*. New York: Harper & Row.

Goldband, S. 1981: Imposed latencies, interruptions, and dyadic interaction: Physiological response and interpersonal attraction. *Journal of Research in Personality*, **15**, 221–32.

Gottman, J. 1982: Emotional responsiveness in marital conversations. *Journal of Communication*, **32**, 108–20.

Greene, J.O. 1982: On the nature of action schemas: An action-assembly theory. Paper presented to the International Communication Association, Boston, Mass.

—— 1984: Evaluating cognitive explanations of communication phenomena. *Quarterly Journal of Speech*, **70**, 241–54.

Greene, J.O. and Sparks, G. 1983: Explication and test of a cognitive model of communication apprehension: A new look at an old construct. *Human Communication Research*, **9**, 349–66.

Grice, H.P. 1975: Logic and conversation. In Cole, P. and Morgan, J.L., editors, *Syntax and semantics: Speech Acts* (New York: Academic Press).

Haas, A. 1979: Male and female spoken language differences: Stereotypes and evidence. *Psychological Bulletin*, **86**, 616–26.

Hamilton, D. 1979: A cognitive-attributional analysis of stereotyping. In Berkowitz, L., editor, *Advances in experimental social psychology 12* (New York: Academic Press) 53–84.

Harper, R.G., Wiens, A.N. and Matarazzo, J.D., editors, 1978: *Nonverbal communication: The state of the art*. New York: John Wiley.

Harvey, J.H. and Weary, G. 1984: Current issues in attribution theory and research. *Annual Reviews in Psychology*, **35**, 427–59.

Helfrich, H. 1979: Age markers in speech. In Scherer, K.R. and Giles, H., editors, *Social markers in speech* (Cambridge: Cambridge University Press) 63–107.

Hershey, S. and Werner, E. 1975: Dominance in marital decision-making in women's liberation and non-women's liberation families. *Family Processes*, **14**, 223–33.

Hewes, D.E. 1979: The sequential analysis of social interaction. *Quarterly Journal of Speech*, **65**, 56–73.

Hopper, R. 1981: The taken-for-granted. *Human Communication Research*, **7**, 195–211.

Ickes, W.J., Patterson, M.L., Rajecki, D.W. and Tanford, S. 1982: Behavioral and cognitive consequences of reciprocal versus compensatory responses to pre-interaction expectancies. *Social Cognition*, **1**, 160–90.

Jaffe, J. and Feldstein, S. 1970: *Rhythms of dialogue*. New York: Academic Press.

Jaffe, J., Stern, D. and Peery, J.C. 1973: Conversational coupling of gaze behaviour in prelinguistic human development. *Journal of Psycholinguistic Research*, **2**, 321–9.

Johnson-Laird, P.N. 1983: *Mental models: Toward a cognitive science of language, inference, and consciousness*. Cambridge, Mass: Harvard University Press.

Kahneman, D. 1973: *Attention and effort*. Englewood Cliffs, NJ: Prentice-Hall.

King, M.R. and Manaster, G.J. 1977: Bossy image, self-esteem, expectations, self-assessments, and actual success in a simulated job interview. *Journal of Applied Psychology*, **62**, 589–94.

Knapp, M.L. 1978: *Nonverbal communication in human interaction*, 2nd edition. New York: Holt, Rinehart & Winston.

LaFrance, M. 1979: Nonverbal synchrony and rapport: Analysis by the cross-lag panel technique. *Social Psychology Quarterly*, **42**, 66–70.

LaFrance, M. and Broadbent, M. 1976: Group rapport: Posture sharing as a nonverbal indicator. *Group and Organization Studies*, 1, 328–33.

Larsen, K.S., Martin, H.J. and Giles, H. 1977: Anticipated social cost and interpersonal accommodation. *Human Communication Research*, 3, 303–8.

Libby, W.L. 1970: Eye contact and direction of looking as stable individual differences. *Journal of Experimental Research in Personality*, 4, 303–12.

Lowery, C.R., Snyder, C.R. and Denney, N.W. 1976: Perceived aggression and predicted counteraggression as a function of sex of dyad participants: When males and females exchange verbal blows. *Sex Roles*, **2**, 339–46.

Matarazzo, J.D. and Wiens, A.N. *The interview: Research on its anatomy and structure*. Chicago: Aldine-Atherton.

McDowell, K.V. 1972: Violations of personal space. *Canadian Journal of Behavioural Science*, 4, 210–17.

McLaughlin, M.L. 1984: *Conversation: How talk is organized*. Beverly Hills, Cal: Sage.

McLaughlin, M.L., Cody, M.J. and Rosenstein, N.E. 1983: Account sequences in conversations between strangers. *Communication Monographs*, **50**, 102–25.

Mead, G.H. 1934: *Mind, self and society*, Chicago: University of Chicago Press.

Mehrabian, A. and Williams, M. 1969: Nonverbal concomitants of perceived and intended persuasiveness. *Journal of Personality and Social Psychology*, **13**, 37–58.

Meltzer, L., Morris, W. and Hayes, D. 1971: Interruption outcomes and vocal amplitude: Explorations in social psychophysics. *Journal of Personality and Social Psychology*, **18**, 392–402.

Minsky, M.A. 1975: A framework for representing knowledge. In Winston, P., editor, *The psychology of computer vision* (New York: McGraw-Hill) 211–77.

Murray, D.C. 1971: Talk, silence, and anxiety. *Psychological Bulletin*, **75**, 224–60.

Natale, M. 1975a: Convergence of mean vocal intensity in dyadic communication as a function of social desirability. *Journal of Personality and Social Psyschology*, **12**, 790–804.

—— 1975b: Social desirability as related to convergence of temporal speech patterns. *Perceptual and Motor Skills*, **40**, 827–30.

—— 1976: A Markovian model of adult gaze behaviour. *Journal of*

Psycholinguistic Research, **5**, 53–61.

Neisser, U. 1976: *Cognition and reality: Principles and implications for cognitive psychology*. San Francisco, Cal: W.H. Freeman.

Nisbett, R.E. and Ross, L. 1980: *Human inference: Strategies and shortcomings of social judgment*. Englewood Cliffs, NJ: Prentice-Hall.

Nisbett, R.E. and Wilson, T.D. 1977: The halo effect: Evidence for the unconscious alteration of judgments. *Journal of Personality and Social Psychology*, **35**, 250–6.

Noller, R. 1980: Gaze in married couples. *Journal of Nonverbal Behaviour*, **5**, 115–29.

Norman, D.A. 1981: Categorization of action slips. *Psychological Review*, **88**, 1–15.

O'Keefe, B.J. and Delia, J.G. 1982: Impression formation and message production. In Roloff, M.E. and Berger, C.R., editors, *Social cognition and communication* (Beverly Hills, Cal. Sage) 33–72.

Patterson, M.L. 1973: Compensation in nonverbal immediacy behaviours: A review. *Sociometry*, **36**, 237–52.

——. 1976: An arousal model of interpersonal intimacy. *Psychological Review*, **83**, 235–45.

——. 1982: Personality and nonverbal involvement: A functional analysis. In Ickes, W.J. and Knowles, E.S., editors, *Personality, roles and social behaviour* (New York: Springer-Verlag).

——. 1983: *Nonverbal behaviour: A functional perspective*. New York: Springer Verlag.

Petty, R.E., Cacioppo, J.T. and Heesacker, M. 1981: The use of rhetorical questions in persuasion: A cognitive response analysis. *Journal of Personality and Social Psychology*, **40**, 432–40.

Planalp, S. and Tracy, K. 1980: Not to change the topic but . . .: A cognitive approach to the management of conversation. In Nimmo, D., editor, *Communication Yearbook 4* (New Brunswick, NJ: Transaction) 237–58.

Putman, W.B. and Street, R.L., Jr 1984: The conception and perception of noncontent speech performance. Implications for speech accommodation theory. *International Journal of the Sociology of Language*, **46**, 97–114.

Ragan, S. 1983: A conversational analysis of alignment talk in job interviews. In Bostrom, R.N., editor, *Communication Yearbook 7* (Beverly Hills, Cal. Sage) 502–16.

Robinson, W.P. 1979: Speech markers and social class. In Scherer, K.R. and Giles, H., editors, *Social Markers in Speech* (Cambridge: Cambridge University Press) 211–49.

Roloff, M.E. 1981: *Interpersonal communication: The social exchange approach*. Beverly Hills, Cal. Sage.

Ryan, E.B. and Giles, H., editors: 1982: *Attitudes toward language variation: Social and applied contexts*. London: Edward Arnold.

Sabin, E.J., Clemmer, E.J., O'Connell, D.C. and Kowal, S. 1979: A pausological approach to speech development. In Siegman, A.W. and Feldstein, S., editors, *Of speech and time* (Hillsdale, NJ: Erlbaum), 35–55.

Sackett, G.P., Holm, R., Crowley, C. and Henkins, A. 1979: A FORTRAN program for lag sequential analysis of contingency and cyclicity in behavioural data. *Behaviour Research Methods and Instrumentation*, **11**, 366–78.

Schank, R.C. and Abelson, R.P. 1977: *Scripts, plans, goals, and understanding.* Hillsdale, NJ: Erlbaum.

Scherer, K.R. 1979: Personality markers in speech. In Scherer, K.R. and Giles, H., editors, *Social markers in speech* (Cambridge: Cambridge University Press) 147–209.

Schneider, F.W. and Hansvick, C.L. 1977: Gaze and distance as a function of changes in interpersonal gaze. *Social Behaviour and Personality*, 5, 49–53.

Schulz, R. and Barefoot, J. 1974: Nonverbal responsiveness and affiliative conflict theory. *British Journal of Social and Clinical Psychology*, 13, 237–43.

Shaw, M.E. 1981: *Group dynamics: The psychology of small group behaviour*, 3rd ed. New York: McGraw-Hill.

Shrout, P.E. and Fiske, D.W. 1981: Nonverbal behaviours and social evaluation. *Journal of Personality*, 49, 115–28.

Siegman, A.W. 1978: The telltale voice: Nonverbal messages of verbal communication. In Siegman, A.W. and Feldstein, S., editors, *Nonverbal behaviour and communication* (Hillsdale, NJ: Erlbaum) 183–243.

Sillars, A. 1980: Attributions and communication in roommate conflicts. *Communication Monographs*, 47, 180–200.

—— 1982: Attribution and communication: Are people 'naive scientists' or just naive? In Roloff, M.E. and Berger, C.R., editors, *Social cognition and communication* (Beverly Hills, Cal: Sage) 73–106.

Simard, L., Taylor, D.M. and Giles, H. 1976: Attribution processes and interpersonal accommodation in a bilingual setting. *Language and Speech*, 19, 374–87.

Smith, A.A., Malmo, R.B. and Shagass, C. 1954: An electromyography study of listening and talking. *Canadian Journal of Psychiatry*, 8, 219–27.

Smith, M.J. 1984: Contingency rules theory, context, and compliance behaviours. *Human Communication Research*, 10, 489–512.

Smith, P.M. 1979: Sex markers in speech. In Scherer, K.R. and Giles, H., editors, *Social markers in speech* (Cambridge: Cambridge University Press) 109–46.

Street, R.L., Jr 1982: Evaluation of noncontent speech accommodation. *Language and Communication*, 2, 13–31.

—— 1983: Noncontent speech convergence in adult–child interactions. In Bostrom, R.N., editor, *Communication Yearbook 7* (Beverly Hills, Cal. Sage) 369–95.

—— in press: Speech convergence and speech evaluation in fact-finding interviews. *Human Communication Research*.

—— in preparation: Participant-observer differences among social evaluations of interview participants. Texas Tech University.

Street, R.L., Jr and Brady, R.M. 1982: Speech rate acceptance ranges as a function of evaluative domain, listener speech rate, and communicative context. *Communication Monographs*, 49, 290–308.

Street, R.L.. Jr, Brady, R.M. and Lee, R. 1984: Evaluative responses to communicators: The effects of speech rate, sex, and interaction context. *Western Journal of Speech Communication*, 48, 14–27.

Street, R.L., Jr, Brady, R.M. and Putman, W.B. 1983: The influence of speech rate stereotypes and rate similarity on listeners' evaluations of speakers.

Journal of Language and Social Psychology, **2**, 37–56.

Street, R.L., Jr and Giles, H. 1982: Speech accommodation theory: A social-cognitive approach to language and speech behaviour. In Roloff, M.E. and Berger, C.R., editors, *Social cognition and communication* (Beverly Hills, Cal: Sage) 193–226.

Street, R.L., Jr and Hopper, R. 1982: A model of speech style evaluation. In Ryan, E.B. and Giles, H., editors, *Attitudes toward language variation: Social and applied contexts* (London: Edward Arnold) 175–88.

Sundstrom, E. 1975: An experimental study of crowding: Effects of room size, intrusion, and goal blocking on nonverbal behaviour, self-disclosure, and self-reported stress. *Journal of Personality and Social Psychology*, **32**, 645–54.

Tajfel, H. 1981: Social stereotypes and social groups. In Turner, J.C. and Giles, H., editors, *Intergroup behaviour* (Oxford: Blackwell).

Tedeschi, J.T., editor, 1974: *Perspectives on social power*. Chicago: Aldine.

Tedeschi, J.T. and Melburg, V. 1984: Impression management and influence in the organization. In Bacharach, S.B. and Lawler, E.J., editors, *Perspectives in organizational psychology: Theory and research* (Greenwich: JAI Press).

Tedeschi, J.T. and Norman, N. in press: Social power, self-presentation, and the self. In Schlenker, B.R., editor, *Self and identity* (New York: McGraw-Hill).

Thakerar, J.N. and Giles, H. 1981: They are – so they speak: Noncontent speech stereotypes. *Language and Communication*, **1**, 251–6.

Thakerar, J.N., Giles, H. and Cheshire, J. 1982: Psychological and linguistic parameters of speech accommodation theory. In Fraser, C. and Scherer, K.R., editors, *Advances in the social psychology of language* (Cambridge: Cambridge University Press) 205–55.

Thomas, E.A.C. and Martin, J.A. 1976: An analysis of parent–infant interaction. *Psychological Review*, **83**, 141–56.

Tracy, K. 1982: On getting the point: Distinguishing 'issues' from 'events', an aspect of conversational coherence. In Burgoon, M., editor, *Communication Yearbook 5* (New Brunswick, NJ: Transaction) 279–301.

—— 1983: The issue–event distinction: A rule of conversation and its scope condition. *Human Communication Research*, **9**, 320–34.

Trevarthen, C. 1977: Descriptive analysis of infant communicative behaviour. In Schaffer, H.R., editor, *Studies in mother–infant interaction*. (New York: Academic Press).

Tronick, E.D., Als, H. and Brazelton, T.B. 1974: Mutuality is mother–infant interaction. *Journal of Communication*, **27**, 74–9.

Trout, D.L. and Rosenfeld, H.M. 1980: The effect of postural lean and body congruence on the judgment of psychotherapeutic rapport. *Journal of Nonverbal Behaviour*, **4**, 176–90.

von-Raffler-Engel, W. 1980: The unconscious element in intercultural communication. In St Clair, R.N. and Giles, H., editors, *The social and psychological contexts of language* (Hillsdale, NJ: Erlbaum) 101–29.

Warner, R. 1979: Activity pattern, personality, and social interaction. Unpublished manuscript, Department of Psychology, University of Miami.

Watzlawick, P., Beavin, J. and Jackson, D.D. 1967: *Pragmatics of human communication*. New York: W.W. Norton.

Weary, G. and Arkin, R.M. 1981: Attitudinal self-presentation. In Harvey, J.H., Ickes, W.J. and Kidd, R., editor, *New directions in attribution theory and research 3* (Hillsdale, NJ: Erlbaum).

Webb, J.T. 1972: Interview synchrony: An investigation of two speech rate measures. In Siegman, A.W. and Pope, B., editors, *Studies in dyadic communication* (New York: Pergamon).

Welkowitz, J. and Kuc, M. 1973: Interrelationships among warmth, genuineness, empathy, and temporal speech patterns in interpersonal interaction. *Journal of Consulting and Clinical Psychology*, **41**, 472–3.

Williams, F. 1976: *Explorations of the linguistic attitudes of teachers*. Rowley, Mass: Newbury.

Williams, F., Whitehead, J.L. and Miller, L. 1972: Relations between attitudes and teacher expectancy. *American Educational Research Journal*, **9**, 263–377.

Worthy, M.A., Gary, I. and Kahn, G.M. 1969: Self-disclosure as an exchange process. *Journal of Personality and Social Psychology*, **13**, 59–63.

Zajonc, R.B. 1980: Feeling and thinking: Preferences need no inferences. *American Psychologist*, **35**, 151–75.

Zimny, G.H. and Weidenfeller, E.W. 1963: Effects of music upon GSR and heart rate. *Journal of Psychology*, **76**, 311–14.

Index